Ancestors, Descendants and Family of
Dr. Rufus Clarence Hall of Marshall, Texas
Hall Family - Vol. 1
by Ronald C. Hall

Beginning with William Hall (c. 1715 - 1758)
and a study of selected children:
John, Hezekiah and Elisha

Dedication

These books are dedicated to my cousins, collaborators, friends and of course, my wife: Scotty and Jill Hall, Jan and Ed Peine, Fay Yates, Jena Costello, Lou Ellen Smih, Albert Minter, Mittie U. Rose and Jane Hall.

Thanks for contributing and listening.

Ronald C. Hall - October, 2013

Preface

This work is an attempt to satisfy a curiosity that was probably first expressed when I was about nine years old. I remember sitting at the kitchen table asking "PaPa" about his parents and grandparents. He told me a little about his father, Dr. Rufus C. Hall and said his grandfather died in the Civil War, but he could not remember his name. He knew the Taylor family was important but it was not clear to me how. I came away somewhat disappointed in what little he seemed to remember or was willing to relate. My grandmother gave the impression of wanting to be more helpful but I noticed that they tended to be unable to agree on the story being told. After a number of attempts (probably to their annoyance), I decided that better answers to my questions would have to be found elsewhere or at another time. My inquiry was thus stymied and put to the "back-burner" of a child's list of things to do. I have recently discovered that this frustration was also experienced and recorded by my grandmother's nephew, George W. Glass who worked diligently on the "Glass" side of the family. He spent several days with his aunt in 1963 and wrote in his notes: *"after spending several days in the anti-genealogical atmosphere of Mrs. Hall's residence..."*

Apparently, I did make an impression. I can remember some mild excitement and discomfort when it was announced that I would be getting a visit from a "relative," Aunt Clare (Hall) Farrar, who had been studying the family's genealogy. My grandparents had contacted her. But, my curiosity had been previously squelched and I was not up to the opportunity that was before me even though this was someone (I could not figure out at the time how she was related.) that might know the answers to my questions. A mixture of fear of what I might find out, a desire to go play outside and a new discomfort regarding why the family history had to be "studied" rendered me mute. It was too much to contemplate at the time. No doubt to her disappointment, I ran off to enjoy the afternoon.

That dormant and unresolved curiosity was sparked alive late in 1994. My mother's illness with throat cancer had returned. As I reflected on the amount of time I was spending with her, it was clear that I had better come up with some topics of mutual interest for conversation. At that point, she was already unable to speak due to the insertion of the "trache" but she could and did write well. We started with her family. She was able to provide valuable clues from the family lore that she recounted. She remembered Virginia Thorpe, a cousin, who had been working on her family's genealogy and she reminded me of Aunt Clare with respect to my father's side. A call to my uncle, Conway G. Hall, confirmed Clare's address and a letter was dispatched. A similar letter was sent to Virginia Thorpe after confirming her address with my mother's sister, Jeanne Shively. Soon, I had plenty of material from both sides of the family. A lively correspondence was begun with Virginia Thorpe and what a pleasant surprise it was to receive a phone call from Fay (Farrar) McGraw (now Yates), Clare's daughter, who has been so helpful in sharing the information she had from her mother's work.

The Dallas Public Library became my third home. Through my research at the library I was able to find pictures of my mother's father, uncle, great grandfather and a great-great grandmother. Unfortunately, mother's condition deteriorated to the point that she was "out" most of the time due to the amount of pain medication being administered. I know that she really wanted to see that picture of her great grandfather. I described it to her in detail about a month before her death. Meanwhile, the project had taken a life of its own.

It was Aunt Kay (Hall) Tharp, at my mother's funeral, that insisted that if I wanted to find out about the Halls "just go to Marshall" (Texas). Everything I would want to know would be there. I found true treasures in the Harrison County Historical Museum. These include an unpublished report on the Hall Family, <u>The Hell Raisin Halls of Texas by George</u>, also known as "W. W. Hall - Shropshire Families" written between 1950-1977 by George Cross Hall and William T. Hall, Jr., both cousins of Dr. Rufus Clarence Hall and various smaller reports written by W. T. Vawter, another cousin. And, it was there that William "Scotty" H. Hall, Jr. and I began to cross paths. His interest and perspectives regarding this project and especially the 17th Texas Cavalry Regiment (dismounted) during the Civil War has contributed much to the overall work. What a great pleasure it is to have developed such close friendships with my cousins, Scotty and Fay.

Many of my mother's ancestors emigrated from England to Massachusetts during the 1600's. I noticed from Aunt Clare's notes, that Mary B. (Holman) Taylor, one of my father's ancestors, was said to have been born in Petersham, Massachusetts. One evening while researching Massachusetts material on my mother's side, I decided to take a quick survey regarding this lady. I was able to find quite rapidly a record of her birth and of her parents. Her mother's Morse family has been well researched and documented. So many doors opened so quickly that I decided to redirect my efforts toward collecting and consolidating this information while it was at hand. Even today, doors are still opening on all sides of the family.

Dr. Rufus Clarence Hall is the earliest ancestor of my Hall family line that can be remembered in life with detail by his great-grandchildren and grandchildren. The work includes as many of his paternal ancestors and family that I could trace to date. This work is one of a series of drafts of a catalogue of Hall descendants for future generations to maintain and to fill. I hope this exercise will provide the basis for a satisfactory answer to another child's question regarding his grandparent's parents. I regret that I have not been able to document every success.

Table of Contents

Introduction

I am a descendant of Dr. Rufus Clarence Hall of Marshall, Texas. The earliest Hall ancestor that I have firmly identified for Dr. Rufus Clarence Hall is Charles Merryman Hall (born about 1748). He lived in Virginia and Tennessee. This story starts earlier. Charles's parents appear to be William (born about 1715 in England) and Mary (Merryman) (born 1719 in Baltimore) Hall. The documented linkage to them is a bit tenuous but I gain confidence with every push into the records and present my case. Reasons for making this connection include: a naming tradition of Merryman, William, John, Charles and Mary; assertions in some sources that the "brothers", Charles and William were from Maryland; proximity to many family "in-laws" once William and Mary moved from Maryland to Virginia; a close documented (in many recorded transactions) relationship with his nephew, William who's documentation to his father, John and grandfather, William is solid; Charles and William (nephew) married sisters; and a good date fit.

After selling off their land in Maryland, William Hall and his wife, Mary Merryman moved to Lunenburg County, Virginia near the Falling River about 1748. The portion of the county they settled in was made a part of Bedford County in 1754 and that became Campbell County in 1782. Charles Merryman Hall is mentioned in records that would place him in Bedford/ Campbell Counties as an orphan in 1759 and as an adult resident around 1777. His name appears in court records in Davidson County, Tennessee beginning in 1798. By that time, he had sold most of his land in Virginia and moved his family to the Clover Bottoms along the Stones River just outside of Nashville.

As early settlers of Virginia and Tennessee, the extended Hall family suffered their share of depredations from the area's Indian inhabitants. Charles was orphaned at about age 10. His father, William, was killed by Cherokee Indians in Bedford County, Virginia during a local militia effort to recover some stolen horses in the spring of 1758. Hearings were held and testimony was given to investigate that incident. Probate Court proceedings do not mention William's wife, Mary, and it is presumed that she had died earlier. In 1759, court records indicate that the orphans of William Hall, including Charles, were to be bound out for adoption by the local church wardens as was the custom. No record has been found so far that states what family Charles may have been placed with. I think it is likely that Charles remained with his older brother, John, who was managing his father's estate; thereby creating an opportunity for Charles and his nephew, William, to become close.

Charles Merryman Hall married three times. The children from his first marriage (to Agnes Campbell) included: John B., William, Mary "Polly", Elizabeth, Nancy C. and Martha. After Charles died in 1826, these children asserted a vigorous effort in court to sway the division of the assets of his estate away from their father's third wife, Nancy B. (Steele) Hall and children: Charles M., Aristin and Elizabeth Hall. They presented a will in court which was denied. Time passed finding witnesses, hearing testimony and other delays. The court determined that it would divide the estate equally between the parties after the widow had received her portion. The assets were inventoried and sold and the estate was divided. The benefit to us today is that we have clear documentation of how all of the named parties in the dispute are related.

The children of Charles Merryman Hall went their separate ways from their homestead in Tennessee. John B. moved his family with his cousin, William Hall, to Mississippi. The Cross's, along with the William W. Hall family moved to Alabama. William W. Hall later moved on to Texas. Elizabeth (Hall) London and her family settled in Missouri and some of her children later came to Texas. Nancy C. (Hall) (Russell) and her husband, John Neely bounced between Tennessee and Alabama. Martha married William Williams and apparently died within a few years as she was not mentioned in the legal battles over her father's estate. The family of the third wife, Nancy (Steele), remained in Tennessee for awhile before moving off to Texas.

The grandparents of Dr. Rufus Clarence Hall, William W. and Pamela (Shropshire) Hall, came to the Republic of Texas in 1844 from Jackson County, Alabama. There must have been some sadness as William was not to see his sister, Mary "Polly" and brother-in-law, Maclin Cross again. They had been close for many years. And, there may have been some excitement too, given the promotions they no doubt heard from Sterling Robertson (1785-1842), a cousin of Maclin Cross and the empresario of Robertson's Colony in Texas.

Each generation has its story and memories to share and tell. There have been many hardships and many successes. Interspersed among the statistics, I have tried to capture some of the great wit that abounds in this family and note that we do have our share of good cooks. Many of the family stories and traditions that I have uncovered have been dusted off and recorded here. The information I have compiled is captured in multiple volumes. This being the first which covers the earliest ancestors of Dr. Hall and migrations from Virginia into Ohio, Illinois, Missouri, Mississippi, Tennessee, Alabama and Texas. There is some overlap between volumes which should facilitate tracking the family lines through the generations and these books.

Ronald C. Hall
Ft. Worth, Texas
October 2013

Descendants of William Hall (c. 1715 - 1758)

First Generation

1. William Hall was born about 1715 in England[1] and died on 9 May 1758 in Bedford County, Virginia[2] about age 43. The cause of his death was reported in sworn testimony. He was shot and killed by Indians while participating in a local militia effort to recover some stolen horses.[3]

Death Notes:

From: The History of Pittsylvania County, Virginia

The French and Indian War began about 1754 over boundary disputes between the French and English regarding their colonies in the Americas. Many of the northern Indians took sides with the French in waging war on the English settlers in Virginia. In 1756, Governor Dinwiddie of the Virginia Colony pursued a peace treaty with friendly Cherokee and Catawba Indians. Terms of the treaty required Virginia to build a fort for the protection of the Indian children and their wives from the northern tribes. The Indians were to provide 500 warriors to defend the settlers. By October 1757, the fort at Winchester was completed. Some 400 Indian warriors arrived soon after. However, only 180 remained. Those that left were *"disaffected toward the Virginians through French influence"* and as a consequence began wrecking havoc on the settlers as they passed through the English settlements. They had become particularly aggressive by the time they reached western Halifax and Bedford Counties. The settlers were generally restrained from attacking the Indians because it was well known that the Cherokees were friendly and the English wanted to avoid outright, open warfare. The Indians knew this and took advantage of the settlers by attacking, robbing and insulting the inhabitants. The citizens of Bedford County petitioned to be allowed to kill the Indians and asked for soldiers to be stationed among them for protection. This petition was denied in hopes of preventing open conflict. The Indian attacks continued.

In 1758, Mr. Blair, the presiding official of the Virginia Colony prior to the arrival of Governor Fauquier ordered an investigation into the origins of the troubles in Halifax and Bedford Counties with the Cherokees. A special court was held at Mayes Ferry on the Staunton River on June 1, 1758. Depositions were taken of *"those who had suffered from Indian outrages or taken part in conflicts with them."* The inquiry was specifically focused on three engagements between militia of Halifax and Bedford Counties in conjunction with part of Captain Hawkins' men and several bands of Indians in their march through those settlements.

John Wheeler, William Verdiman, John Hall, Richard Thompson, William Verdiman, Jr., Robert Jones, Jr., and Henry Snow were sworn with regard to the first engagement. John Wheeler, aged 50, John Hall and Richard Thompson, each about 25 years old, swore they had been robbed of some horses at the beginning of May. They were informed by a neighbor that several Indians had passed through with a great number of packed horses and that several horses (at least 20) had gone missing throughout the neighborhood. Additionally, several houses had been robbed and at least one family had been captured and feared murdered as they were missing. It was said that the Indians had called themselves Shawnees. Wheeler, Hall and Thompson and four others agreed to go after the Indians *"and in a friendly manner demand the horses and other things stolen."* Wheeler, Hall and Thompson went on horseback, the others were on foot. They found the Indians *"and the deponent, Wheeler calling them brothers, desired to treat with them. The Indians, painted and sullen, put themselves in a posture for battle, and sternly asked if they were for War."* The deponents replied that they were not and that they were *"friends and brothers"* and desired peace and quiet delivery of their horses. They asked the Indians of what Nation they were. The Indians *"instantly set up a War Whoop."* The Indians seized the bridle of Wheeler's horse and after receiving several blows from their tomahawkes; Wheeler abandoned his horse and fled on foot. He was pursued by three Indians. Three guns were fired. Wheeler heard a bullet whistle by him. He and his companions escaped without any other loss or injuries excepting two horses were taken by the Indians. In their retreat, they met up with the rest of the company who were on foot. They decided to follow the Indians. They were then joined by a few other men making their number about eleven. Not all of the men had guns. When they arrived at the river bank of the Staunton River they heard an Indian *"WarHallo"* on the other side. They proceeded to cross the river and found a small fire "just kindled" as they came up the bank on the other side. A short distance away, they observed *"the enemy."* Old William Verdiman, about age 60, led the group who followed close at his heels up to the enemy encampment. The Indians had tied their horses (*"pretty many in number"*) to the bushes. Most of the Indians were painted; others were painting, some red but mostly black. As he came near, Old Verdiman pulled off his hat and bowed and called out to them in terms of peace and friendship. He said, *"Gentlemen we come in a brotherly manner to ask of you for our horses and other goods that you have taken from us."* The Indians gave a kind of grunt and presented a mischievous demeanor. They stripped themselves and *"through out the priming of their guns, fresh primed and cocked them."* They then struck their tomahawks against the trees and demanded in an angry manner if the deponents would fight. *"Whilst Verdiman who was still uncovering, bowing and treating with them, the enemy indeavored to inviron them and had actually got them into a half circle before the deponents were aware."* Young Verdiman observed that two Indians were pointing their guns at them. The deponents then began to retreat backwards with their faces towards the Indians. They took to the trees. The Indians threw their tomahawks and narrowly missed two of the men. Another tomahawk would have hit Old Verdiman but he deflected the blow with his Elder stick. He was one of the group that had no gun. The Indians drove the men almost to the river bank when a gun was fired and then many guns were discharged on both sides. Three Indians were wounded.   It was at this time that the father of John Hall [William] was mortally wounded.   Ammunition was scarce among the men and they *"were obliged to fly from tree to tree for a shott of powder and lead."*   They escaped across the river and reorganized at a neighbor's house with more supplies and ammunition. They went back to the place of the engagement to look for their wounded friend, *"who they found expiring."* Three Indians were dead and there was much plunder. They scalped the Indians and threw their bodies into the river. They took away their dying friend, who died soon after, and the plunder which consisted of horses, saddles, bridles and clothing. This was detailed in an inventory presented to the court.

The second engagement (there were three being investigated) involved Captain Pinkethman Hawkins's militia company who were sent out by Colonel Talbot to join Captain Mead in finding the enemy who had killed **Hall**, stole horses and plundered the residents of Halifax and Bedford counties.

--

From: George Washington Papers Series 4. General Correspondence. 1697-1799
Transcription of the testimony of Timothy Dalton, May 9, 1758:
[Note 1: 1 Sent by President Blair to Washington.]
"BEDFORD COUNTY
This Day Timothy Dalton made Oath before me one of his majestyes Justices of the peace for the Said County: that yesterday there Came to his house three Indians and Quickly after Came four white men in Pursuit of the Said Indians namely John Wheeler Robt. Dalton Henry Wooddy William Hall from whom the Said Indians had Stollen horses from the Demanded the horses of the Said Indians but they Refused to let them have them on which the Said Wheeler went to take one of the horses on which they Shot at the Said Wheeler three times but Missed him on which the Said Indians went away and the Said white men in a Small time Joined with Seven more white men and went in Pursuit of the Said Indians again and them Indians being Joined by ten more Indians went over Stanton River a mile above the mouth of Pigg River and Threw off their Packs and Prepared them Selves for Battle then William Vardeman Sener and Some of the Rest went up to them and told them they Did not want to fight they only wanted their Horses and Did not want to hurt them on which the Indians told them they Should fight for them and Immediately the Indians fired on them three Guns Still the white men would not Shoot at them then the Indians fired three Guns more at them on that the Battle Began in which William Hall was mortally wounded of which wound he Died this Morning: and Likewise Richard Thompson was wounded in the Shoulder and Buttock; and that the white men Like Wise Killed and Scalped three Indians on which the Rest of the Indians Ran away and Left the horses and the Chief of the Plunder they had Stolen; and farther this Deponent Saith not Certified under my hand this the 9 Day of May 1758
ROBT. BABER"
--

From: George Washington Papers Series 4. General Correspondence. 1697-1799
Letter of William Callaway to George Washington, May 15, 1758
BEDFORD 15th May 1758
SIR
The Circumstances of afairs at this time causes my Boldness in hopes To Receive Information what was ye. Reason of our frend Indions as we Call them Returning Home if they are Returned & To inform you how we are opressd & what has hapened Last week by several Parties of Indions by Computation about 70 or 80 which Cald themselves Sumtimes Cherokees and sumtimes Shonees & has acted Vilinously Robing & Stealing, Plundering houses; Puling men of their horses striping & whiping Beating with tomahoaks & Stoning many People in so much that the People Gathering demanded Reasons & their Horses to be Returned On that they have had two scrimidges There was four white men folowed & Come up with three Indions who Put our men to defianc & shott at them several runs & then went of our white men being Joynd by seven other white men folowed ye Indions who when they Came to them was Joynd by Ten more Indions Our men Told ye Indions they were brothers & that they wanted their horses The Indions told them that they must fight for them and Prepared themselves for Battle Our People Told ye. Indions they did not want to fight they were Brothers they only wanted their horses ye Indions called themselves Shawnees & fird three guns at our men & omediatly three more & shot down **Wm Hall** *one of our men on which although our men had not all got guns & sum of them wood not fire they Returned ye. fire so Brisk that they Kild three Indions & wounded several Took the stolen Horses & plunder there was one white man kild. & one wounded--Likewise another Party Comited ye. same vilony with Cuting open beds & throughing out ye. fithers & was folowed & when the white men Came near a Cap of Luningburg and a Leutenant of this County went up to talk with ye. Indions & Cald them Brothers & desird to be in frend ship with them. The Indions answd. no Brothers no Cherokees they were Shonese Took the Cap & Leutenant & strapd them & Beat Them That they were Glad to Got off naked to save Life on which the Rest of their men Pursued & Gott before the Indions & had a scurmidge with them But ye. number of Indions computed sixty or Seventy & white men about forty & sum Part of ye. white men Run before a gun fird Others Broke soon after without being of any service the Indions Kept the grounds when the white men went ye. next day there was but one Indion But many Horses & sum Bagidg The Consequence of this time only Is to determine If the Indions*

4

should be Cherokees Acting this to open a War It may Hasten the Crises if not they must Explain their frendship on better tirms Our County as well as the Neighbouring Countys is in the greatest Consternation Imaginable I thought it most Expedient to Comunicate this to you & hope you will mutely consider the Case & as we are not aprised Whether those Indions if Cherokees is diserted or not that its Quite nesary you should know their behavour you may the better deal with those still at that place though the distance was great it must be Expedient to Comunicate the Case which I hope you will give your self the Trouble to send an answer by ye. bearer & other news if not agst. your athoritys Intrests
I shall subscribe my self your most
... oblid your Hume. sert.
... WM. CALLAWAY

Research Notes:

William Hall and Mary Merryman were married in Baltimore, Baltimore County, Maryland. Two children, John and Mary, were born in Baltimore. Their births are recorded in the registers of St. Paul's Parish in Baltimore. William and Mary sold their land in Baltimore and moved to Lunenburg County, Virginia (later to become Bedford County) around 1747-1748. They settled with a large contingent of Mary's Merryman family and in-laws and business partners. William Hall is listed among a number of his "in-laws" on several yearly Tithes Lists for Lunenburg County, Virginia beginning in 1748. I suppose it is possible that the William Hall identified here, residing in Lunenburg County, Virginia in the middle of a large contingent of Merrymans, Hailes, Talbots and Choates (all related in family or business) all from Baltimore, Maryland is unrelated. My speculation is that this is William Hall and his wife, Mary (Merryman) Hall who had decided to join the family migration.

In 1758, William and his son, John, participated in a militia effort to recover some stolen horses from a band of Indians. William Hall was killed in that skirmish. A detailed report was compiled by a tribunal in June 1758 regarding the incident. John Hall and others gave testimony. Later, in Probate Court, John was made the administrator of his father's estate. It would appear that William's wife, Mary, had died before 1759 as she is not mentioned in the probate proceedings.

In 1759, Bedford County, Virginia Court orders indicate that William Hall's underaged children were assigned out into the community as orphans. Records are scant regarding where the children were placed. Transactions and relationships can be observed in later records that identify and tie some of the children together.

Documentation on my line of Halls is solid to a Charles Merryman Hall of Campbell County, Virginia and Davidson, County, Tennessee. Campbell County came out of Bedford County, Virginia when is was formed. Charles is the name of one of the orphans of William Hall (d. 1758). Charles is found in multiple records in Davidson County, Tennessee participating in transactions with William Hall, a son of John Hall as well as his children. Charles and William are married to sisters, Agnes and Elizabeth Campbell. My documentation clearly points to the family of William Hall, Sr. (d. 1758). My DNA test should stand as a marker for that family.

In December 2007, Ronald C. Hall participated in a DNA study analyzed by Family Tree DNA of Houston, Texas and organized by the "Hall DNA Project". Those results are published under the name of the "earliest known ancestor," William Hall, Kit Number: 108353. The original test was upgraded to a 67 marker test. Results so far have produced at least one very close match to date. That gentleman's name is Timothy E. Hall. Research on Timothy's ancestors has progressed. A current survey points to an early ancestor named John Hall, farmer and wagon-maker, born in Virginia about 1780. He was living in Texas in 1850. This John appears to me to be a great grandson of William Hall (d. 1758) through William's eldest son, John. His line is attached in this report to John's son, John, Jr.

Haplogroup R1b1 is the most common haplogroup in European populations. It is believed to have expanded throughout Europe as humans re-colonized after the last glacial maximum 10-12 thousand years ago. This lineage is also the haplogroup containing the Atlantic modal haplotype. The haplogroup, R1b1 would include and may indicate English/Irish origins.

This brings us to family lore. John Hall, of Missouri in 1832, a great -grandson of John Hall, brother of Charles (sons of William), is said to have written the following: *"Hall - William Hall of England settled in Pennsylvania, and was killed by the Indians."* Further stories from another source add: *"Four Hall brothers were brought to America by their mother in 1725 to escape military service. They came from Birmingham, England and settled among the Quakers in the Philadelphia area. Among these sons was one named Matthew."*

A Mathew Hall in Pennsylvania has been identified by other researchers as a candidate. *"Matthew Hall came to this country when quite young from Staffordshire, England as stated by his grandson John Hall, son of Mahlon & Jane (Higgs) Hall. He settled in Bucks County, Pa. but no relationship has been established between him and other Halls of that county.....*" Staffordshire is where Birmingham, England is located. It is asserted that descendants of that family also settled in Bedford County, Virginia, years later.

There is current speculation among researchers that naming traditions would imply that the name of William Hall's father was "John." See endnotes for correspondence.

A Thomas Hall who lived in Lunenburg/Bedford County should be looked into as well as a Durham Hall of Norfolk, Virginia who died in 1750. Durham Hall's will was witnessed by Archibald Campbell and Elizabeth Campbell and mentions his brother, William, and land to be sold in Lunenburg County, Virginia. Note: There is more than one Archibald Campbell and William Hall out there and there is lots of land in Lunenburg County. It just seems coincidental that all of these names and places show up on one document at the right time frame. We will see what further research bears out.

The family may have come to America from England (DNA tests indicate that.) and settled initially in Pennsylvania as described above. A move to Baltimore by William Hall, once old enough, would have been quite manageable. So, the story above could well be ours. Proof is elusive.[4]

Noted events in his life were:
- He owned land from 1742 to 1745 in Baltimore County, Maryland.[5]
  Deed records show that William Hall and Mary Hall conveyed land in Baltimore County, Maryland to Christopher Choate on May 23, 1742.
  "23 May, 1742, William & Mary Hall, planter, of Baltimore Co., Maryland to Christopher Choate, of same, £3.5, 50 acres ...patented by John Lane. Signed William Hall. Wit. John Risteau and Nathaniel Gist."

Notes from a Choate family researcher state that this property was known as Hall's Approach and Christopher and Flora Choate raised hogs and corn on the property.

Deed records show that William and Mary Hall sold land in Baltimore County, Maryland on July 27, 1745.
"July 27, 1745 William & Mary Hall and Christopher & Flora Choate, planters of Baltimore Co., Maryland to Amon Butler, £54, 50 acres...line of John Lane. Signed William Hall and Christopher (x) Choate. Wit: William Rogers and Emanuel Teal."

Notes from a Choate family researcher state that Mary Hall and Flora Choate relinquished their dower rights to this property and the 54 pounds paid for the property included *"20 head of hoggs and one moity of corn now growing on said land, for which the said Butler had a bill of sale."*

Choate family researchers wonder if Mary Hall was Mary Choate, daughter of Christopher and Flora Choate. No record has been found to support that speculation.

Children of Christopher and Flora Choate settled in Lunenburg County, Virginia at about the same time as William and Mary Hall (1747-1748).

- He owned land on the Patapsco River from 1744 to 1746 in Baltimore County, Maryland.[6]
  "A tract of fifty acres called "The Level Bottom" surveyed for William Hall of Baltimore County, July 10, 1744 is described as situated *"upon the main falls of Patapsco River...beginning at a bounded hickory and a bounded chesnut tree standing by the Indian Road on the west side of Patapsco Falls..."*"

Deed records show that William Hall (weaver) and his wife, Mary of Baltimore County sold land to William Cross, planter, of same, on 4 August 1746. He paid £5 and 3000 pounds of tobacco for 50 acres on the west side of Patapsco River. The transaction was witnessed by Samuel Owings and Urath Owings.

"Cross, William ...in Aug. 1746 bought 50 a. Level Bottom from William Hall, weaver, and w. Mary..."

William Cross already owned at least 23 acres on the east side of Patapsco Falls.

William Cross may be a brother of Joseph Cross who married Elizabeth Merryman, sister of Mary Merryman, wife of William Hall.

- He owned land in 1750 in Baltimore County, Maryland.[7]
  Deed records indicate that in 1750 William Hall owned part of Pleasant Meadows and 50 a. of Hall's Range. This <u>may</u> be our William Hall.

- He had a residence in 1748 in Lunenburg County, Virginia.[8]
  Tithes List taken by John Phelps in 1748 *"from the mouth of the Falling River upwards."* His area includes land that would later become a part of western Bedford and Campbell Counties. Names include:
  Nicholas Hail III (brother-in-law of Charles Merryman III, brother of Mary Merryman)
  Charles Morreman (brother of Mary Merryman)
  William Mead (future son-in-law of Nicholas Haile III)
  William Hall (husband of Mary Merryman)
  John Beard (future father-in-law of Archibald Campbell)
  Adum Beard (future brother-in-law of Archibald Campbell)

  Other Halls in this same area on John Phelps's list include:
  Thomas Hall and John Hall, relationship unknown.

  Additional names of interest on Phelps list, all deponents in the investigation of the Indian depredations and killing of William Hall in 1758:
  Robert Baber, Timothy Dalton, William Vardeman, William Vardeman, Jr., John Wheler, Robert Jones (this may be the father of Robert Jones, Jr., deponent)
  --
  Mathew Talbot's Tithes List dated June 19, 1748
  Mathew Talbot (son-in-law of Nicholas Haile III)
  Mathew Talbot, Jr.
  Charles Talbot (Mathew Talbot's older brother)
  Moses, Thomas and William Hall are listed on Mathew Talbot's List. There is a will in Lunenburg County, Virginia records, of a William Hall who apparently died in 1753 that mentions his sons, Thomas and Moses Hall and granddaughter, Elliball Hall. (I have not found a connection to this family. See Research notes. --rch)
  --
  William Caldwell's Tithes List for 1748
  Richard Lane (brother-in-law of William Merryman, brother of Mary Merryman Hall)
  Tidence and John Lane (sons of Richard Lane).

- He had a residence in 1749 in Lunenburg County, Virginia.[9]
  Tithes List taken by William Caldwell in 1749 *"from Falling River to Little Ronoke River."* Names include:
  Archibald Campbell (future father-in-law of Charles M. Hall, son of William)
  Moses and Thomas Hall (relationship to William Hall, next line below, unknown)
  William Hall (husband of Mary Merryman)
  William Rutherford (husband of Agnes Beard, daughter of John Beard, sister of Elizabeth Beard Campbell)
  Charles Talbot (brother of Mathew Talbot)
  --
  Tithes List taken by Nicholas Haile in 1749 *"from Goose Creek to the extent of the County upwards."* Names include:
  Nicholas Haile III (brother-in-law of Charles Merryman III, brother of Mary Merryman Hall)
  Nicholas Haile, Jr.
  Charles Merryman, Senr. Constable (brother of Mary Merryman Hall)
  Charles Merryman, Jr.
  Joseph Clark
  William Merryman (or Clark) (brother of Mary Merryman Hall)
  Sabret Choat, Christopher Choat, Jr., Richard Choat (Children of Charles Choat, Sr. who engaged in land transactions with William Hall in Maryland)
  Thomas Hall, Sr., John Hall, Thomas Hall, Jr. (relationship to William Hall unknown)
  Robert Jones (perhaps the father of Robert Jones, Jr., deponent in 1758)
  --
  Tithes List taken by Mathew Talbot in 1749 *"from Falling Creek to Goose Creek."* Names include:
  Robert Baber (deponent in 1758)
  William Mead (future son-in-law of Nicholas Haile III)
  Matw Talbot (son-in-law of Nicholas Haile III)
  Matw Talbot, Jr.
  Wm. Verdemon (deponent in 1758)
  John Wheeler (deponent in 1758)

- He had a residence in 1750 in Lunenburg County, Virginia.[10]
  Tithes List taken by Nicholas Haile in 1750 *"from Goose Creek to the extent of the county upwards."* Names include:

Nicholas Haile, Jr.

Charles Merryman (brother of Mary Merryman Hall)

Charles Merryman, Jr.

Richard Choat, Sabret Choat, Christopher Chote, Jr. (children of Christopher and Flora Choate of Baltimore, Maryland)

William Merryman (brother of Mary Merryman Hall)

William Hall (husband of Mary Merryman Hall)

John Beard (father-in-law of Archibald Campbell)

Nicholas Haile III (brother-in-law of Charles Merryman III, brother of Mary Merryman Hall)

Thomas Hall, Jr., Thomas Hall, Sr., John Hall (Not thought to be related to William Hall above.--rch)

Robert Jones (perhaps the father of Robert Jones, Jr. deponent in 1758)

--

Tithes List taken by William Caldwell in 1750 *"from Little Roanoke up the Fork"*

Wm. Rutherford (husband of Agnes Beard, daughter of John Beard, sister of Elizabeth Beard Campbell)

Chas. Talbot (brother of Mathew Talbot, who was a son-in-law of Nicholas Haile III)

Jno. Beard (father-in-law of Archibald Campbell)

--

Tithes List taken by Abra. Martin in 1750 *"from Blew Stone to Little Roanoke"*

Thomas, Moses and William Hall (thought to be unrelated to William Hall and Mary Merryman Hall--rch)

--

Tithes List taken by John Phelps in 1750 *"from Falling River to Goose Creek"*

Matw. Talbot, Jr.

Wm. Verdsman (deponent in 1758)

Wm. Verdsman, Junr. (deponent in 1758)

William Mead (son-in-law of Nicholas Haile III)

Timy. Dalton (deponent in 1758)

Jno. Wheeler (deponent in 1758)

Robert Baber (deponent in 1758)

--

Tithes List taken by Richard Witton in 1750

Richd. Thompson (deponent in 1758)

- He had a residence in 1752 in Lunenburg County, Virginia.[11]
Tithes List taken by William Caldwell in 1752. Names include:

Archibal Cambil (father-in-law of Charles Merryman Hall)

John Baird (father-in-law of Archibald Campbell)

Chas. Talbot (brother of Mathew Talbot II)

Wm. Hall (husband of Mary Merryman)

--

Tithes List taken by John Phelps in 1752. Names include:

Sabrit Choat, Christopher Choat, Jr., Richd. Choat (children of Christopher Choate of Baltimore, Maryland)

Matw. Talbot, Jr.

--

Tithes List taken by Mattw. Talbot in 1752. Names include:

Mattw. Talbot (son-in-law of Nicholas Haile III)

Jno. Talbot

Abm. Chandler

Danl. Krins

Mrs. Nichs Hail (widow of Nicholas Haile III)

Shadrick Hail

Nichs Hail, Junr.

Chs. Merriman (brother of Mary Merryman Hall)

Chs. Merriman, Jr.

Adam Baird (son of John Beard)

Robt. Baber (deponent in 1758)

William Verdeman (deponent in 1758)

William Verdeman, Jr. (deponent in 1758)

Timy. Dalton (deponent in 1758)

--

Tithes List taken by Cornelius Cargill in 1752. Names include:

Wm. Rutherford (husband of Agnes Beard, daughter of John Beard, sister of Elizabeth Beard Campbell)
Robert Jones, Jr. (deponent in 1758)
--
Tithes List taken by Field Jefferson in 1752. Names include:
Richard Thompson (deponent in 1758)

- He had an estate probated from 1758 to 1769 in Bedford County, Virginia.[12]
  Bedford County, Virginia Order Book 1-B, 1754 - 1761
  page 96 - *"On the motion of John Hall, who made oath and entered into bond with John Quarles, John Board and Mathew Talbot... of £500. Certificate is granted him for obtaining administration of the estate of William Hall."*

  James Callaway, Augustin Leftwich, William Verdemen and John Wheeler, or any three, being first sworn are appointed to appraise the estate of William Hall, deceased. Recorded: November Court 1758.

  Bedford County, Virginia Order Book 1-B, 1754 - 1761
  page 103 - *"Ordered that the churchwardens bind out Elisha, **Charles**, William, Thomas, Sarah, Rebecca, and Susanna Halls, orphans of William Hall."* Recorded: 23 January 1759.

  Bedford County, Virginia Deed Book A-1, 1754-1762
  page 243 - Hall, William Inventory of the Estate of William Hall on December 29, 1758 by Augustin Leftwich, Wm. Verdman and John Wheeter. Lists cattle, farm tools, kitchen utensils, furniture, food products and a 30 pound note. Recorded: 26 November 1759.

  Bedford County, Virginia Order Book 1-B, 1754 - 1761
  page 156 - Robert Baber, John Quarles, William Irvine are appointed to settle the estate of William Hall, deceased. Recorded: April Court 1761

  Bedford County, Virginia Will Book 1, 1759 - 1787
  page 76 - Settlement of accounts of William Hall; by: John Quarles, Robert Baber. Recorded: 23 May 1769.

William married **Mary Merryman,** daughter of **Charles Merryman, Jr.** and **Jane Long,** on 17 Dec 1734 in Patapsco River, St. Paul's Parish, Baltimore County, Maryland.[13] Mary was born on 27 Mar 1719 in Baltimore County, Maryland[14] and died before 1759 in Bedford County, Virginia.

Death Notes:
She is not mentioned in the 1759 probate proceedings of her husband, William Hall in Bedford County, Virginia. It is presumed she had died before that time. John Hall was named administrator of his father's estate. --rch, 2010

General Notes:
Mary was mentioned in her father's (Charles Merryman) will. Disbursements were made to her through her husband, William Hall. Her married sisters (Ann m. Benjamin Richards and Elizabeth m. Joseph Cole) received disbursements from the estate in the same manner. --rch[15]

Research Notes:
There are at least two Mary Halls that appear in Baltimore, Maryland records of 1715-1760. One is older, one younger. Ours is the younger.

The older Mary was married to a William Hall as well. She may be the Mary Hall, widow, who married John Chapman in Baltimore County, Maryland in 1746. The older Mary had at least three husbands: She was widow and adminx. of the estate of Thomas Gwin in 1726 in Anne Arundel County. She posted an administrative bond for William Hall's estate on July 20, 1749 with Robert and John Chapman. She married John Chapman as her third husband by November 7, 1750. The estate of William Hall was administered by Mary Hall on 31 Oct. 1750 and 7 Nov. 1850. This is not the Mary who moved with her husband, William Hall to Lunenburg, Virginia by 1747.[16]

Children from this marriage were:

2 M   i.   **John Hall** was born on 31 Jul 1735 in Baltimore County, Maryland[17] and died about Aug 1794 in Bedford County, Virginia about age 59.

       Noted events in his life were:
       - He served in the military in 1758 in Bedford County, Virginia.[18]
          An act of assembly, passed March 1758, the 31st year of the reign of King George II, some of the militia were

called out for service in the early days of the French and Indian War, Annexed to this act, was a schedule of the names of the militia officers and soldiers, and the citizens who furnished provisions to that militia. This is the schedule pertaining to Bedford County.

Names listed include: <u>John Hall</u>, Archibald Campbell, John Hunter, James M'Reynalds, Robert Ogelsby, Thomas Ogelsby, Adam Beard, Edward Choat, Augustine Choat, Edward Ohair (Phair).

- He signed a will on 10 May 1794 in Bedford County, Virginia.[19]
"IN THE NAME OF GOD AMEN May 10th, 1794, I John Hall of Bedford County and State of Virginia being weak in body but of Perfect mind and memory thanks be to God for the same but calling to mind the mortality of men & knowing that it appointed to all men once to die, do make and Ordain this my Last Will & Testament. (Viz) in the manner & form as followeth Princepally & first of all I give & recommend my soul to God that First give it a being, & and my body to the earth from whence it was taken to be buried in decent form and that at the Discretion of my executors nothing doubting but <u>but</u> that I shall receive it again by the mighty Power of God at the General Resurrection and as Touching such Worldley Estate as the Lord hath blest me with in this life I give Demise & Dispose of the same in the following manner & form; first I give & bequeath unto my beloved wife Magdalane Hall all my Negroes that I possess. (to wit) Jamis Patt Jude frank Joe Bitte Patt Pegge as long as she lives & at her death I give & bequeath unto my son Mathew Hall a Negroe Man James and a Negroe Woman named Patt, Item I give unto my son William Hall a Negro man named Joe. Item I give unto my son Elisha Hall a Negroe Wooman named <u>Judge</u> and a Negro man named Frank. Item I give unto my son Jesse Hall one feather bed & Cow & Calf. Item Give unto my son Hezekiah Hall one horse & saddle & 1 cow and calf. Item I give unto my son John Hall one shilling starling and no more Item I give to my Daughter Tabitha Hall one Negroe Girl named Pegge at my wife's death Likewise one Feather bed & cow & calf. Item I give unto my Daughter Keziah Hall, one Negroe Girl named Patt at my wife's death Likewise one Feather Bed & Cow & Calf. Item I give to my Beloved wife Magdalen Hall a third part of my land as long as she lives and to fall to Mathew Hall & Elisha Hall my two sons to be divided as followeth to with Mathew Hall is to have the upper end, beginning at the old mill seat and then down the said creek to the fence & then along sd. Fence to the branch that comes down from John Owens then up the said branch to owen's line, and then follow his Line round to the beginning. Item I give unto my son Elisha Hall the balance of all the Land I now Possess together with the mill, and also an equal part of all my moveable property. And it is my Will & Pleasure that the rest of my moveable properties be left in the hands of my wife, that she may divide it as she sees cause - Between Hezekiah Tabitha & Keziah Hall. & Lastly I nominate & appoint my wife magdalen Hall as Executer of this my Last Will & Testament. I do hereby utterly Disanull Revoke all & every other former Testament, Will Legases bequeaths and Executors by me in any wise before named willed & bequeathed. Rattifying & confirming this & no other to be my last will & testament."
John Hall
Signed sealed & Delivered
In the Presents of us -
William Hancock
John Hancock
John Hall, Junr.
At a Court held for Bedford County the 22nd day of September 1794 This Last Will & Testament of John Hall, Deceased was proved by oath of William Hancock & John Hancock Witnesses whose names are there unto subscribed & Ordered to be recorded.
Teste:
Ja Steptoe CBC
Will Book 2, Page 140

- He had an estate probated from 1794 to 1799 in Bedford County, Virginia.[20]
Will Book 2 - page 262, 20 Nov 1799
Inventory of the Estate of John Hall was submitted by Thomas Leftwich, Thomas Williams and John Clayton. Recorded 23 Dec 1799.

John married **Mary Magdalene Smith,** daughter of _____ **Smith** and _____ **Evans,** about 1759 in Bedford County, Virginia. Mary was born about 1745 in Virginia and died about 1833 in Bedford County, Virginia[21] about age 88.

Noted events in her life were:
- She appeared on the United States census in 1830 in Bedford County, Virginia.[22]
Presumably the female age 80-90 in the household of Elisha Hall.
Males: 15-20 (1); 50-60 (2). Females: 10-15 (2); 50-60 (1); 80-90 (1).

3 F ii. **Mary Hall** was born on 31 May 1737 in Baltimore County, Maryland.[23]

4 M iii. **Hezekiah Hall** was born about 1740 in Baltimore County, Maryland[24] and died about Jul 1811 in Bedford County, Virginia[25] about age 71.

Birth Notes:
William and Mary (Merryman) Hall did not move to Lunenburg, Virginia before 1747. It is presumed that Hezekiah was born in Maryland.--rch 2010

Noted events in his life were:
• He served in the military militia about 1756 in Lunenburg County, Virginia.[26]
From: Hening's Statutes, Volume 7
pages 21-22 - Act of Assembly for the State of Virginia, Mar 1756: *"Payment for services rendered for the defence and protection of the frontiers of the colony against the incursions and depredations of the French and their Indian allies..."*

September 1758, page 225 - Lunenburg County: Hezekiah and Aquilla Hall, £4 5s. each

• He owned land in Jan 1762 in Bedford County, Virginia.[27]
Hezekiah purchased 200 acres of land on Back Creek in January, 1762. The land was purchased for 100 pounds from a land speculator named, John Hall who had acquired it in 1758. Hezekiah's brother, John Hall, witnessed the transaction and guaranteed the payments. Witnesses to the transaction were: Thos. Christian, John Callaway, William Verdeman, William Callaway and Henry Snow.

Recorded Bedford Deed Book A-1 1754-1762; March 23, 1762; Page 535.

When Campbell County was formed from Bedford in 1782, Back Creek was part of the diving line. Hezekiah's land fell in both counties.

• He signed a will on 9 Mar 1811 in Bedford County, Virginia.[28]
"The Will is a short, terse document. Keziah, his wife, received one-third of the land, 170 acres. For Samuel, James, Abner and Keziah, his daughter, this amounted to a little over 60 acres for each of them. The older children, William, Thomas, Elisha, Sarah and Tabitha a token bequest - five shillings each." --Carrol Carmen Hall

"Will of Hezekiah Hall
I, Hezekiah Hall of Bedford County do hereby make this my last will and testament in manner and form following, that is to say, I desire that all my Just debts be first paid. I lend one third of my estate both real and personal to my wife Kiziah Hall during her natural life, and after her decease, I give the same to my four first mentioned children equally to be divided among them and to be enjoyed forever. Item, I give unto Samuel Hall, James Hall, Abner Hall and Kiziah Hall which are my beloved sons and daughter, all my estate both real and personalty not otherwise disposed of. Item, I give unto William Hall five shillings. Item, I give unto Sarah Smith my daughter five shillings. Item, I give unto Thomas Hall five shillings, Item, I give unto Elisha Hall five shillings. Item, I given unto Tabitha Dalton my daughter five shillings which I give to the, their heirs, executors, administrators and assigns forever. I do hereby constitute my friends Jesse Leftwich, Burwel Lee and Ralph Smith executors of this my last will and testament hereby revoking all other or former wills or testaments by me heretofore made. In Witness whereof I have set my hand and seal this ninth day of March one thousand eight hundred and eleven.

Hezekiah Hall {seal}
Signed sealed in the presence of
John Overstreet
Francis {X} his mark Wood
Littleberry {X} his mark Dixon

At a court held for Bedford County at the courthouse the 22nd day of July, 1811.
This last will and testament of Hezekiah Hall, dec'd, was exhibited in Court and proven by the oaths of Francis Wood and Littleberry Dixon subscribing witnesses thereto and ordered to be recorded. And at ____ held for said County at the Courthouse the 26th day of August following - on the motion of Burwell Lee one of the executors therein mentioned certificate is granted him for obtaining a probate thereof in due form, liberty being reserved the other executors to join in the probate when they shall think fit.

Teste,
J. Steptoe, C.B.C.
Clerk Bedford County"

- He had an estate probated in 1813 in Pittsylvania County, Virginia.[28]
In 1813 a suit was filed in Pittsylvania County by Litterbery Dixon to become the Executor. In the same year the suit was dismissed and Burwel Lee was retained. Land in the estate was divided by court order in March 1813.

Hezekiah married **Keziah Smith,** daughter of _____ _____ and _____ _____,
about 1774 in Bedford County, Virginia.[29] Keziah was born about 1750 in Virginia[29] and died about 1820 in
Lawrence County, Ohio[29] about age 70.

Marriage Notes:
Some sources suggest that Keziah and Mary Magdalene Smith, wife of John, are sisters and daughters of Gideon
Smith. Some sources suggest that Keziah may have married a Banks first. These issues are presently unresolved.
--rch 2011

Noted events in her life were:
- She had a residence in 1815 in Ohio.[30]
Widow Hall who owned land in Bedford County, Virginia noted on the 1815 Land Tax that her principal
residence was in Ohio.

5 M iv. **Elisha Hall** was born before 1748 in Lunenburg County, Virginia.

Noted events in his life were:
- He was involved in a court case about his apprenticeship to Jeremiah Early about 1762 in Bedford County,
Virginia.[31] Elisha sought to obtain his release.

- He was involved in a court case about regarding his apprenticeship in Jul 1766 in Bedford County, Virginia.[32]
Elisha was bound over to a new "master", "Donathan".

Elisha married **Caroline Estes,** daughter of _____ _____ and _____ _____,
about 1774 in Virginia.

6 M v. **Maj. Charles Merryman Hall** was born about 1748 in Lunenburg County, Virginia, died about 7 Oct 1826 in
Davidson County, Tennessee[33] about age 78, and was buried in Oct 1826 in Davidson County, Tennessee.

Research Notes:
Charles M. Hall was a landowner, farmer and builder in the early rural/wilderness areas of Bedford and Campbell
Counties in Virginia. The portion of Bedford County, Virginia that Charles lived in became part of Campbell
County when it was formed in 1782.

In 1759, Bedford County, Virginia Court orders indicate that William Hall's underage children were farmed out in
the community as orphans. Charles Hall was on that list of orphans. No record has been found so far that
names the family that Charles was assigned to. It is my opinion that he remained in his brother John's
household and during that time established a strong bond with his nephew, William (John's son). Reasons for
this assertion include: Charles and William married Agnes and Elizabeth Campbell, daughters of Archibald and
Elizabeth (Beard) Campbell. To date, no record has been found for Charles's marriage to Agnes. But, she is
named in her father's will, **Agnes Hall.** Charles Hall witnessed Agnes's grandfather's (John Beard) will in
1780. The marriage record for William indicates that Charles Hall posted a surety bond for William's marriage to
Elizabeth Campbell. Several land transactions and various other property transactions are recorded between
William Hall (who married Elizabeth Campbell) and his children and Charles Hall in Davidson County,
Tennessee. About 1821, William and his family sold their land in Davidson County and the family made their
move to Yazoo County, Mississippi. John B. Hall, a son of Charles, moved with them.

While there is a William listed as a brother of Charles among the orphans, the William Hall that married Elizabeth
would be too young to have been Charles's brother. Charles's father was killed in 1758. The William Hall who
married Elizabeth Campbell was born about 1763.

Further court transactions and communications recorded in Bedford County, Virginia; Bedford County,
Tennessee and Maury County, Tennessee reveal that William Hall, son of John, and William's children, all of
whom had moved to Yazoo County, Mississippi in the 1820's and 1830's, were heirs and distributees of the
estates of John Hall, Hezekiah B. Hall and a Dr. Elisha S. Hall. John was William's father. Hezekiah B. Hall was

William's unmarried brother. Elisha S. Hall was a son of William. Dr. Elisha S. Hall died before 1828, lived in Yazoo County, Mississippi in 1823 and left a legacy (a lot in Louisiana) to his brothers and sisters for an administrator in Bedford County, Tennessee to distribute.

It is said that Charles Hall and his "brother", William, built some now historic homes in Davidson County, Tennessee in partnership with the Buchannans. These are known as the "Old Blue Brick" and the "McCampbell House." That may be, though I think it was his nephew (who was also his brother-in-law) that he was in business with rather than his "brother". However, the recent discovery of a marriage of a William Hall to Archibald Buchannan's sister, Rebecca in Augusta County, Virginia may turn out to be a significant clue.

Charles Merryman Hall died in 1826 in Davidson County, Tennessee. A bitter dispute over the distribution of Charles's considerable estate was played out in the Davidson County Courts over the course of several years. Charles had married at least three times and had two sets of children. The widow, Nancy (Steele) Hall (Charles's 3rd wife) and her three children were pitted against the children from the "first" marriage to Agnes Campbell. The court ended up dividing the estate equally among the heirs after the widow got her portion. The court case is of benefit to us in that all of the family members (descendants) were identified in the proceedings. As a result, our connection to Charles Merryman Hall can be well documented.

Noted events in his life were:
• He served in the military probably as a Private in the Continental Line during the Revolutionary War from 1777 to 1778 in Virginia.[34]
In the book, <u>Lest it be Forgotten - A Scrapbook of Campbell County, Virginia</u> compiled by The Historical Committee of the Bicentennial Commission of Campbell County, Virginia, the name Charles Hall appears on a list of men from Bedford County, Virginia that have been identified as Revolutionary War soldiers. A scant line entry also appears in Gwathmey's <u>Historical Register of Virginians in the Revolution 1775-1783</u>.

A review of the microfilmed payroll and muster rolls of Capt. John Willis's Company of the 2nd Virginia Regiment, Commanded by Christian Febiger shows a Charles Hall on the payroll from October 1777 through February 1778. On the Muster Roll of December 1777, he is noted to be in the hospital. Charles appears on an additional payroll form in February 1778 for "extraordinary pay." In March 1778, his name is on the "Account of Money due the dead, deserted and prisoners of the 2nd Virginia Regiment." There are no notations beside his name indicating the specifics of his status (most every other soldier on the list has a note of some sort). I have not found any further record of active service for Charles Hall.

The 2nd Virginia Regiment was part of the Southern Army that spent the winter of 1777-1778 at Valley Forge. In December of 1777, the 2nd Regiment had 406 men on its rosters, 245 of them were sick. The roster had lost 160 men by March 1778. On December 23, 1777, of the whole army encamped at Valley Forge, 2,898 men were reported sick or unfit for duty due to the lack of clothing. By February 1778, the number of incapacitated increased to 3,989. Small Pox and "the itch" were the predominant illnesses reported. Typhus, typhoid, dysentery and pneumonia were among the other diseases that challenged the troops. Sickness, lack of: supplies, clothing and payroll caused many men to go home.

An additional perspective is given in <u>The Grandfathers, The Hall and Overstreet Families</u> by Carrol Carmen Hall:

"Another letter to the Governor of Virginia stated: Captain Leftwich and Capt. Early's Co's from Bedford, after six weeks service, claiming a discharge at the end of that term, to be dated from the Time of Marching from their County, upon refusal, deserted. The pretext for their claims was a Promise from the County Lt. that they should not be compelled to serve longer than six weeks. As the Orderly Sergeants belonging to the different Companies, deserted with them and carried off their Lists, it is impossible to make an accurate Return of their names or numbers.

This last communication to the Governor of Virginia is of particular significance to the story of <u>The Grandfathers</u>. Capt. Leftwich was from the area in which a number of the Halls lived. He and his family were neighbors of the Halls; the Leftwich name appears on several family legal papers. As militia groups came from the same neighborhoods, it could well be that a number of the Halls, Overstreets and their kin were in his group."

In May of 1780, the General Assembly of Virginia passed an act authorizing the governor to impress supplies needed by the American army. Charles Hall of Bedford County, Virginia appears on a list of claimants of impressed property compiled by the county courts. Certificates were issued by the local Commissioner, when he impressed property. They were presented at the county courts between 1781 and 1783 to be authenticated and compiled. The claims were then sent to Richmond for settlement. On September 11th and 12th 1781 "Charls" Hall submitted for reimbursement his receipts for beef (1 beeve - 300 (lbs.) and another entry 8 (lbs.)) and 8 pecks of oats that had been requisitioned by the army. His neighbors (Hunter, Oglesby and Steele) appear on the list with similar claims.

From the Campbell County, Virginia Circuit Court Order Book, Vol. 2 - July 1786
"Charles Hall came into Court and proved he furnished Christopher Irvin, Commissioner of the Provisional ---- with three hundred pound weight of beef and that he has lost the certificate for the same which is ordered to be certified to the treasury."

- He had a residence in 1778 in Bedford County, Virginia.[35]
In a Bill of Sale recorded in the Campbell County Deed Book No. 4 1796-1799 on September 11, 1797, Charles M. Hall paid 100 *"pounds current money of Virginia"* to Samuel Hunter for the purchase of 200 acres of land located on Wreck Island Creek. It is noted that Charles M. Hall has resided on this land for ***"upwards of twenty years"*** and that the land was sold to Hall prior to his taking up residence there. Additionally, Charles M. Hall had *"instituted a suit in Chancery in the County Court of Campbell"* to perfect the title to the land and premises. This transaction arose out of the decree obtained in that Court during the May Term of 1797. This portion of Bedford County became Campbell County in 1782.

- He appraised the estate of Thomas Helm on 1 Aug 1781 in Bedford County, Virginia.[36]
Bedford County, Virginia Will Book 1, 1759-1787, page 398
Appraisal submitted by: Thomas McReynolds, Charles Hall and William Brown. Recorded August 28, 1781.

Thomas Carson Helm, son of Moses and Sarah Helm was killed at the battle of "Guilford Courthouse, North Carolina [some accounts say at the Battle of Cowpens] (March 15, 1781). He was a Lt. or Captain in the Revolutionary War serving in the militia from Bedford County, Virginia." His first wife was Elizabeth Oglesby, a daughter of Thomas Oglesby. He owned land along the Falling River in Bedford County. Both the Helm and Oglesby families were close neighbors of Charles Hall.

- He had a residence in 1785 in Campbell County, Virginia.[37]
Charles M. Hall was listed on the 1785 Campbell County Personal Tax List as transcribed by Jeffrey C. Weaver, July 23, 1998.
Information includes:
Name; White Males 21+; Blacks under 16; Blacks over 16; Total Blacks; Horses; Cattle

Thomas Jones' Tax List
Steel, George 1, , , 4, 5
Dixon, John 1, , , , 4, 7
Hall, David 1, , , 4, 1

District No. 2
Campbell, Archibald 1, 1, 7, 8, 7, 21
McReynolds, James 1, 3, 4, 7, 9, 28
Hall, Charles 1, 3, 3, 6, 10, 5
Steel, Alexander 1, 2, 5, 7, 12, -
Campbell, John 1, , , , 3, 4
Campbell, James 1, , , , 3, 5
Beard, Elizabeth -, 2, 3, 5, 2, 14
Dixon, James 1, 2, 6, 8, 4, 18
Dixon, James 1, 4, 1, 5, 6, 9

Burton's (5th) District
Campbell, James 1, 3, 3, 6, 2, 20
Campbell, Wm. 1, -, -, -, 4, -

Clement's Tax List

Hall, John (Glover)* 1, 1, -, 1, 1, 5 | *[His trade. --rch]

- He was involved in a court case on 10 Jan 1786 in Campbell County, Virginia.[38]
...at a Court held at the Campbell County Court House on *"Thursday the 10th day of January in the year of our Lord, one thousand seven hundred and eighty six and the tenth year of our Independence for the trial of George, a Negroe man, slave, the property of Charles Hall on suspicion of his feloniously broken open the kitchen of Mary Wilson of this county on the night of the tenth day of December last past and stealing thereout a bed cover and piece of linsey out of the loom, five small briddlings of bacon, a quantity of beef and a knife."*

  Testimony was given. George was found guilty and sentenced to five lashes on his back at the public whipping post. He apparently had an accomplice who received 39 lashes in a separate trial.

- He owned land in 1787 in Campbell County, Virginia.[39]
Campbell County, Virginia Deed Book 2, Page 191. January 1, 1787
"From Andrew Turner in the county of Buckingham to Charles Hall of Campbell, for 10 pounds, one tract of land of 100 acres in Campbell County on the head branch of Wreck Island Creek, bounded by Phelps, Hunter's Road, Larson. Signed Andrew (w his mark) Turner. Witnessed John Hunter, James Robinson, Thomas Carson, Robert Hunter. Recorded February 1, 1787."

  It is possible that this land was part of the parcels sold in 1797. See Campbell County Deed Book 4, pages 251 and 297.

- He was elected to office from 1793 to 1794 in Campbell County, Virginia.[40]
Charles M. Hall appears on The Register of the General Assembly of Virginia for Campbell County from 1793-1794 as a Member of the House of Delegates. The dates of the terms were: October 21 - December 12, 1793 and November 11- December 27, 1794.

  For timeline reference:
  * George Washington's second inauguration was in 1793.
  * George Washington proclaimed that the United States would be neutral in the matters of war and trade between France and Great Britain and its allies in 1793.
  * Thomas Jefferson resigned as Secretary of State in 1793.
  * There was a Yellow Fever epidemic particularly in the northeast in1793-1794.
  * The Whiskey Rebellion (against Federal Excise Taxes) was under way and resolved in 1794 in Pennsylvania.
  * The U. S. Post Office was founded about 1792.
  * Throughout this time period there were debates between Alexander Hamilton, Thomas Jefferson, James Madison and John Adams over the shape of the new government and foreign policy. George Washington often served as mediator.
  * In 1794, the scalp of Captain Robert Benge, Cherokee Indian, was sent to the Virginia governor as proof that *"he was no more."* The General Assembly of Virginia sent Lt. Hobbs a silver-mounted rifle to acknowledge his services.

- He owned land as evidenced in the following transactions on 11 Sep 1797 in Campbell County, Virginia.[41]
"This indenture made the eleventh day of September in the year one thousand seven hundred and ninety seven between Samuel Hunter of the one part and Charles M. Hall of the County of Campbell of the other part. Witnesseth that the said Samuel Hunter for and in consideration of the sum of one hundred pounds current money of Virginia to him in hand paid the receipt of which he doth hereby acknowledge hath granted bargained and sold and by these presents doth grant bargain and sell unto the said Charles M. Hall one certain tract or parcel of land situate lying and being in the said county of Campbell on Wreck Island Creek containing two hundred acres be the same more or less it being the land whereon the said Hall hath resided upwards of twenty years and the land which the said Hunter sold unto the said Hall before the s^d Halls residence thereon which land the said Hunter had _____ unto him by his father Alexander Hunter it being the residue of the said Alex Hunter tract which he had reserved unto himself in his lifetime after giving to his several sons their respective portions of land -- and for the perfection of the title to and in the land and premises aforesaid the said Hall instituted a suit in Chancery in the County Court of Campbell and in pursuance thereof obtained a decree at the last May Term now according to the known and reputed bounds and land marks which are as follows (to wit) beginning _____."
--
"This indenture made the eleventh day of September one thousand seven hundred and ninety seven between Charles M. Hall, Thomas Oglesby and Martha Oglesby, his wife of the County of Campbell of the one part and

John M. Walker of the County of Bedford of the other part. Witnesseth that the said Charles M. Hall and Thomas Oglesby for and in consideration of the sum of one hundred and ninety four pounds current money of Virginia to them in hand paid the receipt whereof they do hereby acknowledge have granted bargained and sold and by these presents doth grant bargain and sell unto the said John M. Walker a tract of land on the waters of Wreck Island Creek containing one hundred ninety four acres be the same more or less and bounded as follows (to wit)..." The property is bounded by Thomas Oglesby, Obadiah Patterson and William Stills' old line.

The relationship of Charles Hall to the Oglesby family (beyond neighbors) is not known at this time. For purposes of the above transaction, they may have had overlapping deeds to the property. Charles Hall was active in the probate of the will of Thomas Oglesby, Sr. in 1787. He also served in various capacities in the administration of the estate of Richard Oglesby in 1790, brother of Thomas, Jr. and son of Thomas, Sr.

A suit was filed in Campbell County Chancery Court: *"Charles Hall against the heirs of Walter West, deceased."* A summons document for the West heirs in the file is dated March 18, 1796. An official notice was published dating the suit in process on November 15, 1797. A trial was set for the March Term 1798. The testimony presented by Charles Hall was that he had negotiated a purchase agreement for some land with Walter West. Charles states that he fulfilled the agreement and paid all of the money due, but he never received a title to the land. Meanwhile, Walter West had departed Campbell County for Georgia and passed away there. Charles Hall instituted this suit to have the heirs of Walter West present a valid title to the property. The heirs were no longer in Campbell County; hence there were multiple delays of the trial. A notation in the file indicates that an attorney for S. Hunter apparently made a presentation to the court. On one document the plaintiff is named Charles M. Hall. (--rch)

- He owned land described in various parcels on Land Tax Lists from 1797 to 1810 in Campbell County, Virginia.[42]

A Summary of the tax lists of 1797 to 1810 follows:

1797 - Land Book North

Name	Acres
p. 2 Arch'd Campbell	421
p. 6 Charles Hall	200
	100
	7
	25
	326

1798-1799 - Books missing

1800 - North

p. 3 Arch'd Campbell	421
p. 7 Charles Hall	276
	25
	7

1801 - North

p. 2 Archibald Campbell	33
p. 6 Charles Hall	276
	25
	7

1802 - North, Book missing
1803 - Land Books missing
1804 - North, Book missing
1805 - North

p. 2 Archibald Campbell	33
p. 7 Charles Hall	14
**?	??? - illegible (could be John Hall? - 372?)

1806-1808 Land Books missing
1809 - North

p. 10 Charles Hall	14

1810 - North

p. 13 Charles Hall	14

1811 - North, Book missing
1812 - North

no listing for Charles Hall
1813 - Land Books missing.

- He moved about 1797 to Davidson County, Tennessee.[43]
In October 1797, he designated John M. Walker as his attorney to act in his name in all business transactions that may arise in the State of Virginia. *"Know all men by these presents that I Charles M. Hall for divers good causes and considerations me hereunto moving have made ordained constituted and appointed John M. Walker my true and lawful attorney..."* In transactions thereafter, Charles M. Hall is referred to as *"Charles M. Hall, of the <u>State of Tennessee</u> by John M. Walker of..."*

Though the record is hard to decipher, a notation in the index of Volume 6 of the Campbell County, Virginia Order Book, dated in October 1797 on page 3 indicates that a deed (probably) for land was transacted between Hall and Walker. Nancy (Hall's wife) was first privately examined. Nancy and Agnes were names that were often used as nicknames for each other. Her examination by the Court would indicate that she was verifying that she entered into the transaction of her own free will and that the property may have been an inheritance.

In September of 1798 Charles M. Hall relinquished his post as an "Overseer of the Poor" in Campbell County. *"Jno. M. Walker appt'd an Overseer of the Poor in this cty in the room of Chas M Hall who [qualified as required by] law."* Generally, prior to the Revolutionary War, the duties of an Overseer of the Poor were handled by the church; afterwards it became a civic position. Overseers of the Poor were responsible for collecting taxes from indigent residents. They would "levy poor taxes [on the general population], distribute public money and deal with the underprivileged as they thought best." Assistance to the poor was meager and usually came in the form of shelter, clothing, food, a little money, poor notes (similar to food stamps), education and apprenticeships, medical care and burials. The overseers operated the poorhouse (if there was one) and bound out orphans and illegitimate children as apprentices. To date I have not found the entry documenting the appointment of Charles M. Hall to the post as an Overseer of the Poor. It would have to have happened after Campbell County was formed in 1782 and probably after his service as a state assemblyman in 1794. My guess is that he did not hold the post long, perhaps five years. Given that Charles was an orphan himself, this was likely a significant duty for him. --rch 2011

Charles M. Hall appears frequently in the legal documents and records of Davidson County, Tennessee. He regularly served as a juror during the years 1801-1802.

Other recorded transactions of interest include:

Davidson County, Tennessee
County Court Minute Book page 313 - July 12, 1802
"..ordered that Charles M. Hall oversee the road from John Buchanan's Mill to Buchanan's Ferry on the Stone's River with those to work there-on that worked under the late overseer..."

Davidson County, Tennessee
Page 88 - Bill of Sale - June 16, 1806
"I, Maclin Cross of Davidson County sold unto Charles M. Hall of same place a number of Negroes, namely, Charles, Phil, Patty, Claiborne, Henry, a girl named Aicy and Polly. This 8 Jan 1806. Wit: Thomas Harney, Robert Hays, William London." Sale price: $1525.00. (Excepting Charles, Maclin Cross inherited these Negroes from his father in 1802. Charles was given to him by his grandfather, William Maclin, Sr. in 1798.--rch 2009)

From the **Papers of Andrew Jackson**
--Page 529 - March 1805, A bale of cotton from Charles M. Hall was delivered to Andrew Jackson's cotton gin (Jackson and Hutchins) at the Clover Bottoms by William Hall.
--Page 564 - 26 November 1811, Charles M. Hall sold a slave named David to Andrew Jackson for $450.00. [This may be one of the slaves that Charles's 2nd wife, Elizabeth, deceased, received from the estate of her late husband, Lewis Green. --rch]

Additional newspaper postings include:

From: *The Tennessee Gazette and Metro District Advertiser* - Jan. 31, 1807 - Vol. 6, No. 41

"Reward $5.00. A new saddle lost or stolen on the 29th of Dec. last at Maj. Chas. M. Hall's near the Clover Bottom. Clement Hall"

From: *The Impartial Review and Cumberland Repository* 1805-1808 Oct. 27, 1808, Vol. 3, No. 51
"A dark brown horse was taken up by Charles M. Hall in Davidson County, near the Clover Bottom. The horse was appraised at $20.00. Thos. Dillahunty"

- He owned land in the Clover Bottoms along the Stones River, just south and east of Nashville along the Old Lebanon Road in 1799 in Davidson County, Tennessee.
Index to Warranty Deeds Davidson County, Tennessee
Land Genealogy of Davidson County, Tennessee 1797-1803 Vol. 3, by Marsh, Helen C. and Timothy Grantor: John Caffrey - Grantee: Charles M. Hall 7 July 1799: 27 Nov 1799 - Book E, page 136 - 440 acres near Stones River. John Caffrey conveyed unto Charles Merryman Hall a tract of land containing 440 acres in Davidson County on the waters of Stones River, originally granted to William Moore the same being conveyed to Benjamin Knox and from said Knox to John Caffrey, adjoining a corner made for Christopher Waggoner's land. He paid 2500.00 dollars in Virginia currency. Wit: William Sanders and John Erwine. Oct Term 1799.
Also recorded in Davidson County, Tennessee, County Court Minutes 1799-1803, Minute Book, page 46, October 19, 1799. Proven by John Erwine.

Davidson County, Tennessee Deeds - Deed Book E - 11 November 1800, page 245
"This indenture made 7 Feb 1800 between Charles M. (Merryman) Hall of Davidson County of the one part and William Hall of the same place of the other part. Charles M. Hall conveyed unto William Hall a tract of land containing 177 acres in Davidson County, being part of William Moore's preemption lying between Stones River and McCrory's Creek adjoining McMurray's line and Thomas Gallaspie's line. Wit: John Hogartt and John Bowls. Oct. Term 1800."
Also recorded in Davidson County, Tennessee, County Court Minutes 1799-1803, Minute Book, page 136, October 14, 1800. Proven by John Hoggartt and John Bowls.

Davidson County, Tennessee Deeds - 11 June 1801, page 290
James Wills
It is mentioned in this record that the property of Archibald Buchannan and Charles M. Hall adjoins that of James Todd, John Hoggart and James Mulherrin along the Stones River.

Davidson County, Tennessee Deeds - Book F, December 28, 1805, page 304
Charles M. Hall
It is recorded in this entry that on 3 Feb 1801, Charles M. Hall purchased from James Wills 117 acres of land on Moore's north boundary line and adjacent the property of Captain Hoggat, "to a sugartree and redbud on Archibald Buchanon's south boundary line", the Stone's River and Mulherrin. He paid *"seven hundred and twenty-nine dollars and a half good and lawful money Virginia currency."* Witnessed by William London, McL Cross and William Hall.

Davidson County, Tennessee Deeds - Book F, March 20, 1806, page 318-319
Charles M. Hall
It is recorded in this entry that on 31 July 1804, Charles M. Hall purchased from Maclin Cross 640 acres of land in Davidson County along the Stone's River south from William Moore's south most corner. He paid two thousand dollars. Witnessed by William London, John Hall and William Hall.

Davidson County, Tennessee Deeds - Book G, April 3, 1807, page 126
Charles M. Hall
It is recorded in this entry that on 17 January 1807, Charles M. Hall purchased 170 acres along the waters of the Stones River from Thomas Gallaspie of Tazwell, Virginia for four hundred and five dollars. The land was bounded among others by James Buchanon. Witnessed by B. F. Bradford and John E. Beck.

Davidson County, Tennessee Deeds - Book G, April 2, 1807, page 129
Thomas Gillespy
It is recorded in this entry that, Thomas Gillespy purchased 480 acres along the waters of the Stones River from Charles M. Hall for $1955.00. The land was bounded among others by Samuel McMurry and William Hays.

It is likely that he had a keen interest in horse racing. Charles Hall's property near Nashville was located close to the horse racing track at Clover Bottom.

- He worked as a contractor/builder in 1799 in Davidson County, Tennessee.[44]
The Hall "brothers", partners of Archibald Buchanan, are recollected to be the builders of two old houses in Davidson County in the Clover Bottom Plantation. The "Old Blue Brick" and the "Hall-McCampbell" house were both built before 1800. It is said that the "Old Blue Brick" received its name because one wall was painted blue. At one time it was a tavern and it may have been painted blue at that time. Andrew Jackson is also said to have used the grounds for the staging of his troops.

[Hard fired bricks were also called blue brick because of the color they turned after being fired in the kiln. The Buchanan family lived in the "Old Blue Brick" home for awhile.--rch] William Hall lived in the McCampbell House until he sold it to Thomas Harding in 1820 prior to his move to Mississippi. In 1847 the house was sold to James Anderson of Kentucky. In 1852, Anderson sold it to Thomas McCampbell. It remained in the McCampbell family until 1946.

"Major Hall and his brother built the two houses. The land must have been a grant to Major Hall for services in the Revolutionary War. The house was built by slaves with bricks made on the place. The bricks were different sizes." As told by Miss Maggie McCampbell on July 7, 1936 - History of the McCampbell Home.

The "Old Blue Brick" was torn down in 1951. On March 4, 2010, the Hall-Harding-McCampbell House had been nominated to be listed on the National Registry of Historic Places.

- He served in the military as a "Patroller in Bounds" of the Davidson County Militia 1802 to 1803 in Davidson County, Tennessee.[45]
Captain William Hall was the commander of his militia company.

- He served in the military in Captain Jesse Thomas' Militia Company in 1812 in Davidson County, Tennessee.[46]
His (Capt. Thomas's) muster ground was William McMurray's farm, near Todd's Knob on the Lebanon Turnpike.
"I was a child twelve years old and was delighted when I saw him (Capt. Thomas) dress in his uniform. He wore white pants, white vest, blue cloth coat trimmed in red and brass buttons. His hat was crescent shaped with a cockade with a silver edge on one side and a large white feather tipped with red. He wore a sword and belt and a ruffled shirt and high boots." Jane H. Thomas.

Charles Hall's listing in the 1812 Census in Captain Thomas's Company is not necessarily an indicator of "military" service. He lived in the area and could be called upon to serve and /or pay <u>taxes</u>.

- He had a residence in 1816 in Davidson County, Tennessee.[47]
Charles M. Hall and John B. Hall paid taxes on their lands lying within District 4 of Davidson County, Tennessee. Neighbors included: David Abernethy, John Anderson, Anthony Clopton, Joseph Cook, N. Drew, David and Thomas Edmiston, Edward East, Jeremiah Ezell, John Hoggatt, William Huggins, Stockley D. and Jane Hays, John and P. H. Jones, James Lee, James McFerrin, Zachariah Noel, Francis Sanders, John Tait, Sr., Spencer Payne.

- He appeared on the United States census on 7 Aug 1820 in Davidson County, Tennessee.[48]
Charles M. Hall. Head of household.
Males: (<10) - 1, (>45) - 1; Females: (<10) - 1, (10-16) - 1, (16-26) - 1; Number of persons engaged in agriculture: 10; Slaves: 20.
--
I have not been able to identify who the mid-aged female is in the household. All of Charles M. Hall's daughters had been married by 1820. The other individuals would appear to be his family with his third wife, Nancy S. Hall. --rch, 2012

- He filed for divorce about 1826 in Davidson County, Tennessee.
Davidson County Circuit Court - November Term 1826
9 December 1826, page 96
Charles M. Hall - Pet. vs. Nancy B. Hall - Def.
"The petitioner having departed this life since the filing of said petition. It is ordered by the court that the same abate."

This dispute may be connected to an official inquiry regarding the sanity of Charles M. Hall:

Davidson County Court Minutes - Book 1824-1826 January Session
21 January 1826, page 371
"Be it remembered that on this day there was produced and read in this court an affidavit in the following words and figures to wit: In the matter of Charles M. Hall a citizen and resident in the county of Davidson Zachariah Noell makes oath that he is now and has been long acquainted with said Hall and that he verily believes his mind is so much decayed by age and other causes that he is wholly incompetent to manage his own affairs that he has a large real and personal estate liable to be lost or injured greatly for want of some person legally authorized to protect the same. Z. Noell."

The court ordered that the Sheriff summon a jury to conduct an inquisition regarding the idiocy or lunacy of Charles M. Hall and submit a report by the next court session; also they were to report what lands or chattel, if any, that Charles may possess (if he be found an idiot or lunatic).

Davidson County Court Minutes - Book 1824-1826 April Session
18 April 1826, page 427
"The jurors who were summoned and sworn by the Sheriff of this county to enquire into the idiocy or lunacy of Charles M. Hall having made their report to this court. On motion of John H. Martin esquire in behalf of Charles M. Hall said report is set aside and motion made by Ephraim H. Foster to have the former order revised."

Davidson County Court Minutes - Book 1824-1826 July Session
25 July 1826, page 516
"The jurors summoned by the Sheriff in pursuance of an order to inquire into the idiocy or lunacy of Charles M. Hall returned into court their report. And thereupon came hereunto court James Rucks Esquire and moved the court for leave to show cause why the said report should be quashed and to him it is granted. And the said rule is extended and continued until next court."

- His obituary was published in the National Banner and Nashville Whig on 14 Oct 1826 in Nashville, Davidson County, Tennessee.[49]
  "In this county, Mr. Charles M. Hall, aged 78."

- He had an estate probated from 1826 to 1830 in Davidson County, Tennessee.[50]
  Davidson County Court, October Session, October 16, 1826, page 557-558. A purported will of Charles M. Hall was submitted to the court by William Hall, John B. Hall, John G. Neely and his wife, Nancy C., Elizabeth Shropshire and Polly Cross (children of Charles M. Hall). The will was contested by Nancy B. Hall, widow and mother of three additional Hall children: Charles M. Hall, Eliza Ann Hall and Aristen Hall. She maintained this was not his last will. The will presented was found by the court to be invalid. Another document was not submitted to the court. Nancy B. Hall was granted administration of the estate and posted a $25,000.00 bond. Andrew Jackson, Edward H. East, John W. Jones, Zachariah Noel and Absalom Gleaves were named Commissioners to lay off and set apart one year's support for the widow and her family from the estate. On the next day, October 17th, it is recorded that Nancy B. Hall granted her brother's firm, Christopher Brooks and Samuel Steele, Power of Attorney over the estate of Charles M. Hall. Pages 550, 555, 561.

  John B. Hall, William Hall, B. Shropshire, John C. Neely and Maclin Cross, legatees of Charles M. Hall, dec'd, secured an Indemnity Bond by assigning their interest in the estate to Robertson & Earhart on 28 October 1826. Recorded on 17 Nov 1826 [p. 354]

  Davidson County, Tennessee - Minutes of the First Circuit Court Vol. F 1826-1827 - November 21, 1826 - page 18
  The dispute became quite contentious and apparently erupted into violence as John C. Hall, Ellen Cason (Nancy's sister), Nancy B. Hall and James Buchanan were arrested, charged by the Sheriff and indicted by a grand jury for an affray (fight or riot), assault and battery. Everyone was required to pay court costs and excepting James Buchanan an additional fine. John C. Hall's fine was the largest at $49.00. The case was finally closed out when Ellen Cason and Betsy Hall were again arrested for failure to pay their fines in May 1827. They stated that they did not have $2.00 between them. The court discharged the debt.

  Davidson County, Tennessee - Will Book 9 - January Term 1827 - page 98

An inventory of the estate of Charles M. Hall dated 27 December 1826 was filed in court on 19 March 1827 by Nancy B. Hall. The property included: 27 Negroes, 12 horses, 18 head of cattle, 40 head of hog, 13 sheep, geese, a set of blacksmith tools, a wagon, a cotton spinning wheel and more... The property was sold in December and the sale was recorded on 20 March 1827. Nancy B. Hall purchased most of the items. Other names appearing on the list of purchasers included Samuel and Archibald Hall.

The court's ruling invalidating the will was appealed by the children. Depositions were taken throughout 1827 and 1828. The case was frequently delayed. Finally, a trial was held in the First Circuit Court in Davidson County, Tennessee (November Term 1828, December 6, 1828) and a jury decided the will was not the last will and testament of Charles M. Hall. Apparently, there was no other written will. Since the parties could not come to an agreement, the court appointed Commissioners were assigned to evaluate the estate for the purpose of dividing it equally between all of the claimants/heirs after debts were paid. On June 3, 1829 the court divided the remaining property of the estate (primarily slaves, land and cash) equally among the heirs. Remnants of the case continued to spring up over the years. After Nancy B. Hall's death, her children, represented by their guardian, Samuel Steele pursued a claim in court to collect cash that was to have been distributed by the court's partition (December 25, 1830). See also the contested estate of Elizabeth Hall London Shropshire in Schuyler County, Missouri, 1852.

- He had an estate probated from 1831 to 1838 in Yazoo County, Mississippi.[51]
About January of 1831, John B. Hall petitioned the Probate Court in Yazoo County, Mississippi as follows:

"To the Honorable William E. Parker Judge of Probate for Yazoo County. Your petitioner, John B. Hall ____ respectfully ____unto your honor that in the year 1827 the father of your petitioner, Charles M. Hall, died in the State of Tennessee, Davidson County. That letters of Administration of decedent's estate were granted in the State aforesaid and that a final settlement was there made. In that the administratrix is since deceased your petitioner would further express unto your honor that there is accounts due to said descendant in this State which were not administrated upon in the State of Tennessee. Your petitioner would therefore request your Honor to grant unto him letters of Administration upon the Estate of said deceased in this State to assist your petitioner is duty bound___ every prayer ____ --John B. Hall."
--
Apparently, the heirs were noted to be John B. Hall, Wm. Hall and Maclin Cross in right of his wife, Mary Hall.
--
An Administrator's Notice was published in the Manchester Whig an early newspaper in Yazoo County on December 25th 18??. A bond dated 28 March 1831, in the amount of $1,000.00, secured by John B. Hall, William Ward and Morgan Fitch was presented to the court as security for the Letters of Administration issued to John B. Hall.
--
Apparently, the principal asset to be collected was a note due from J. C. Hall, son of William Hall. J. C. Hall died in 1834. The note is recorded as paid in the final accounting submitted on 26 January 1838. The net value after numerous expenses related to court costs and costs of collection was $335.48.

Yazoo County, Mississippi Probate Court - February Term 1838, Thursday. p. 493; Case #153
"John B. Hall, administrator of the Estate of Charles M. Hall, deceased, having applied and presented his account with said estate for final settlement and allowance, the same having been audited and allowed, it is ordered adjudged and decreed that the same be received, filed and recorded."

Charles married **Agnes Campbell,** daughter of **Archibald Campbell** and **Elizabeth Beard,** about 1779 in Bedford County, Virginia.[52] Agnes was born about 1757 in Bedford County, Virginia,[53] died from about 1805 to 1807 in Davidson County, Tennessee about age 48, and was buried in Davidson County, Tennessee.

Marriage Notes:
Deed records indicate that Archibald Campbell and his family and Charles M. Hall were in Bedford County, Virginia at the estimated date of marriage of Charles and Agnes.

Charles Hall witnessed the will of John Beard, Agnes's maternal grandfather, in Bedford County, Virginia on April 20, 1780. In that will, Agnes's sister, Elizabeth Campbell is listed as a granddaughter and her mother, Elizabeth Campbell is listed as the executrix of the estate of her father, John Beard. The will was recorded November 26, 1780 in the Bedford County, Virginia Will Book 1, page 384.

Agnes (Campbell) Hall and her sister, Elizabeth are mentioned in their father's will (Archibald Campbell's will of Sep 8, 1801, Knox County, Tennessee).

It is my opinion that Charles and Agnes were married prior to the signing of John Beard's will. --rch, 2009[54]

Death Notes:
There seems to be several land transactions in this time slot (1805-1807) that may indicate an effort by Charles M. Hall to settle the estate of Agnes (Campbell) Hall with his children. (rch 2009)

Charles next married **Elizabeth Crawley,** daughter of _____ _____ and _____ _____, on 20 Nov 1809 in Davidson County, Tennessee.[55] Elizabeth died in Oct 1811 in Davidson County, Tennessee[56] and was buried in Davidson County, Tennessee.

Marriage Notes:
She was a widow, previously married to Lewis Green.

Lewis Green died Oct. 18, 1806, leaving a widow, Elizabeth and four children: Horace, Eldridge, Robert and Lewis, Jr.
--
Davidson County, Tennessee - Will Book 4, July Term 1810, page 116:
Settlement of the Estate of Lewis Green. deceased.
Elizabeth Hall is the admrx.
--
page 116
Division of Negroes of the estate of Lewis Green. They were divided among the heirs. To Mrs. Elizabeth Hall, Davey, Carey and two children.[57]

Noted events in her life were:
• Her obituary was published in The Democratic Clarion and Tennessee Gazette on 22 Oct 1811 in Nashville, Davidson County, Tennessee.[58]
  "Died a few days since, Mrs. Hall. She was the partner of Maj. Hall, near Clover Bottom."

Charles next married **Nancy Buchanan Steele,** daughter of **Andrew Steele** and **Martha Buchanan,** on 12 Mar 1816 in Davidson County, Tennessee.[59] Nancy was born about 1781 in Virginia, died on 23 Dec 1829 in Davidson County, Tennessee[60] about age 48, and was buried in Davidson County, Tennessee.

Death Notes:
From: Minutes of the First Circuit Court in Davidson County, Tennessee - Vol. G 1828-1831 - November Term 1829, page 211 - January 14, 1830.
John B. Hall announces and the court notices that Nancy B. Hall has died. No one denied it.

General Notes:
Nancy's sister, Mary Steele, was the wife of Perry Magness. Perry was nearby when his brother, David Magness shot and killed Patton Anderson (a friend and business associate of Andrew Jackson). See the discussion under William W. Hall.[61]

Noted events in her life were:
• She appeared on the United States census on 7 Aug 1820 in Davidson County, Tennessee.[48]
  Nancy S. Hall. Probably the oldest female listed in the Charles M. Hall household. [I believe the enumerator listed her in the wrong age column though. --rch, 2012)
  --
  Charles M. Hall. Males: (<10) - 1, (>45) - 1; Females: (<10) - 1, (10-16) - 1, (16-26) - 1; Number of persons engaged in agriculture: 10; Slaves: 20.

• She had an estate probated in Davidson County, Tennessee.
  See: Davidson County Will Book Vol. 9
  Dec. 23, 1829, recorded March 9, 1930 - page 409
  Inventory of the Estate of Nancy B. Hall
  Items included: 6 Negroes, 39 acres of land, 2 horses, 4 head of cattle, 15 geese, 3 spinning wheels and more.

  Nancy B. Hall - Sale of Inventory - Jan. 30, 1830, recorded May 15, 1830.
  Buyers included: Hugh Hayes, Samuel Steele, Ellender Cason, Thomas Gleaves and Wm. H. Williams. Samuel

Steele, Administrator of the Estate.

7 M vi. **William Hall, Jr.** was born after 1748 in Lunenburg County, Virginia.

Research Notes:
An interesting lead for further research:
"Collins - Glass Connection

On 16 October 1775 in Halifax County, Virginia, Edward Stokes conveyed to William Glass, Jr. a 246 acre tract of land in Halifax County. Witnesses to this deed were Thomas Turnstall, Thomas Hope, Michael Roberts and <u>*William Hall, Jr.*</u>

I believe that ***William Hall, Jr.*** *was married* <u>ante</u> *16 October 1775 to a Miss Glass, a sister of William Glass, Jr. [and Thomas Glass] and a daughter of William Glass, Sr. and Joyce, his wife. In the 1782 census of Halifax County the name* ***William Hall, Jr.*** *appears three names above that of William Glass, Sr.*

On 2 December 1778 in Halifax County, Virginia, William Laws and Mary, his wife, conveyed to William Glass, Sr. a 500 acre tract on the Banister River in both Halifax and Pittsylvania Counties. Witnesses to this deed were Benjamin Lankford, <u>*Joseph Collins*</u>*, Dudley Glass, John Glass,* <u>*Thomas Glass*</u> *and Robert Weakley.*

I believe that Joseph Collins (born <u>circa</u> *1747) was married ante 2 December 1778 to a Miss Glass, a daughter of William Glass, Sr. and Joyce, his wife. But it is possible that I am wrong in this presumption; that the Joseph Collins named as a witness in the 1778 deed was Joseph Collins, Sr.; and that his eldest son, Stephen Collins, born* <u>circa</u> *1745 (?) was the one who married a daughter of William Glass, Sr.*

Very soon after the execution of the 1778 deed, Stephen Collins, Robert Bowmar (who married Chloe Collins), Elisha Prewitt (who married Tabitha Collins), Robert Prewitt, Joshua Prewitt, ***William Hall***, *James Cox, and Thomas Glass and the families of those who were married, set out for Kentucky, reaching Bowman's Station late in February 1779. Herman Bowmar, son of Robert, was a boy around 10 or 11 at the time. In 18___ he recalled that three members of the group decided not to remain at Bowman's Station and went instead to the vacinity of present day Lexington, Fayette County, Kentucky. These three were Stephen Collins,* ***William Hall***, *and Thomas Glass. So, I have reason to believe that both Stephen Collins and* ***William Hall*** *married sisters of Thomas Glass."* --George W. Glass, 22 January 1975

[I have seen no record to bring this marriage speculation, Hall m. Glass into reality and later in his writings, George Glass indicates that the journey to Kentucky appeared to be more of a Collins family affair. --rch, 2011]
--
The Collins family set up an <u>iron manufacturing</u> business in what was then Fayette County. *"Two brothers, Stephen and Joel Collins had by 1783 acquired a total of around 1,200 acres of the best bottom land on the Red River, a small tributary flowing into the Kentucky River, in what is now Fayette County. Several years later the brothers found a good grade of iron ore on Cow, Catamount and other creeks. With several associates, men who were familiar with iron-making, Stephen Collins started the construction of a bloomery forge [to be known as the Collins forge] on his 200 acre grant in the "great north bend" of the Red River in the early summer of 1787. Here he produced in his smelting forge on Red River the first commercial iron made in Kentucky..."* --George W. Glass, 26 Dec 1974
--
The Collins brothers sold their forge to Clark and Smith in 1805. It was the forerunner of the Red River Iron Works in Clay City, Powell County, Kentucky.

The questions include:
Was this the orphan, William Hall, Jr., who was the apprentice to the iron manufacturer, Robert Clark in Bedford County in 1766? There is implication that he is the right age and as a resident of Halifax, Virginia, he is in close proximity to Bedford. If he is William Hall, Jr., brother of Charles M. Hall, then his marriage to a Glass could be a "first" marriage and imply that he returned to Virginia from Kentucky to marry Rebecca Buchanan in 1787. Given his age, not an unreasonable timeline. **However,** early court documents from Halifax County indicate that there was a William Hall and William Hall, Jr. who resided along the Banister River in Halifax County, Virginia. Among other things, they applied for permission to build a grist mill along the Banister River. Did that project fall apart? Further review of the court documents of Halifax

may help pin this down.[62]

Noted events in his life were:
- He was involved in a court case about regarding his apprenticeship in Jul 1766 in Bedford County, Virginia.[63]
  William asked to be removed from his master, George Grundy. George Grundy was an Englishman and a member of the Bedford militia in September 1758. A wagon-maker, he also held a license to operate an "ordinary." Later in life he traded real estate. He was the father of Felix Grundy, a Congressman and Senator from Tennessee. He was also the 13th Attorney General of the United States.

  The court placed William Hall with Robert Clark, an iron manufacturer. This may be Capt. Robert Clark (1738-1810) who moved to Bedford County, Virginia in 1765-1766. He and his family moved on to Kentucky in 1779. "The first iron manufacturer in Kentucky." He was a cousin of William Clark of the Lewis & Clark Expedition.

William married **Rebecca Buchanan,** daughter of **James Buchanan** and **Martha Allison,** on 16 Jun 1787 in Augusta County, Virginia.[64] Rebecca was born about 1734 in Chester County, Pennsylvania.[65]

Marriage Notes:
Debie Cox reports: *"note ...**Archibald Buchanan's** sister Rebecca married a William Hall, Jr. in Augusta Co. VA. She was married first to Robert Brafford 1787--June 11, Wm. Hall and Robert McChesney, surety. Wm. Hall and Rebecca Brafford, widow."*

[This becomes important as a William Hall and Charles M. Hall are said to be brothers and partners with Archibald Buchanan in the construction of some now historic, houses in Nashville, Tennessee in the late 1790's. However, William Hall, nephew and brother-in-law of Charles M. Hall, has a definite presence in Nashville in proximity to Charles M. Hall about that same time period.] --rch[66]

8 M vii. **Thomas Hall** was born after 1748 in Bedford County, Virginia.

Noted events in his life were:
- He was involved in a court case about regarding his apprenticeship in Aug 1768 in Bedford County, Virginia.[67]
  The churchwardens took Thomas Hall away from Nicholas Hayes. A new master was not named.

- He served in the military perhaps as a soldier in Capt. Thomas Buford's Volunteer Company in Oct 1774 in Bedford County, Virginia.[68]
  Capt. Thomas Buford's volunteers *"formed part of the army led by General Andrew Lewis at the battle with the Indians at Point Pleasant, the 10th of October, 1774."*

  The name, Thomas Hall appears on a listing of volunteers along with, William Overstreet and John and William Campbell.

9 F viii. **Sarah Hall** was born in Lunenburg County, Virginia.

10 F ix. **Rebecca Hall** was born in Lunenburg County, Virginia.

Noted events in her life were:
- She was involved in a court case about regarding her foster parents from 1763 to 1771 in Bedford County, Virginia.[69]
  She was bound out to a new family, Ben Butterworth.

11 F x. **Susannah Hall** was born in Bedford County, Virginia.

Descendants of John Hall (1735 - 1794)
of Bedford County, Virginia

First Generation

1. John Hall, son of **William Hall** and **Mary Merryman,** was born on 31 Jul 1735 in Baltimore County, Maryland[17] and died about Aug 1794 in Bedford County, Virginia about age 59.

Noted events in his life were:

- He served in the military in 1758 in Bedford County, Virginia.[18]
An act of assembly, passed March 1758, the 31st year of the reign of King George II, some of the militia were called out for service in the early days of the French and Indian War, Annexed to this act, was a schedule of the names of the militia officers and soldiers, and the citizens who furnished provisions to that militia. This is the schedule pertaining to Bedford County.
Names listed include: <u>John Hall</u>, Archibald Campbell, John Hunter, James M'Reynalds, Robert Ogelsby, Thomas Ogelsby, Adam Beard, Edward Choat, Augustine Choat, Edward Ohair (Phair).

- He signed a will on 10 May 1794 in Bedford County, Virginia.[19]
"IN THE NAME OF GOD AMEN May 10th, 1794, I John Hall of Bedford County and State of Virginia being weak in body but of Perfect mind and memory thanks be to God for the same but calling to mind the mortality of men & knowing that it appointed to all men once to die, do make and Ordain this my Last Will & Testament. (Viz) in the manner & form as followeth Princepally & first of all I give & recommend my soul to God that First give it a being, & and my body to the earth from whence it was taken to be buried in decent form and that at the Discretion of my executors nothing doubting but <u>but</u> that I shall receive it again by the mighty Power of God at the General Resurrection and as Touching such Worldley Estate as the Lord hath blest me with in this life I give Demise & Dispose of the same in the following manner & form; first I give & bequeath unto my beloved wife Magdalane Hall all my Negroes that I possess. (to wit) Jamis Patt Jude frank Joe Bitte Patt Pegge as long as she lives & at her death I give & bequeath unto my son Mathew Hall a Negroe Man James and a Negroe Woman named Patt, Item I give unto my son William Hall a Negro man named Joe. Item I give unto my son Elisha Hall a Negroe Wooman named <u>Judge</u> and a Negro man named Frank. Item I give unto my son Jesse Hall one feather bed & Cow & Calf. Item Give unto my son Hezekiah Hall one horse & saddle & 1 cow and calf. Item I give unto my son John Hall one shilling starling and no more Item I give to my Daughter Tabitha Hall one Negroe Girl named Pegge at my wife's death Likewise one Feather bed & cow & calf. Item I give unto my Daughter Keziah Hall, one Negroe Girl named Patt at my wife's death Likewise one Feather Bed & Cow & Calf. Item I give to my Beloved wife Magdalen Hall a third part of my land as long as she lives and to fall to Mathew Hall & Elisha Hall my two sons to be divided as followeth to with Mathew Hall is to have the upper end, beginning at the old mill seat and then down the said creek to the fence & then along sd. Fence to the branch that comes down from John Owens then up the said branch to owen's line, and then follow his Line round to the beginning. Item I give unto my son Elisha Hall the balance of all the Land I now Possess together with the mill, and also an equal part of all my moveable property. And it is my Will & Pleasure that the rest of my moveable properties be left in the hands of my wife, that she may divide it as she sees cause - Between Hezekiah Tabitha & Keziah Hall. & Lastly I nominate & appoint my wife magdalen Hall as Executer of this my Last Will & Testament. I do hereby utterly Disanull Revoke all & every other former Testament, Will Legases bequeaths and Executors by me in any wise before named willed & bequeathed. Rattifying & confirming this & no other to be my last will & testament."
John Hall
Signed sealed & Delivered
In the Presents of us -
William Hancock
John Hancock
John Hall, Junr.
At a Court held for Bedford County the 22nd day of September 1794 This Last Will & Testament of John Hall, Deceased was proved by oath of William Hancock & John Hancock Witnesses whose names are there unto subscribed & Ordered to be recorded.
Teste:
Ja Steptoe CBC
Will Book 2, Page 140

- He had an estate probated from 1794 to 1799 in Bedford County, Virginia.[20]
Will Book 2 - page 262, 20 Nov 1799
Inventory of the Estate of John Hall was submitted by Thomas Leftwich, Thomas Williams and John Clayton. Recorded 23 Dec 1799.

John married **Mary Magdalene Smith,** daughter of _____ **Smith** and _____ **Evans,** about 1759 in Bedford

County, Virginia. Mary was born about 1745 in Virginia and died about 1833 in Bedford County, Virginia[21] about age 88.

Noted events in her life were:
- She appeared on the United States census in 1830 in Bedford County, Virginia.[22]
Presumably the female age 80-90 in the household of Elisha Hall.
Males: 15-20 (1); 50-60 (2). Females: 10-15 (2); 50-60 (1); 80-90 (1).

Children from this marriage were:

+ 2 M   i.   **John Hall, Jr.** was born about 1760 in Bedford County, Virginia[70] and died after 1850.[70]

+ 3 M   ii.   **William Hall** was born about 1763 in Bedford County, Virginia, died on 30 Aug 1838 in Yazoo County, Mississippi[71] about age 75, and was buried in Yazoo County, Mississippi.

4 M   iii.   **David Hall** was born about 1765 in Bedford County, Virginia and died before 1786 in Bedford County, Virginia.[72] The cause of his death was "killed as a youth at the mill.".[72] He never married and had no children.

+ 5 M   iv.   **Mathew Hall, Sr.** was born about 1767 in Bedford County, Virginia[73] and died about 1855 in Bedford County, Virginia[70] about age 88.

+ 6 M   v.   **Jesse Hall** was born about 1770 in Bedford County, Virginia[70] and died about 1802 in Bedford County, Virginia[70] about age 32.

7 M   vi.   **Hezekiah B. Hall** was born about 1773 in Bedford County, Virginia[70] and died on 12 Jul 1851 in Bedford County, Virginia[74] about age 78. He never married and had no children.

Noted events in his life were:
- He appeared on the United States census in 1810 in Bedford County, Virginia.[75]
Probably the other male in the household of Elisha Hall aged 26-44.
Males <10 (2); 26-44 (2). Females <10 (3); 10-15 (1); 26-44 (1); >45 (1). Slaves (6).

- He appeared on the United States census in 1830 in Bedford County, Virginia.[22]
Hezekiah B. Hall. Presumably one of the males age 50-60 in the household of Elisha Hall.
Males: 15-20 (1); 50-60 (2). Females: 10-15 (2); 50-60 (1); 80-90 (1).

- He appeared on the United States census on 18 Sep 1850 in Bedford County, Virginia.[76]
Hezikiah. Age 77. Living in his sister's (Keziah Musgrove) household.

- He had an estate probated from about 1851 to 1855 in Bedford County, Virginia.[77]
Hezekiah B. Hall apparently left no will and did not marry. A suit was filed in Chancery Court to determine the distribution of the property in his estate.

Family members mentioned in the suit who appeared before the court included: Kezia Hall (Musgrove) sister of Hezekiah; Children of Jesse Hall, deceased, brother of Hezekiah: Jesse Hall, John Hall, Joel Hall; Children of Elisha Hall, deceased, brother of Hezekiah: Nathaniel and Sarah (Hall) Morgan, Thos. and Tabitha (Hall) Hepstinstall, James N. and Sally (Hall) Shaon, Catherine (Hall) Burnette, (separated from her husband), Elisha Hall (Jr.), not married.

Family members mentioned in the suit who did not appear before the court included: John Hall, son of John Hall, d. 1794, brother of Hezekiah, William Hall, brother of Hezekiah, living in Mississippi [William died in 1838 -rch], Tabitha (Hall) Brown, sister of Hezekiah, in Tennessee, Bird and Drucilla (Hall) Greer, dau. Elisha in Tennessee, John Hall, son of Elisha, deceased, living in Missouri, Banks B. Hall, son of Elisha, deceased living in Missouri.

+ 8 M   vii.   **Elisha Hall** was born about 1776 in Bedford County, Virginia[78] and died about 1840 in Bedford County, Virginia[79] about age 64.

+ 9 F   viii.   **Tabitha Hall** was born about 1779 in Bedford County, Virginia,[70] died about 1863 in Bedford County, Tennessee[70] about age 84, and was buried in Bedford County, Tennessee.

+ 10 F   ix.   **Keziah Hall** was born about 1782 in Bedford County, Virginia,[70] died on 4 May 1865 in Bedford County, Virginia[80] about age 83, and was buried in Bedford County, Virginia.

Descendants of John Hall (1735 - 1794)
of Bedford County, Virginia

Second Generation

2. John Hall, Jr. *(John ¹)* was born about 1760 in Bedford County, Virginia[70] and died after 1850.[70]

General Notes:
It is to this individual, John Hall, Jr. that I am attaching the family of fellow DNA tester, Timothy E. Hall. It seems likely John was the product of a second marriage.
My reasons are:
*The DNA test aligns him with my Hall family line.
*Birth date and place fit well at this location.
*Naming tradition of <u>Jesse</u>, John, William and others through out the family.
See DNA discussion under William Hall, Sr. (d. 1758) --rch

Research Notes:
"A letter received by Alexis Spiritas from Richard Savage contains the following statement and information: "I don't know much about the Halls. They came from Grainger Co. to Bledsoe Co. in 1818 according to the deed books. I believe they were all descendants of John Hall Sr. A second group of unrelated Hall's settled in Bledsoe Co. sometime later. I have these marriages from Grainger Co. John Hall, Jr. -Franky Acuff Feb.17,1802 (bond John Hall, Sr.) William Hall - Nancy Acuff Jan.28, 1804 (bond John Hall, Jr.) Jesse Hall -Poly Defoe Aug. 1, 1807 Joel Hall -Judith Mallicoat Dec.2 1809 I think all these are sons of John Hall, Sr. I know Jesse Hall received land in the will of John Hall, Sr. Also in 1805 Grainger tax lists, list John Hall, Sr. and William Hall. and a 1799 Grainger tax list, lists John Hall. John Hall bought land in Grainger Co. Oct.3,1797 and he and wife Grizell Hall sold land Nov.4,1798." There is no evidence as to who the father is of John Hall (1810). He could be the son of any of the above 4 men, or no relation at all. Any of the marriage dates would fit John Hall's birthday of 1810."[81]

Noted events in his life were:
• He had a residence in 1794 in Bedford County, Virginia.[82]
"to a tract of land on which John Hall, Junior then lived according to the lines mentioned in a Deed from Richard Stith to the said _____ which bond & Deed is here referred."

Mathew Hall had filed suit against his mother and siblings to secure title in land his father, John Hall (d. abt 1794) had promised him before his death. His brother, John Hall, Jr. lived on the land at the time (1794). --rch

• He appeared on the United States census in 1830 in Bledsoe County, Tennessee.[83]
John Hall, Sr. Head of family.
Males: 70 -80 (1). Females: 70 -80 (1).
--
Research:
This appears to be the Census Record for John Hall, [Jr.] in 1830.
There are a number of John Halls in Bledsoe County on the 1830 Census on this page:
John Hall, Jr. age 15 -20; wife 20 -30; 1 child under 5.
*John Hall, age 50 -59; wife: 20 -30; 6 children.
*John Hall, Sr. age 70 -80; wife: 70 -80.
John Hall, Sr. age 60 -70; wife: 60 -70.
William Hall, age 40 -50; wife: 30 -40; 10 children

The John Hall listed here fits in the correct age bracket.

Others on the page may be children and grandchildren from the first marriage. I do not know who the William is. Perhaps a son of the other older John Hall, who I also don't know.

John married **Molly Wills,** daughter of **Euclid Wills** and **Unknown,** on 30 Jan 1778 in Bedford County, Virginia.[84]

John next married someone. _____ _____

His child was:

+ 11 M   i.   **John Hall** was born about 1780 in Virginia and died before Oct 1869 in Collin County, Texas.

3. William Hall *(John ¹)* was born about 1763 in Bedford County, Virginia, died on 30 Aug 1838 in Yazoo County,

Mississippi[71] about age 75, and was buried in Yazoo County, Mississippi.

Death Notes:
The date of death varies in affidavits found in the Probate proceedings: August 30 and August 31. Archibald C. Hall gives the 30th date and Samuel S. Hall gives the 31st date. --rch, 2012.

General Notes:
William Hall is mentioned in various sources:

The Carthage Gazette and Friend of the People, April 3, 1809 Vol. 1 No. 17.
"The following persons have reported estrays in Warren County, per Issac W. Sullivan, for Richard Burke, Ranger: (1) Wm. Hall, on the Stones River, has taken up a Roan horse that was appraised at a value of $6.00."
--

Bedford County, Virginia Deed Book 26, 1836-1837, page 190-191
"To all whom these presents may concern, know ye that I, William Hall of the county of Yazoo in the state of Mississippi did heretofore to wit on the seventh day of April in the year 1836 make and execute to Shadrack Brown of the county of Bedford in the state of Tennessee a deed of all my right, bills, interest, claims or demands against of the _____ _____ of John Hall, dec'd formerly of Bedford County in Virginia and did thereby authorize the said Shadrack Brown to demand and recover of Benjamin Musgrove of the said county of Bedford in Virginia the administrator ...[of] the will of my father (the said John Hall) dec'd, my distributive share of said estate consisting of a Negro girl named Rhoda and twenty-five dollars, which said deed was not duly authenticated according to the laws of Virginia, and the said Benjamin Musgrove upon delivery of the said distributive share hath required of the said Shadrack Brown to procure from me a deed confirming that of this 7th of April aforesaid duly authenticated. Now I the said William Hall do by these presents ratify and confirm the said deed... this 10th day of March 1837 --Wm. Hall"

The document was sworn before J. T. Rountree, J. P. and James F. Erwin, J. P. of Probate Court; recorded by the Yazoo County Clerk, J. S. Young, 11 March 1837; certified by James M. Brantias, Judge of the Probate Court of Yazoo County; verified by Charles Lynch, Governor of Mississippi, 15 March 1837 and transmitted by the Secretary of State of Mississippi, Barry W. Benson, June 7, 1837.[85]

Research Notes:
Carrol Carman Hall presents the following information regarding another son of William, named Thomas (1786 - 1856). The dates he gives overlap slightly and represent a conflict but with minor adjustment this could well be another individual in that family line. The biggest problem with this proposition is that the name Thomas is not mentioned anywhere in the probate records I have surveyed for William Hall. William's estate was substantial. --rch, 2013

"Sometime after 1818, William Hall had migrated from Bedford county in Virginia to Mississippi. +++His son Thomas, 1786 - 1856, had married Orpha May, 1784 - 1834, in Virginia about 1818. Thomas and Orpha lived on their plantation 'Bedford" in Jefferson county, Miss., near Natchez. They are buried in the Greenwood churchyard near Stanton, Miss. Both the Wickliffe and Throckmorton families were distinguished; the Throckmortons can be traced back to nobility. The connection of these two families came in the marriage of Rhoda Hall, 1819 - 1884, (presumably a daughter of Thomas-- rch) who in 1837 married the Hon. Robert Logan Wickliffe of Bardston, Ky. Wickliffe at one time was a member of the Kentucky Legislature and had many honors. Rhoda and Robert, in turn, had a daughter, Fanny, 1838 - 1921, who in 1863 married Major Charles B. Throckmorton, 1842 - 1915." --The Grandfathers, Vol. I, Section VI.[86]

Noted events in his life were:
• He worked as a contractor/builder about 1799 in Davidson County, Tennessee.[44]
Possibly one of the Hall "brothers", who were partners of Archibald Buchanan, and are recollected to be the builders of two old houses in Davidson County in the Clover Bottom Plantation. (This William Hall is a brother-in-law and nephew of Charles M. Hall.) The "Old Blue Brick" and the "Hall-McCampbell" house were both built before 1800. It is said that the "Old Blue Brick" received its name because one wall was painted blue. At one time it was a tavern and it may have been painted blue at that time. Andrew Jackson is also said to have used the grounds for the staging of his troops.

[Hard fired bricks were also called blue brick because of the color they turned after being fired in the kiln. The Buchanan family lived in the "Old Blue Brick" home for awhile.--rch] William Hall lived in the McCampbell House until he sold it to Thomas Harding in 1820 prior to his move to Mississippi. In 1847 the house was sold to James Anderson of Kentucky. In 1852, Anderson sold it to Thomas McCampbell. It remained in the McCampbell family until 1946.

Descendants of John Hall (1735 - 1794)
of Bedford County, Virginia

"Major Hall and his brother built the two houses. The land must have been a grant to Major Hall for services in the Revolutionary War. The house was built by slaves with bricks made on the place. The bricks were different sizes."
As told by Miss Maggie McCampbell on July 7, 1936 - History of the McCampbell Home.

The "Old Blue Brick" was torn down in 1951. On March 4, 2010, the Hall-Harding-McCampbell House had been nominated to be listed on the National Registry of Historic Places.

- He owned land one hundred eighty two acres and thirty eight poles on 2 Jul 1807 in Davidson County, Tennessee.[87]
  William Hall, Senior
  September 8, 1807 - Davidson County, Tennessee Deed Book G, page 201
  "This indenture made...between Charles M. Hall and William London both of Davidson County and state of Tennessee of the one part and William Hall, Senior of the other part. Witnesseth that the said Charles M. Hall and William London for and in consideration of the sum of thirteen hundred dollars to them in hand paid by the said William Hall, Senior ...conveyed a parcel of land situate lying and being in the county of Davidson in the state of Tennessee on the waters of the Stones River ...bounded as follows to wit: William Hays, McMurry... Witnessed by John Hall, Joh W. East and Peyton Jackson."

- He owned land 18 acres plus 66 poles on 27 Jul 1816 in Davidson County, Tennessee.[88]
  Deed Book "L" - Davidson County Court, page 263
  Registered 7 August 1816
  William Hall purchased from John B. Hall 18 acres plus 66 poles for $221.00. This was a part of the land John bought from Charles M. Hall.
  --
  Charles M. Hall bought a number of parcels of land a few years after he came to Davidson County, Tennessee. Charles sold a portion of this land (177 acres) to his brother-in-law and nephew, William, in 1800. In 1820, probably in anticipation of his move to Mississippi the following year, William sold most of his purchase (171 acres) to his son, John C., who quickly turned the property for a profit. William also sold (donated) the remainder of his property to the Baptist Church of McCory's Creek *"for the purpose of a meeting house and school house."* See Davidson County, Tennessee Court Register of Deeds, land transactions recorded in March, May and June of 1821, pages 205-206, 262-268, 296

- He had a residence in 1816 in Davidson County, Tennessee.[89]
  William Hall paid taxes on the lands he owned in District 16 (once a part of District 4) in Davidson County, Tennessee in 1816. Neighbors included: James and Eleazer Hamilton and John Thompson.

- He appeared on the United States census on 7 Aug 1820 in Davidson County, Tennessee.[90]
  William Hall. Head of household.
  Males (16-26) - 1, (45+) - 1; Females (16-26) - 1, (45+) - 1; Agricultural workers: 31, manufacturing: 13.

- He appeared on the United States census in 1830 in Yazoo County, Mississippi.[91]
  William Hall. Head of household.
  Males: (30-40) - 1, (60-70) - 1; Females: 0; Slaves: 49

- He moved in 1821 to Yazoo County, Mississippi.[92]
  Found in the testimony regarding the Probate of the Estate of William Hall, dec'd is a deposition of John B. Hall given on 24 January 1842, who answers questions regarding William Hall, dec'd. *"William Hall came to Mississippi [from Tennessee] in 1821."* He further stated that William Hall had sold all of his lands in Tennessee prior to his move except for the land he gave to his son, John C. Hall.

- He worked as an Associate Justice from 1823 to 1824 in Yazoo County, Mississippi.[93]

- He worked as a Judge of Probate in 1826 in Yazoo County, Mississippi.[93]

- He had a residence from 1823 to 1825 in Yazoo County, Mississippi.[94]
  He appeared on a Tax List in 1823 and 1825.

- He owned land on 4 Jun 1833 in Yazoo County, Mississippi.[95] He purchased 79.97 acres.

- He owned land on 25 Sep 1835 in Yazoo County, Mississippi.[96] He purchased 39.97 acres.

- His obituary was published in the Arkansas Gazette on 19 Sep 1838 in Little Rock, Pulaski County, Arkansas.[97]
  "William Hall, about 75, d. Aug 31, 1838 in Mississippi; son is Samuel S. Hall, Pulaski Co."

- He had an estate probated in Chancery Court from 1838 to 1852 in Yazoo County, Mississippi.[98]

Descendants of John Hall (1735 - 1794)
of Bedford County, Virginia

"Archibald C. Hall granted letters of administration on the estate of William Hall, Sr." In his petition, he stated that William Hall of Yazoo County died the 30th day of August 1838. Yazoo County Probate Minute Book B, October Term 1838.

--

The Personal Inventory of the Estate of William Hall, deceased, was submitted by Archibald C. Hall. The report was accepted by the court. Yazoo County Probate Minute Book B, November Term 1838.

--

"Application of Samuel S. Hall; Archibald C. Hall; Tabitha Russell, formerly Tabitha Hall; Marcus Pierce and Rhoda, his wife, formerly Rhoda Hall; Campbell Hall; Mary Jane Hall and Nancy Ann Hall, children of John C. Hall; heirs and distributees of the estate of William Hall, deceased, to divide the personal estate of said deceased." Michael Hooter, Robert Spear, David W. Brazeale, Jonathan Bonney and William Mills were appointed Commissioners for the aforesaid purpose. At this same hearing Samuel Marley was appointed guardian of the minor heirs of John C. Hall, deceased. Yazoo County Probate Minute Book B, November Term 1838.

--

Archibald C. Hall petitioned the court to sell the Real Estate of the Estate of William Hall, deceased. All lands were listed in detail. All located in Yazoo County. All parties were to be notified and a court date was set for the March Term 1839 for anyone to show why the sale should not go forward. Publication of the sale was to be made in the Yazoo Banner and the Carrollton Enquirer. Yazoo County Probate Minute Book B, January Term 1839. This case was continued in March and April to allow for summons to be served in Carroll County.

--

"Application of Robt. M. Maben in right of his wife, Mary Jane, formerly Mary Jane Hall, heir and one of the distributees jointly with Campbell C. and Nancy Hall, minors in the right of their father, John C. Hall, one of the distributees of William Hall, deceased for a division of property. Lorenzo Maben, Moses Munholland, Freeland Cook, Samuel Marley, and William Lester were appointed commissioners to allot and divide the personal property of William Hall, deceased." November Term 1839, page 256.

"Samuel S. Hall; Archibald C. Hall; R. M. Maben as guardian of Nancy Ann Hall, infant heir of John C. Hall, deceased; Tabitha Russell; Marcus Pierce and Rhoda Pierce; distributees of the estate of William Hall, deceased, applied for partition of the real estate of William Hall, deceased." Probate Minute Book B, Oct Term 1841, page 558.

Division of real estate of William Hall, in equal parts per heirs listed previously. Probate Minute Book C, April Term 1842, page 21.

A. C. Hall published a notice in the Yazoo Banner on 24 August 1844 and 31 August 1844 advising that he was the administrator of the Estate of William Hall, dec'd and would present a final settlement and ask for allowance.

A division of Real Estate was agreed upon among the five heirs of William Hall and dated December 1843. This was confirmed by the Probate Court of Yazoo County in a Mississippi Supreme Court Case "William W. Wildey v. Moses H. Bonney's Lesse" in the October Term 1856.

William married **Elizabeth Campbell,** daughter of **Archibald Campbell** and **Elizabeth Beard,** on 5 Mar 1787 in Campbell County, Virginia.[99] Elizabeth was born about 1763 in Bedford County, Virginia and died before 1830 in Davidson County, Tennessee.

Marriage Notes:
"Consent by Archibald Campbell, father of the bride." Bonds posted by William Hall and Charles Hall. Witnessed by William Campbell and Samuel Campbell. Marriage return, 5 March 1787 by Archibald McRoberts.[99]

Death Notes:
She does not appear in the household of William Hall on the 1830 Census in Yazoo, Mississippi.

General Notes:
Elizabeth Campbell is listed as a granddaughter and her mother, Elizabeth Campbell is listed as the executrix of the estate of her father, John Beard. Agnes (Campbell) Hall is Elizabeth's sister. Charles Hall witnessed the will of John Beard, his wife's maternal grandfather, in Bedford County, Virginia on April 20, 1780. The will was recorded November 26, 1780 in the Bedford County, Virginia Will Book 1, page 384.[100]

Noted events in her life were:
• She appeared on the United States census on 7 Aug 1820 in Davidson County, Tennessee.[90]
  Elizabeth C. Hall. Presumably the oldest female listed in the household of William Hall.

--
William Hall. Head of household.
Males (16-26) - 1, (45+) - 1; Females (16-26) - 1, (45+) - 1; Agricultural workers: 31, manufacturing: 13.

Children from this marriage were:

+ 12 M   i.   **John C. Hall** was born about Apr 1788 in Campbell County, Virginia, died on 20 Dec 1834 in Yazoo County, Mississippi[101] about age 46, and was buried in Yazoo County, Mississippi (Bradshaw Cemetery).

+ 13 M   ii.   **Samuel S. Hall** was born about 1789 in Campbell County, Virginia, died on 24 May 1842 in Yazoo County, Mississippi[102] about age 53, and was buried in May 1842 in Yazoo County, Mississippi (Wesley Chapel Cemetery).[103]

   14 M   iii.   **Lindsey C. Hall** was born about 1790 in Campbell County, Virginia, died about 1835 in Carroll County, Mississippi[104] about age 45, and was buried in Mississippi. He never married and had no children.

General Notes:
"We usually had an Easter fishing party on Easter Monday. We went fishing at Capt. Hoggett's mill. We took lunch and stayed all day and would go to Mr. Hoggett's for supper and to spend the evening. We played games and danced. Standifer Hoggett played the violin and James played the flute. We always had some very good music. We never stayed past ten o'clock and then the young men would go home with the girls. The young ladies in our neighborhood were Misses Jones, Cooper, Hall, Thomas. The young men were the three sons of Capt. Hoggett, Standifer, James, Jack; William, Henry, James and Langston Cooper; Jack and Ben Clopton; **John, Charles, Eliza, and Lindsley Hall**, *the Flournoys, Buchanons, Jones and..."* others. --From stories told by Jane Henry Thomas of Nashville.[105]

Noted events in his life were:

• He was educated at Major Exum's School on Mr. Clopton's land before 1818 in Davidson County, Tennessee.[106] *"Lindsley Hall went to Princeton from Maj. Exum's school and studied law."* --Jane Henry Thomas

• He was educated at Princeton University from 13 May 1818 to 17 May 1819 in Princeton, New Jersey.[107] *"Dear Mr. Hall, Thank you for your inquiry concerning information on Lindsey C. Hall, Class of 1820. Mr. Hall's non-graduate card file states his place of residence as being Nashville, Tennessee. Mr. Hall entered Princeton University as a Sophomore on May 13, 1818. He was dismissed as per his own request on May 17, 1819. I was unable to locate any other information pertaining to his undergraduate life in our collections."* --Rosalba D. Varallo

• He was educated at Union College in 1820 in Schenectady, New York.[108]
Lindsey C. Hall of Nashville, Tennessee appears on a list of officers, graduates and students for the year 1820.

• He was involved in a court case related to a claim of Nancy (Hall) (Russell) Neely and John C. Hall in Davidson County, Tennessee.[109]
Lindsey C. Hall of Charles M. Hall - Bill of Sale - 8 Dec 1825
"I have sold to L. C. Hall a Negro woman and female infant at her breast. The woman, named Dilley, about twenty two years of age." 1 Aug. 1823 Charles M. Hall. Test: John Braughton, John B. Hall.
Bill of sale proven in open Court - Nov. Term 1825 - John Braughton states that John B. Hall witnessed at the time he signed but now lives beyond the bounds of this state.

Lindsey C. Hall vs. John G. Neely and wife
Davidson County Court - Nov Term 1827, page 430.
In summary: John G. Neely's wife (formerly Nancy C. Russell, formerly Nancy C. Hall, dau. of Charles M. Hall) had a claim and judgment against John C. Hall. She had a lien on his property. John C. Hall was borrowing a slave (see above) that was owned by Lindsey C. Hall. The Neely's had the Sheriff take the slave to be sold. An injunction was filed in the case in November 1826.
Davidson County Court - May Term 1828, page 439.
The judge ordered everyone involved including the Sheriff to be prevented from enforcing the judgment against the slave and her increase. John G. Neely to pay all costs.

• He had a residence in 1825 in Yazoo County, Mississippi.[110]
He appeared on a Tax List in 1825.

- He owned land from 1826 to 1832 in Yazoo County, Mississippi.[111]
  Tracts were purchased in 1826, 1828, 1829, 1830 and 1832. The tract purchased in 1832 appears to be a joint venture with Robert T. Goddard.

  --

  In a deposition given by Marcus Pierce on 24 January 1842, regarding the real estate transactions of Lindsey C. Hall and his father, William Hall, the following information was presented: Marcus Pierce stated that he was acquainted with William Hall and his son, John C. Hall, both deceased. He knew that William Hall gave John C. Hall about 160 acres of land. He thought the land was given in 1830 or 1831. Land was selling for about $10.00 per acre at that time. Lindsey C. Hall purchased lands at the land sales. He used the moneys of William Hall and by his (William's) direction purchased the land. The lands were purchased in the name of Lindsey C. Hall not William Hall. Apparently, there was some "opposition" (competition) at the sales. Lindsey had employed another man to bid on the land and he entered Lindsey's name not knowing they were for William. The Registrar did not want to change the entries and recommended that Lindsey convey the land to William Hall. The land was conveyed to William Hall excepting the lands now being contested which were transferred to John C. Hall per William's instruction. So far as Marcus Pierce knew, John C. Hall did not pay for the land.

- He was elected as State Representative in 1826 in Yazoo County, Mississippi.[112]
  Lindsey C. Hall appears on a list of Senators and Representative for Yazoo County.

- He owned land in 1833 in Carroll County, Mississippi.[113]
  Between October 1 and December 31, 1833, he is listed as purchasing 79.56 acres (He was the assignee.) and 146.4 acres for $1.25 per acre at the land office in Columbus, Mississippi.

- He owned land on 1 Feb 1841 in Holmes County, Mississippi.[114]
  Inexplicably, this land purchase of 146.46 acres is recorded after Lindsey Hall's death. My speculation is that the estate was settling its affairs. On the same day additional land was acquired from Elias Fisher.

- He owned land on 1 Feb 1841 in Leflore County, Mississippi.[115]
  Another 73.77 acres was purchased after Lindsey's date of death.

- He had an estate probated in Court from 1835 to 1841 in Carroll County, Mississippi.[116]
  Archibald C. Hall and Marcus Pierce were appointed administrators of the Estate of Lindsey C. Hall, deceased. Carroll County, MS Probate Records - Book A 1834-1848. August Term 1835, page 15.

  A citation was issued against the legal heirs of L. C. Hall, dec'd. They were identified as: Samuel S. Hall, Archibald C. Hall, Tabitha Russell, Rhoda Pierce, and Robert Maben, guardian of the minor heirs of John C. Hall, dec'd. They were ordered to appear in court. Probate Book B 1841-1845 May Term, page 13.

+ 15 M iv. **Archibald C. Hall** was born on 25 Oct 1792 in Campbell County, Virginia,[117] died on 30 Jun 1863 in Yazoo County, Mississippi[118] at age 70, and was buried in Yazoo County, Mississippi (Bradshaw Cemetery).

+ 16 F v. **Tabitha Hall** was born about 1795 in Campbell County, Virginia,[119] died on 20 Jun 1851 in Carroll County, Mississippi[120] about age 56, and was buried in Mississippi.

+ 17 M vi. **Dr. Elisha S. Hall** was born about 1798 in Bedford County, Virginia and died about 1827 in Bedford County, Tennessee about age 29.

+ 18 F vii. **Rhoda Hall** was born about 1803 in Davidson County, Tennessee, died in Dec 1879 in Montgomery County, Mississippi[121] about age 76, and was buried in Mississippi.

5. Mathew Hall, Sr. *(John¹)* was born about 1767 in Bedford County, Virginia[73] and died about 1855 in Bedford County, Virginia[70] about age 88.

General Notes:
On October 25, 1845, Mathew Hall signed an affidavit attesting to the residency and character of Abram Blankenship, deceased. This was to supplement an application for a Revolutionary War pension. Mathew states that he is 78 years old. He remembers the Blankenship family in Bedford County, Virginia as early as 1789, the year he traveled to the "western country" (probably Kentucky to visit his brother). He distinctly remembers them in 1794, the year his (Mathew's) father died. The Justice of the Peace who witnessed the document attested to Mathew's good health and "clear, distinct recollection." He noted that Mathew was a member of the "babtist" church and a "man of good standing in his neighborhood and full faith and

reliance ought to be placed in his testimony..."[122]

Noted events in his life were:
- He appeared on the United States census in 1810 in Bedford County, Virginia.[123]
  Mathew Hall. Head of household. Presumably the male aged 26-44. Shown living next door to Elisha Hall and Elizabeth Hall.
  Males <10 (1); 26-44 (1). Females <10 (1); 10-15 (1); 26-44 (1). Slaves (2).

- He appeared on the United States census in 1820 in Bedford County, Virginia.[124]
  Mathew Hall. Head of household. Presumably the male aged 45+.
  Males <10 (1); 16-26 (1); > 45 (1). Females <10 (3); 45+ (1).

  Elizabeth Hall, widow of Jesse Hall, lives nearby.

- He appeared on the United States census on 22 Aug 1850 in Bedford County, Virginia.[125]
  Mathew Hall. Age 80. Farmer. Living with his wife, Mary and son, Mathew, Jr.

- He had an estate probated on 27 Jun 1856 in Bedford County, Virginia.[70]
  An inventory of his personal property was filed on this date.

Mathew married **Mary "Polly" Elizabeth Banks,** daughter of **Samuel Banks** and **Unknown,** on 1 Jan 1795 in Bedford County, Virginia.[126] Polly was born about 1774 in Virginia[70] and died about 1860 in Bedford County, Virginia[70] about age 86. She was usually called Polly.

Marriage Notes:
The marriage bond date is given as 29 December 1794 on a different page in the Hall-Overstreet manuscript.[70]

Noted events in her life were:
- She appeared on the United States census in 1810 in Bedford County, Virginia.[123]
  Presumably the female aged 26-44 living in the household of Mathew Hall.
  Males <10 (1); 26-44 (1). Females <10 (1); 10-15 (1); 26-44 (1). Slaves (2).

- She appeared on the United States census in 1820 in Bedford County, Virginia.[124]
  Presumably the female aged 45+. Living in the household of Mathew Hall.
  Males <10 (1); 16-26 (1); > 45 (1). Females <10 (3); 45+ (1).
  Elizabeth Hall lives nearby.

- She appeared on the United States census on 22 Aug 1850 in Bedford County, Virginia.[127]
  Mary E. Hall. Age 76. Living with her husband, Mathew and son, Mathew, Jr.

Children from this marriage were:

  19 M   i.   **Mathew Hall, Jr.** was born about 1800 in Bedford County, Virginia[70] and died about 1860 in Bedford County, Virginia[70] about age 60. He never married and had no children.

               Noted events in his life were:
               - He appeared on the United States census on 22 Aug 1850 in Bedford County, Virginia.[125]
                 Mathew Hall. Age 50. Laborer. Living with his parents, Mathew and Mary.

               - He appeared on the United States census on 7 Aug 1860 in Bedford County, Virginia.[128]
                 Mathew Hall, Jr. Age 50(?) Farmer. Also in household, M. Ayers (age 22), Farm hand.

+ 20 F   ii.   **Magdalena Hall** was born about 1802 in Bedford County, Virginia[70] and died about 1859 in Bedford County, Virginia[70] about age 57.

+ 21 F   iii.   **Melinda A. Hall** was born about 1810 in Bedford County, Virginia[70] and died about 1886 in Bedford County, Virginia[70] about age 76.

+ 22 F   iv.   **Mary E. Hall** was born about 1812 in Bedford County, Virginia[70] and died about 1875 in Bedford County, Virginia[70] about age 63.

+ 23 F   v.   **Keziah Hall** was born about 1817 in Bedford County, Virginia[70] and died about 1857 in Bedford County, Virginia[70] about age 40.

Descendants of John Hall (1735 - 1794)
of Bedford County, Virginia

6. Jesse Hall *(John [1])* was born about 1770 in Bedford County, Virginia[70] and died about 1802 in Bedford County, Virginia[70] about age 32.

Noted events in his life were:
- He had an estate probated on 20 Oct 1802 in Bedford County, Virginia.[70]
  An inventory of his estate was recorded on this date.

Jesse married **Elizabeth Williams,** daughter of _____ _____ and _____ _____, on 1 Mar 1797 in Bedford County, Virginia.[129] Elizabeth died before 1850 in Bedford County, Tennessee.[70]

Noted events in her life were:
- She appeared on the United States census in 1810 in Bedford County, Virginia.[130]
  Elizabeth Hall. Head of household.
  Presumably the female aged 26-44.
  Males: 10-15 (3). Females: 26-44 (1). Slaves: (0).
  Living next door to Elisha Hall and Mathew Hall.

- She appeared on the United States census in 1820 in Bedford County, Virginia.[131]
  Elizabeth Hall. Head of household.
  Presumably the female aged 45+.
  Males: 16-26 (1). Females: 45+ (1).
  Mathew Hall lives nearby.

Children from this marriage were:

　24　M　　i.　**Jesse Hall, Jr.** was born about 1797 in Bedford County, Virginia.

Noted events in his life were:
- He appeared on the United States census in 1810 in Bedford County, Virginia.[130]
  Presumably one of the males aged 10-15. Living with their mother, Elizabeth Hall.
  Males: 10-15 (3). Females: 26-44 (1). Slaves: (0).

- He owned land in 1838 in Bedford County, Virginia.[132]
  From: Bedford County, Virginia Deed Book 27, November 19, 1838, Page 337.

  Jesse Hall of Patrick County, Virginia sold a 10 acre tract of land in Bedford County, along the waters of Rock Castle Creek and adjoining the lands of Mathew and Elisha Hall to John Hall [his brother] for six dollars. This land was part of the estate of Jesse Hall, deceased, father of Jesse Hall. The transaction was witnessed by: Nicholas Robertson and Wm. W. Reese.

- He appeared on the United States census in 1840 in Patrick County, Virginia.[133]
  Jesse Hall. Head of household.
  Males: 40 <50 - 1. Females: 20 <30 - 1.

　+ 25　M　　ii.　**John Hall** was born about 1798 in Bedford County, Virginia and died after 1860 in Bedford County, Virginia.

　+ 26　M　　iii.　**Joel Hall** was born about 1799 in Bedford County, Virginia.

8. Elisha Hall *(John [1])* was born about 1776 in Bedford County, Virginia[78] and died about 1840 in Bedford County, Virginia[79] about age 64.

Noted events in his life were:
- Elisha Hall served as the guardian of his brother's children: Jesse, John and Joel after 1802 in Bedford County, Virginia.

- He appeared on the United States census in 1810 in Bedford County, Virginia.[75]
  Elisha Hall. Head of household. Presumably one of the males aged 26-44.
  Males <10 (2); 26-44 (2). Females <10 (3); 10-15 (1); 26-44 (1); >45 (1). Slaves (6).

- He appeared on the United States census in 1820 in Bedford County, Virginia.[134]
  Elisha Hall. Head of household. Presumably the male aged 26-45.
  Males <10 (1); 10-16 (1); 16-26 (1); 26-45 (1). Females <10 (3); 10-16 (1); 16-26 (1); 26-45 (1).

- He appeared on the United States census in 1830 in Bedford County, Virginia.[22]
  Elisha Hall. Head of household. Presumably one of the males age 50-60 in this household.
  Males: 15-20 (1); 50-60 (2). Females: 10-15 (2); 50-60 (1); 80-90 (1).

Elisha married **Sarah Best,** daughter of **John Best** and **Drucilla Banks,** on 24 Nov 1800 in Bedford County, Virginia.[135] Sarah was born about 1776 in Virginia.[134]

Marriage Notes:
"Elisha Hall and Sarah Best, November 24, 1800. Levi Best, surety. Consent of Drusala Best, mother of Sarah."[136]

Noted events in her life were:
- She appeared on the United States census in 1810 in Bedford County, Virginia.[75]
  Presumably the female aged 26-44 living in the household of Elisha Hall.
  Males <10 (2); 26-44 (2). Females <10 (3); 10-15 (1); 26-44 (1); >45 (1). Slaves (6).

- She appeared on the United States census in 1820 in Bedford County, Virginia.[134]
  Presumably the female aged 26-45. Living in the household of Elisha Hall.
  Males <10 (1); 10-16 (1); 16-26 (1); 26-45 (1). Females <10 (3); 10-16 (1); 16-26 (1); 26-45 (1).

- She appeared on the United States census in 1830 in Bedford County, Virginia.[22]
  Presumably the female age 50-60 in the household of Elisha Hall.
  Males: 15-20 (1); 50-60 (2). Females: 10-15 (2); 50-60 (1); 80-90 (1).

Children from this marriage were:

+ 27 F   i.   **Tabitha Hall** was born about 1796 in Virginia and died before 1850 in Virginia.

+ 28 F   ii.   **Drucilla Hall** was born about 1804 in Bedford County, Virginia and died before 1870 in Henry County, Tennessee.

+ 29 M   iii.   **John Hall** was born about 1806 in Bedford County, Virginia and died in Missouri.

+ 30 F   iv.   **Katherine Hall** was born in Bedford County, Virginia.

+ 31 F   v.   **Mary "Polly" Hall** was born about 1811 in Bedford County, Virginia.

+ 32 M   vi.   **Banks B. Hall** was born about 1813 in Bedford County, Virginia and died before 1870 in Audrain County, Missouri.

+ 33 F   vii.   **Sarah Hall** was born in Bedford County, Virginia.

+ 34 F   viii.   **Keziah Hall** was born in Bedford County, Virginia.

   35 M   ix.   **Elisha Hall, Jr.** was born in Bedford County, Virginia.

+ 36 F   x.   **Magdalena Hall** was born in Bedford County, Virginia.

9. Tabitha Hall *(John¹)* was born about 1779 in Bedford County, Virginia,[70] died about 1863 in Bedford County, Tennessee[70] about age 84, and was buried in Bedford County, Tennessee.

Noted events in her life were:
- She appeared on the United States census in 1840 in Bedford County, Tennessee.[137]
  Presumably the female in the household of S. S. Brown, age 60-70

- She appeared on the United States census on 18 Nov 1850 in Bedford County, Tennessee.[138]
  Tabitha Brown. Age 71. Head of household. Living with her daughter, Mary M. Hall Sanders and grandchildren.

- She appeared on the United States census on 2 Jun 1860 in Bedford County, Tennessee.[139]
  Tabitha Brown. Age 82. Farmer. Living next door to her son, G. W. Brown and family.

- She signed a will on 30 Mar 1858 in Bedford County, Tennessee.[140]
  Her will mentions sons: Geo. W., Thomas J. and daughters: Eliz. Robinson, Naomi Tilford, Tabitha Locke, Magdaline Sanders. Also children: Sterling Brown, deceased and Keziah Sudurth, deceased.

The estate was probated in August 1863.

Tabitha married **Shadrack S. Brown,** son of **Daniel Brown, Jr.** and **Lucy Leftwich,** on 17 Oct 1799 in Bedford County, Virginia.[141] Shadrack was born about 1778 in Bedford County, Virginia,[142] died about 1848 in Bedford County, Tennessee[143] about age 70, and was buried in Bedford County, Tennessee.

Marriage Notes:
"Shadrack Brown and Tabitha Hall, October 14, 1799. Elisha Hall, surety. Consent of Magdalean Hall, mother of Tabitha."[144]

General Notes:
A number of slaves were sold by Shadrack Brown to his wife Tabitha and then to a third party according to an index of the Bedford County, Tennessee, County Court Minute Book, Volume 1, 1848-1852. All of the transactions were recorded on pages 375 and 382. This appears to be a settlement of property from his estate. An index of these transactions would include:

Alick / Ellick (slave) -Slave of Shadrack S. Brown, to his wife, Tabitha. Then sold to T. J. Brown.
Easter / Easther (slave) -Slave of Shadrack S. Brown, to his wife, Tabitha. Then sold to N.B. Suddarth.
Ezekiel / Zeke (slave) -Slave of Shadrack S. Brown, to his wife, Tabitha. Then sold to James Ogilvie.
Grundy (slave) -Slave of Shadrack S. Brown, to his wife, Tabitha. Then sold to Robert Cannon.
James (slave) -Slave of Shadrack S. Brown, to his wife, Tabitha. Then sold to Jno. W. Rutledge.
Mason (slave) -Slave of Shadrack S. Brown, to his wife, Tabitha. Then sold to B. G. Green.
Nancy (slave) -Slave of Shadrack S. Brown, to his wife, Tabitha. Then sold to Naomi Tilford.
Sarah (slave) -Slave of Shadrack S. Brown, to his wife, Tabitha. Then sold to J.B. Suddarth.
Sylvia (slave) -Slave of Shadrack S. Brown, to his wife, Tabitha. Then sold to N.B. Suddarth.[145]

Noted events in his life were:
- He appeared on the United States census in 1840 in Bedford County, Tennessee.[137]
  S. S. Brown, head of household, age 60-70

- He had an estate probated from 1848 to 1851 in Bedford County, Tennessee.[146]
  His will proved Sept. 1848 names Richard Warner as the administrator of the estate. Tabitha Brown is his wife. The children are not named. See Bedford County Court Minutes.

Children from this marriage were:

+ 37 M   i.   **William H. Brown** was born on 14 Nov 1800 in Bedford County, Virginia.[147]

+ 38 F   ii.   **Mary Magdalene Hall Brown** was born about 1801 in Bedford County, Virginia.[148] (Twin)

+ 39 F   iii.   **Naomi Brown** was born about 1801 in Bedford County, Virginia.[147] (Twin)

+ 40 M   iv.   **Sterling Brown** was born about 1803.

+ 41 F   v.   **Kezia Brown** was born about 1805.

+ 42 F   vi.   **Lucy Brown** was born about 1806.[147]

+ 43 F   vii.   **Elizabeth Brown** was born about 1810 in Tennessee.[147]

+ 44 M   viii.   **George W. Brown** was born about 1813 in Tennessee.[147]

+ 45 F   ix.   **Tabitha Brown** was born about 1815 in Tennessee[147] and died about 1861 about age 46. (Twin)

+ 46 M   x.   **Thomas Jefferson Brown** was born about 1815 in Tennessee.[147] (Twin)

+ 47 F   xi.   **Emily M. Brown** was born about 1819 in Tennessee.[147]

10. Keziah Hall *(John ¹)* was born about 1782 in Bedford County, Virginia,[70] died on 4 May 1865 in Bedford County, Virginia[149] about age 83, and was buried in Bedford County, Virginia.

Noted events in her life were:
- She appeared on the United States census in 1820 in Bedford County, Virginia.[150]
  Presumably the female age 26-45 in the household of Benjamin Musgrove.
  Males: 10-16 (1); 16-26 (1); 45+ (1). Females: <10 (4); 10-16 (1); 16-26 (2); 26-45 (1).

- She appeared on the United States census in 1830 in Bedford County, Virginia.[151]
  Presumably the female age 40-50 in the household of Benjamin Musgrove.

Males: <5 (1); 5-10 (1); 20-30 (1); 50-60 (1). Females: 10-15 (3); 40-50 (1).

- She appeared on the United States census on 18 Sep 1850 in Bedford County, Virginia.[152]
Kizia Musgrave. Age 68. Living next door to her sons, D. P. Musgrove, Benjamin B. Musgrove and Christopher Musgrove. Also shown in her household: Milerson Anthony (age 30) and Hezikiah (age 77). Millicent Anthony is her widowed daughter. Hezikiah is probably her brother, Hezikiah Hall.

- She appeared on the United States census on 1 Aug 1860 in Bedford County, Virginia.[153]
Keziah Musgrove. Age 79.

Keziah married **Benjamin Barton Musgrove**, son of **Henry Musgrove** and **Rachel Owen,** on 25 Dec 1796 in Bedford County, Virginia.[154] Benjamin was born on 22 Nov 1780 in Prince Georges County, Maryland,[155] died on 14 Feb 1840 in Bedford County, Virginia[155] at age 59, and was buried in Bedford County, Virginia.

Marriage Notes:
"Benjamin Musgrove and Kezia Hall, December 15, 1796. Elisha Hall, surety. Consent of Magdalean Hall, mother of Kezia.".[156]

Birth Notes:
There is some discussion about his birth date. It may be about 1780.

Noted events in his life were:
- He appeared on the United States census in 1820 in Bedford County, Virginia.[150]
Benjamin Musgrove. Head of household. Presumably the male 45+.
Males: 10-16 (1); 16-26 (1); 45+ (1). Females: <10 (4); 10-16 (1); 16-26 (2); 26-45 (1).

- He appeared on the United States census in 1830 in Bedford County, Virginia.[151]
Benjamin Musgrove. Head of household. Presumably the male age 50-60 in this household.
Males: <5 (1); 5-10 (1); 20-30 (1); 50-60 (1). Females: 10-15 (3); 40-50 (1).

- He appeared on the United States census in 1840 in Bedford County, Virginia.[157]
Benjamin Musgrove. Head of household. Presumably the male age 60-70.
Males: 10-15 (1); 15-20 (1); 60-70 (1). Females: 20-30 (1); 40-50 (1).
Listed next is Christopher Musgrove.

Children from this marriage were:

+ 48 M   i.   **Christopher Musgrove** was born on 9 Feb 1798 in Bedford County, Virginia[158] and died on 19 Mar 1870 in Bedford County, Virginia[159] at age 72.

+ 49 M   ii.   **Rev. Henry Musgrove** was born on 3 May 1800 in Bedford County, Virginia[160] and died on 4 Sep 1869 in Henry County, Iowa[160] at age 69.

   50 F   iii.   _____ **Musgrove** was born about 1801 in Bedford County, Virginia. She never married and had no children.

+ 51 F   iv.   **Mary Magdalean Smith Musgrove** was born on 16 Jul 1804 in Bedford County, Virginia[161] and died on 20 Feb 1885 in Bedford County, Virginia[162] at age 80.

+ 52 F   v.   **Rebekah Hall Musgrove** was born on 15 May 1805 in Bedford County, Virginia[163] and died on 29 Mar 1877 in Bedford County, Virginia[164] at age 71.

+ 53 M   vi.   **John Hall Musgrove** was born on 27 Jun 1806 in Bedford County, Virginia,[165] died on 23 Apr 1888 in Bedford County, Virginia[166] at age 81, and was buried in Bedford County, Virginia.

+ 54 F   vii.   **Rachel Musgrove** was born on 11 Dec 1808 in Bedford County, Virginia[167] and died on 18 Feb 1879 in Lynchburg, Virginia[168] at age 70.

+ 55 F   viii.   **Keziah Stover Musgrove** was born on 31 Aug 1811 in Bedford County, Virginia[77] and died on 30 Nov 1892 in Bedford County, Virginia[169] at age 81.

+ 56 F   ix.   **Tabitha Musgrove** was born on 11 Dec 1813 in Bedford County, Virginia[170] and died on 15 Dec 1875 in Franklin County, Virginia[171] at age 62.

+ 57 F   x.   **Minerva Naomi Musgrove** was born on 21 May 1816 in Bedford County, Virginia[172] and died on 9 Apr 1875 in Independence County, Arkansas[173] at age 58.

+ 58 F xi. **Millicent Musgrove** was born on 10 May 1817 in Bedford County, Virginia[174] and died on 3 Jun 1883 in Bedford County, Virginia[175] at age 66.

+ 59 M xii. **Benjamin Barton Musgrove, Jr.** was born on 1 Jul 1822 in Bedford County, Virginia[176] and died on 3 May 1902 in Bedford County, Virginia[177] at age 79.

+ 60 M xiii. **Demetrious Polyclitus Musgrove** was born on 1 Mar 1826 in Bedford County, Virginia[178] and died on 22 May 1862 in Bedford County, Virginia[179] at age 36.

Descendants of John Hall (1735 - 1794)
of Bedford County, Virginia

Third Generation

11. John Hall *(John, Jr.* [2], *John* [1]*)* was born about 1780 in Virginia and died before Oct 1869 in Collin County, Texas.

General Notes:
On September 25, 1843, John Hall appeared before John Wood a Judge of the of the County Court at Hamilton, Tennessee. He stated that Nancy Crawford was the widow of Moses Crawford, deceased [his father-in-law], a Revolutionary War pensioner of the United States. He had gathered materials and papers regarding Moses Crawford including the original Pension Certificate and mailed them to James Standifer. The writing is unclear, but the papers have either been lost or James Standifer died. John Hall was unable to recover the papers. This created delays and problems with the pursuit of the Pension Claims for Moses Crawford and his widow.

On the same day, Johnathan Wood certified that John Crawford, Delilah Hall and John Hall submitted their affidavits in support of said pension declaration and that they were found to be of "undoubtable veracity."

John Hall apparently spent some time and effort securing statements and affidavits on behalf of his mother-in-law's pension claims. She was not successful in recovering bounty land but support payments were approved.[180]

Noted events in his life were:
- He appeared on the United States census in 1830 in Bledsoe County, Tennessee.[181]
John Hall. Head of family. Presumably the oldest male in the houshold.
Males: <5 (1), 10 -14 (1), 15 -19 (1), 50 -59 (1). Females: <5 (1), 10 -14 (1), 20 -29 (1).
--
Research:
This appears to be the Census Record for John Hall in 1830.
There are a number of John Halls in Bledsoe County on the 1830 Census on this page:
John Hall, Jr. age 15 -20; wife 20 -30; 1 child under 5.
*John Hall, age 50 -59; wife: 20 -30; 6 children.
*John Hall, Sr. age 70 -80; wife: 70 -80.
John Hall, Sr. age 60 -70; wife: 60 -70.
William Hall, age 40 -50; wife: 30 -40; 10 children

The John Hall listed here fits in the correct age bracket. I speculate that the other members of this household are his family from a first marriage. He is living next door to a John Hall, Sr. who fits the correct age bracket to be his father and mother.

Others on the page may be children and grandchildren from the first marriage. I do not know who the William is. Perhaps a son of the other older John Hall, who I also don't know.
--
The Moses Crawford family including Delilah, John Hall's future wife, lived in Bledsoe County, Tennessee in 1826 when Moses died. Nancy Crawford, his widow is listed on the 1830 Bledsoe County, Tennessee. Living nearby is Jesse Hall (40 - 50). His age would place him as a brother to John Hall. This has not been confirmed.

- He appeared on the United States census in 1840 in Bledsoe County, Tennessee.[182]
John Hale [Hall]. Head of family. Presumably the oldest male.
Males: 5 -10 (1), 10 -15 (2), 50 -60 (1). Females: 10 -15 (1), 50 -60 (1).

I have not identified the younger female. --rch

- He appeared on the United States census on 12 Sep 1850 in Meigs County, Tennessee.[183]
John Hall. Age 69. Farmer. Living with his wife, Delilah and children: Jessee F., Joseph M., William H., Martha D. and Andrew J. Hall.

- He appeared on the United States census on 7 Jun 1860 in Collin County, Texas.[184]
John Hall. Age 80. Farmer. Living with his wife, Delila and children: J. F., Martha D. and A. J., and Wm. H. Hall.

John married **Franky Acuff,** daughter of _____ _____ and _____ _____, on 17 Feb 1802 in Grainger County, Tennessee.[185]

The child from this marriage was:

  61 M   i.   **John Hall, Jr.** was born about 1810 in Tennessee.

John next married **Delilah Crawford,** daughter of **Moses B. Crawford** and **Nancy Dorsey,** in Bledsoe County, Tennessee. Delilah was born about 1799 in Virginia[180] and died in Oct 1869 in Collin County, Texas[186] about age 70.

> **General Notes:**
> On September 25, 1843, Delilah Hall age 55, appeared before John Wood a Judge of the of the County Court at Hamilton, Tennessee. She stated that Nancy Crawford was the widow of Moses Crawford, deceased, a Revolutionary War pensioner of the United States and that he died on the 17 day of December 1826.[180]
>
> **Noted events in her life were:**
> - She appeared on the United States census on 12 Sep 1850 in Meigs County, Tennessee.[183]
>   Delilah Hall. Age 48. Living with her husband, John Hall and children: Jessee F., Joseph M., William H., Martha D. and Andrew J. Hall.
>
> - She appeared on the United States census on 7 Jun 1860 in Collin County, Texas.[184]
>   Delilah Hall. Age 58. Living with her husband, John Hall and children: J. F., Martha D. and A. J., and Wm. H. Hall.

Children from this marriage were:

+ 62 M   i.   **Jesse F. Hall** was born on 5 Feb 1832 in Tennessee,[187] died on 20 Mar 1884 in Collin County, Texas[187] at age 52, and was buried in Mar 1884 in Collin County, Texas (Forest Grove Cemetery).[187]

+ 63 M   ii.   **Joseph Marion Hall** was born on 8 Aug 1833 in Tennessee[188] and died on 19 May 1905 in McKinney, Collin County, Texas[189] at age 71.

+ 64 M   iii.   **William Houston Hall** was born about 1837 in Tennessee and died on 1 Mar 1894 in Collin County, Texas[190] about age 57.

+ 65 F   iv.   **Martha Delilah Hall** was born on 10 Feb 1841 in Tennessee,[191] died on 4 Sep 1921 in Bowie, Montague County, Texas[191] at age 80, and was buried on 5 Sep 1921 in Clay County, Texas (Vashti Cemetery).[191]

  66 M   v.   **Andrew J. Hall** was born about 1843 in Tennessee.

> **Noted events in his life were:**
> - He appeared on the United States census on 12 Sep 1850 in Meigs County, Tennessee.[183]
>   Andrew J. Hall. Age 7. Living with his parents.
>
> - He appeared on the United States census on 7 Jun 1860 in Collin County, Texas.[184]
>   A. J. Hall. Age 17. Living with his parents.

12. John C. Hall *(William ³, John ¹)* was born about Apr 1788 in Campbell County, Virginia, died on 20 Dec 1834 in Yazoo County, Mississippi[101] about age 46, and was buried in Yazoo County, Mississippi (Bradshaw Cemetery).

> **Noted events in his life were:**
> - He worked as a Deputy Sheriff from 1809 to 1810 in Nashville, Davidson County, Tennessee.
>
> - He appeared on the United States census on 7 Aug 1820 in Davidson County, Tennessee.[192]
>   John Hall. Head of household.
>   Males (<10) - 2, (26-44) - 1; Females (<10) - 2, (26-44) - 1; Foreigners not Naturalized -1; Agricultural workers: 1.
>   --
>   It is my opinion that the entry for "Foreigners not Naturalized" is a smudge or an erasure and not an valid entry. --rch, 2012.
>
> - He moved in 1827 to Yazoo County, Mississippi.[92]
>   Found in the testimony regarding the Probate of the Estate of William Hall, dec'd is a deposition of John B. Hall given on 24 January 1842, who answers questions regarding John C. Hall, dec'd. , son of William Hall, dec'd. *"John C. Hall came to Mississippi* [from Tennessee] *in 1826 or 1827."* He further stated that William Hall gave John C. Hall about 100 acres of land (in Tennessee) in about 1820. John C. Hall informed John B. Hall that he lived on that land for several years before he sold it to Tom Hardin at $20.00 per acre.
>
> - He appeared on the United States census in 1830 in Yazoo County, Mississippi.[193]
>   J. C. Hall - Head of household. Probably the oldest male in the household.

Descendants of John Hall (1735 - 1794)
of Bedford County, Virginia

Males (>5) -1, (5-10) -1, (10-15) -1, (15-20) -1, (20-30) -1, (30-40) -1, (40-50) -1; Females (5-10) -1, (10-15)-1, (15-20) -1, (30-40) -1.

There are several unidentified children enumerated in this record. Perhaps a second family.

- He had an estate probated from 1836 to 1844 in Yazoo County, Mississippi.[194]
  A petition was presented to the court to allow a Public Sale of the Personal Estate of John C. Hall, deceased. The Administrator was ordered to advertise the sale. Yazoo County Probate Court - February Term 1837.

  --

  Application of Samuel Dilly and Elizabeth Hall, Administrators of the Estate of John C. Hall, deceased, to sell Personal Property, including cattle and hogs and to hire out Negroes of said estate. Yazoo County Probate Court - November Term 1837.

  --

  Petition of Samuel Dilly and Elizabeth Hall, Administrators of the Estate of John C. Hall, deceased, to sell land. Campbell, Jane and Nancy Ann Hall are ordered to appear to show why the sale should not go forward. Notices were to be published in two public newspapers. A lease of the lands and hiring Negroes for one year was allowed by the court. Yazoo County Probate Court - December Term 1837.

  --

  The administration of his estate was first granted to his wife Elizabeth and Samuel Dilley[?]. Elizabeth died and possibly for a short time she was succeeded by son, Campbell. He died. The court became aware of the minor status of daughter, Nancy Ann, at which time a guardian was chosen, Thomas Maben.

John married **Elizabeth Marshall,** daughter of **Daniel Marshall** and **Unknown,** on 1 Oct 1810 in Rutherford County, Tennessee.[195] Elizabeth was born before 1794, died about 1838 in Yazoo County, Mississippi,[196] and was buried in Mississippi.

Noted events in her life were:
- She appeared on the United States census on 7 Aug 1820 in Davidson County, Tennessee.[192]
  Elizabeth M. Hall. Presumably the oldest female listed in the household of John Hall.

  --

  John Hall. Head of household.
  Males (<10) - 2, (26-44) - 1; Females (<10) - 2, (26-44) - 1; Foreigners not Naturalized -1; Agricultural workers: 1.

  --

  It is my opinion that the entry for "Foreigners not Naturalized" is a smudge or an erasure and not an valid entry. --rch, 2012.

- She appeared on the United States census in 1830 in Yazoo County, Mississippi.[193]
  Elizabeth Hall. Probably the oldest female in the household of her husband, J. C. Hall.
  Males (>5) -1, (5-10) -1, (10-15) -1, (15-20) -1, (20-30) -1, (30-40) -1, (40-50) -1. Females (5-10) -1, (10-15)-1, (15-20) -1, (30-40) -1.

Children from this marriage were:

67   M   i.   **Campbell Hall** was born before 1820 in Davidson County, Tennessee and died before Apr 1842 in Yazoo County, Mississippi. He never married and had no children.

Noted events in his life were:
- He appeared on the United States census on 7 Aug 1820 in Davidson County, Tennessee.[192]
  Campbell Hall. Presumably one of the two young males listed in the household of John Hall.

  --

  John Hall. Head of household.
  Males (<10) - 2, (26-44) - 1; Females (<10) - 2, (26-44) - 1; Foreigners not Naturalized -1; Agricultural workers: 1.

  --

  It is my opinion that the entry for "Foreigners not Naturalized" is a smudge or an erasure and not an valid entry. --rch, 2012.

- He was involved in a court case about the division and sale of the properties of the Estate of William Hall, deceased in 1839 in Yazoo County, Mississippi.[197]
  ...Samuel Marley is appointed guardian of the said Campbell, Mary Jane and Nancy Ann Hall, minor heirs of John C. Hall, deceased and distributees in the right of the John C. Hall, their father, of the said William Hall, deceased... Yazoo County Probate Court November Term 1838.

  --

31 January 1839 - Chancery Court of Yazoo County, Mississippi
Estate of William Hall, deceased
Summons
Samuel Marley, the guardian of Campbell, Mary Jane and Nancy Ann Hall, minor heirs of John C. Hall and distributees in the right of the said John C. Hall, their father, of the estate of William Hall, dec'd is to appear on the 4th Monday of March 1839. He is to show why a sale of the lands of William Hall cannot go forward.

+ 68   F   ii.   **Mary Jane Hall** was born about 1820 in Davidson County, Tennessee and died before 1866 in Mississippi.

+ 69   F   iii.   **Nancy Ann Hall** was born on 4 Sep 1830 in Yazoo County, Mississippi,[198] died on 22 Apr 1860 in Yazoo County, Mississippi[199] at age 29, and was buried in Yazoo County, Mississippi (Bradshaw Cemetery).

13. Samuel S. Hall *(William³, John¹)* was born about 1789 in Campbell County, Virginia, died on 24 May 1842 in Yazoo County, Mississippi[102] about age 53, and was buried in May 1842 in Yazoo County, Mississippi (Wesley Chapel Cemetery).[103]

Noted events in his life were:

• He served in the military as a soldier on Gen. Andrew Jackson's staff at the Battle of New Orleans from 1814 to 1815.[200]

• He worked as a Judge of the 3rd Judicial Circuit from 1823 to 1828 in Arkansas.[201]
On October 31, 1827 the General Assembly of the Territory of Arkansas passed an act entitled: "An Act For the Relief of Samuel S. Hall." This act directed the auditor draw a warrant on the treasurer for $50.00 to compensate Samuel S. Hall *"for holding the court in Crittenden [county], in the first judicial circuit, on the first Monday in November, 1826,..."* -- Arkansas Gazette, 1827

Apparently, the bill was a topic of some budgetary debate as an amendment to increase a contingency fund to $1,000.00 was added. --Arkansas Gazette, 1827

• He had a residence on 13 Apr 1824 in Little Rock, Pulaski County, Arkansas.[202]
An advertisement published in the Arkansas Gazette Newspaper in Little Rock, Arkansas on April 13, 1824 reads:
"SAMUEL S. HALL
WILL PRACTICE LAW in the Circuit Courts south of the Arkansas River, and in the Superior Court of this Territory. His residence is at Little Rock. April 13, 1824."
--
50 Dollars Reward
STRAYED or STOLEN from the subscriber, about the first of December last, a Dark Brown Horse, about 15 -1/2 hands high, five years old last spring, and had on a dollar bell. He is of uniform color and has no marks or spots on him by which he can be more particularly described.
Said horse was turned into the range in the vicinity of this place, and was seen about the middle of Dec. about two miles below Little Rock, and has not been heard of since.
If said horse has been stolen, I will pay a reward of Fifty Dollars to any person who will return him to me and secure the thief so that he can be brought to justice; or if strayed, I will pay a reward of Ten Dollars to the person taking him up, and delivering him to me at this place. Samuel S. Hall, Little Rock, Jan. 11, 1825."

• He joined a church: The Christian Church, in 1832, in Little Rock, Pulaski County, Arkansas.[203]
A story is told of how Dr. Benjamin Franklin Hall (1803-1873) came to Little Rock in the summer of 1832. Dr. Hall was known as the strolling dentist who often took preaching journeys. He came to visit his "brother" Judge Samuel Hall.
"Little Rock had only three churches at the time: a Regular Baptist, a Cumberland Presbyterian and a Methodist. Hall decided to worship with his brother and thirteen other members of the Regular Baptists. All but three of the small group were women, but Hall knew the men from his travels. The congregation asked Hall to preach for them, and he did so. Hall's Restoration messages soon caused considerable excitement in the congregation and in the community. Invited to speak to the Little Rock Temperance Society on July 4, 1832, Hall spoke on "Christian Unity." Later that same day, Hall organized Arkansas's first Restoration church with a congregation of eight, all drawn from the other churches in the city. On the fourth Sunday in August 1832, the entire Regular Baptist congregation renounced the Philadelphia Confession of Faith and were all baptized in the Arkansas River, becoming part of the Restoration church. The new congregation now numbered twenty-two. Among the new members were Colonel Charles A. Caldwell, the speaker of the State Legislative Council, and William W. Stevenson, the Cumberland Presbyterian preacher for the last decade, who now became the new congregation's preacher. The group took the name Christian Church."

• He worked as a Partner, Business Owner and Retail Merchant in 1835 in Davidson County, Tennessee.[204]
Samuel S. Hall and his cousin, John B. Hall, operated a business as "traders and merchants" in partnership with Andrew J.

Blakemore in Davidson County, Tennessee. The business was known as Hall, Blakemore & Co. This information came to light in a Tennessee Supreme Court case heard in 1835-36. A man named Mansel Hite (yeoman) was accused and convicted of stealing a five dollar bank note that was the property of Hall, Blakemore & Co. The crime was committed at a business known as Morgan's in a town named Haysborough. The conviction was appealed on the grounds that the location of the business and therefore the crime was not committed in Davidson County proper but a neighboring county (Rutherford) due to changes in the legal boundaries of the adjoining counties. The original trial and related court proceedings were therefore held in the wrong court. Further, since the accused was acquitted (on a previous appeal), a second trial for the same offense was not proper. Finally, the detailed description of the bank note stolen was inconsistent and perhaps miscopied. This led to some question regarding just exactly what was stolen.

- He worked as a Lawyer, United States Attorney and Circuit Court Judge from 1836 to 1838 in Arkansas.[205]
In 1887, General Albert Pike (1809-1891) wrote a series of biographical sketches of early jurists and law makers in Arkansas. These were men he knew from the mid 1830's. His sketch of Samuel S. Hall follows.

"Among the lawyers who were of the Little Rock bar while Arkansas was a territory, one of the most amusing was Samuel S. Hall, a rather small, dried up, old man of some sixty years, queer and quaint, who came there from Satartia, in Mississippi, a lawyer pretty well read and not without ability, but whose peculiarities were often the cause of merriment.

He knew nothing about Latin, but was fond of picking up and using scraps of it. Once, I was told, in a case before Judge William Trimble, in which Parrott, who died before 1833, was opposed to him as counsel, Judge Hall, as we always called him, fired off at the jury all the scraps of Latin that he could remember; when Parrott replied he uttered half a dozen long sentences in Choctaw. Hall appealed to Judge Trimble against this, insisting that Parrott should use language fit to be quoted from and which others understood. Parrott gravely replied that the language which he had used was Latin, and it was not his fault if Judge Hall did not understand it. Hall resented this and indignantly denied that the gibberish used by Parrott was Latin; and Parrott proposed to leave it to the Court to decide, to which Judge Hall consented; and the Judge decided that, to the best of his knowledge, Parrott's Latin was as good as Hall's.

The old gentleman told some of us once that he intended soon to retire, and to travel through the United States incog.

He exploded some of his Latin against me once, I think it was these lines from Horace, which, whether he used them on that particular occasion or not, he was fond of repeating ore rotundo: "Si quem mobilium turba Quiritium, Certat tergeminis tollere honoribus."

And in replying to him I repeated, knowing he would not understand it, the passage said in "Ten Thousand a Year," or "The Diary of a Physician," to be in Persius, but which is not to be found there: "Eandem semper canens cantilenam, Ad nauseam usque."

This staggered and confounded the old gentleman, and after court adjourned he had me write it down for him, with a translation, and it afterward did him good service.

In the trial of a man in the circuit court of Pulaski County, Judge Hall, for the defense, in his speech to the jury, inveighed with some sharpness, at the expense of Absalom Fowler, who had been hired to prosecute, and who had, of course, done it savagely, against the taking of money by counsel to prosecute innocent men for their lives, and was evidently well satisfied with himself and the supposed effect of that part of his speech upon the jury. Fowler, a hard, harsh, dry man, listened apathetically, and following Hall, spoke so long before alluding to his denunciation of hired counsel, that the judge became radiant with the conviction that he would not venture to comment upon it, when, all at once, Fowler coldly and slowly said, "you have heard, gentlemen of the jury, what one of the counsel for the defense said in regard to the impropriety of counsel consenting to be employed to assist the officer of the State in the prosecution of persons guilty of crimes, the punishment of which is hanging. I remember that the same gentleman, a few years ago, was hired to prosecute, and did prosecute an innocent and poor countryman indicted for murder. He fulfilled his contract to the utmost of his ability, while I defended the prisoner, whom he did his best to hang, and who was acquitted. He earned his wages, gentlemen, and he received them, according to the contract of hiring, in the shape of a little, old, scrawny, roached-mane, bob-tailed, clay-bank pony, which with pride he led from court in Saline county to his home in Little Rock." Discomfited by what he could not deny, the judge collapsed.

He rode, when going upon the circuit, an old, white, lean mare, that could seldom do more than strike a slow trot for a few minutes at a time, then subsiding to her usual walk. Once I left Little Rock with him, to go to the court at Greenville, Clark county, where, I remember, landlord Sloan fed us on boiled fresh pork, corn bread without butter, and sweet potatoes for a week. The judge rode the mare, and I my sorrel horse Davy, as well known on the roads to Washington and Van Buren as I myself was. During the first day I stayed with the judge as he plodded along, to the immense weariness of myself and the great disgust of my horse, it was taking us all day to ride to Mrs. Lockhart's on the Saline. The next day after we had got out of the horrible bottom of the Saline, and were upon the gravel hills beyond, I said to the judge, "my horse is fretting, and I will ride ahead for a piece, and wait for you to come up;" and without waiting for an answer put Davy to his best pace and let him enjoy himself. At the end of a ride of five or six miles I stopped, and sitting down upon a log waited nearly an hour until the judge came up, and I jogged on with him a few miles further, and then left him again with a simple "good-bye." Again he over took me, and we rode on for five or six miles until he saw that I was about to repeat the performance, when wheeling his old mare across the rode in front of me, he said, "see here! you are a young man, and I am an old one. Let me tell you something. I used, in my younger days, to push and hurry to get to court and be there before it opened, and I always found that I might just as well have taken my time on the road, for my business would not have suffered if I had not hurried. So I used to ride hard, as soon as court adjourned, to get home; and it never happened that Mrs. Hall did not say to me when I got home, "why, judge, I did not look for you until tomorrow or next day." Now you take my advice and remember that nobody makes anything by hurrying through life. You'll always get to the end of your journey soon enough, and may-be be more welcome if you don't get there too soon."

I kept the old man company until we reached Greenville, and I remembered his advice always afterward; but I never rode in company with Judge Hall again.

I see the good, honest, honorable, fair, old man now, as I often saw him arguing to court or jury. he would begin with his feet close together, and holding in one hand a piece of tobacco, from which, as he talked, he would pick off a small bit, put it into his mouth and forthwith spit it out, his feet gradually farther and farther apart from each other until he would have to bring hem together again to keep himself from toppling over. Then he would pause, look with shrewdly twinkling eyes at judge or jury, and say, "how does my case stand now?""

--

An additional mention of Judge Hall of the Third Judicial Circuit is found in this story by Albert Pike:

"In the winter of 1835-6 I went from Little Rock with Judge Johnson, Colonel Fowler and Judge Hall, to Crawford Old Court-House, on the Arkansas river, some twenty-five miles below Fort Smith, where Judge Johnson, then of the superior court of the territory, was to hold the circuit court. It was a terribly cold journey, so cold that when we left Fletcher's, on Point Remove creek, where there was a bridge then, after staying there all night, we were compelled to forego traveling, after getting through the bottom, and to remain at the first house until the next day. We crossed the river at the court-house on foot upon the ice, leaving our horses, getting over safely, though with difficulty, the ice consisting of rough fragments packed and frozen together. Archibald Yell, who crossed the same day with other lawyers from Fayetteville, broke through, and but for a pole which he carried would have been drowned. Nineteen of us, the judge being one, slept in one room over the improvised court-room, during the term. Here I saw Jesse Turner for the first time, who was then living and had an office there. "While we were there the landlord, Hungerford (I think), became demented through jealousy, it was said, Judge Johnson, good, innocent man, being the object of his suspicions without knowing it. On our way home we came, late in the evening of a very cold day, to Old Dwight in Pope county, and stopped there for the night. "We gathered round the fire in the big fireplace, and were sitting there talking, when a citizen "mul-fathered" with whisky came in, got a chair, and sitting near the fire soon seemed to be dozing. But after a little, some one speaking to Judge Hall, who sat near the fellow, called him "judge," and the man opened his eyes and said to the judge: "You're the judge, are you. Then it's you that Hungerford went crazy about, 'cause you was too fond of his wife." "Sir," said Judge Hall, "I don't know what you mean. My name is Samuel S. Hall, sir." "Oh," said the man, "t'aint you then." When I hearn it canvassed about they said 'twas Judge Johnson." "Get out of here!" roared Judge Johnson [?] [Hall], "get out of here! I'll bet that story has got to Little Rock, and Matilda has heard it before now. Get out of here quick if you don't want to get killed!" The chap "lit out" in a hurry; but the judge was evidently disturbed all the way home, fearing that the report had preceded him."

--

Prior to his position as United States Attorney, Samuel S. Hall was a candidate for the position of delegate from Pulaski, White and Saline Counties to the Constitutional Convention held in Little Rock Arkansas on January 4, 1836. The meeting took place in the Baptist Meeting House, the customary place at the Capital for holding legal assemblies, there being no Hall obtainable. The Convention proceeded to frame a Constitution and adjourned January 30, 1836. Arkansas became a State on June 15-16, 1836. In a newspaper article advertising his candidacy, he mentions his *"nearly twenty years residence among you."* See Arkansas Advocate, November 20, 1835 and the Arkansas Gazette, November 24, 1835.

- He owned land on 23 Jun 1836 in Randolph County, Arkansas.[206] 80 Acres

- He appeared on the United States census in 1830 in Pulaski County, Arkansas.[207]
Samuel S. Hall. Head of household. He is the older male in the household. He is living with his wife, Matilda, son and daughter.
Males (<5) -1, (30-40) -1; Females (10-15) -1, (20-30) -1, (40-50) -1.

Presumably one of the grandmothers are in the household. Due to the age listed, she is probably Samuel's mother-in-law.

There are 3 slaves in the household.

- He appeared on the State Tax List census in 1835 in Pulaski County, Arkansas.[208]

- He appeared on the United States census in 1840 in Yazoo County, Mississippi.[209]
Samuel S. Hall. Head of household.
Males (>5) - 2, (10-15) - 1, (15-20) - 1, (40-50) - 1. Females (20-30) - 1, (30-40) - 1. Slaves: 21.

Living near John B. Hall, William Hall, W. W. Wildy, Jonathan Bonney

- He had an estate probated from 1842 to 1844 in Yazoo County, Mississippi.[210]
Yazoo County Probate Minute Book C, Sept Term 1842, September 26, 1842
"W. W. Wildy was granted letters of administration on the estate of Samuel S. Hall, deceased." In the petition of William W. Wildy for appointment as administrator of the estate of Samuel S. Hall, he states that Samuel S. Hall died on 24th of May 1842 leaving a widow, Matilda and 2 children: Laurena (Hall) Wildy and William C. Hall, a minor aged 14 years. Sixty days had passed since he petitioned the court. He was instructed to file a bond with approved security.
--
Yazoo County Probate Minute Book C, Oct Term 1844, October 30, 1844
"Letters of guardianship granted Wm. W. Wildy for Wm. Hall, a minor." William and Laurena Wildy were named guardians and provided a $600.00 bond. In the petition of William W. Wildy to James R. Brown, Probate Judge, Wildy states that William Hall, a son of Samuel S. Hall deceased is a minor under the age of 16 years. Wildy asked to be appointed William Hall's guardian.
--
An Administrator's notice was published on July 22, 1848 in the <u>Yazoo Democrat</u> in Yazoo City, Mississippi.

Samuel married **Matilda Garrett**,[211] daughter of **Jacob Garrett** and **Charity Taylor,** about 1819 in Davidson County, Tennessee. Matilda was born about 1803 in Davidson County, Tennessee and died from 1843 to 1847 in Yazoo County, Mississippi about age 40.

Death Notes:
In a letter to the Probate Court in Yazoo County, Mississippi as part of the testimony in the hearings regarding the settlement of the Estate of William Hall, deceased, Robert Maben states that Samuel S. Hall has died leaving a widow, Matilda Hall and two children, William Hall and Lavinia, wife of William W. Wildy.

General Notes:
Jacob Garrett, Matilda Garrett's father, was a representative from the Municipality of St. Augustin to the Consultation of Texas held in the town of San Felipe de Austin in October 1835. Among other notable founders of the Republic of Texas attending this convention was General Samuel Houston.[212]

Noted events in her life were:
- She appeared on the United States census in 1830 in Pulaski County, Arkansas.[207]
Matilda Garrett Hall. Presumed to be the female 20-30 years old in Samuel S. Hall's household.
Males (<5) -1, (30-40) -1; Females (10-15) -1, (20-30) -1, (40-50) -1
Presumably one of the grandmothers are in the household. Due to the age listed, perhaps she is the mother of Matilda.

- She appeared on the United States census in 1840 in Yazoo County, Mississippi.[209]
Matilda Garrett. Presumably the female 30-40 years old in the household of:
Samuel S. Hall. Head of household.
Males (>5) - 2, (10-15) - 1, (15-20) - 1, (40-50) - 1. Females (20-30) - 1, (30-40) - 1. Slaves: 21.

Living near John B. Hall, William Hall, W. W. Wildy, Jonathan Bonney

Children from this marriage were:

+ 70 F   i.   **Laurena Matilda Hall** was born on 31 Aug 1819 in Davidson County, Tennessee,[213] died on 13 Nov 1871 in Yazoo County, Mississippi[214] at age 52, and was buried in Nov 1871 in Yazoo County, Mississippi (Wesley Chapel Cemetery).[215]

+ 71 M   ii.   **William C. Hall** was born about 1828 in Arkansas and died before 1870 in Mississippi.

15. Archibald C. Hall *(William ³, John ¹)* was born on 25 Oct 1792 in Campbell County, Virginia,[117] died on 30 Jun 1863 in Yazoo County, Mississippi[216] at age 70, and was buried in Yazoo County, Mississippi (Bradshaw Cemetery).

Noted events in his life were:

- He served in the military during the War of 1812.[217] He was a Private in the Vol. Mounted Gunmen Regiment under Col. R. H. Dyer and Capt Thos. Jones. He enlisted on 28 Sept 1814.

- He worked as an Attorney in 1822 in Carroll County, Tennessee.[218]
He was approved to practice as an attorney before the court in Carroll County and Madison County, Tennessee in 1822.

- He had a residence in 1823 in Yazoo County, Mississippi.[94]
He appeared on a Tax List in 1823.

- He owned land on 1 May 1828 in Choctaw County, Mississippi.[219] He purchased 159.06 acres and 79.72 acres on the same date.

- He owned land on 27 Feb 1841 in Choctaw County, Mississippi.[220] He purchased 40.37 acres.

- He appeared on the United States census in 1830 in Yazoo County, Mississippi.[221]
A. C. Hall - Head of household. Living near the households of J. B. Hall and J. C. Hall.
Male under five, 1; male thirty-forty, 1;
Female under five, 1; female five-ten, 1; female twenty-thirty, 1

- He appeared on the United States census in 1840 in Carroll County, Mississippi.[222]
Archibald Hall. Head of household.

  Males- 5 < 10: 2; Male- 40 < 50: 1. Females- < 5: 2; Female- 10 < 15: 1; Female- 30 < 40: 1. Slaves: 39.

- He appeared on the United States census on 17 Sep 1850 in Yazoo County, Mississippi.[223]
Archibald C. Hall. Age 58. Planter. Living with his wife, Mary B. and children: Elvira Wallace (daughter), Samuel S. Hall, Octavia E. and Laurina M. Hall.

- He appeared on the United States census on 21 Aug 1860 in Yazoo County, Mississippi.[224]
A. C. Hall. Age 68. Planter. Living with wife, Mary B. and daughter, Lorena Hall. W. W. Wildy household on same page.

Archibald married **Mary B. Hamilton,** daughter of _____ _____ and _____ _____, on 23 Mar 1826 in Wilkinson, Mississippi.[225] Mary was born about 29 Nov 1804 in Tennessee,[226] died on 10 Apr 1882 in Yazoo County, Mississippi about age 77, and was buried in Yazoo County, Mississippi (Bradshaw Cemetery).

Noted events in her life were:

- She appeared on the United States census in 1830 in Yazoo County, Mississippi.[221]
Presumably the oldest female in the household of her husband:
A. C. Hall - Head of household. Living near the households of J. B. Hall and J. C. Hall.
Male under five, 1; male thirty-forty, 1;
Female under five, 1; female five-ten, 1; female twenty-thirty, 1

- She appeared on the United States census in 1840 in Carroll County, Mississippi.[227]
Mary B. Hall. Living in the household of Archibald Hall.

  Males- 5 < 10: 2; Male- 40<50: 1. Females- < 5: 2; Female- 10 < 15: 1; Female- 30 < 40: 1.

- She appeared on the United States census on 17 Sep 1850 in Yazoo County, Mississippi.[223]
Mary B. Hall. Age 47. Living with her husband, Archibald C. Hall and children: Elvira Wallace (daughter), Samuel S. Hall, Octavia E. and Laurina M. Hall.

- She appeared on the United States census on 21 Aug 1860 in Yazoo County, Mississippi.[224]

Mary B. Hall. Age 55 Living with her husband and daughter, Lorena.

- She appeared on the United States census on 1 Aug 1870 in Yazoo County, Mississippi.[228]
Mary D. Hall. Age 65. Keeping house. Living in the household of S. B. and Bessie Hart. Relationship unknown. The Harrison Hart family were next door neighbors in the 1850 Census. Hart daughters married the Childress boys. This appears to be the census listing for Mary B. Hall, widow of Archibald Hall. --rch

Children from this marriage were:

72 M   i.   **Archibald C. Hall** was born on 21 Oct 1826 in Tennessee, died on 5 May 1840 in Yazoo County, Mississippi[226] at age 13, and was buried in Yazoo County, Mississippi (Bradshaw Cemetery). He never married and had no children.

         Noted events in his life were:
- He appeared on the United States census in 1830 in Yazoo County, Mississippi.[221]
Presumably the male under five shown in the household of Archibald Hall.

         A. C. Hall - Head of household. Living near the households of J. B. Hall and J. C. Hall.
Male under five, 1; male thirty-forty, 1;
Female under five, 1; female five-ten, 1; female twenty-thirty, 1

+ 73 F   ii.   **Elvira E. Hall** was born about Dec 1827 in Davidson County, Tennessee,[229] died about 1902 in Yazoo County, Mississippi[229] about age 75, and was buried in Yazoo County, Mississippi.

74 M   iii.   **Samuel S. Hall** was born about 1831 in Tennessee.

         Noted events in his life were:
- He appeared on the United States census in 1840 in Carroll County, Mississippi.[227]
Samuel S. Hall. Living with his parents in the household of Archibald Hall.

         Males- 5 < 10: 2; Male- 40<50: 1. Females- < 5: 2; Female- 10 < 15: 1; Female- 30 < 40: 1.

- He appeared on the United States census on 17 Sep 1850 in Yazoo County, Mississippi.[223]
Samuel S. Hall. Age 19. Student. Living with his parents.

75 M   iv.   _____ **Hall** was born about 1834 in Tennessee. He never married and had no children.

         Noted events in his life were:
- He appeared on the United States census in 1840 in Carroll County, Mississippi.[227]
Hall. Living with his parents in the household of Archibald Hall.

         Males- 5 < 10: 2; Male- 40<50: 1. Females- < 5: 2; Female- 10 < 15: 1; Female- 30 < 40: 1.

+ 76 F   v.   **Octavia E. Hall** was born on 26 Feb 1838 in Tennessee, died on 18 Aug 1856 in Yazoo County, Mississippi at age 18, and was buried in Yazoo County, Mississippi (Bradshaw Cemetery).

+ 77 F   vi.   **Laurena M. Hall**[230] was born on 16 Dec 1839 in Mississippi, died on 25 Jul 1863 in Yazoo County, Mississippi[231] at age 23, and was buried in 1863 in Yazoo County, Mississippi (Bradshaw Cemetery).

78 F   vii.   **Almira E. Hall** was born on 29 Mar 1845 in Yazoo County, Mississippi, died on 18 Jun 1846 in Yazoo County, Mississippi[231] at age 1, and was buried in Yazoo County, Mississippi (Bradshaw Cemetery). She never married and had no children.

16. Tabitha Hall *(William³, John¹)* was born about 1795 in Campbell County, Virginia,[119] died on 20 Jun 1851 in Carroll County, Mississippi[120] about age 56, and was buried in Mississippi.

     Death Notes:
Hand written in the Family Register of the William Ross Russell Bible: *"Tabitha Rufsell Departed this life the 20th day of June 1851 aged _____"*

Noted events in her life were:
- She appeared on the United States census in 1830 in Yazoo County, Mississippi.[232]
Probably the lone female in this household.
Wm. Russell. Head of household.
Males: (<5) -3, (5-10) -1, (10-15) -2, (15-20) -2, (40-50) -1
Females: (30-40) -1

- She appeared on the United States census in 1840 in Carroll County, Mississippi.[233]
Tabitha (Hall) Russell is probably the female listed in the household of her son, William Russell:
Males: age 10 < 15 - 1; 15 < 20 - 1; 20 < 30 - 1. Females: age 40 < 50 -1. Slaves: 24.
--
This family is living next door to the William Morehead family.

- She appeared on the United States census on 1 Oct 1850 in Carroll County, Mississippi.[234]
Tobitha Ross. Age 55. Living with her son, Linsey H. Russell and next door to son, William R. Russell and family.

Tabitha married **William Russell,** son of **James Russell** and **Rosannah Rutherford,** on 15 Feb 1810 in Davidson County, Tennessee.[235] William was born on 16 Sep 1782 in Campbell County, Virginia,[120] died about 1836 in Yazoo County, Mississippi about age 54, and was buried in Mississippi.

Noted events in his life were:
- He appeared on the United States census in 1830 in Yazoo County, Mississippi.[232]

  Wm. Russell. Head of household.
  Males: (<5) -3, (5-10) -1, (10-15) -2, (15-20) -2, (40-50) -1
  Females: (30-40) -1

- He had an estate probated from before 1837 to 1839 in Yazoo County, Mississippi.[236]
Marcus Pierce Administrator of the Estate of William Russell, deceased, presented in the Yazoo County Probate Court an appraisal of the Personal Estate of William Russell, deceased in Carroll County. The court accepted the report. A petition was presented to allow the sale of stock, cattle, hogs and sheep. The Court ordered that public notice be given of the sale. Yazoo County Probate Court - October Term 1837.
--
Marcus Pierce Administrator of the Estate of William Russell, deceased, filed an accounting of the sale of Personal property of the estate. The court accepted the report. Yazoo County Probate Court - December Term 1837.
--
Marcus Pierce, Administrator of the Estate of William Russell, deceased, was granted a continuance to file an annual settlement report. Yazoo County Probate Court - October Term 1838.
--
Marcus Pierce, Administrator of the Estate of William Russell, deceased, filed an annual settlement report. The court accepted the report. Yazoo County Probate Court - April Term 1839.

- He had an estate probated from 1840 to 1841 in Carroll County, Mississippi.[237]
Tabitha Russell was appointed guardian of Lindsey A. and Felix G. Russell, minor children of Wm. Russell. Probate Book A, December Term 1840, page 213.

  Camp P. Merritt and Marcus Pierce gave testimony that Tabitha Russell, Wm. R. Russell and Lindsey H. Russell are the only surviving heirs of Wm. Russell, dec'd. late of Yazoo, Mississippi. Probate Book A, June Term, 1841, Page 19.

Children from this marriage were:

+ 79 M   i.   **William Ross Russell** was born on 29 Dec 1817 in Tennessee[238] and died on 27 Jun 1852 in Carroll County, Mississippi[239] at age 34.

   80 M   ii.   **James R. Russell** was born about 1820 in Tennessee and died before 1840 in Carroll County, Mississippi.[240] He never married and had no children.

   81 M   iii.   **Felix G. Russell** was born about 1822 in Tennessee and died about 1840 in Carroll County, Mississippi[240] about age 18. He never married and had no children.

   82 M   iv.   **Wesley Russell** was born about 1825 in Tennessee and died before 1841 in Carroll County, Mississippi.[241] He never married and had no children.

Noted events in his life were:

- He appeared on the United States census in 1840 in Carroll County, Mississippi.[233]
  Wesley Russell. Probably the male Age 15 < 20. Living with his mother, Tabitha (Hall) Russell and brothers in the household of his brother:

  William Russell:
  Males: age 10 < 15 - 1; 15 < 20 - 1; 20 < 30 - 1. Females: age 40 < 50 -1. Slaves: 24.

+ 83 M v. **Lindsey H. Russell** was born about 1827 in Yazoo County, Mississippi[119] and died between 1864 and 1870 in Mississippi.

Tabitha next married **Jesse S. Ross,** son of _____ _____ and _____ _____, on 20 Aug 1843 in Carroll County, Mississippi.[119] Jesse died about 1849 in Mississippi.[242] They had no children.

Death Notes:
Mention of the death of Jesse S. Ross was made in an application of Archibald C. Hall, Administrator of the Estate of William Hall, deceased to the Yazoo County Probate Court. The application for first settlement of his accounts as Administrator of said estate was made during the February Term 1850.

Noted events in his life were:

- He was involved in a court case about the division of Real Estate among the heirs of William Hall, Deceased. in 1849 in Yazoo County, Mississippi.[242]

  A summons was issued on 28 April 1849 for Jesse E. Ross and Tabitha his wife to appear in the Yazoo County Probate Court on the 4th Monday of July 1849. The summons was delivered to Tabitha on 11 May 1849. The Sheriff noted that Jesse S. Ross was not found in his county (Carroll County, Mississippi).

17. Dr. Elisha S. Hall *(William³, John¹)* was born about 1798 in Bedford County, Virginia and died about 1827 in Bedford County, Tennessee about age 29.

Noted events in his life were:

- He appeared on the United States census on 7 Aug 1820 in Davidson County, Tennessee.[90]
  Elisha S. Hall. Presumably the younger male in the household of William Hall.
  --
  William Hall. Head of household.
  Males (16-26) - 1, (45+) - 1; Females (16-26) - 1, (45+) - 1; Agricultural workers: 31, manufacturing: 13.

- He had a residence in 1823 in Yazoo County, Mississippi.[243]
  He appears on a Tax List for 1823 in Yazoo County, Mississippi.

- He signed a will in 1825 in Bedford County, Tennessee.[244]
  From a series of depositions made in early 1828 regarding the ownership of a slave considered by the plaintiffs to be the property of the estate of Dr. Elisha S. Hall:

  "R. C. Thompson called in 1825 by Doctor Elisha S. Hall to write his last will and testament as he was about to take a trip to the lower country."

  Apparently, the plaintiffs were A. C. Hall and Sterling Brown, administrators of the estate of E. S. Hall. Archibald C. Hall, an attorney, was a brother of Elisha and son of William Hall then living in Yazoo County, Mississippi. Sterling Brown, was a cousin; a son of Shadrack Brown, an uncle (in-law) of Elisha S. Hall.

  The living children of William Hall were given a legacy by Dr. Elisha S. Hall, deceased:

  Bedford County, Tennessee Register of Deeds Vol. X-BB, April 1827 - March 1832
  John C. Hall and others from A. B. Morton 1830 Vol. X-BB, page 397-398
  "1 December 1831; Abraham B. Morton of Shelbyville to "...John C. Hall, Jr., Archibald C. Hall, Samuel Hall, Lindsey Hall, William Russell his wife Tabitha Russell formerly Tabitha Hall, and Rhody Hall now married to a gentleman whose name is not known, heirs and distributees of Dr. Elisha S. Hall..."; for $700 paid by Elisha S. Hall "in his lifetime and his administrator since his death" for Town Lot #1 in St. Francisville, Louisiana; witness: William Gilchrist, Shad. S. Brown."

Elisha married **Jane Gillespie Brown,** daughter of **Joseph Brown** and **Sarah Thomas,** on 27 Oct 1822 in Bedford County, Tennessee.[245] Jane was born on 22 Jan 1806 in Davidson County, Tennessee[246] and died on 7 Sep 1826 in Shelbyville, Bedford County, Tennessee[246] at age 20. They had no children.

Noted events in her life were:
• Her obituary was published in the National Banner and National Whig newspaper on 30 Sep 1826 in Davidson County, Tennessee.[247]
"Mrs. Jane Hall, wife of Dr. E. S. Hall, died in Bedford County, Tennessee."

18. Rhoda Hall *(William[3], John[1])* was born about 1803 in Davidson County, Tennessee, died in Dec 1879 in Montgomery County, Mississippi[121] about age 76, and was buried in Mississippi. The cause of her death was Fever.

General Notes:
*"In 1812 [21?-rch], Mr. Richard Drake kept a tavern at Clover Bottom. On the Fourth of July he gave ball...The young ladies who went were: Misses Martha and Virginia Jones, **Rody and Betsy Hall**, Jane Sandifer, Lucinda Lunden, Agnes and Emeline Clopton, Sarah Priestly, Sallie Cook, Thomas, Harriet and Fannie Drake."* --Jane Henry Thomas[248]

Noted events in her life were:
• She appeared on the United States census on 7 Aug 1820 in Davidson County, Tennessee.[90]
Rhoda Hall. Presumably the yougest female in the household of William Hall.
--
William Hall. Head of household.
Males (16-26) - 1, (45+) - 1; Females (16-26) - 1, (45+) - 1; Agricultural workers: 31, manufacturing: 13.

• She appeared on the United States census in 1830 in Yazoo County, Mississippi.[249]
Probably the oldest female in the household of Marcus Pierce.
Males (>5) -1, (30-40) -1; Females (>5) -2, (20-30) -1
A. C. Hall, J. B. Hall and J. C. Hall are nearby.

• She appeared on the United States census in 1840 in Carroll County, Mississippi.[250]
Probably the oldest female listed in the household of Marcus Pierce.
Males: (<5) -1, (5-10) -1, (10-15) -1, (40-50) -1
Females: (5-10) -1, (10-15) -2, (30-40) -1
Slaves: 16

• She appeared on the United States census on 11 Oct 1850 in Carroll County, Mississippi.[251]
Rhoda Pierce. Age 46. Head of household. Living with her son and children. Additionally, there are two children in the household, Eugenia Harbuck, age 4; and Ursella Harbuck, age 2 who's relationship is unknown (rch 2007).

• She appeared on the United States census on 20 Jun 1860 in Choctaw County, Mississippi.[252]
Rhoda Pierce. Age 55. Farmer. Head of household. Living with her children: William, James C., Benjamin F., and Henry M.

• She appeared on the United States census on 19 Oct 1870 in Choctaw County, Mississippi.[253]
Roda Pierce. Age 69. Living in the household of her son, Benjamin. Also in the household is William Pierce and his wife, Nancy and their son, Briler.

Rhoda married **Marcus Pierce,** son of _____ _____ and _____ _____, about 1825 in Yazoo County, Mississippi.[254] Marcus was born about 1795 in Massachusetts, died about Apr 1844 in Carroll County, Mississippi[255] about age 49, and was buried in Mississippi.

Marriage Notes:
Found in the testimony regarding the Probate of the Estate of William Hall, dec'd is a deposition of Marcus Pierce given on 24 January 1842, who answers questions regarding John C. Hall, dec'd. , son of William Hall, dec'd. Among his responses, he states that he married a daughter of William Hall, dec'd. (Rodah) and that the court had assigned the couple a fractional share in the property of the estate. He further stated that they had signed over their share of the real estate to Archibald C. Hall.[256]

Noted events in his life were:
• He appeared on the United States census in 1830 in Yazoo County, Mississippi.[249]
Marcus Pierce. Head of household. Probably the oldest male in the household.

Males (>5) -1, (30-40) -1; Females (>5) -2, (20-30) -1
A. C. Hall, J. B. Hall and J. C. Hall are nearby.

- He appeared on the United States census in 1840 in Carroll County, Mississippi.[250]
Marcus Pierce. Head of household:
Males: (<5) -1, (5-10) -1, (10-15) -1, (40-50) -1
Females: (5-10) -1, (10-15) -2, (30-40) -1
Slaves: 16

- He had an estate probated in County Court in 1844 in Yazoo County, Mississippi.[257]
Yazoo County Probate Court Probate Minute Book C, May Term 1843[4], May 30, 1843[4] *"Application of Rhoda Pierce, widow of Marcus Pierce, deceased, for allotment of dower."* *"It is ordered that publication of said petition be made in the Hornet, a paper published in Carrollton, Carroll County and the nearest paper published to the residence of the said Rhoda Pierce for four successive weeks."*

- He had an estate probated in County Court in 1844 in Carroll County, Mississippi.[258]
"William Sanders was appointed Administrator of the Estate of Marcus Pierce, dec'd." From May Term, 1844; page 205.

"Rhoda Pierce, widow of Marcus Pierce, deceased petitioned to allot dower to her in a certain parcel of land." From December Term, 1844; page 242.

Children from this marriage were:

+ 84 M   i.   **William Pierce** was born about 1826 in Yazoo County, Mississippi and died after 1880 in Mississippi.

   85 F   ii.   **Elizabeth Pierce** was born about 1828 in Yazoo County, Mississippi.

Noted events in her life were:
- She appeared on the United States census in 1830 in Yazoo County, Mississippi.[249]
Probably one of the young females in the household of Marcus Pierce.
Males (>5) -1, (30-40) -1; Females (>5) -2, (20-30) -1
Next door to A. C. Hall, J. B. Hall and J. C. Hall are nearby.

- She appeared on the United States census in 1840 in Carroll County, Mississippi.[250]
Living with her parents in the household of Marcus Pierce.
Males: (<5) -1, (5-10) -1, (10-15) -1, (40-50) -1
Females: (5-10) -1, (10-15) -2, (30-40) -1

- She appeared on the United States census on 12 Oct 1850 in Carroll County, Mississippi.[259]
Elizabeth Pierce. Age 22. Living with her mother, brothers and sisters.

   86 F   iii.   **Julia W. Pierce** was born about 1830 in Yazoo County, Mississippi.

Noted events in her life were:
- She appeared on the United States census in 1830 in Yazoo County, Mississippi.[249]
Probably one of the young females in the household of Marcus Pierce.
Males (>5) -1, (30-40) -1; Females (>5) -2, (20-30) -1
Next door to A. C. Hall, J. B. Hall and J. C. Hall are nearby.

- She appeared on the United States census in 1840 in Carroll County, Mississippi.[250]
Living with her parents in the household of Marcus Pierce.
Males: (<5) -1, (5-10) -1, (10-15) -1, (40-50) -1
Females: (5-10) -1, (10-15) -2, (30-40) -1.

- She appeared on the United States census on 12 Oct 1850 in Carroll County, Mississippi.[259]
Julia W. Pierce. Age 20. Living with her mother, brothers and sisters.

+ 87 F   iv.   **Eliza Pierce** was born about 1833 in Yazoo County, Mississippi and died before 1880 in Louisiana.

   88 M   v.   **James C. Pierce** was born about 1835 in Mississippi.

Noted events in his life were:
- He appeared on the United States census in 1840 in Carroll County, Mississippi.[250]
  Living with his parents in the household of Marcus Pierce.
  Males: (<5) -1, (5-10) -1, (10-15) -1, (40-50) -1
  Females: (5-10) -1, (10-15) -2, (30-40) -1.

- He appeared on the United States census on 12 Oct 1850 in Carroll County, Mississippi.[259]
  James Pierce. Age 15. Living with his mother, brothers and sisters.

- He appeared on the United States census on 20 Jun 1860 in Choctaw County, Mississippi.[252]
  James C. Pierce. Age 23. Farmer. Living with his mother and brothers.

+ 89 M   vi.   **Benjamin Franklin Pierce** was born about 1838 in Mississippi and died after 1880 in Mississippi.

   90 M   vii.   **Henry M. Pierce** was born about 1842 in Carroll County, Mississippi.

Noted events in his life were:
- He appeared on the United States census on 12 Oct 1850 in Carroll County, Mississippi.[259]
  Henry Pierce. Age 8. Living with his mother, brothers and sisters.

- He appeared on the United States census on 20 Jun 1860 in Choctaw County, Mississippi.[260]
  Henry M. Pierce. Age 19. Farmer. Living with his mother and brothers.

- He appeared on the United States census on 18 Jun 1880 in Montgomery County, Mississippi.[261]
  Henry Pierce. Age 38. Farmer. Living near his brother, Frank.

20. Magdalena Hall *(Mathew, Sr.* [5], *John* [1]*)* was born about 1802 in Bedford County, Virginia[70] and died about 1859 in Bedford County, Virginia[70] about age 57.

Magdalena married **John D. Carter,** son of **John Carter, Sr.** and **Frances DuPriest,** on 6 Jan 1820 in Bedford County, Virginia.[262] John was born about 1795 in Bedford County, Virginia and died about 1856 in Bedford County, Virginia about age 61.

21. Melinda A. Hall *(Mathew, Sr.* [5], *John* [1]*)* was born about 1810 in Bedford County, Virginia[70] and died about 1886 in Bedford County, Virginia[70] about age 76.

Noted events in her life were:
- She appeared on the United States census on 13 Sep 1850 in Bedford County, Virginia.[263]
  Malinda A. Hall. Age 40. Living with her husband, John and children: Andrew J., John W., Sally Ann, F. F., Mary C., Malinda A., Thomas B., Mathew and Martha M. B.

- She appeared on the United States census on 9 Aug 1860 in Bedford County, Virginia.[264]
  M. A. Hall. Age 52. Living with her husband, Jno. Hall and children: J. W., S. A. G., K. F., M. E., M. A., Thos. B., M. V., M. M. V., R. J., W. C.

Melinda married **John Hall,** son of **Jesse Hall** and **Elizabeth Williams,** on 18 Feb 1830 in Bedford County, Virginia.[265] John was born about 1798 in Bedford County, Virginia and died after 1860 in Bedford County, Virginia.

Noted events in his life were:
- He appeared on the United States census in 1810 in Bedford County, Virginia.[130]
  Presumably one of the males aged 10-15. Living with their mother, Elizabeth Hall.
  Males 10-15 (3). Females 26-44 (1). Slaves (0).

- He appeared on the United States census on 13 Sep 1850 in Bedford County, Virginia.[263]
  John Hall. Age 52. Laborer. Living with his wife, Malinda A. Hall and children: Andrew J., John W., Sally Ann, F. F., Mary C., Malinda A., Thomas B., Mathew and Martha M. B.

- He appeared on the United States census on 9 Aug 1860 in Bedford County, Virginia.[266]
  Jno. Hall. Age 62. Farmer. Living with his wife, M. A. and children: J. W., S. A. G., K. F., M. E., M. A., Thos. B., M. V., M. M. V., R. J., W. C.

- He owned land in 1838 in Bedford County, Virginia.[132]
  From: Bedford County, Virginia Deed Book 27, November 19, 1838, Page 337.

Descendants of John Hall (1735 - 1794)
of Bedford County, Virginia

Jesse Hall of Patrick County, Virginia sold a 10 acre tract of land in Bedford County, along the waters of Rock Castle Creek and adjoining the lands of Mathew and Elisha Hall to John Hall [his brother] for six dollars. This land was part of the estate of Jesse Hall, deceased, father of Jesse Hall. The transaction was witnessed by: Nicholas Robertson and Wm. W. Reese.

Children from this marriage were:

91 M   i. **Andrew J. Hall** was born about 1831 in Bedford County, Virginia.

     Noted events in his life were:
- He appeared on the United States census on 13 Sep 1850 in Bedford County, Virginia.[263]
  Andrew J. Hall. Age 19. Laborer. Living with his parents and siblings.

- He appeared on the United States census on 9 Aug 1860 in Bedford County, Virginia.[267]
  A. J. Hall. Age 29. Farmer. Living with his children: A. A. J.(7), L. G. C.(6), G. J.(3). Living next door to his parents.

92 M   ii. **John W. Hall** was born about 1833 in Bedford County, Virginia.

     Noted events in his life were:
- He appeared on the United States census on 13 Sep 1850 in Bedford County, Virginia.[263]
  John W. Hall. Age 17. Laborer. Living with his parents and siblings.

- He appeared on the United States census on 9 Aug 1860 in Bedford County, Virginia.[266]
  J. W. Hall. Age 27. Farmer. Living with his parents and siblings.

93 F   iii. **Sally Ann Hall** was born about 1835 in Bedford County, Virginia.

     Noted events in her life were:
- She appeared on the United States census on 13 Sep 1850 in Bedford County, Virginia.[268]
  Sally Ann Hall. Age 15. Living with her parents and siblings.

- She appeared on the United States census on 9 Aug 1860 in Bedford County, Virginia.[266]
  S. A. G. Hall. Age 26. Living with her parents and siblings.

94 F   iv. **F. F. Hall** was born about 1837 in Bedford County, Virginia.

     Noted events in her life were:
- She appeared on the United States census on 13 Sep 1850 in Bedford County, Virginia.[268]
  F. F. Hall. Age 13. Living with her parents and siblings.

- She appeared on the United States census on 9 Aug 1860 in Bedford County, Virginia.[266]
  K. F. Hall. Age 22. Living with her parents and siblings.

95 F   v. **Mary E. Hall** was born about 1839 in Bedford County, Virginia.

     Noted events in her life were:
- She appeared on the United States census on 13 Sep 1850 in Bedford County, Virginia.[268]
  Mary C. Hall. Age 11. Living with her parents and siblings.

- She appeared on the United States census on 9 Aug 1860 in Bedford County, Virginia.[266]
  M. E. Hall. Age 19. Living with her parents and siblings.

96 M   vi. **Mathew Hall** was born about 1839 in Bedford County, Virginia.

     Noted events in his life were:
- He appeared on the United States census on 13 Sep 1850 in Bedford County, Virginia.[268]
  Mathew Hall. Age 11. Living with his parents and siblings.

97 F   vii. **Malinda S. Hall** was born about 1841 in Bedford County, Virginia.

     Noted events in her life were:
- She appeared on the United States census on 13 Sep 1850 in Bedford County, Virginia.[268]
  Malinda S. Hall. Age 9. Living with her parents and siblings.

- She appeared on the United States census on 9 Aug 1860 in Bedford County, Virginia.[266]
  M. A. Hall. Age 17. Living with her parents and siblings.

98 M viii. **Thomas B. Hall** was born about 1844 in Bedford County, Virginia.

Noted events in his life were:
- He appeared on the United States census on 13 Sep 1850 in Bedford County, Virginia.[268]
  Thomas B. Hall. Age 6. Living with his parents and siblings.

- He appeared on the United States census on 9 Aug 1860 in Bedford County, Virginia.[266]
  Thos. B. Hall. Age 15. Living with his parents and siblings.

99 M ix. **M. V. Hall** was born about 1847 in Bedford County, Virginia.

Noted events in his life were:
- He appeared on the United States census on 9 Aug 1860 in Bedford County, Virginia.[266]
  M. V. Hall. Age 13. Living with his parents and siblings.

100 F x. **Martha M. B. Hall** was born about 1849 in Bedford County, Virginia.

Noted events in her life were:
- She appeared on the United States census on 13 Sep 1850 in Bedford County, Virginia.[268]
  Martha M. B. Hall. Age 1. Living with her parents and siblings.

- She appeared on the United States census on 9 Aug 1860 in Bedford County, Virginia.[266]
  M. M. V. Hall. Age 12. Living with her parents and siblings.

101 F xi. **R. J. Hall** was born about 1850 in Bedford County, Virginia.

Noted events in her life were:
- She appeared on the United States census on 9 Aug 1860 in Bedford County, Virginia.[266]
  R. J. Hall. Age 10. Living with her parents and siblings.

102 M xii. **W. C. Hall** was born about 1853 in Bedford, Bedford County, Virginia.

Noted events in his life were:
- He appeared on the United States census on 9 Aug 1860 in Bedford County, Virginia.[266]
  W. C. Hall. Age 7. Living with his parents and siblings.

22. Mary E. Hall *(Mathew, Sr.⁵, John¹)* was born about 1812 in Bedford County, Virginia[70] and died about 1875 in Bedford County, Virginia[70] about age 63.

Mary married **John R. Marshall,** son of _____ _____ and _____ _____, on 30 Oct 1846 in Bedford County, Virginia.[70]

23. Keziah Hall *(Mathew, Sr.⁵, John¹)* was born about 1817 in Bedford County, Virginia[70] and died about 1857 in Bedford County, Virginia[70] about age 40.

Keziah married **Elisha C. Jacobs,** son of **A. Jacobs** and **Unknown,** about 14 Dec 1846 in Bedford County, Virginia.[70]

25. John Hall *(Jesse⁶, John¹)* was born about 1798 in Bedford County, Virginia and died after 1860 in Bedford County, Virginia.

Noted events in his life were:
- He appeared on the United States census in 1810 in Bedford County, Virginia.[130]
  Presumably one of the males aged 10-15. Living with their mother, Elizabeth Hall.
  Males 10-15 (3). Females 26-44 (1). Slaves (0).

- He appeared on the United States census on 13 Sep 1850 in Bedford County, Virginia.[263]
  John Hall. Age 52. Laborer. Living with his wife, Malinda A. Hall and children: Andrew J., John W., Sally Ann, F. F., Mary C., Malinda A., Thomas B., Mathew and Martha M. B.

- He appeared on the United States census on 9 Aug 1860 in Bedford County, Virginia.[266]
Jno. Hall. Age 62. Farmer. Living with his wife, M. A. and children: J. W., S. A. G., K. F., M. E., M. A., Thos. B., M. V., M. M. V., R. J., W. C.

- He owned land in 1838 in Bedford County, Virginia.[132]
From: Bedford County, Virginia Deed Book 27, November 19, 1838, Page 337.

Jesse Hall of Patrick County, Virginia sold a 10 acre tract of land in Bedford County, along the waters of Rock Castle Creek and adjoining the lands of Mathew and Elisha Hall to John Hall [his brother] for six dollars. This land was part of the estate of Jesse Hall, deceased, father of Jesse Hall. The transaction was witnessed by: Nicholas Robertson and Wm. W. Reese.

John married **Melinda A. Hall,** daughter of **Mathew Hall, Sr.** and **Mary "Polly" Elizabeth Banks,** on 18 Feb 1830 in Bedford County, Virginia.[265] Melinda was born about 1810 in Bedford County, Virginia[70] and died about 1886 in Bedford County, Virginia[70] about age 76.

Noted events in her life were:
- She appeared on the United States census on 13 Sep 1850 in Bedford County, Virginia.[263]
Malinda A. Hall. Age 40. Living with her husband, John and children: Andrew J., John W., Sally Ann, F. F., Mary C., Malinda A., Thomas B., Mathew and Martha M. B.

- She appeared on the United States census on 9 Aug 1860 in Bedford County, Virginia.[264]
M. A. Hall. Age 52. Living with her husband, Jno. Hall and children: J. W., S. A. G., K. F., M. E., M. A., Thos. B., M. V., M. M. V., R. J., W. C.

(Duplicate Line. See Person 21 on Page 52)

26. **Joel Hall** *(Jesse* [6]*, John* [1]*)* was born about 1799 in Bedford County, Virginia.

Noted events in his life were:
- He appeared on the United States census in 1810 in Bedford County, Virginia.[130]
Presumably one of the males aged 10-15. Living with their mother, Elizabeth Hall.
Males 10-15 (3). Females 26-44 (1). Slaves (0).

- He appeared on the United States census in 1830 in Bedford County, Virginia.[269]
Joel Hall. Head of household. Presumably the male age 30-40 in this household.
Males: <5 (1); 30-40 (1). Females: <5 (1); 20-30 (1).

- He appeared on the United States census on 5 Sep 1850 in Bedford County, Virginia.[270]
Joel Hall. Age 51. Farmer. Living with his wife, Sally B. and children: Elizabeth, Jesse M. S., David O., John Q. A., Nancy C., Abner J., William H., James M. C. F., Albun S., Sally B.

Joel married **Sally B. Jones,** daughter of **Unknown** and **Elizabeth _____,** on 24 Apr 1826 in Bedford County, Virginia.[271] Sally was born about 1806 in Virginia.

Noted events in her life were:
- She appeared on the United States census in 1830 in Bedford County, Virginia.[269]
Presumably the female age 20-30 in the household of Joel Hall.
Males: <5 (1); 30-40 (1). Females: <5 (1); 20-30 (1).

- She appeared on the United States census on 5 Sep 1850 in Bedford County, Virginia.[270]
Sally B. Hall. Age 44. Living with her husband, Joel and children: Elizabeth, Jesse M. S., David O., John Q. A., Nancy C., Abner J., William H., James M. C. F., Albun S., Sally B.

Children from this marriage were:
    103   F   i.   **Elizabeth Hall** was born about 1827 in Bedford County, Virginia.

Noted events in her life were:
- She appeared on the United States census on 5 Sep 1850 in Bedford County, Virginia.[270] Elizabeth Hall. Age 23. Living with her parents and siblings.

104 M ii. **Jesse M. S. Hall** was born about 1829 in Bedford County, Virginia.

Noted events in his life were:
- He appeared on the United States census on 5 Sep 1850 in Bedford County, Virginia.[270] Jesse M. S. Hall. Age 21. Laborer. Living with his parents and siblings.

+ 105 M iii. **David O. Hall** was born about 1831 in Bedford County, Virginia.

106 M iv. **John Q. S. Hall** was born about 1833 in Bedford County, Virginia.

Noted events in his life were:
- He appeared on the United States census on 5 Sep 1850 in Bedford County, Virginia.[270] John Q. S. Hall. Age 17. Laborer. Living with his parents and siblings.

107 F v. **Nancy C. Hall** was born about 1835 in Bedford County, Virginia.

Noted events in her life were:
- She appeared on the United States census on 5 Sep 1850 in Bedford County, Virginia.[270] Nancy C. Hall. Age 15. Living with her parents and siblings.

108 M vi. **Abner J. Hall** was born about 1837 in Bedford County, Virginia.

Noted events in his life were:
- He appeared on the United States census on 5 Sep 1850 in Bedford County, Virginia.[270] Abner J. Hall. Age 13. Living with his parents and siblings.

109 M vii. **William H. Hall** was born about 1840 in Bedford County, Virginia.

Noted events in his life were:
- He appeared on the United States census on 5 Sep 1850 in Bedford County, Virginia.[270] William H. Hall. Age 10. Living with his parents and siblings.

110 M viii. **James M. C. F. Hall** was born about 1842 in Bedford County, Virginia.

Noted events in his life were:
- He appeared on the United States census on 5 Sep 1850 in Bedford County, Virginia.[270] James M. C. F. Hall. Age 8. Living with his parents and siblings.

111 M ix. **Albun S. Hall** was born about 1844 in Bedford County, Virginia.

Noted events in his life were:
- He appeared on the United States census on 5 Sep 1850 in Bedford County, Virginia.[270] Albun S. Hall. Age 6. Living with his parents and siblings.

112 F x. **Sally B. Hall** was born about Dec 1849 in Bedford County, Virginia.

Noted events in her life were:
- She appeared on the United States census on 5 Sep 1850 in Bedford County, Virginia.[270] Sally B. Hall. Age 10/12. Living with her parents and siblings.

27. Tabitha Hall *(Elisha [8], John [1])* was born about 1796 in Virginia and died before 1850 in Virginia.

Tabitha married **Thomas Heppenstall,** son of **Caleb Heppenstall** and **Liza Trege Greer,** on 13 Dec 1815 in Bedford County, Virginia.[79] Thomas was born about 1788 in Virginia.

Children from this marriage were:

+ 113 F i. **Sarah Ann Heppenstall** was born about 1825 in Franklin County, Virginia[272] and died about 1916 about age 91.

+ 114 M   ii. **Thomas Heppenstall** was born about 1831 in Bedford County, Virginia.

28. Drucilla Hall *(Elisha [8], John [1])* was born about 1804 in Bedford County, Virginia and died before 1870 in Henry County, Tennessee.

    Noted events in her life were:
- She appeared on the United States census on 16 Sep 1850 in Henry County, Tennessee.[273]
  Drusilla Greer. Age 47. Living with her husband, Bird Greer and children: Calloway, Mary C., Caroline, Louisa, Martha, Bird Greer, Jr., Washington, Amanda, Tabitha and James.

- She appeared on the United States census on 4 Aug 1860 in Henry County, Tennessee.[274]
  Drucilla Greer. Age 56. Living with her husband, Bird Greer and children: Calvin, Martha A., Washington, Josaphine, Tabitha and James K. P.

Drucilla married **William Bird Greer,** son of **Nathan Greer** and **Lucy Arthur,** on 16 Jun 1819 in Bedford County, Virginia.[79] William was born about 1797 in Franklin County, Virginia and died before 1870 in Henry County, Tennessee.

    Noted events in his life were:
- He appeared on the United States census on 16 Sep 1850 in Henry County, Tennessee.[273]
  Bird Greer. Age 52. Farmer. Living with his wife, Drusilla and children: Calloway, Mary C., Caroline, Louisa, Martha, Bird Greer, Jr., Washington, Amanda, Tabitha and James.

- He appeared on the United States census on 4 Aug 1860 in Henry County, Tennessee.[274]
  Bird Greer. Age 62. Farmer. Living with his wife, Drucilla and children: Calvin, Martha A., Washington, Josaphine, Tabitha and James K. P.

29. John Hall *(Elisha [8], John [1])* was born about 1806 in Bedford County, Virginia and died in Missouri.

    Noted events in his life were:
- He appeared on the United States census in 1830 in Bedford County, Virginia.[275]
  John Hall. Head of household. Presumably one of the males age 20-30 in this household.
  Males: <5 (1); 5-10 (1); 20-30 (3). Females: <5 (1); 20-30 (1).

John married **Elizabeth Moon,** daughter of **Christopher Moon** and **Unknown,** on 17 Aug 1824 in Pittsylvania County, Virginia.[276] The marriage ended in divorce. Elizabeth was born about 1805.

    Noted events in her life were:
- She appeared on the United States census in 1830 in Bedford County, Virginia.[275]
  Presumably the female age 20-30 in the household of John Hall.
  Males: <5 (1); 5-10 (1); 20-30 (3). Females: <5 (1); 20-30 (1).

John next married **Sarah Ann Woodard,** daughter of _____ _____ and _____ _____, on 17 Jun 1839 in Clinton County, Ohio.[277]

30. Katherine Hall *(Elisha [8], John [1])* was born in Bedford County, Virginia.

Katherine married **William Burnett,** son of **Williamson Burnett** and **Priscilla Carter,** on 10 Jan 1827 in Bedford County, Virginia.[278] The marriage ended in separation about 1855. William was born in Virginia and died before 1851.

    Marriage Notes:
Marriage Bond: 25 Dec. 1826.

31. Mary "Polly" Hall *(Elisha [8], John [1])* was born about 1811 in Bedford County, Virginia. She was usually called Polly.

    Noted events in her life were:
- She appeared on the United States census on 17 Sep 1850 in Bedford County, Virginia.[279]
  Mary Shaon. Age 39. Living with her husband, James and children: Sarah J. J., Martha K. E., Missouri, Josephine, Rebecca. Also in the household: Manerva Overstreet, Thomas H. Miles, Will. S. Williams.

Polly married **James K. Shaon,** son of _____ _____ and _____ _____, about 17 Apr 1827 in Bedford County, Virginia.[79] James was born about 1800 in Virginia.

Noted events in his life were:
- He appeared on the United States census on 17 Sep 1850 in Bedford County, Virginia.[279]
James K. Shaon. Age 50. Farmer. Living with his wife, Mary and children: Sarah J. J., Martha K. E., Missouri, Josephine, Rebecca. Also in the household: Manerva Overstreet, Thomas H. Miles, Will. S. Williams.

32. Banks B. Hall *(Elisha⁸, John¹)* was born about 1813 in Bedford County, Virginia and died before 1870 in Audrain County, Missouri.

Noted events in his life were:
- He appeared on the United States census in 1840 in Audrain County, Missouri.[280]
B. B. Hall. Head of household. Presumably the oldest male listed.
Males: < 5 - 1; 20 <30 - 1. Females: 20 <30 - 1.

- He appeared on the United States census on 3 Sep 1850 in Audrain County, Missouri.[281]
Banks B. Hall. Age 37. Farmer. Living with his wife, Mary and children: Wm. (age 13), Sarah (age 6), Kissiah (age 2).

- He appeared on the United States census on 3 Jul 1860 in Audrain County, Missouri.[282]
Bank Hall. Age 48. Farmer. Living with his wife, Mary and children: Sarah, Kassiah, Mary J., Banks, Chls. and Madosa. Also listed in the household is John Adams, insane.

Banks married **Mary H. Reed,** daughter of _____ _____ and _____ _____, on 21 May 1835 in Callaway County, Missouri.[283] Mary was born about 1816 in Kentucky and died in Missouri.

Noted events in her life were:
- She appeared on the United States census in 1840 in Audrain County, Missouri.[280]
Mary Hall. Presumably the oldest female listed in the household of her husband, B. B. Hall.
Males: < 5 - 1; 20 <30 - 1. Females: 20 <30 - 1.

- She appeared on the United States census on 3 Sep 1850 in Audrain County, Missouri.[281]
Mary Hall. Age 37. Living with her husband, Banks B. Hall and children: Wm. (age 13), Sarah (age 6), Kissiah (age 2).

- She appeared on the United States census on 3 Jul 1860 in Audrain County, Missouri.[282]
Mary Hall. Age 44. Living with her husband, Bank Hall and children: Sarah, Kassiah, Mary J., Banks, Chls. and Madosa. Also listed in the household is John Adams, insane.
Her birthplace is listed as Kentucky on this record.

- She appeared on the United States census on 6 Jul 1870 in St. Louis, Missouri.[284]
Mary H. Hall. Age 55. Widow. Keeps Boarders. Living with her children: Sarah E., Kessiah C., Mollie G., Banks B., Charles T. and Medera A. Hall.

- She appeared on the United States census on 9 Nov 1880 in St. Louis, Missouri.[285]
Mary H. Hall. Age 64. Keeping house. Living with her children and grandchildren: Sallie E., Mollie J. B., Medora A., Charles T., Banks B., Emma M. (daughter-in-law), Alice G. (grand daughter).

33. Sarah Hall *(Elisha⁸, John¹)* was born in Bedford County, Virginia.

Sarah married **Nathaniel Morgan,** son of **Reece Morgan** and **Lavina Snider** _____, about 7 Jul 1834 in Bedford County, Virginia.[79] Nathaniel was born about 1811 in Bedford County, Virginia.

34. Keziah Hall *(Elisha⁸, John¹)* was born in Bedford County, Virginia.

Keziah married **Charles Lewellen,** son of _____ _____ and _____ _____, on 12 Mar 1835 in Bedford County, Virginia.[79]

36. Magdalena Hall *(Elisha⁸, John¹)* was born in Bedford County, Virginia.

Magdalena married **James W. Greer,** son of _____ _____ and _____ _____, about 22 Jan 1827 in Bedford County, Virginia.[79]

37. William H. Brown *(Tabitha Hall⁹, John¹)* was born on 14 Nov 1800 in Bedford County, Virginia.[147]

William married **Mollie Fuquin,** daughter of _____ _____ and _____ _____, about 1818 in

Tennessee.[147] Mollie was born about 1799 in Kentucky.[147]

38. Mary Magdalene Hall Brown *(Tabitha Hall[9], John[1])* was born about 1801 in Bedford County, Virginia.[148]

> **Noted events in her life were:**
> • She appeared on the United States census on 18 Nov 1850 in Bedford County, Tennessee.[138]
> Mary M. Hall Sanders. Age 49. Living with her mother, and children: Mary L., George W., Eliza H___,

Mary married someone _____ **Sanders,** son of _____ _____ and _____ _____.
_____ Sanders died before 1850.

Children from this marriage were:

115 F i. **Mary L. Sanders** was born about 1836 in Arkansas.

> **Noted events in her life were:**
> • She appeared on the United States census on 18 Nov 1850 in Bedford County, Tennessee.[138]
> Mary L. Sanders. Age 14. Living with her grandmother, mother and siblings.

116 M ii. **George W. Sanders** was born about 1839 in Arkansas.

> **Noted events in his life were:**
> • He appeared on the United States census on 18 Nov 1850 in Bedford County, Tennessee.[138]
> George W. Sanders. Age 11. Living with his grandmother, mother and siblings.

117 F iii. **Eliza H. Sanders** was born about 1845 in Arkansas.

> **Noted events in her life were:**
> • She appeared on the United States census on 18 Nov 1850 in Bedford County, Tennessee.[138]
> Eliza H. Sanders. Age 5. Living with her grandmother, mother and siblings.

39. Naomi Brown *(Tabitha Hall[9], John[1])* was born about 1801 in Bedford County, Virginia.[147]

Naomi married **David Tilford,** son of _____ _____ and _____ _____.

40. Sterling Brown *(Tabitha Hall[9], John[1])* was born about 1803.

Sterling married **Mary Locke,** daughter of _____ _____ and _____ _____.

41. Kezia Brown *(Tabitha Hall[9], John[1])* was born about 1805.

Kezia married **Samuel Suddarth,** son of _____ _____ and _____ _____.

42. Lucy Brown *(Tabitha Hall[9], John[1])* was born about 1806.[147]

Lucy married **Col. Richard Warner,** son of _____ _____ and _____ _____.

43. Elizabeth Brown *(Tabitha Hall[9], John[1])* was born about 1810 in Tennessee.[147]

> **Noted events in her life were:**
> • She appeared on the United States census on 18 Nov 1850 in Bedford County, Tennessee.[286]
> Elizabeth Robertson. Age 40. Head of household. Living with her children: Amanda, Michael, John and Jas. M.

Elizabeth married _____ **Robertson,** son of _____ _____ and _____ _____, about 1830
in Tennessee. _____ Robertson died before 1850.

Children from this marriage were:

118 F i. **Amanda Robertson** was born about 1831 in Tennessee.

Noted events in her life were:
- She appeared on the United States census on 18 Nov 1850 in Bedford County, Tennessee.[286]
  Amanda Robertson. Age 19. Living with her mother and siblings: Michael, John and Jas. M.

119 M   ii. **Michael Robertson** was born about 1835 in Tennessee. (Twin)

Noted events in his life were:
- He appeared on the United States census on 18 Nov 1850 in Bedford County, Tennessee.[286]
  Michael Robertson. Age 15. Living with his mother and siblings: Amanda, John and Jas. M.

120 M   iii. **John Robertson** was born about 1835 in Tennessee. (Twin)

Noted events in his life were:
- He appeared on the United States census on 18 Nov 1850 in Bedford County, Tennessee.[286]
  John Robertson. Age 15. Living with his mother and siblings: Amanda, Michael and Jas. M.

121 M   iv. **James M. Robertson** was born about 1839 in Tennessee.

Noted events in his life were:
- He appeared on the United States census on 18 Nov 1850 in Bedford County, Tennessee.[286]
  James M. Robertson. Age 11. Living with his mother and siblings: Amanda, Michael and John.

44. George W. Brown *(Tabitha Hall [9], John [1])* was born about 1813 in Tennessee.[147]

Noted events in his life were:
- He appeared on the United States census on 18 Nov 1850 in Bedford County, Tennessee.[287]
  George W. Brown. Age 37. Head of household. Living with his wife, Nancy A. and children: King S., Glenn, Harless, Joseph and Nancy T.
- He appeared on the United States census on 2 Jun 1860 in Bedford County, Tennessee.[288]
  G. W. Brown. Age 46. Farmer. Living next door to his mother, Tabitha Brown. Living with his wife, Nancy Brown and children: Billy, Sterling, Jos., J. R. P., and Geo. M. D. (twins), Wm. W.

George married **Nancy A. Winn,** daughter of _____ _____ and _____ _____, in Tennessee. Nancy was born about 1822 in Tennessee.

Noted events in her life were:
- She appeared on the United States census on 18 Nov 1850 in Bedford County, Tennessee.[287]
  Nancy A. Brown. Age 28. Living with her husband, George W. Brown and children: King S., Glenn, Harless, Joseph and Nancy T.
- She appeared on the United States census on 2 Jun 1860 in Bedford County, Tennessee.[288]
  Nancy Brown. Age 37. Living with her husband, G. W. Brown and children: Billy, Sterling, Jos., J. R. P., and Geo. M. D. (twins), Wm. W.

45. Tabitha Brown *(Tabitha Hall [9], John [1])* was born about 1815 in Tennessee[147] and died about 1861 about age 46.

Tabitha married **Robert Weakley Locke,** son of **William Locke** and **Martha Carothers,**. Robert was born on 13 Mar 1813 in Bedford County, Tennessee[289] and died on 14 Aug 1883[289] at age 70.

46. Thomas Jefferson Brown *(Tabitha Hall [9], John [1])* was born about 1815 in Tennessee.[147]

Thomas married **Elizabeth Jane Stoker,** daughter of _____ _____ and _____ _____.

47. Emily M. Brown *(Tabitha Hall [9], John [1])* was born about 1819 in Tennessee.[147]

Emily married **Loton S. Shofner,** son of _____ _____ and _____ _____.

48. Christopher Musgrove *(Keziah Hall [10], John [1])* was born on 9 Feb 1798 in Bedford County, Virginia[158] and died on 19 Mar 1870 in Bedford County, Virginia[159] at age 72.

Noted events in his life were:

- He appeared on the United States census on 18 Sep 1850 in Bedford County, Virginia.[290]
Christopher Musgrove. Age 53. Farmer. Living with his wife, Eliza and children: Juliet, Rachel, Christopher C., Jordan Martin and Kizia. Nearby are his brothers, Benjamin B. Musgrove and Christopher Musgrove and mother.

Christopher married **Eliza Emily Ann Jones,** daughter of _____ _____ and _____ _____, on 27 Mar 1826 in Bedford County, Virginia.[159] Eliza was born about 1806 in Bedford County, Virginia[159] and died on 17 Jul 1858 in Bedford County, Virginia[159] about age 52.

Noted events in her life were:

- She appeared on the United States census on 18 Sep 1850 in Bedford County, Virginia.[290]
Eliza Musgrove. Age 44. Living with her husband, Christopher and children: Juliet, Rachel, Christopher C., Jordan Martin and Kizia.

- Her obituary was published in the Staunton Spectator on 27 Jul 1858 in Bedford County, Virginia.[291]
Shocking Murder in Bedford
Mrs. Musgrove, wife of Christopher Musgrove, was murdered on 7/17/1858. Prime suspect was one her female slaves.

Christopher next married **Harriet Ann Ashworth,** daughter of _____ _____ and _____ _____, on 17 Feb 1859 in Bedford County, Virginia.[159] Harriet was born about 1834 in Bedford County, Virginia[159] and died in Bedford County, Virginia.

49. Rev. Henry Musgrove *(Keziah Hall [10], John [1])* was born on 3 May 1800 in Bedford County, Virginia[160] and died on 4 Sep 1869 in Henry County, Iowa[160] at age 69.

General Notes:
Left home at age 16.

Noted events in his life were:

- He appeared on the United States census on 16 Aug 1850 in Clark County, Illinois.[292]
Henry Musgrove. Age 56. Farmer. Living with his wife, Elizabeth and children: Tabitha, Henry and Elizabeth.

Henry married **Elizabeth Croy,**[293] daughter of **John Croy** and **Susannah Huston,** on 11 Nov 1821 in Montgomery Co, Ohio.[293] Elizabeth was born on 3 Nov 1798 in Bedford County, Pennyslvania.

Noted events in her life were:

- She appeared on the United States census on 16 Aug 1850 in Clark County, Illinois.[292]
Elizabeth Musgrove. Age 57. Living with her husband, Henry and children: Tabitha, Henry and Elizabeth.

51. Mary Magdalean Smith Musgrove *(Keziah Hall [10], John [1])* was born on 16 Jul 1804 in Bedford County, Virginia[161] and died on 20 Feb 1885 in Bedford County, Virginia[162] at age 80.

Noted events in her life were:

- She appeared on the United States census on 11 Sep 1850 in Bedford County, Virginia.[294]
Mary M. Wilkerson. Age 45. Living with her husband, Wm. and children: Pannis (age 20), Margaret (age 18), Ulisses (age 16) and Martha (age 24).

Mary married **William Wilkerson,** son of _____ _____ and _____ _____, on 28 Aug 1827 in Bedford County, Virginia.[162] William was born on 15 May 1802 in Bedford County, Virginia and died on 13 Jul 1867 in Bedford County, Virginia[162] at age 65.

Noted events in his life were:

- He appeared on the United States census on 11 Sep 1850 in Bedford County, Virginia.[294]
Wm. Wilkerson. Age 45. Farmer. Living with his wife, Mary M., and children: Pannis (age 20), Margaret (age 18), Ulisses (age 16) and Martha (age 24).

52. Rebekah Hall Musgrove *(Keziah Hall [10], John [1])* was born on 15 May 1805 in Bedford County, Virginia[163] and died on 29 Mar 1877 in Bedford County, Virginia[164] at age 71.

Noted events in her life were:
- She appeared on the United States census on 11 Sep 1850 in Bedford County, Virginia.[295]
  Rebecca Pearson. Age 45. Living with her husband, Hall and children: Rizy (age 19), Chris. W. (age 14) and John (age 10).

Rebekah married **Hal L. Pearson,** son of _____ _____ and _____ _____, on 30 Mar 1824 in Bedford County, Virginia.[164] Hal was born about 1803 in Bedford County, Virginia and died in Bedford County, Virginia.

Noted events in his life were:
- He appeared on the United States census on 11 Sep 1850 in Bedford County, Virginia.[295]
  Hall Pearson. Age 45. Farmer. Living with his wife, Rebecca and children: Rizy (age 19), Chris. W. (age 14) and John (age 10).

53. John Hall Musgrove *(Keziah Hall [10], John [1])* was born on 27 Jun 1806 in Bedford County, Virginia,[165] died on 23 Apr 1888 in Bedford County, Virginia[166] at age 81, and was buried in Bedford County, Virginia.

Noted events in his life were:
- He appeared on the United States census on 24 Aug 1850 in Franklin County, Virginia.[296]
  John H. Musgrove. Age 44. Farmer. Living with his wife, Lucy and children: Christopher, John, Keziah and Ulises.

John married **Lucy Lazenby,** daughter of _____ _____ and _____ _____, on 1 Nov 1836 in Bedford County, Virginia.[166] Lucy was born about 1817 in Bedford County, Virginia[166] and died in Bedford County, Virginia.

Noted events in her life were:
- She appeared on the United States census on 24 Aug 1850 in Franklin County, Virginia.[296]
  Lucy Musgrove. Age 33. Living with her husband, John H. Musgrove and children: Christopher, John, Keziah and Ulises.

54. Rachel Musgrove *(Keziah Hall [10], John [1])* was born on 11 Dec 1808 in Bedford County, Virginia[167] and died on 18 Feb 1879 in Lynchburg, Virginia[168] at age 70.

Noted events in her life were:
- She appeared on the United States census on 5 Aug 1850 in Bedford County, Virginia.[297]
  Rachiel Wilkerson. Age 37. Living with her husband, Owin and children: Kiziah (age 19), William O., (age 15), Joseph B., (age 13) and Chris. H., (age 11).

Rachel married **Owen Wilkerson, Sr.,** son of **Joseph B. Wilkerson** and **Penelope Parsons,** on 4 Mar 1830 in Bedford County, Virginia.[168] Owen was born in 1774 in Bedford County, Virginia[168] and died about 1852 in Lynchburg, Virginia about age 78.

Noted events in his life were:
- He appeared on the United States census on 5 Aug 1850 in Bedford County, Virginia.[297]
  Owin Wilkerson. Age 75. Farmer. Living with his wife, Rachiel and children: Kiziah (age 19), William O., (age 15), Joseph B., (age 13) and Chris. H., (age 11).

55. Keziah Stover Musgrove *(Keziah Hall [10], John [1])* was born on 31 Aug 1811 in Bedford County, Virginia[77] and died on 30 Nov 1892 in Bedford County, Virginia[298] at age 81.

Noted events in her life were:
- She appeared on the United States census on 11 Sep 1850 in Bedford County, Virginia.[299]
  Kisiah S. Wilkerson. Age 38. Living with her husband, Wm. L., and children: Wm. (age 18), Kisah H. (age 16), Rachel J. (age 13), Rebecca (age 10), Jno. C., (age 7), Jas. P. (age 5), and Rhoda L. P., (age 2).

Keziah married **William Lockett Wilkerson,** son of **Joseph Wilkerson** and **Rhoda Lockett,** on 1 Apr 1828 in Bedford County, Virginia.[298] William was born on 11 Dec 1811 in Bedford County, Virginia[300] and died on 1 Nov 1883 in Bedford County, Virginia[300] at age 71.

Noted events in his life were:
- He appeared on the United States census on 11 Sep 1850 in Bedford County, Virginia.[299]
  Wm. L. Wilkerson. Age 38. Farmer. Living with his wife, Keziah S., and children: Wm. (age 18), Kisah H. (age 16), Rachel J. (age 13), Rebecca (age 10), Jno. C., (age 7), Jas. P. (age 5), and Rhoda L. P., (age 2).

56. Tabitha Musgrove *(Keziah Hall [10], John [1])* was born on 11 Dec 1813 in Bedford County, Virginia[170] and died on 15 Dec 1875 in Franklin County, Virginia[171] at age 62.

Noted events in her life were:
- She appeared on the United States census on 24 Aug 1850 in Franklin County, Virginia.[301]
  Tabitha English. Age 33. Living with her husband, Parmenas English and children: James English (age 15, step-son) and Ann R. Gill (age 5, daughter). William B. Hippenstall is also shown in the household.

Tabitha married **John Sun Gill,** son of _____ _____ and _____ _____, on 3 Nov 1836 in Bedford County, Virginia.[171] John was born about 1811 in Bedford County, Virginia[171] and died in Bedford County, Virginia.

Tabitha next married **Parmenias English,** son of _____ _____ and _____ _____, on 12 Nov 1849 in Bedford County, Virginia.[171] Parmenias was born about 1798 in Bedford County, Virginia.

Noted events in his life were:
- He appeared on the United States census on 24 Aug 1850 in Franklin County, Virginia.[301]
  Parmenas English. Age 52. Farmer. Living with his wife, Tabitha and children: James English (age 15, son) and Ann R. Gill (age 5, step-daughter). William B. Hippenstall is also shown in the household.

57. Minerva Naomi Musgrove *(Keziah Hall [10], John [1])* was born on 21 May 1816 in Bedford County, Virginia[172] and died on 9 Apr 1875 in Independence County, Arkansas[173] at age 58.

Noted events in her life were:
- She appeared on the United States census on 18 Oct 1850 in Independence County, Arkansas.[302]
  Manerva Baker. Age 30. Living with her husband, Harrison and children: William (age 12), Benj. J., (age 10), Henry C. (age 8), Mildred K. (age 6), John C. (age 1).

Minerva married **Judge Harrison William Baker,** son of _____ _____ and _____ _____, on 9 May 1837 in Bedford County, Virginia.[173] Harrison was born about 1813 in Bedford County, Virginia[173] and died about 1852 in Independence County, Arkansas[173] about age 39.

Noted events in his life were:
- He appeared on the United States census on 18 Oct 1850 in Independence County, Arkansas.[302]
  Harrison Baker. Age 36. Farmer. Living with his wife, Manerva and children: William (age 12), Benj. J., (age 10), Henry C. (age 8), Mildred K. (age 6), John C. (age 1).

Minerva next married **Benjamin Franklin Ball,** son of _____ _____ and _____ _____, on 21 Oct 1853 in Independence County, Arkansas.[173] Benjamin was born on 30 Aug 1806 in Loudon County, Virginia and died on 4 Jun 1889 in Independence County, Arkansas at age 82.

58. Millicent Musgrove *(Keziah Hall [10], John [1])* was born on 10 May 1817 in Bedford County, Virginia[174] and died on 3 Jun 1883 in Bedford County, Virginia[175] at age 66.

Noted events in her life were:
- She appeared on the United States census on 18 Sep 1850 in Bedford County, Virginia.[152]
  Milerson Anthony. Age 30. Living with her mother, Kezia Musgrove. She is probably a widow at this time.

Millicent married **Henry B. Anthony,** son of _____ _____ and _____ _____, on 31 Jan 1843 in Bedford County, Virginia.[175] Henry was born about 1815 in Bedford County, Virginia[175] and died before 1850 in Bedford County, Virginia.

Millicent next married **Thomas Albert Mitchell,** son of _____ _____ and _____ _____, on 17 Jun 1851 in Bedford County, Virginia.[175] Thomas was born about 1815 in Bedford County, Virginia.[175]

59. Benjamin Barton Musgrove, Jr. *(Keziah Hall [10], John [1])* was born on 1 Jul 1822 in Bedford County, Virginia[176] and died on 3 May 1902 in Bedford County, Virginia[177] at age 79.

Noted events in his life were:
- He appeared on the United States census on 18 Sep 1850 in Bedford County, Virginia.[303]
  Benjamin B. Musgrove. Age 27. Farmer. Living with his wife, Sarah and children: Martha, Sarah, Mary, Gloria and

Stephen. Next door is his mother and nearby are his brothers, Benjamin B. Musgrove and Christopher Musgrove.

Benjamin married **Sarah Ann English,** daughter of _____ _____ and _____ _____, on 14 Dec 1842 in Bedford County, Virginia.[177] Sarah was born about 1822 in Bedford County, Virginia[177] and died about 1894 in Bedford County, Virginia[177] about age 72.

> **Noted events in her life were:**
> • She appeared on the United States census on 18 Sep 1850 in Bedford County, Virginia.[303]
> Sarah Musgrove. Age 26. Living with her husband, Benjamin and children: Martha, Sarah, Mary, Gloria and Stephen.

60. Demetrious Polyclitus Musgrove *(Keziah Hall [10], John [1])* was born on 1 Mar 1826 in Bedford County, Virginia[178] and died on 22 May 1862 in Bedford County, Virginia[179] at age 36.

> **Noted events in his life were:**
> • He appeared on the United States census on 18 Sep 1850 in Bedford County, Virginia.[304]
> D. P. Musgrove. Age 24. Farmer. Living with his wife, Martha and daughters: Frances and Elizabeth Ann. Next door is his mother and nearby are his brothers, Benjamin B. Musgrove and Christopher Musgrove.

Demetrious married **Martha Ann Watson,** daughter of _____ _____ and _____ _____, on 3 Nov 1846 in Bedford County, Virginia.[179] Martha was born about 1828 in Bedford County, Virginia.

> **Noted events in her life were:**
> • She appeared on the United States census on 18 Sep 1850 in Bedford County, Virginia.[304]
> Martha Musgrove. Age 25. Living with her husband, D. P. Musgrove and daughters: Frances and Elizabeth Ann.

Descendants of John Hall (1735 - 1794)
of Bedford County, Virginia

Fourth Generation

62. Jesse F. Hall *(John [11], John, Jr. [2], John [1])* was born on 5 Feb 1832 in Tennessee,[187] died on 20 Mar 1884 in Collin County, Texas[187] at age 52, and was buried in Mar 1884 in Collin County, Texas (Forest Grove Cemetery).[187]

> **Noted events in his life were:**
> - He appeared on the United States census on 12 Sep 1850 in Meigs County, Tennessee.[183]
> Jessee F. Hall. Age 18. Farmer. Living with his parents.
>
> - He appeared on the United States census on 7 Jun 1860 in Collin County, Texas.[184]
> J. F. Hall. Age 28. Waggoner. Living with his parents.
>
> - He appeared on the United States census on 8 Sep 1870 in Collin County, Texas.[305]
> Jesse Hall. Age 38. Farmer. Living with his wife, Jane and children: John and James. Also in the household is James Houston, farm laborer.
>
> - He appeared on the United States census on 2 Jun 1880 in Collin County, Texas.[306]
> Jesse Hall. Age 48. Farmer. Living with his wife, Jane D. Hall and children: John. J. T., Phidella, Kate, and Rob't. L. Hall.

Jesse married **Elizabeth Jane Houston,** daughter of _____ _____ and _____ _____, about 1866 in Texas. Elizabeth was born about 1838 in Tennessee, died on 22 Aug 1896 in Collin County, Texas[307] about age 58, and was buried in Aug 1896 in Collin County, Texas (Forest Grove Cemetery).[307]

> **Noted events in her life were:**
> - She appeared on the United States census on 8 Sep 1870 in Collin County, Texas.[305]
> Jane Hall. Age 32. Keeping house. Living with her husband, Jesse and children: John and James.
>
> - She appeared on the United States census on 2 Jun 1880 in Collin County, Texas.[306]
> Jane D. Hall. Age 42. Keeping house. Living with her husband, Jesse Hall and children: John, J. T., Phidella, Kate, and Rob't. L. Hall.

Children from this marriage were:

122 M   i. **John Hall** was born about 1867 in Texas.

> **Noted events in his life were:**
> - He appeared on the United States census on 8 Sep 1870 in Collin County, Texas.[305]
> John Hall. Age 3. Living with his parents.
>
> - He appeared on the United States census on 2 Jun 1880 in Collin County, Texas.[306]
> John Hall. Age 13. Living with his parents.

123 M   ii. **James T. Hall** was born about 1869 in Texas.

> **Noted events in his life were:**
> - He appeared on the United States census on 8 Sep 1870 in Collin County, Texas.[305]
> James Hall. Age 1. Living with his parents.
>
> - He appeared on the United States census on 2 Jun 1880 in Collin County, Texas.[306]
> J. T. Hall. Age 10. Living with his parents.

+ 124 F   iii. **Phidella "Della" Hall** was born on 14 Aug 1873 in Collin County, Texas,[308] died on 10 Jun 1962 in Collin County, Texas[308] at age 88, and was buried in Jun 1962 in Collin County, Texas (Forest Grove Cemetery).[308]

125 F   iv. **Kate Hall** was born about 1877 in Collin County, Texas.

> **Noted events in her life were:**
> - She appeared on the United States census on 2 Jun 1880 in Collin County, Texas.[306]
> Kate Hall. Age 3. Living with her parents.

126 M   v. **Robert L. Hall** was born about 1879 in Collin County, Texas.

Noted events in his life were:
- He appeared on the United States census on 2 Jun 1880 in Collin County, Texas.[306]
  Rob't. L. Hall. Age 1. Living with his parents.

63. Joseph Marion Hall *(John* [11]*, John, Jr.* [2]*, John* [1]*)* was born on 8 Aug 1833 in Tennessee[188] and died on 19 May 1905 in McKinney, Collin County, Texas[189] at age 71.

Noted events in his life were:
- He appeared on the United States census on 12 Sep 1850 in Meigs County, Tennessee.[183]
  Joseph M. Hall. Age 17. Farmer. Living with his parents.

- He appeared on the United States census on 7 Jun 1860 in Collin County, Texas.[309]
  J. M. Hall (indexed as Holl). Age 25. Waggonmaker. Living with his wife, Polly A. and children: John A. H., Bluford C., and William J. Hall.
  --
  Living next door appears to be his father, John Hall (80) and his wife, Delila (58).

- He appeared on the United States census on 1 Jun 1870 in Limestone County, Texas.[310]
  Joseph M. Hall. Age 37. Wagon maker. Living with his wife, Polly A. and children: Jno. A. H., Bluford C., William G., Gabe W., Geo. L., and Harriet D. B. M. Hall.

- He appeared on the United States census on 2 Jun 1880 in Lampasas County, Texas.[311]
  James Hall. Age 47. Farmer. Livng with his wife, Polley and children: John, William, Gabe, George and Harriett.
  --
  On the same page below is a William C. Hall (52) with wife, Sarah (48) and children; and his son(?) William T. Hall (28) with wife, Louisa (21) and new born daughter, Polley.

- He appeared on the United States census on 5 Jun 1900 in Collin County, Texas.[312]
  Joseph M. Hall. Age 66. Birth date: Aug, 1833. Married 48 years. Farmer. Living with his wife, Pollie A. Hall and children: Gabe W. Hall and Harriet H. Murphy and her husband and children.

Joseph married **Mary "Polly" Ann Estes,** daughter of **Bluford Estes** and **Rebecca _____**, on 20 Apr 1853 in Dent County, Missouri.[313] Polly was born on 30 Sep 1834 in Missouri,[314] died on 20 Mar 1912 in Collin County, Texas[315] at age 77, and was buried in Mar 1912 in Collin County, Texas (Scalf Cemetery).[315] She was usually called Polly.

Birth Notes:
Another source in an apparent typo has her birth date as: July 9, 1823.

Research Notes:
On 17 October 1908, Mrs. Polly Ann Hall, aged 73 years and a resident of Collin County, Texas filed an Application of Indigent widow of soldier or sailor of the late Confederacy for Pension under the Act of May 12, 1899. She stated that she was the widow of Joseph M. Hall who died on 18 May 1905. She married J. M. Hall on 17 April 1853 in Missouri. She had been a resident of McKinney, Collin County, Texas for 53 years. She noted her husband's service with Co. B of the 16th Texas Cavalry Regiment from February 1892 to November 1863. She stated that she owned "one old cow worth $25.00."

A review of his official records (found in the file) indicate that he had not been properly discharged. Despite letters of appeal written by Mrs. Hall <u>and</u> fellow soldiers that indicate that he had been wounded in the hip and sent home. The Board denied her application and viewed him as a deserter. --rch, 2013.[316]

Noted events in her life were:
- She appeared on the United States census on 29 Oct 1850 in Lawrence County, Arkansas.[317]
  Polly A. Estes. Age 14. Living with her parents.

- She appeared on the United States census on 7 Jun 1860 in Collin County, Texas.[318]
  Polly A. Hall (indexed as Holl). Age 28. Living with her husband, J. M. and children: John A. H., Bluford C., and William J. Hall. This record lists her place of birth as Illinois.

- She appeared on the United States census on 1 Jun 1870 in Limestone County, Texas.[310]
  Polly A. Hall. Age 35. Keeping house. Living with her husband, Joseph M. Hall and children: Jno. A. H., Bluford C., William G., Gabe W., Geo. L., and Harriet D. B. M. Hall.

- She appeared on the United States census on 2 Jun 1880 in Lampasas County, Texas.[311]

Polley Hall. Age 45. Keeping house. Livng with her husband, James and children: John, William, Gabe, George and Harriett.

- She appeared on the United States census on 5 Jun 1900 in Collin County, Texas.[312]
Pollie A. Hall. Age 65. Birth date: Sep 1834. Married 48 years. Children: 10; Living: 5. Living with her husband, Joseph M. Hall and children: Gabe W. Hall and Harriet H. Murphy and her husband and children.

- She appeared on the United States census on 18 Apr 1910 in Collin County, Texas.[319]
Polly A. Hall. Age 75. Widow. Living in the household of her daughter, Harriet Murphy with her husband, William and children.

Children from this marriage were:

+ 127 M   i.   **John Andrew Houston Hall** was born on 31 Jan 1854 in Lafayette County, Arkansas,[320] died on 11 Feb 1943 in San Angelo, Tom Green County, Texas[321] at age 89, and was buried in Feb 1943 in Tom Green County, Texas (Mereta Cemetery).[322]

128 M   ii.   **Bluford C. Hall** was born about 1856 in Collin County, Texas.

      Noted events in his life were:
- He appeared on the United States census on 7 Jun 1860 in Collin County, Texas.[318]
Bluford Hall (indexed as Holl). Age 3. Living with his parents.

- He appeared on the United States census on 1 Jun 1870 in Limestone County, Texas.[310]
Bluford C. Hall. Age 14. Living with his parents, Joseph M. and Polly A. Hall.

129 M   iii.   **William J. G. Hall** was born on 5 Sep 1857 in Collin County, Texas,[323] died on 11 Dec 1955 in Haskell, Haskell County, Texas[323] at age 98, and was buried on 12 Dec 1955 in Haskell County, Texas (Willow Cemetery).[323]

      Birth Notes:
His death certificate says he was born in Grayson County, Texas.

      Noted events in his life were:
- He appeared on the United States census on 7 Jun 1860 in Collin County, Texas.[318]
William J. (G.?) Hall (indexed as Holl). Age 1. Living with his parents.

- He appeared on the United States census on 1 Jun 1870 in Limestone County, Texas.[310]
William G. Hall. Age 12. Living with his parents, Joseph M. and Polly A. Hall.

- He appeared on the United States census on 2 Jun 1880 in Lampasas County, Texas.[311]
William Hall. Age 21. At home. Livng with his parents.

130 M   iv.   **Gabe W. Hall** was born in Nov 1862 in Collin County, Texas.

      Noted events in his life were:
- He appeared on the United States census on 1 Jun 1870 in Limestone County, Texas.[310]
Gabe W. Hall. Age 8. Living with his parents, Joseph M. and Polly A. Hall.

- He appeared on the United States census on 2 Jun 1880 in Lampasas County, Texas.[311]
Gabe Hall. Age 16. At home. Livng with his parents.

- He appeared on the United States census on 5 Jun 1900 in Collin County, Texas.[312]
Gabe W. Hall. Age 37. Birth date: Nov. 1862. Married 14 years. No wife or children listed. Farm Laborer. Living with his parents and his sister and her family.

131 M   v.   **George L. Hall** was born about 1865 in Texas.

      Noted events in his life were:
- He appeared on the United States census on 1 Jun 1870 in Limestone County, Texas.[310]
Geo. L. Hall. Age 5. Living with his parents, Joseph M. and Polly A. Hall.

- He appeared on the United States census on 2 Jun 1880 in Lampasas County, Texas.[311]
George Hall. Age 14. At home. Livng with his parents.

+ 132 F   vi.   **Harriett D. B. M. Hall** was born on 5 Jan 1867 in Lampasas County, Texas,[324] died on 18 Jan 1959 in McKinney,

Collin County, Texas[324] at age 92, and was buried on 19 Jan 1959 in Collin County, Texas (Scalf Cemetery).[324]

133   M   vii.   **J. W. Hall**.

64. William Houston Hall *(John [11], John, Jr. [2], John [1])* was born about 1837 in Tennessee and died on 1 Mar 1894 in Collin County, Texas[190] about age 57.

Noted events in his life were:
- He appeared on the United States census on 12 Sep 1850 in Meigs County, Tennessee.[183]
  William H. Hall. Age 13. Living with his parents.

- He appeared on the United States census on 7 Jun 1860 in Collin County, Texas.[325]
  Wm. H. Hall. Age 23. Wagon maker. Living with his parents.

William married **Lucitia** _____, daughter of _____ _____ and _____ _____, on 7 Jun 1860 in Collin County, Texas.[190] Lucitia was born about 1838 in Pettis County, Missouri.[190]

65. Martha Delilah Hall *(John [11], John, Jr. [2], John [1])* was born on 10 Feb 1841 in Tennessee,[191] died on 4 Sep 1921 in Bowie, Montague County, Texas[191] at age 80, and was buried on 5 Sep 1921 in Clay County, Texas (Vashti Cemetery).[191]

Noted events in her life were:
- She appeared on the United States census on 12 Sep 1850 in Meigs County, Tennessee.[183]
  Martha D. Hall. Age 9. Living with her parents.

- She appeared on the United States census on 7 Jun 1860 in Collin County, Texas.[184]
  Martha D. Hall. Age 18. Living with her parents.

Martha married **William Basil Brown,** son of _____ _____ and _____ _____, in Texas. [326] William died before 1921 in Texas.

Martha next married **William Amos Lovelady,** son of _____ _____ and _____ _____. William was born in Texas and died in Arkansas.

68. Mary Jane Hall *(John C. [12], William [3], John [1])* was born about 1820 in Davidson County, Tennessee and died before 1866 in Mississippi.

Noted events in her life were:
- She appeared on the United States census on 7 Aug 1820 in Davidson County, Tennessee.[192]
  Mary Jane Hall. Presumably one of the two young females listed in the household of John Hall.
  --
  John Hall. Head of household.
  Males (<10) - 2, (26-44) - 1; Females (<10) - 2, (26-44) - 1; Foreigners not Naturalized -1; Agricultural workers: 1.
  --
  It is my opinion that the entry for "Foreigners not Naturalized" is a smudge or an erasure and not an valid entry. --rch, 2012.

- She appeared on the United States census in 1840 in Yazoo County, Mississippi.[327]
  Robert Mabane. One of two males in the household age 20<30. Presumably the other male is his brother, Thomas. Others in the household include two females: 1- 10<15 and 1- 15<20. Presumably, the Hall sisters, **Mary Jane** and Nancy Ann Hall, daughters of John C. Hall.

- She appeared on the United States census on 16 Sep 1850 in Yazoo County, Mississippi.[328]
  Mary J. Mabin. Age 29. Living with her husband, Robert M. and son, Benjamin Mabin.

- She appeared on the United States census on 25 Aug 1860 in Yazoo County, Mississippi.[329]
  Mary J. Maben. Age 37. Living with her husband, R. M. Maben. Also in the household are two women: Eliza Farour (50) and Anna Lester. Relationships are unknown.

- She was involved in a court case about the division and sale of the properties of the Estate of William Hall, deceased in 1839 in Yazoo County, Mississippi.[197]
  ...Samuel Marley is appointed guardian of the said Campbell, Mary Jane and Nancy Ann Hall, minor heirs of John C. Hall, deceased and distributees in the right of the John C. Hall, their father, of the said William Hall, deceased... Yazoo County Probate Court November Term 1838.

--
31 January 1839 - Chancery Court of Yazoo County, Mississippi
Estate of William Hall, deceased
Summons
Samuel Marley, the guardian of Campbell, Mary Jane and Nancy Ann Hall, minor heirs of John C. Hall and distributees in the right of the said John C. Hall, their father, of the estate of William Hall, dec'd is to appear on the 4th Monday of March 1839. He is to show why a sale of the lands of William Hall cannot go forward.

Mary married **Robert M. Maben,** son of **William Maben** and **Charity Smith,** about 1840 in Yazoo County, Mississippi. Robert was born about 1812 in Adams County, Mississippi and died after 1870 in Louisiana.

Noted events in his life were:
• He appeared on the United States census in 1840 in Yazoo County, Mississippi.[327]
Robert Mabane. One of two males in the household age 20<30. Presumably the other male is his brother, Thomas. Others in the household include two females: 1- 10<15 and 1- 15<20. Presumably, the Hall sisters, Mary Jane and Nancy Ann Hall, daughters of John C. Hall.

• He appeared on the United States census on 16 Sep 1850 in Yazoo County, Mississippi.[328]
Robert M. Mabin. Age 38. Planter. Living with his wife, Mary J. and son, Benjamin. They are not far from his brother, Thomas and the Wildy family.

• He appeared on the United States census on 25 Aug 1860 in Yazoo County, Mississippi.[329]
R. M. Maben. Age 48. Planter. Living with his wife, Mary J. Maben. Also in the household are two women: Eliza Farour (50) and Anna Lester. Relationships are unknown.

• He appeared on the United States census on 11 Jun 1870 in Vermillion Parish, Louisiana.[330]
Robert Maben. Age 59. Farmer. Living with his wife, Mary. A new born child, William Maben and an 18 year old female, Sarah Maben are listed in the household. The relationship is unclear.
--
This would appear to be a second wife, Mary Jane Caldwell, whom he married in Louisiana in 1866. --rch, 2012

Children from this marriage were:
134   M   i.   **Robert M. Maben** was born on 13 Oct 1840 in Yazoo County, Mississippi and died on 22 Nov 1840 in Yazoo County, Mississippi.[331] He never married and had no children.

135   M   ii.   **Benjamin F. Maben** was born about 1849 in Yazoo County, Mississippi[331] and died before 1860 in Mississippi. He never married and had no children.

Noted events in his life were:
• He appeared on the United States census on 16 Sep 1850 in Yazoo County, Mississippi.[328]
Benjamin F. Mabin. Age 1. Living with his parents.

69. Nancy Ann Hall *(John C.* [12], *William* [3], *John* [1]*)* was born on 4 Sep 1830 in Yazoo County, Mississippi,[198] died on 22 Apr 1860 in Yazoo County, Mississippi[199] at age 29, and was buried in Yazoo County, Mississippi (Bradshaw Cemetery). The cause of her death was Consumption.

Birth Notes:
Taken from the Yazoo County Probate Minute Book C - October Term 1843, page 275.
"Nancy Ann Hall, a minor over the age of 14 years, chose Robert M. Maben as her guardian."
This fact was repeated again in the Feb Term 1844, page 319.

Noted events in her life were:
• She was involved in a court case about the division and sale of the properties of the Estate of William Hall, deceased in 1839 in Yazoo County, Mississippi.[197]
Yazoo County Probate Court November Term 1838
...Samuel Marley is appointed guardian of the said Campbell, Mary Jane and Nancy Ann Hall, minor heirs of John C. Hall, deceased and distributees in the right of the John C. Hall, their father, of the said William Hall, deceased...
--
Chancery Court of Yazoo County, Mississippi - 31 January 1839
Estate of William Hall, deceased

Summons

Samuel Marley, the guardian of Campbell, Mary Jane and Nancy Ann Hall, minor heirs of John C. Hall and distributees in the right of the said John C. Hall, their father, of the estate of William Hall, dec'd is to appear on the 4th Monday of March 1839. He is to show why a sale of the lands of William Hall cannot go forward.

- She appeared on the United States census in 1840 in Yazoo County, Mississippi.[327]
  Robert Mabane. One of two males in the household age 20<30. Presumably the other male is his brother, Thomas. Others in the household include two females: 1- 10<15 and 1- 15<20. Presumably, the Hall sisters, Mary Jane and **Nancy Ann Hall**, daughters of John C. Hall.

- She appeared on the United States census on 16 Sep 1850 in Yazoo County, Mississippi.[332]
  Nancy A. Mabin. Age 19. Living with her husband, Thomas S. and children: Mary, William and Andrew.

Nancy married **Thomas S. Maben,** son of **William Maben** and **Charity Smith,** about 1842 in Yazoo County, Mississippi. Thomas was born about 1819 in Mississippi.

Noted events in his life were:
- He appeared on the United States census in 1840 in Yazoo County, Mississippi.[327]
  Robert Mabane. One of two males in the household age 20<30. Presumably the other male is his brother, **Thomas**. Others in the household include two females: 1- 10<15 and 1- 15<20. Presumably, the Hall sisters, Mary Jane and Nancy Ann Hall, daughters of John C. Hall.

- He appeared on the United States census on 16 Sep 1850 in Yazoo County, Mississippi.[332]
  Thomas S. Mabin. Age 31. Planter. Living with his wife, Nancy A. and children: Mary, William and Andrew. Living in the same household is his mother, Charity Mabin and brother, Warren and his children.

- He appeared on the United States census on 25 Aug 1860 in Yazoo County, Mississippi.[333]
  T. S. Maben. Age 41. Planter. Living with children: Julia (10), Louisa (7), John (5) and Frank (3). Also in the household is Thomas Mulkaney, a laborer.

- He appeared on the United States census on 30 Jun 1870 in Carroll Parish, Louisiana.[334]
  Thomas M. Mabin. Age 51. Farmer. Living with his wife, Mary M. and children: Frank (13), Susan (6), Thomas (4) and Maggie (3/12). Frank and Susan appear to be from a previous marriage. Also in the household are: Susan and Elizabeth Mosley; and Black children: Jeff and Lucy Mabin.

Children from this marriage were:

136 F   i.   **Audrey J. Maben** was born on 8 Jan 1843 in Yazoo County, Mississippi,[331] died on 14 Jul 1849 in Yazoo County, Mississippi[331] at age 6, and was buried in Yazoo County, Mississippi (Bradshaw Cemetery). She never married and had no children.

137 F   ii.   **Mary E. Maben** was born on 18 Feb 1846 in Yazoo County, Mississippi, died on 24 Oct 1852 in Yazoo County, Mississippi at age 6, and was buried in Yazoo County, Mississippi (Bradshaw Cemetery). She never married and had no children.

     Noted events in her life were:
     - She appeared on the United States census on 16 Sep 1850 in Yazoo County, Mississippi.[332]
      Mary E. Mabin. Age 4. Living with her parents.

138 M   iii.   _____ **Maben** was born on 29 Jul 1847 in Yazoo County, Mississippi, died on 11 Aug 1847 in Yazoo County, Mississippi, and was buried in Yazoo County, Mississippi (Bradshaw Cemetery). He never married and had no children.

139 M   iv.   **William Maben** was born on 29 Jul 1848 in Yazoo County, Mississippi, died on 10 Aug 1857 in Yazoo County, Mississippi at age 9, and was buried in Yazoo County, Mississippi (Bradshaw Cemetery). He never married and had no children.

     Noted events in his life were:
     - He appeared on the United States census on 16 Sep 1850 in Yazoo County, Mississippi.[332]
      William Mabin. Age 2. Living with his parents.

140 M   v.   **Andrew S. Maben** was born about 1849 in Yazoo County, Mississippi, died before 1860 in Yazoo County, Mississippi, and was buried in Yazoo County, Mississippi (Bradshaw Cemetery).

Noted events in his life were:
- He appeared on the United States census on 16 Sep 1850 in Yazoo County, Mississippi.[332]
  Andrew S. Mabin. Age 1. Living with his parents.

141 F vi. **Julia Maben** was born about 1850 in Yazoo County, Mississippi.

Noted events in her life were:
- She appeared on the United States census on 25 Aug 1860 in Yazoo County, Mississippi.[333]
  Julia Maben. Age 10. Living with her father and siblings.

142 M vii. **Frank Maben** was born about 1857 in Yazoo County, Mississippi.

Noted events in his life were:
- He appeared on the United States census on 25 Aug 1860 in Yazoo County, Mississippi.[333]
  Frank Maben. Age 3. Living with his father and siblings(?). Also in the household is Thomas Mulkaney, a laborer.

- He appeared on the United States census on 30 Jun 1870 in Carroll Parish, Louisiana.[334]
  Frank Mabin. Age 13. Living with his father, Thomas S. and step mother, Mary M. and siblings.

143 F viii. **Nancy J. Maben** was born on 13 Dec 1858 in Yazoo County, Mississippi, died on 18 Jun 1860 in Yazoo County, Mississippi[335] at age 1, and was buried in Yazoo County, Mississippi (Bradshaw Cemetery). She never married and had no children.

70. Laurena Matilda Hall (*Samuel S.* [13], *William* [3], *John* [1]) was born on 31 Aug 1819 in Davidson County, Tennessee,[213] died on 13 Nov 1871 in Yazoo County, Mississippi[214] at age 52, and was buried in Nov 1871 in Yazoo County, Mississippi (Wesley Chapel Cemetery).[215] Another name for Laurena was Rena.

Birth Notes:
Many Census records indicate she was born in Arkansas, not Tennessee.

General Notes:
In the court case of William Garrett vs. William Nash, et als. heard in the St. Augustine County, Texas District Court, Fall Term 1847: William and Laurena Wildy and her brother, William Hall were summoned to appear as heirs at law of Claiborn Garrett, deceased and defendants in the suit. The court noted that they were nonresidents of the State of Texas and ordered that they be cited, by publication, to appear and defend said suit. Notices were to be published for twelve successive weeks in the Texas Union newspaper. They were summoned to appear at the District Court House in St. Augustine, Texas on the first Monday of April 1848.
--
On 8 June 1847, property of the Estates of Jacob and his son, Claiborne Garrett (deceased) was partitioned to the heirs by the Probate Court in St. Augustine County, Texas. In a court document recorded 28 July 1847 William Wildy, in right of his wife Laurena and William Hall (her brother) were awarded a number of named slaves. The respective value of the partition was listed. The actual disposition of the slaves is not clear from the document.
--
These documents clearly connect Laurena and William Hall as the children of Matilda Garrett Hall, wife of Samuel S. Hall. -- rch 2011[336]

Noted events in her life were:
- She appeared on the United States census in 1830 in Pulaski County, Arkansas.[207]
  Laurena Matilda Hall. Living with her parents. Presumed to be the female (10-15) in Samuel S. Hall's household.

  Males (<5) -1, (30-40) -1; Females (10-15) -1, (20-30) -1, (40-50) -1

- She appeared on the United States census in 1840 in Yazoo County, Mississippi.[209]
  Laurena Hall Childress. Presumably the female 20-30 years old in the household of her father:
  Samuel S. Hall. Head of household.
  Males (>5) - 2, (10-15) - 1, (15-20) - 1, (40-50) - 1. Females (20-30) - 1, (30-40) - 1. Slaves: 21.

  Living near John B. Hall, William Hall, W. W. Wildy (future husband), Jonathan Bonney

- She appeared on the United States census on 14 Sep 1850 in Yazoo County, Mississippi.[337]

Laurena Wildy. Age 31. Living with her husband, William W. Wildy and children: Matilda, H., Sally and Ada Wildy. Also in the household are Laurena's sons from her previous marriage: William G. and Samuel Childress. Laurena's brother, William Hall is also living in this household. Her birth state is listed as Arkansas.

- She appeared on the United States census on 21 Aug 1860 in Yazoo County, Mississippi.[338]
Lorena Wildy. Age 41. Living with her husband, W. W. Wildy and children and two sons from her previous marriage to Elisha Robertson Childress.

- She appeared on the United States census on 2 Aug 1870 in Yazoo County, Mississippi.[339]
L. Wildy. Age 50. Living with her husband and children. Her birth state is incorrectly listed as Maryland as it is with all of her children.

Laurena married **Elisha Robertson Childress,** son of **John Childress** and **Elizabeth Robertson,** on 14 Jul 1835 in Little Rock, Pulaski County, Arkansas.[340] Elisha was born on 5 Apr 1807 in Davidson County, Tennessee[341] and died on 7 Aug 1839 in Benton, Saline County, Arkansas at age 32.

Marriage Notes:
Hall, Miss Laurena, dau. of S. S. Hall, Esq. of the Arkansas Territory married in Little Rock on 14th July to Col. Robertson Childress. National Banner & Nashville Whig (Mon. Aug 3, 1835).
--
Childress, Robertson Col., attorney and Miss Laurena Hall, only daughter of S. S. Hall of Little Rock. Tuesday, July 14, 1835, Little Rock, Pulaski County, by Rev. J. W. Moore. See: Arkansas Advocate, July 17, 1835; Little Rock Times, July 18, 1835; Arkansas Gazette, July 21, 1835.[342]

Research Notes:
There are two lines of ancestors for Elisha Childress presented in the Family Search™ Pedigree Resource File - Individual Records and the Family Search™ International Genealogical Index v5.0 - Family Group Record.

One line shows Elisha's parents as Joel Childress and his wife, Elizabeth Winslett. I do <u>not</u> believe this lineage is correct. It is indicated that this family resided in Rutherford County, Tennessee.

The other line shows Elisha's parents as John Childress and his wife, Elizabeth Robertson. I believe this to be correct. It is indicated that this family resided in Nashville, Davidson County, Tennessee.

This appears to be verified by DNA testing. See:
http://freepages.genealogy.rootsweb.ancestry.com/~jpcfamily/childress_observations.htm.

See item 13: *"This posting date of November 9, 2006 reflects an additional three individuals whose extended, 67-marker results have been received. An interesting development of a mutation at marker 534 (the 55th marker) shows up for Samuel Hall Childress, (earliest ancestor is Judge John Childress, m. Elizabeth Robertson) and William A. Childress (earliest ancestor is Robert Childress, b. circa 1758). These two individuals would do well to compare ancestral notes. Carlos St. Clair also shows this marker mutation."*[343]

Noted events in his life were:
- He worked as a Partner in the law firm of S. Hall and R. Childress on 14 Jun 1836 in Little Rock, Pulaski County, Arkansas.[344]
An advertisement in the Arkansas Gazette Newspaper in Little Rock, Arkansas on June 14, 1836 states:
"LAW NOTICE
SAMUEL S. HALL & R. CHILDRESS
HAVE formed a Partnership in the Practice of Law, and will attend the Courts in the Second Judicial Circuit and the Superior Court at Little Rock.

Office in the south room of the white building attached to Jeffries Hotel. Little Rock, April 25, 1835"

- He served in the military as a Brigadier General in the Arkansas Militia in 1837 in Little Rock, Pulaski County, Arkansas.[344]
A notice given in the Arkansas Gazette published April 25, 1837 reads:

"HEAD QUARTERS
2D BRIGADE, 1ST DIVISION,
Arkansas Militia,

Little Rock, April 24, 1837
[Order No. 1]

The Brigadier General commanding the 2d Brigade of the first Division of Arkansas Militia, hereby appoints E. A. More, Brigade Mayor, with the rank of Major, and Samuel H. Hempstead, Aid de Camp with the rank of Captain. The officers and soldiers of the Brigade are required to respect them accordingly.

By order of Robertson Childress, Brigadier General. Samuel H. Hempstead, Aid de Camp"

- His obituary was published in the Arkansas Gazette Newspaper on 14 Aug 1839 in Little Rock, Pulaski County, Arkansas.[344]
  "Died - At Benton, Saline county, on Wednesday last, Gen. Robertson W. Childress, aged about 35 years, formerly of Tennessee."

A correction was printed on August 21, 1839. His age was restated as about 30 years old.

Children from this marriage were:

+ 144 M   i. **William Gordon Childress, Sr.** was born about Aug 1831 in Arkansas, died on 27 Nov 1921 in Yazoo County, Mississippi[345] about age 90, and was buried in Yazoo County, Mississippi (Hart-Childress Cemetery).[346]

+ 145 M   ii. **Samuel Hall Childress** was born on 24 Aug 1838 in Arkansas,[347] died on 27 Dec 1917 in Yazoo County, Mississippi[348] at age 79, and was buried in Yazoo County, Mississippi (Hart-Childress Cemetery).[349]

Laurena next married **Maj. William W. Wildy,** son of **William Wildy** and **Sarah _____**, about 1841 in Yazoo County, Mississippi.[348] William was born on 9 Oct 1809 in Northumberland County, Virginia,[350] died on 7 Feb 1881 in Yazoo County, Mississippi[351] at age 71, and was buried in Feb 1881 in Yazoo County, Mississippi.

Death Notes:
Died at 6 o'clock in the morning at the home of Jas. M. Bonney.

General Notes:
"In 1877, Maj. Wildy also journeyed to New Mexico to seek investment opportunities. Impressed with the Roswell area, Wildy bought the land and buildings — a house and store — upon which Van C. Smith had founded Roswell some seven or eight years earlier. The 480-acre tract was to be the future location of Roswell. Wildy's enthusiasm for Roswell enticed Lea and his bride to come in the fall of 1877 in search of ranch land. Lea bought a quartersection directly west of Wildy's. Wildy gave his land to daughter Sally on Aug. 1, 1878."[352]

Noted events in his life were:
- He had a residence before 1840 in Yazoo County, Mississippi.[200]
  "William W. Wildy likely was part of a migration in the 1830s to take up lands in Yazoo County, Mississippi, that had been noticed by Gen. Andrew Jackson during the War of 1812. Their plantations were south of the town of Satartia. Satartia was the largest active community in southwestern Yazoo County by 1830 and the only one to retain its Indian name ("pumpkin patch"). Typical Southern plantations developed in the Satartia area, unlike the rest of the county. Wildy was a typical planter."

  "A teacher from Michigan, DuPuy Van Buren, visited the Wildy plantation and wrote an insider's account in 1859 [DePuy Van Buren, Jottings of a Sojourn in the South (Battle Creek, Mich., 1859)]. He was surprised that almost everyone, including ladies, rode horseback instead of in carriages. The Wildy plantation was in a valley. The old house was there on a knoll overlooking the plantation, and in 1859 it was the residence of the overseer. The log cabins for slaves were nearby. Van Buren went on to the "Ridge House," the family house some two miles farther back in the uplands. Upon reaching the house, Van Buren "... met a cordial reception from Mrs. W., a lady of true Southern frankness - of a generous and spirited nature, and whose countenance expresses much of the feeling of her heart." Van Buren comments on Southern manners and concludes, "One might say that everything is different here from Northern life."

- He appeared on the United States census in 1840 in Yazoo County, Mississippi.[353]
  W. W. Wildy. Head of household. Presumably the other members of this household include his mother and siblings. Males: age 20 < 30 - 2. Females: age 20 < 30 -1; 40 < 50 -1. Slaves: 36

- He appeared on the United States census on 14 Sep 1850 in Yazoo County, Mississippi.[337]
  William W. Wildy. Age 41. Planter. Living with his wife, Laurena and children: Matilda, H., Sally and Ada Wildy. Also

in the household are Laurena's sons from her previous marriage: William G. and Samuel Childress. Laurena's brother, William Hall is also living in this household.

- He appeared on the United States census on 21 Aug 1860 in Yazoo County, Mississippi.[338]
  W. W. Wildy. Age 50. Planter. Living with his wife, Lorena and children: Matilda, Harry, Sally, Ada, John and Earnest. Also in the household ar his two step-sons, William and Samuel Childress.

- He appeared on the United States census on 2 Aug 1870 in Yazoo County, Mississippi.[339]
  W. W. Wildy. Age 59. Farmer. Living with his wife and children.

- He appeared on the United States census on 15 Jun 1880 in Yazoo County, Mississippi.[354]
  W. W. Wildy. Age 70. Farmer. Head of household. Widowed. Living with his daughter Ada B. Holloman age 30, and her daughter, Ellen.

- He served in the military Private in Capt. H. C. Tyler's Co. of Capt. Gartley's Company of Cavalry Mississippi Volunteers, which was called the "Yazoo Rangers", in 1862 in Yazoo County, Mississippi.[200]
  "Although the Confederate States eventually drafted men up to 50 years old in the Civil War, Wildy was already 51 when the war started. However, he did enlist in a local militia unit. Records show that Wildy enlisted at Yazoo City on April 16, 1862. According to Robert Crook, whose great-great-grandfather was also in the outfit, the Yazoo Rangers were Company "D" of the 2nd Battalion of Mississippi Cavalry that functioned as independent scouts on the Mississippi and Yazoo Rivers. They were frequently under the command of the 1st Mississippi Cavalry. The unit went into active service May 14, 1862, at Liverpool; but two muster rolls in the records indicate that Wildy did not go with them. Remarks on the muster roll for June 14 to November 1, 1862, are "Exempt by Age. No Pay." The roll for December 10, 1862, to February 28, 1863, states, "Absent with leave. No pay." Wildy's enlistment was apparently a show of support for the Confederacy and the local troops."

Children from this marriage were:

+ 146 F   i. **Matilda Wildy** was born on 10 Jul 1842 in Yazoo County, Mississippi,[355] died on 27 Sep 1915 in Yazoo County, Mississippi[356] at age 73, and was buried in Yazoo County, Mississippi (Wesley Chapel Cemetery).[215]

  147 M   ii. **Harry H. Wildy** was born on 21 Feb 1846 in Yazoo County, Mississippi,[357] died in Dec 1878 in San Diego, San Diego County, California[358] at age 32, and was buried on 20 Dec 1878 in San Diego, San Diego County, California.[358]

Noted events in his life were:
- He appeared on the United States census on 14 Sep 1850 in Yazoo County, Mississippi.[337]
  H. Wildy. Age 5. Living with his parents.

- He appeared on the United States census on 21 Aug 1860 in Yazoo County, Mississippi.[338]
  Harry Wildy. Age 14. Living with his parents.

- He appeared on the United States census on 2 Aug 1870 in Yazoo County, Mississippi.[339]
  H. H. Wildy. Age 23. At school. Living with his parents.

- He graduated from the University of Mississippi in 1870 in Oxford, Lafayette County, Mississippi.[359]
  Harry Hill [Hall] Wildy is listed as a member of the graduating class of 1870. He was an Attorney at Law in San Diego, California.

- He had a residence on 13 Jul 1876 in San Diego, San Diego County, California.[360]
  On July 4, 1876 the city of San Diego celebrated "the Centennial Anniversary of American nationality." The day was filled with public events. There were Religious Services, a Procession, Literary Exercises, an Oration and a Grand Ball. H. H. Wildy served as an aid to the Grand Marshall of the Processional Parade.

  An article was published on July 13, 1876 in the *San Diego Union*, a weekly newspaper. The 4th of July activities are described in detail. In an annotated footnote, Mr. Harry Hill Wildy is described as follows: "Harry Hill Wildy was born in Mississippi ca. 1846, arriving in San Diego in about 1873, where he was a practicing attorney. *Great Register, San Diego County, California* (August, 1877), p. 23."

- He worked as a District Attorney from 1875 to 1876 in San Diego, San Diego County, California.[361]
  In 1875, H. H. Wildy was apparently involved in the pursuit of a gang of Mexican bandits and their leader. See the following newspaper article:

"Latest from Campo - Two Gangs of Mexican Bandits - Reported Revolution in Sonora
[Specially telegraphed to the Bulletin]
San Diego, December 23d-- A letter from H. H. Wildy who has charge of the Sheriff's posse at Campo, dated December 21st, says: *"I sent for the Alcade at Trearte yesterday, but he would not come. Several Mexicans have been up today, but I could get no satisfaction from them. I learn that Cruz Lopez is the sucessor of Chavez and leader of these bandits. There are two organized gangs of them -- one around Lone Pine and Panamint and the other on this border, with their quarters in Trearte Valley. Without Cruz the rest are nothing, but I think he will not be taken, not withstanding the statement that the lower California authorities are after him. The honest people of Lower California are reported to be in a state of terror on account of these bandits..."*
--

In an article published in the same newspaper, one week prior, it was announced that at a meeting of businessmen and prominent citizens, funds were raised to *"send a volunteer guard to Campo to protect the border settlements from Mexican bandits. H. H. Wildy, District Attorney elect, was authorized to proceed to Campo and organize a posse."*

- His obituary was published in the San Diego Union on 20 Dec 1878 in San Diego, San Diego County, California.[358]
  "Glimpses of the Past in San Diego's Life"
  "The Union of 40 years ago today (Dec. 20, 1878) said:"

  "The funeral of the late H. H. Wildy will take place this morning at 10 o'clock, from the residence of Dr. W. A. Winder." --republished in the San Diego Union, 20 December 1918
  --

  A follow up article published the net day reported that the funeral was *"largely attended."*

+ 148 F iii. **Sally Edith Wildy** was born on 3 Nov 1848 in Yazoo County, Mississippi,[362] died on 20 Feb 1884 in Chaves County, New Mexico[363] at age 35, and was buried in Feb 1884 in Chaves County, New Mexico (South Side Cemetery).

+ 149 F iv. **Ada Byron Wildy** was born on 21 Mar 1849 in Yazoo County, Mississippi[364] and died on 29 Apr 1924 in Chaves County, New Mexico at age 75.

+ 150 M v. **John Hall Wildy** was born on 18 Oct 1853 in Yazoo County, Mississippi,[365] died on 5 Nov 1893 in Miami, Roberts County, Texas[363] at age 40, and was buried in Nov 1893 in Roberts County, Texas.

+ 151 M vi. **Earnest Linwood Wildy** was born on 29 Apr 1856 in Yazoo County, Mississippi[366] and died in May 1912 in Long Beach, Los Angeles County, California at age 56.

  152 F vii. **Ella Hall Wildy** was born on 18 Apr 1861 in Yazoo County, Mississippi, died on 19 Aug 1862 in Yazoo County, Mississippi[367] at age 1, and was buried in Aug 1862 in Yazoo County, Mississippi (Wesley Chapel Cemetery).[368] She never married and had no children.

  153 M viii. **William "Willie" Wildy** was born on 18 Apr 1861 in Mississippi,[369] died on 19 Aug 1862 in Mississippi[369] at age 1, and was buried in Aug 1862 in Yazoo County, Mississippi (Wesley Chapel Cemetery).[369] He was usually called Willie. He never married and had no children.

71. William C. Hall *(Samuel S.[13], William[3], John[1])* was born about 1828 in Arkansas and died before 1870 in Mississippi.

General Notes:
In the petition of William W. Wildy for appointment as Administrator of the estate of Samuel S. Hall, he states that Samuel S. Hall died on 24th of May 1842 leaving a widow, Matilda and 2 children: Laurena (Hall) Wildy and William C. Hall, a minor aged 14 years. The petition was dated 26 September 1842.
--

In the petition of William W. Wildy to James R. Brown, Probate Judge, Wildy states that William Hall, a son of Samuel S. Hall deceased is a minor under the age of 16 years. Wildy asks to be appointed William Hall's guardian. The petition was dated 30 October 1844. Yazoo County, Mississippi Probate Records: Minute Book A- October Term 1844, page 431. Letters of guardianship granted Wm. W. Wildy for Wm. Hall, a minor. *"Letters of guardianship granted Wm. W. Wildy for Wm. Hall, a minor."* Probate Minute Book C, Oct Term 1844, page 431. William and Laurena Wildy were named guardians and provided a $600.00 bond.
--

In the files of the Probate Court of Yazoo County, Mississippi regarding the estate of William Hall, dec'd. is a letter from

William C. Hall stating *"The undersigned is over twenty years of age and waives service of notice on him or W. W. Wildy his guardian to make his final settlement as guardian."* Signed William C. Hall, undated. This is followed by a document that states that William W. Wildy has paid to William Hall the property that has come into his hands as guardian and for management of the estate. It refers to a final settlement of the estate of Samuel S. Hall by W. W. Wildy administrator. Dated March 21, 1852.

--

According to information gleaned from the files of the Estate of Samuel S. Hall, dec'd., William Hall appears to have been well provided for. Expenses were paid for his boarding (school). There are detailed receipts for clothing and pairs of shoes. He was given money to travel to Texas (perhaps to see his mother's family) and Kentucky (perhaps to see his Hall and Bonney cousins).

In the court case of William Garrett vs. William Nash, et als. heard in the St. Augustine County, Texas District Court, Fall Term 1847: William and Laurena Wildy and her brother, William Hall were summoned to appear as heirs at law of Claiborn Garrett, deceased and defendants in the suit. The court noted that they were nonresidents of the State of Texas and ordered that they be cited, by publication, to appear and defend said suit. Notices were to be published for twelve successive weeks in the Texas Union newspaper. They were summoned to appear at the District Court House in St. Augustine, Texas on the first Monday of April 1848.

--

On 8 June 1847, property of the Estates of Jacob and his son, Claiborne Garrett (deceased) was partitioned to the heirs by the Probate Court in St. Augustine County, Texas. In a court document recorded 28 July 1847 William Wildy, in right of his wife Laurena and William Hall (her brother) were awarded a number of named slaves. The respective value of the partition was listed. The actual disposition of the slaves is not clear from the document.

--

These documents clearly connect Laurena and William Hall as the children of Matilda Garrett Hall, wife of Samuel S. Hall. --rch, 2011[370]

Noted events in his life were:
- He appeared on the United States census in 1830 in Pulaski County, Arkansas.[207]
  William C. Hall. Living with his parents. Presumed to be the young male in Samuel S. Hall's household.

  Males (<5) -1, (30-40) -1; Females (10-15) -1, (20-30) -1, (40-50) -1

- He appeared on the United States census in 1840 in Yazoo County, Mississippi.[209]
  William C. Hall. Presumably the male age 10-15 years old in the household of his father:
  Samuel S. Hall. Head of household.
  Males (>5) - 2, (10-15) - 1, (15-20) - 1, (40-50) - 1. Females (20-30) - 1, (30-40) - 1. Slaves: 21.

  Living near John B. Hall, William Hall, W. W. Wildy, Jonathan Bonney

- He appeared on the United States census on 14 Sep 1850 in Yazoo County, Mississippi.[337]
  William Hall. Age 21. Law Student. Living in the household of his sister, Laurena Wildy, her husband and family.

William married **Mary E. Pace,** daughter of **Elijah H. Pace** and **Unknown,** on 11 May 1858 in Warren County, Mississippi.[371] Mary was born in Aug 1832 in Mississippi, died on 18 Aug 1904 in San Diego, San Diego County, California at age 72, and was buried on 20 Aug 1904 in San Diego, San Diego County, California.

Noted events in her life were:
- She appeared on the United States census on 9 Sep 1850 in Warren County, Mississippi.[372]
  Mary E. Pace. Age 18. Living with her father and siblings.

- She appeared on the United States census on 27 Jul 1870 in Warren County, Mississippi.[373]
  M. E. Hall. Age 36. Living with her daughter, W. E. Hall, age 9.

- She appeared on the United States census on 29 Jun 1900 in Chaves County, New Mexico.[374]
  Mary Hall. Age 67. Birth date: Aug 1832. Widow. Living with her daughter's family, Earnest L. Wildy household. Children: 1; Living: 1. Address in 1900: Missouri Avenue.

- Her obituary was published in the Evening Tribune on 19 Aug 1904 in San Diego, San Diego County, California.[375]
  "Death of Mrs. Hall

Mrs. Mary E. Hall, a native of Mississippi, aged 72 years, died in this city last night after an illness of two weeks. She came here two years ago from New Mexico. Mrs. Hall is survived by one daughter. Mrs. E. L. Wildy and four grandchildren. The funeral service will be held at St. Joseph's Church tomorrow morning at 10 o'clock."

The child from this marriage was:

+ 154 F   i. **Willie Laurena Hall** was born on 14 Nov 1861 in Mississippi[366] and died on 22 May 1940 in Los Angeles County, California[376] at age 78.

73. Elvira E. Hall *(Archibald C. [15], William [3], John [1])* was born about Dec 1827 in Davidson County, Tennessee,[229] died about 1902 in Yazoo County, Mississippi[229] about age 75, and was buried in Yazoo County, Mississippi.

    Noted events in her life were:
- She appeared on the United States census in 1830 in Yazoo County, Mississippi.[221]
  Presumably the female under five shown in the household of Archibald Hall.

  A. C. Hall - Head of household. Living near the households of J. B. Hall and J. C. Hall.
  Male under five, 1; male thirty-forty, 1;
  Female under five, 1; female five-ten, 1; female twenty-thirty, 1

- She appeared on the United States census in 1840 in Carroll County, Mississippi.[227]
  Elvira E. Hall. Living with her parents in the household of Archibald Hall.

  Males- 5 < 10: 2; Male- 40<50: 1. Females- < 5: 2; Female- 10 < 15: 1; Female- 30 < 40: 1.

- She appeared on the United States census on 17 Sep 1850 in Yazoo County, Mississippi.[223]
  Elvira Wallace. Age 22. Living in the household of her parents.

- She appeared on the United States census on 21 Aug 1860 in Yazoo County, Mississippi.[377]
  Elvira Bradshaw. Age 33. Living with her husband, Jas. N. Bradshaw and children: James, Samuel and Mary Bradshaw and her daughter from a previous marriage, Lauretta Wallace.

- She appeared on the United States census on 2 Aug 1870 in Yazoo County, Mississippi.[378]
  E. Bradshaw. Age 38. Keeping house. Living with her husband, J. N. Bradshaw and children: James, Sarah, Wesley and Laura Bradshaw.

- She appeared on the United States census on 1 Jun 1900 in Yazoo County, Mississippi.[379]
  Elvira Bradshaw. Age 72. Birth date: Dec 1827. Head of household. Widow. Living with her son, John N. and daughter, Laura Bradshaw. Children: 9; Living: 3.

Elvira married **Robert Wallace,** son of _____ _____ and _____ _____, on 21 May 1847 in Yazoo County, Mississippi.[380]

The child from this marriage was:

  155 F   i. **Loretta R. Wallace** was born about 1850 in Yazoo County, Mississippi and died after 1865 in Mississippi.

        Noted events in her life were:
      - She appeared on the United States census on 21 Aug 1860 in Yazoo County, Mississippi.[381]
        Lauretta Wallace. Age 10. Living with her mother and step-father, Jas. K. Bradshaw.

Elvira next married **James Nathaniel Bradshaw,** son of **John Wesley Bradshaw** and **Sarah Harrison,** on 19 May 1855 in Yazoo County, Mississippi.[382] James was born on 7 Aug 1815 in Rodney, Jefferson County, Mississippi,[229] died on 3 Jun 1883 in Phoenix, Yazoo County, Mississippi[229] at age 67, and was buried in Jun 1883 in Yazoo County, Mississippi.

    Noted events in his life were:
- He appeared on the United States census on 21 Aug 1860 in Yazoo County, Mississippi.[383]
  Jas. K. Bradshaw. Age 45. Planter. Living with his wife, Elvira Bradshaw, and children: James, Samuel and Mary Bradshaw and his step-daughter, Lauretta Wallace. Also in the household is Minerva Peers (sister?).

- He appeared on the United States census on 2 Aug 1870 in Yazoo County, Mississippi.[378]
  J. N. Bradshaw. Age 55. Farmer. Living with his wife, E. Bradshaw and children: James, Sarah, Wesley and Laura

Bradshaw. This census record says he was born in Louisiana.

- He served in the military as a PVT. Gartley's Co.-Yazoo Rangers-Miss Cav-CSA.[229]

Children from this marriage were:

156 M i. **James H. Bradshaw** was born about 1856 in Yazoo County, Mississippi.

Noted events in his life were:
- He appeared on the United States census on 21 Aug 1860 in Yazoo County, Mississippi.[383]
James Bradshaw. Age 4. Living with his parents.

- He appeared on the United States census on 2 Aug 1870 in Yazoo County, Mississippi.[378]
James Bradshaw. Age 14. At home. Living with his parents.

157 M ii. **Samuel Bradshaw** was born about 1858 in Mississippi and died before 1870 in Mississippi. He never married and had no children.

Noted events in his life were:
- He appeared on the United States census on 21 Aug 1860 in Yazoo County, Mississippi.[383]
Samuel Bradshaw. Age 2. Living with his parents.

158 F iii. **Sarah Bradshaw** was born about 1859 in Yazoo County, Mississippi.

Noted events in her life were:
- She appeared on the United States census on 2 Aug 1870 in Yazoo County, Mississippi.[378]
Sarah Bradshaw. Age 11. At home. Living with her parents.

159 F iv. **Mary Bradshaw** was born about Nov 1859 in Yazoo County, Mississippi and died before 1870 in Mississippi. She never married and had no children.

Noted events in her life were:
- She appeared on the United States census on 21 Aug 1860 in Yazoo County, Mississippi.[383]
Mary Bradshaw. Age 10/12. Living with her parents.

160 M v. **John Wesly Bradshaw** was born on 11 Apr 1865 in Yazoo County, Mississippi,[384] died on 17 Sep 1938[384] at age 73, and was buried in Sep 1938 in Yazoo County, Mississippi (Wesley Chapel Cemetery).[384]

Noted events in his life were:
- He appeared on the United States census on 2 Aug 1870 in Yazoo County, Mississippi.[378]
Wesley Bradshaw. Age 5. At home. Living with his parents.

- He appeared on the United States census on 1 Jun 1900 in Yazoo County, Mississippi.[379]
John W. Bradshaw. Age 35. Birth date: April 1865. Farmer. Living with his mother and sister.

161 F vi. **Laura Bradshaw** was born about 1867 in Yazoo County, Mississippi.

Noted events in her life were:
- She appeared on the United States census on 2 Aug 1870 in Yazoo County, Mississippi.[378]
Laura Bradshaw. Age 3. At home. Living with her parents.

- She appeared on the United States census on 1 Jun 1900 in Yazoo County, Mississippi.[379]
Laura Bradshaw. Age 32. Birth date: August 1867. Teacher. Living with her mother and brother.

76. Octavia E. Hall *(Archibald C. [15], William [3], John [1])* was born on 26 Feb 1838 in Tennessee, died on 18 Aug 1856 in Yazoo County, Mississippi at age 18, and was buried in Yazoo County, Mississippi (Bradshaw Cemetery).

Noted events in her life were:
- She appeared on the United States census in 1840 in Carroll County, Mississippi.[227]
Octavia E. Hall. Living with her parents in the household of Archibald Hall.

Males- 5 < 10: 2; Male- 40<50: 1. Females- < 5: 2; Female- 10 < 15: 1; Female- 30 < 40: 1.

- She appeared on the United States census on 17 Sep 1850 in Yazoo County, Mississippi. [223]
Octavia E. Hall. Age 12. Living in the household of her parents.

Octavia married **W. S. Elkins,** son of _____ _____ and _____ _____, on 22 Nov 1855 in Yazoo County, Mississippi. [385]

77. Laurena M. Hall[230] *(Archibald C. [15], William [3], John [1])* was born on 16 Dec 1839 in Mississippi, died on 25 Jul 1863 in Yazoo County, Mississippi[231] at age 23, and was buried in 1863 in Yazoo County, Mississippi (Bradshaw Cemetery).

Birth Notes:
Her 1850 Census record says she was born in Tennessee.

Noted events in her life were:
- She appeared on the United States census in 1840 in Carroll County, Mississippi. [227]
Laurena M. Hall. Living with her parents in the household of Archibald Hall.

  Males- 5 < 10: 2; Male- 40<50: 1. Females- < 5: 2; Female- 10 < 15: 1; Female- 30 < 40: 1.

- She appeared on the United States census on 17 Sep 1850 in Yazoo County, Mississippi. [223]
Laurina M. Hall. Age 10. Living in the household of her parents and siblings.

- She appeared on the United States census on 21 Aug 1860 in Yazoo County, Mississippi. [224]
Lorena Hall. Age 21. Living with her parents.

- She signed a will on 19 Mar 1861 in Yazoo County, Mississippi. [230]
The Last Will and Testament of Laurena M. Hall was witnessed by her parents, Archibald and Mary B. Hall. The will specified that her property go to her children, if any. If she had no children then all of her property was to go to her niece, Loretia R. Wallace. I. I. (or J. J.) Hall of Louisiana was to be the executor.

- She had an estate probated in the March Term of the Probate Court on 23 Mar 1865 in Yazoo County, Mississippi. [386]
The will was proved on 23 March 1865 by Mary B. Hall, her mother. Archibald C. Hall(her father and other witness) had died. Mary B. Hall attested to his signature as well.

Laurena married _____ **More,** son of _____ _____ and _____ _____.

79. William Ross Russell *(Tabitha Hall [16], William [3], John [1])* was born on 29 Dec 1817 in Tennessee[238] and died on 27 Jun 1852 in Carroll County, Mississippi[239] at age 34.

Birth Notes:
Hand written in the Family Register of the William Ross Russell Family Bible: *"William Rofs Rufsell son of William and Tabitha Rufsell was Born the 29th day of December AD 1817"*

Death Notes:
Hand written in the Family Register of the William Ross Russell Family Bible: *"William R Russell departed this life on Sunday morning the 27th of June AD 1852 aged thirty-five years six months and two days."*

Noted events in his life were:
- He appeared on the United States census in 1840 in Carroll County, Mississippi. [233]
William Russell. Age 20 < 30. Head of household. Living with his mother, Tabitha (Hall) Russell and brothers.
Males: age 10 < 15 - 1; 15 < 20 - 1; 20 < 30 - 1. Females: age 40 < 50 -1. Slaves: 24.
--
This family is living next door to the William Morehead family. William's future "in-laws."

- He appeared on the United States census on 1 Oct 1850 in Carroll County, Mississippi. [387]
William R. Russell. Age 32. Farmer. Head of household. Living with his wife, Susan and children: Tobitha, Donna and Roxannah. Next door to brother, Lindsey H. Russell and mother, Tabitha.

William married **Elizabeth Morhead,** daughter of **William Morhead** and **Ann** _____, on 24 Dec 1840 in Carroll County, Mississippi. [388] Elizabeth was born on 5 Sep 1818 in Mississippi[120] and died on 11 May 1847 in Mississippi[120] at age 28.

Marriage Notes:
Wm Ross Russell Bible Family Register - Elizabeth Morehead and W R Russell Marriage Record
Hand written in the Family Register of the William Ross Russell Family Bible: *"William R. Rufsel and Elizabeth Morehead*

Daughter of William and Anna Morehead were Married the 24th Day of December AD 1840."[120]

Birth Notes:
Hand written in the Family Register of the William Ross Russell Family Bible: *"Elizabeth Rufsell wife of William Ross Rufsell was Born the 5th day of September AD 1818"*

Death Notes:
Hand written in the Family Register of the William Ross Russell Bible: *"Elizabeth Rufsell wife of William R. Rufsell Departed this life the 11th day of May in the year of our Lord AD 1847 aged 28 years 8 months and 6 days."*

Noted events in her life were:
- She appeared on the United States census in 1840 in Carroll County, Mississippi.[389]
  Elizabeth Morehead may be the female Age 15 < 20 listed in the household of William Morehead.
  --
  This family is living next door to the William Russell family. Elizabeth's future "in-laws."

Children from this marriage were:

+ 162 F i. **Tabitha Ann Russell** was born on 13 Oct 1841 in Carroll County, Mississippi.[390]

163 F ii. **Donna Julia Russell** was born on 4 Jan 1844 in Carroll County, Mississippi,[120] died on 2 Sep 1928 in Carroll County, Mississippi[119] at age 84, and was buried in Carroll County, Mississippi (Liberty Baptist Church Cemetery).[119] She never married and had no children.

Birth Notes:
Hand written in the Family Register of the William Ross Russell Family Bible: *"Donnah Julia Rufsell Daughter of William and Elizabeth was Born the 4th day of January AD 1844."*

Noted events in her life were:
- She appeared on the United States census on 1 Oct 1850 in Carroll County, Mississippi.[387]
  Dona Russell. Age 6. Living with her father and stepmother, Susan.

- She appeared on the United States census on 14 Aug 1860 in Carroll County, Mississippi.[391]
  Donna Russell. Age 16. Living with her grandmother, Ann Morhead, age 64 in the household of William Morhead, age 32. Also in the household is her brother, W. L. Russell.

- She appeared on the United States census on 10 Apr 1910 in Carroll County, Mississippi.[392]
  Donna Russell. Age 66. Living in the household of her cousin, William K. Mohead.

- She appeared on the United States census on 28 Jan 1920 in Carroll County, Mississippi.[393]
  Donna Russell (Indexed as Konna). Age 70. Boarder. Living with her cousin, William K. Mohead and his sisters.

164 M iii. **William L. Russell** was born about 1846 in Carroll County, Mississippi and died in Mississippi.

Noted events in his life were:
- He appeared on the United States census on 16 Oct 1850 in Carroll County, Mississippi.[394]
  William Russell. Age 4. Living with his mother's parents, William and Ann Morehead.

- He appeared on the United States census on 14 Aug 1860 in Carroll County, Mississippi.[395]
  W. L. Russell. Age 14. Living with his grandmother, Ann Morhead, age 64 in the household of William Morhead, age 32. Also in the household is his sister, Donna Russell.

William next married **Susan Thomas Caperton,** daughter of **Green Caperton** and **Annie Hudspeth,** on 26 Oct 1847 in Carroll County, Mississippi.[396] Susan was born on 4 Mar 1829 in Tennessee[397] and died about 1861 in Mississippi about age 32.

Marriage Notes:
Hand written in the Family Register of the William Ross Russell Family Bible: *"William R. Rufsell and Susan T Caperton Daughter of Green and Any Caperton were Married the 26th day of October AD 1847."*[120]

Birth Notes:
Hand written in the Family Register of the William Ross Russell Family Bible: *"Susan Thomas Caperton Daughter of Green and Any Caperton was Born the 4th of March 1829 in the year of our lord 1829."*

Noted events in her life were:
- She appeared on the United States census on 1 Oct 1850 in Carroll County, Mississippi.[387]
  Susan Russell. Age 21. Living with husband, William, his children and their new daughter, Roxannah.

- She appeared on the United States census on 18 Sep 1860 in Carroll County, Mississippi.[398]
  Susan Beene. Age 30. Living with her second husband, Rufus K. Beene and his sons from a previous marriage. Shown also are her children, Peter and Mary Beene and son, Thomas Russell.

Children from this marriage were:

165 F   i.   **Roxannah Green Russell** was born on 8 Aug 1848 in Carroll County, Mississippi[399] and died on 6 Dec 1851 in Carroll County, Mississippi[397] at age 3. She never married and had no children.

       Birth Notes:
       Wm Ross Russell Bible Family Register - Roxana Green Russell Birth Record
       Hand written in the Family Register of the William Ross Russell Family Bible: *"Roxana Green Rufsell Daughter of William R and Susan T Rufsell was Born the 8th day of August AD 1848."*

       Death Notes:
       Hand written in the Family Register of the William Ross Russell Family Bible: *"Roxana Green Rufsell Departed this life on Saturday the 6th day of December 1851 aged 3 years 4 months 28 days."*

       Noted events in her life were:
       - She appeared on the United States census on 1 Oct 1850 in Carroll County, Mississippi.[387]
         Roxannah Russell. Age 1. Living with her parents.

166 M   ii.   **Lambert Hudson Russell** was born on 17 Aug 1850 in Mississippi[397] and died on 19 Nov 1851 in Mississippi[397] at age 1. He never married and had no children.

       Birth Notes:
       Wm Ross Russell Bible Family Register - Lambert Hudson Russell Birth Record
       Hand written in the Family Register of the William Ross Russell Family Bible: *"Lambert Hudson Rufsell Son of William R and Susan T Rufsell was born the 17th day of August AD 1850."*

       Death Notes:
       Hand written in the Family Register of the William Ross Russell Family Bible: *"Lambert Hudson Rufsell Departed this life 19th day of November 1851 aged 15 months."*

+ 167 M   iii.   **Thomas Shelton Russell** was born on 20 Mar 1852 in Mississippi[400] and died on 31 Aug 1912 in Fort Worth, Tarrant County, Texas[401] at age 60.

83. Lindsey H. Russell *(Tabitha Hall [16], William [3], John [1])* was born about 1827 in Yazoo County, Mississippi[119] and died between 1864 and 1870 in Mississippi.

Noted events in his life were:
- He appeared on the United States census in 1840 in Carroll County, Mississippi.[233]
  Lindsey H. Russell. Probably the male Age 10 < 15. Living with his mother, Tabitha (Hall) Russell and brothers in the household of his brother:

  William Russell:
  Males: age 10 < 15 - 1; 15 < 20 - 1; 20 < 30 - 1. Females: age 40 < 50 -1. Slaves: 24.

- He appeared on the United States census on 1 Oct 1850 in Carroll County, Mississippi.[234]
  Linsey H. Russell. Age 23. Farmer. Head of household. Living with his mother, Tabitha Ross and next door to brother, William R. Russell.

- He appeared on the United States census on 21 Jul 1860 in Fayette County, Texas.[402]
  L. W. Russell. Age 34. Head of household. Living with his wife, Louisa A. Russell and daughters, Mary and Sarah.

Lindsey married **Louisa A. Simmons,** daughter of _____ _____ and _____ _____, on 21 Aug 1855 in Yalobusha County, Mississippi.[403] Louisa was born about 1837 in Georgia and died between 1870 and 1880 in Mississippi.

Noted events in her life were:

- She appeared on the United States census on 21 Jul 1860 in Fayette County, Texas.[402]
Louisa A. Russell. Age 23. Living with her husband, L. H. Russell and daughters, Mary and Sarah. A close next door neighbor, as indicated on the census record, is the family of Ira and Anna Mullins. Perhaps a relation, or not.

- She appeared on the United States census on 20 Aug 1870 in Tallahatchie County, Mississippi.[404]
Louisa A. Russell. Age 35. Living in the household of Smith Murphy. Children include: Mary W., Virginia and Lindsey H. Russell, Jr.

Children from this marriage were:

168 F   i.   **Mary W. Russell** was born about 1856 in Texas.

> **Noted events in her life were:**
>
> - She appeared on the United States census on 21 Jul 1860 in Fayette County, Texas.[402]
> Mary W. Russell. Age 4. Living with her parents.
>
> - She appeared on the United States census on 20 Aug 1870 in Tallahatchie County, Mississippi.[404]
> Mary W. Russell. Age 14. Living with her mother and siblings in the household of Smith Murphy.

169 F   ii.   **Sarah M. Russell** was born about 1859 in Texas and died before 1870. She never married and had no children.

> **Noted events in her life were:**
>
> - She appeared on the United States census on 21 Jul 1860 in Fayette County, Texas.[402]
> Sarah M. Russell. Age 1. Living with her parents

170 F   iii.   **Virginia Russell** was born about 1860 in Mississippi.

> **Noted events in her life were:**
>
> - She appeared on the United States census on 20 Aug 1870 in Tallahatchie County, Mississippi.[404]
> Virginia Russell. Age 10. Living with her mother and siblings in the household of Smith Murphy.

171 M   iv.   **Lindsey H. Russell, Jr.** was born about 1864 in Mississippi.

> **Noted events in his life were:**
>
> - He appeared on the United States census on 20 Aug 1870 in Tallahatchie County, Mississippi.[404]
> Lindsey H. Russell. Age 6. Living with his mother and siblings in the household of Smith Murphy.

84. William Pierce *(Rhoda Hall [18], William [3], John [1])* was born about 1826 in Yazoo County, Mississippi and died after 1880 in Mississippi.

Noted events in his life were:

- He appeared on the United States census in 1830 in Yazoo County, Mississippi.[249]
Probably the youngest male in the household of Marcus Pierce.
Males (>5) -1, (30-40) -1; Females (>5) -2, (20-30) -1
Next door to A. C. Hall, J. B. Hall and J. C. Hall are nearby.

- He appeared on the United States census in 1840 in Carroll County, Mississippi.[250]
Living with his parents in the household of Marcus Pierce.
Males: (<5) -1, (5-10) -1, (10-15) -1, (40-50) -1
Females: (5-10) -1, (10-15) -2, (30-40 -1.

- He appeared on the United States census on 11 Oct 1850 in Carroll County, Mississippi.[251]
William Pierce. Age 24. Living with his mother.

- He appeared on the United States census on 20 Jun 1860 in Choctaw County, Mississippi.[252]
William Pierce. Age 35. Farmer. Living with his mother and brothers.

- He appeared on the United States census on 19 Oct 1870 in Choctaw County, Mississippi.[253]
William Pierce. Age 42. Farmer. Living in the household of his brother, Benjamin. Also in the household are his mother, Roda and his wife, Nancy and son, Briler.

- He appeared on the United States census on 11 Jun 1880 in Montgomery County, Mississippi.[405]

William Pierce. Age 53. Working in a water mill. Single. Boarder in the household of J. Hornbrick.

William married **Nancy** _____, daughter of _____ _____ and _____ _____, about 1868 in Mississippi. Nancy was born about 1843 in Georgia.

> **Noted events in her life were:**
> • She appeared on the United States census on 19 Oct 1870 in Choctaw County, Mississippi.[253]
> Nancy Pierce. Age 27. Living in the household of her brother-in-law, Benjamin Pierce. Also in the household are her mother-in-law, Roda and her husband, William and son, Briler.

The child from this marriage was:

172 F i. **Briler Pierce** was born about 1869 in Mississippi.

> **Noted events in her life were:**
> • She appeared on the United States census on 19 Oct 1870 in Choctaw County, Mississippi.[253]
> Briler Pierce. Age 1. Living in with his parents.

87. Eliza Pierce *(Rhoda Hall [18], William [3], John [1])* was born about 1833 in Yazoo County, Mississippi and died before 1880 in Louisiana.

> **Noted events in her life were:**
> • She appeared on the United States census in 1840 in Carroll County, Mississippi.[250]
> Living with her parents in the household of Marcus Pierce.
> Males: (<5) -1, (5-10) -1, (10-15) -1, (40-50) -1
> Females: (5-10) -1, (10-15) -2, (30-40) -1.
>
> • She appeared on the United States census on 12 Oct 1850 in Carroll County, Mississippi.[259]
> Eliza Pierce. Age 17. Living with her mother, brothers and sisters.
>
> • She appeared on the United States census on 19 Jun 1860 in Carroll Parish, Louisiana.[406]
> Eliza Munholland. Age 27. Living with her husband, Moses; 3 children and an orphan, William Merchant, age 12; born in Mississippi.

Eliza married **Moses M. Munholland,** son of _____ _____ and _____ _____, on 26 Feb 1853 in Yazoo County, Mississippi.[403] Moses was born about 1835 in Mississippi.

> **Noted events in his life were:**
> • He appeared on the United States census on 19 Jun 1860 in Carroll Parish, Louisiana.[406]
> Moses M. Munholland. Age 25. Planter. Living with his wife, Eliza; 3 children and an orphan, William Merchant, age 12; born in Mississippi. Also in the household are three carpenters: Stephen L. Kamberlin, James M. Smith and William B. Smith, all from Mississippi.

Children from this marriage were:

173 F i. **Julia L. Munholland** was born about 1854 in Mississippi.

> **Noted events in her life were:**
> • She appeared on the United States census on 19 Jun 1860 in Carroll Parish, Louisiana.[406]
> Julia L. Munholland. Age 6. Living with her parents.

174 F ii. **Gesisim Munholland** was born about 1856 in Louisiana.

> **Noted events in her life were:**
> • She appeared on the United States census on 19 Jun 1860 in Carroll Parish, Louisiana.[406]
> Gesisim C. Munholland. Age 4. Living with her parents.

175 M iii. **Moses M. Munholland, Jr.** was born about 1859 in Louisiana.

Noted events in his life were:
- He appeared on the United States census on 19 Jun 1860 in Carroll Parish, Louisiana.[406]
  Moses M. Munholland, Jr. Age 1. Living with his parents.

89. Benjamin Franklin Pierce *(Rhoda Hall [18], William [3], John [1])* was born about 1838 in Mississippi and died after 1880 in Mississippi.

Noted events in his life were:
- He appeared on the United States census in 1840 in Carroll County, Mississippi.[250]
  Living with his parents in the household of Marcus Pierce.
  Males: (<5) -1, (5-10) -1, (10-15) -1, (40-50) -1
  Females: (5-10) -1, (10-15) -2, (30-40) -1.

- He appeared on the United States census on 11 Oct 1850 in Carroll County, Mississippi.[259]
  Franklin Pierce. Age 12. Living with his mother, brothers and sisters.

- He appeared on the United States census on 20 Jun 1860 in Choctaw County, Mississippi.[252]
  Benjamin F. Pierce. Age 22. Farmer. Living with his mother and brothers. The Crook family are close neighbors.

- He appeared on the United States census on 19 Oct 1870 in Choctaw County, Mississippi.[253]
  Benjamin Pierce. Age 37. Farmer. Head of household. Living with his mother, brother and family.

- He appeared on the United States census on 18 Jun 1880 in Montgomery County, Mississippi.[407]
  Frank Pierce. Age 43. Farmer. Living with his wife, Adnett Pierce and five children.

Benjamin married **Antoinette T. Crook,** daughter of **Valentine Crook** and **Temperance _____**, about 1870 in Mississippi. Antoinette was born about 1843 in Georgia and died about 1928 in Montgomery County, Mississippi[408] about age 85.

Noted events in her life were:
- She appeared on the United States census on 21 Jun 1860 in Choctaw County, Mississippi.[409]
  Antinett T. Crook. Age 17. Spinster. Living in the household of her parents, Valentine and Temperance Crook along with her brothers and sister.

- She appeared on the United States census on 18 Jun 1880 in Montgomery County, Mississippi.[407]
  Adnett Pierce. Age 37. Keeping house. Living with her husband, Frank Pierce and five children.

Children from this marriage were:

+ 176 F   i.   **Ada Beatrice Pierce** was born on 2 Jun 1870 in Choctaw County, Mississippi and died on 8 Dec 1962 in Clinton, East Feliciana Parish, Louisiana[410] at age 92.

  177 M   ii.   **Charles Pierce** was born about 1872 in Mississippi.

        Noted events in his life were:
        - He appeared on the United States census on 18 Jun 1880 in Montgomery County, Mississippi.[407]
         Charlie Pierce. Age 8. Living with his parents.

  178 M   iii.   **Walter Pierce** was born about 1874 in Mississippi.

        Noted events in his life were:
        - He appeared on the United States census on 18 Jun 1880 in Montgomery County, Mississippi.[407]
         Walter Pierce. Age 6. Living with his parents.

  179 F   iv.   **Anah Pierce** was born about 1876 in Mississippi.

        Noted events in her life were:
        - She appeared on the United States census on 18 Jun 1880 in Montgomery County, Mississippi.[407]
         Anah Pierce. Age 4. Living with her parents.

  180 F   v.   **Emma Pierce** was born about 1878 in Mississippi.

Noted events in her life were:
- She appeared on the United States census on 18 Jun 1880 in Montgomery County, Mississippi.[407]
  Emma Pierce. Age 2. Living with her parents.

105. David O. Hall *(Joel* [26]*, Jesse* [6]*, John* [1]*)* was born about 1831 in Bedford County, Virginia.

    Noted events in his life were:
- He appeared on the United States census on 5 Sep 1850 in Bedford County, Virginia.[270]
  David O. Hall. Age 19. Laborer. Living with his parents and siblings.

David married **Minerva A. Overstreet,** daughter of _____ _____ and _____ _____, on 19 Feb 1852 in Bedford County, Virginia.[411] Minerva was born about 1831 in Virginia.

    Noted events in her life were:
- She appeared on the United States census on 17 Sep 1850 in Bedford County, Virginia.[412]
  Manerva Overstreet. Age 19. Living in the household of James K. and Mary (Hall) Shean [Shaon]. Also in the household: Thomas H. Miles, Will. S. Williams.
  --
  In technical parlance, Manerva would become the wife of Mary (Hall) Shaon's first cousin once removed. (Mary's father and David's grandfather were brothers.) The common ancestor was John Hall.

113. Sarah Ann Heppenstall *(Tabitha Hall* [27]*, Elisha* [8]*, John* [1]*)* was born about 1825 in Franklin County, Virginia[272] and died about 1916 about age 91.

Sarah married **Elijah Harrison Turner,** son of _____ _____ and _____ _____, on 1 Nov 1847 in Franklin County, Virginia.[272]

114. Thomas Heppenstall *(Tabitha Hall* [27]*, Elisha* [8]*, John* [1]*)* was born about 1831 in Bedford County, Virginia.

Thomas married **Martha K. Shaon,** daughter of _____ _____ and _____ _____.

Descendants of John Hall (1735 - 1794)
of Bedford County, Virginia

Fifth Generation

124. Phidella "Della" Hall *(Jesse F.* [62]*, John* [11]*, John, Jr.* [2]*, John* [1]*)* was born on 14 Aug 1873 in Collin County, Texas,[308] died on 10 Jun 1962 in Collin County, Texas[308] at age 88, and was buried in Jun 1962 in Collin County, Texas (Forest Grove Cemetery).[308] She was usually called Della.

> **Noted events in her life were:**
> • She appeared on the United States census on 2 Jun 1880 in Collin County, Texas.[306]
>   Phidella Hall. Age 6. Living with her parents.

Della married **Fountain Lee Myrick,** son of _____ _____ and _____ _____, in 1893 in Collin County, Texas. Fountain was born on 1 Jan 1867 in Kentucky,[413] died on 13 Feb 1923 in Collin County, Texas[413] at age 56, and was buried in Feb 1923 in Collin County, Texas (Forest Grove Cemetery).[413]

127. John Andrew Houston Hall *(Joseph Marion* [63]*, John* [11]*, John, Jr.* [2]*, John* [1]*)* was born on 31 Jan 1854 in Lafayette County, Arkansas,[320] died on 11 Feb 1943 in San Angelo, Tom Green County, Texas[321] at age 89, and was buried in Feb 1943 in Tom Green County, Texas (Mereta Cemetery).[322]

> **Noted events in his life were:**
> • He appeared on the United States census on 7 Jun 1860 in Collin County, Texas.[318]
>   John A. H. Hall (indexed as Holl). Age 5. Living with his parents.
>
> • He appeared on the United States census on 1 Jun 1870 in Limestone County, Texas.[310]
>   Jno. A. H. Hall. Age 16. Living with his parents, Joseph M. and Polly A. Hall.
>
> • He appeared on the United States census on 2 Jun 1880 in Lampasas County, Texas.[311]
>   John Hall. Age 25. School teacher. Living with his parents.
>
> • He appeared on the United States census on 30 Jun 1900 in Lampasas County, Texas.[414]
>   Jno. A. Hall. Age 45. Birth date: Jan 1855. School teacher. Widower. Living with his children: Ida A., Jessie E., Callie E., Bell, Sweet O., Jno. R., Dewey, and Jno. Hall.
>
> • He appeared on the United States census on 27 Apr 1910 in Burnet County, Texas.[415]
>   John A. Hall. Age 55. "Own Income." Widower. Living with his children: Belle, Ora, John R., Dewie, and Archie A. Hall.

John married **Ora Bean,** daughter of **Charles Bean** and **Frances Turner,** on 9 Jun 1881 in Burnet County, Texas.[416] Ora was born on 19 Mar 1867 in Texas,[417] died on 22 Apr 1900 in Lampasas County, Texas[417] at age 33, and was buried in Apr 1900 in Lampasas County, Texas (Bend Sand Hill Cemetery).[417]

> **Burial Notes:**
> Notes on Tombstone:
>
> "In Memory of Ora Hall Wife of J. A. Hall Born March 18, 1867 Died April 22, 1900 - Farewell till the millinium dawns"
>
> *"God bless you today, God bless you forever. Dear gentle wife, and Precious Mother"* - Inscription written at the bottom of the marker
>
> **Noted events in her life were:**
> • She appeared on the United States census on 15 Aug 1870 in Burnet County, Texas.[418]
>   Ora Bean. Age 3. Living with her parents, Charles and Frances Bean and siblings: Alace and Allen.
>
> • She appeared on the United States census on 1 Jun 1880 in Lampasas County, Texas.[419]
>   Ora Bean. Age 13. Going to school. Living with her parents, Charles and Francis Bean and siblings: Daniel, Eva and Tilford.

Children from this marriage were:

   181   F   i.   **Ida A. Hall** was born in Sep 1882 in Lampasas County, Texas.

Noted events in her life were:
- She appeared on the United States census on 30 Jun 1900 in Lampasas County, Texas.[414]
  Ida A. Hall. Age 17. Birth date: Sep 1882. At school. Living with her father and siblings.

+ 182 F   ii.   **Jessie Lena Hall** was born on 20 Oct 1884 in Lampasas County, Texas,[420] died on 22 Sep 1986 in Tom Green County, Texas[420] at age 101, and was buried in Sep 1986 in Tom Green County, Texas (Mereta Cemetery).[420]

   183 F   iii.   **Callie E. Hall** was born in Apr 1886 in Lampasas County, Texas.

Noted events in her life were:
- She appeared on the United States census on 30 Jun 1900 in Lampasas County, Texas.[414]
  Callie E. Hall. Age 14. Birth date: Apr 1886. At school. Living with her father and siblings.

+ 184 F   iv.   **Belle Hall** was born on 30 Oct 1890 in Lampasas County, Texas,[421] died on 9 May 1927 in Garland, Dallas County, Texas[421] at age 36, and was buried in Garland, Dallas County, Texas (Mills Cemetery).[421]

+ 185 F   v.   **Sweet Ora Hall** was born on 14 May 1892 in Lampasas County, Texas,[422] died on 4 Dec 1977 in New York[422] at age 85, and was buried in Warren County, Virginia (Prospect Hill Cemetery).[423]

   186 M   vi.   **John Reagan Hall** was born on 8 Oct 1893 in Lampasas County, Texas[424] and died on 15 Oct 1972 in Tom Green County, Texas[425] at age 79.

Noted events in his life were:
- He appeared on the United States census on 30 Jun 1900 in Lampasas County, Texas.[414]
  Jno. R. Hall. Age 6. Birth date: Oct 1893. Living with his father and siblings.

- He appeared on the United States census on 27 Apr 1910 in Burnet County, Texas.[426]
  John R. Hall. Age 15. Living with his father, John A. Hall and siblings.

+ 187 M   vii.   **George Dewey Hall** was born on 5 Feb 1898 in Lampasas County, Texas,[427] died on 22 Dec 1946 in Edinburg, Hidalgo County, Texas[427] at age 48, and was buried on 25 Dec 1946 in Hidalgo County, Texas (Edinburg Cemetery).[427]

+ 188 M   viii.   **Archie Andrew Hall** was born on 16 Feb 1899 in Lampasas County, Texas,[428] died on 29 Jul 1960 in Crocket County, Texas[428] at age 61, and was buried on 31 Jul 1960 in Rankin County, Texas (Rankin Cemetery).[428]

132. Harriett D. B. M. Hall (*Joseph Marion [63], John [11], John, Jr. [2], John [1]*) was born on 5 Jan 1867 in Lampasas County, Texas,[324] died on 18 Jan 1959 in McKinney, Collin County, Texas[324] at age 92, and was buried on 19 Jan 1959 in Collin County, Texas (Scalf Cemetery).[324]

Birth Notes:
She was living on the 1870 United States Census, age 3 and was age 13 on the 1880 Census. This conflicts with the Birth Date information given on the 1900 Census: May 1875 and her Death Certificate: 1869. --rch, 2013.

Noted events in her life were:
- She appeared on the United States census on 1 Jun 1870 in Limestone County, Texas.[310]
  Harriett D. B. M. Hall. Age 3. Living with her parents, Joseph M. and Polly A. Hall.

- She appeared on the United States census on 2 Jun 1880 in Lampasas County, Texas.[311]
  Harriett Hall. Age 13. At home. Living with her parents.

- She appeared on the United States census on 5 Jun 1900 in Collin County, Texas.[312]
  Harriet H. Murphy. Age 25. Birth date: May 1875. Married 2 years. Children: 2; Living 2. Living with her parents and her husband, William S. Murphy and children: Bossa A. (6) and Bettie Murphy (1). Both listed as grandchildren of Joseph M. Hall.

- She appeared on the United States census on 18 Apr 1910 in Collin County, Texas.[319]
  Harriet D. Murphy. Age 40. Living with her husband, William S. Murphy and children: Bessie A, Robert H., Jessie B., William D. and Alvin C. Murphy. Married 11 years. Children: 5; Living: 5.
  --
  Also in the household is her mother, Polly A. Hall. Age 75.

Harriett married **William Stephen Murphy,** son of **Stephen S. Murphy** and **Laura Almada McCreary Thomas,** about 1898 in

Texas. William was born in Sep 1877 in Texas,[429] died on 27 Sep 1960 in McKinney, Collin County, Texas[429] at age 83, and was buried in Sep 1960 in Collin County, Texas (Scalf Cemetery).[429]

Birth Notes:
Other sources list his date of birth as May 3, 1876. This differs from the date given in the 1900 census. --rch, 2013

Noted events in his life were:
• He appeared on the United States census on 5 Jun 1900 in Collin County, Texas.[312]
William S. Murphy. Age 22. Birth date: Sep 1877. Married 2 years. Farm Laborer. Living in his father-in-law's household with his wife, Harriet and children: Bossa A. and Bettie Murphy. Both listed as grandchildren of Joseph M. Hall.

144. William Gordon Childress, Sr. *(Laurena Matilda Hall ⁷⁰, Samuel S. ¹³, William ³, John ¹)* was born about Aug 1831 in Arkansas, died on 27 Nov 1921 in Yazoo County, Mississippi[345] about age 90, and was buried in Yazoo County, Mississippi (Hart-Childress Cemetery).[349]

Noted events in his life were:
• He appeared on the United States census in 1840 in Yazoo County, Mississippi.[209]
William G. Childress. Probably listed as a male under 5, living with his mother in the household of his grandfather: Samuel S. Hall. Head of household.
Males (<5) - 2, (10-15) - 1, (15-20) - 1, (40-50) - 1. Females (20-30) - 1, (30-40) - 1. Slaves: 21.

Living near John B. Hall, William Hall, W. W. Wildy, Jonathan Bonney. Also living nearby is the Harrison Hart family, future "in-laws."

• He appeared on the United States census on 14 Sep 1850 in Yazoo County, Mississippi.[337]
William G. Childress. Age 14. Living with his mother and brother in the household of W. W. Wildy.

• He appeared on the United States census on 21 Aug 1860 in Yazoo County, Mississippi.[338]
William Childress. Age 24. Living with his mother, brother and stepfather, W. W. Wildy.

• He appeared on the United States census on 15 Jun 1880 in Yazoo County, Mississippi.[430]
W. G. Childress. Age 43. Farmer. Head of household. Living with his wife, S. E. Childress and five children.

• He appeared on the United States census on 1 Jun 1900 in Yazoo County, Mississippi.[431]
W. G. Childress. Age 68. Birth date: Aug 1831. Widower. Living with his son, E. G. Childress. This record lists his birth state as Mississippi.

• He appeared on the United States census on 16 Apr 1910 in Yazoo County, Mississippi.[432]
W. G. Childress, Sr. Age 74. Widower. Living in his son's household, S. A. Childress.

• He appeared on the United States census on 2 Jan 1920 in Yazoo County, Mississippi.[433]
Wm. Gordon Childress, Sr. Age 84. Living with his son, Samuel A. Childress and daughter-in-law, Flora B.

• He served in the military CO I, 12th Mississippi Infantry, CSA.[349]

William married **Susan E. Hart,** daughter of **Harrison Hart** and **Eliza A. Buford,** on 11 Jul 1866 in Yazoo County, Mississippi.[403] Susan was born about 1845 in Mississippi, died before 1900, and was buried in Yazoo County, Mississippi (Hart-Childress Cemetery).[434]

Noted events in her life were:
• She appeared on the United States census on 17 Sep 1850 in Yazoo County, Mississippi.[435]
Susan E. Hart. Age 5. Living with her parents, Harrison and Eliza A. Hart; brothers, sisters and grandmother.

• She appeared on the United States census on 15 Jun 1880 in Yazoo County, Mississippi.[430]
S. E. Childress. Age 33. House keeper. Living with her husband, W. G. Childress and five children.

Children from this marriage were:
189 F i. **Ann L. Childress** was born about 1870 in Yazoo County, Mississippi.

Noted events in her life were:
• She appeared on the United States census on 15 Jun 1880 in Yazoo County, Mississippi.[430]
An L. Childress. Age 10. At home. Living with her parents.

+ 190 M ii. **Edward G. Childress** was born about Jul 1872 in Yazoo County, Mississippi.

+ 191 M iii. **Samuel Arthur Childress** was born on 18 Jul 1875 in Yazoo County, Mississippi.[436]

  192 F iv. **Veara Childress** was born about 1877 in Yazoo County, Mississippi.

Noted events in her life were:
- She appeared on the United States census on 15 Jun 1880 in Yazoo County, Mississippi.[430]
  Veara Childress. Age 3. Living with her(?) parents. This record indicates that this child is a "son" (male). The M/F designation is jumbled. The word "son" is slightly smudged.

+ 193 F v. **Lillie Childress** was born on 20 Jul 1879 in Yazoo County, Mississippi, died on 3 Mar 1971 in Yazoo County, Mississippi at age 91, and was buried in Yazoo County, Mississippi (Hart-Childress Cemetery).[437]

145. Samuel Hall Childress *(Laurena Matilda Hall [70], Samuel S. [13], William [3], John [1])* was born on 24 Aug 1838 in Arkansas,[438] died on 27 Dec 1917 in Yazoo County, Mississippi[348] at age 79, and was buried in Yazoo County, Mississippi (Hart-Childress Cemetery).[349]

Burial Notes:
"Mason"

Noted events in his life were:
- He appeared on the United States census in 1840 in Yazoo County, Mississippi.[209]
  Samuel H. Childress. Probably listed as a male under 5, living with his mother in the household of his grandfather: Samuel S. Hall. Head of household.
  Males (<5) - 2, (10-15) - 1, (15-20) - 1, (40-50) - 1. Females (20-30) - 1, (30-40) - 1. Slaves: 21.

  Living near John B. Hall, William Hall, W. W. Wildy, Jonathan Bonney

- He appeared on the United States census on 14 Sep 1850 in Yazoo County, Mississippi.[337]
  Samuel Childress. Age 12. Living with his mother and brother in the household of W. W. Wildy.

- He appeared on the United States census on 21 Aug 1860 in Yazoo County, Mississippi.[338]
  Samuel Childress. Age 22. Living with his mother, brother and stepfather, W. W. Wildy.

- He appeared on the United States census on 29 Jun 1870 in Yazoo County, Mississippi.[439]
  S. H. Childress. Age 31. Farmer. Living with his wife, G. A. Childress and children: William, Ada and Robinson.

- He appeared on the United States census on 15 Jun 1880 in Yazoo County, Mississippi.[440]
  S. H. Childress. Age 41. Farmer. Head of household. Living with his wife, Lula and children: William, Minnie and Harry. Listed on same page as his stepfather, W. W. Wildy. This record lists his birth state as Mississippi.

- He appeared on the United States census on 16 Apr 1910 in Yazoo County, Mississippi.[441]
  Sam Childress (Indexed as Children). Age 72. Farm Manager. Widower. Living with his son, W. G. Childress and family.

- He worked as a Justice of the Peace in 1875 in Yazoo County, Mississippi.[93]

Samuel married **Georgia Ann Hart**, daughter of **Harrison Hart** and **Eliza A. Buford**, on 27 Oct 1860 in Yazoo County, Mississippi.[442] Georgia was born on 8 Oct 1837 in Mississippi,[438] died on 6 Nov 1873 in Yazoo County, Mississippi at age 36, and was buried in Nov 1873 in Yazoo County, Mississippi (Hart-Childress Cemetery).

Noted events in her life were:
- She appeared on the United States census on 17 Sep 1850 in Yazoo County, Mississippi.[443]
  Georgana Hart. Age 12. Living with her parents, Harrison and Eliza A. Hart; brothers, sisters and grandmother.

- She appeared on the United States census on 29 Jun 1870 in Yazoo County, Mississippi.[439]
  G. A. Childress. Age 32. Keeping house. Living with her husband, S. H. Childress and children: William, Ada and Robinson Childress.

Children from this marriage were:

  194 F i. **Ada Viola Childress** was born on 12 Aug 1861 in Yazoo County, Mississippi, died on 24 May 1863 in Yazoo County, Mississippi at age 1, and was buried in May 1863 in Yazoo County, Mississippi (Hart-Childress Cemetery).[444] She never married and had no children.

+ 195 M ii. **William Gordon Childress** was born on 11 Dec 1863 in Yazoo County, Mississippi,[445] died on 5 Mar 1944 in Yazoo County, Mississippi at age 80, and was buried in Mar 1944 in Yazoo County, Mississippi (Hart-Childress Cemetery).[446]

+ 196 F iii. **Ada "Minnie" Childress** was born on 27 Jun 1866 in Yazoo County, Mississippi, died on 26 Feb 1889 in Yazoo County, Mississippi at age 22, and was buried in Yazoo County, Mississippi (Hart-Childress Cemetery).

197 M iv. _____ **Childress** was born on 24 Dec 1866 in Yazoo County, Mississippi, died on 26 Dec 1866 in Yazoo County, Mississippi, and was buried in Yazoo County, Mississippi (Hart-Childress Cemetery).[447] He never married and had no children.

198 M v. **Harry Robertson Childress** was born on 3 Jun 1869 in Yazoo County, Mississippi, died on 23 Jan 1910 in Yazoo County, Mississippi at age 40, and was buried in Jan 1910 in Yazoo County, Mississippi (Hart-Childress Cemetery).[448]

Burial Notes:
"Mason"

Noted events in his life were:
• He appeared on the United States census on 29 Jun 1870 in Yazoo County, Mississippi.[439]
Robertson Childress. Age 1. Living with his parents. This record clearly says his birth place was Missouri.

• He appeared on the United States census on 15 Jun 1880 in Yazoo County, Mississippi.[440]
Harry Childress. Age 9. Living with his father, S. H. Childress and step-mother, Lula.

199 M vi. _____ **Childress** was born on 8 Jul 1871 in Yazoo County, Mississippi, died on 9 Jul 1871 in Yazoo County, Mississippi, and was buried in Jul 1871 in Yazoo County, Mississippi (Hart-Childress Cemetery).[449] He never married and had no children.

Samuel next married **Lula Pegram Kirby,** daughter of _____ _____ and _____ _____, on 21 Dec 1878 in Yazoo County, Mississippi.[403] Lula was born about 1849 in Mississippi and died before 1910 in Mississippi.

Noted events in her life were:
• She appeared on the United States census on 15 Jun 1880 in Yazoo County, Mississippi.[440]
Lula Childress. Age 31. House keeping. Living with her husband, S. H. Childress and his children.

146. Matilda Wildy (*Laurena Matilda Hall [70], Samuel S. [13], William [3], John [1]*) was born on 10 Jul 1842 in Yazoo County, Mississippi,[355] died on 27 Sep 1915 in Yazoo County, Mississippi[356] at age 73, and was buried in Yazoo County, Mississippi (Wesley Chapel Cemetery).[215] Another name for Matilda was Mattie.

Noted events in her life were:
• She appeared on the United States census on 14 Sep 1850 in Yazoo County, Mississippi.[337]
Matilda Wildy. Age 9. Living with her parents and siblings.

• She appeared on the United States census on 21 Aug 1860 in Yazoo County, Mississippi.[338]
Matilda Wildy. Age 18. Student. Living with her parents.

• She appeared on the United States census on 24 Jun 1870 in Yazoo County, Mississippi.[450]
M. W. Bonney. Age 28. Keeping house. Living with her husband, F(?). M. Bonney and daughters Ella and Mary Bonney.

• She appeared on the United States census on 21 Jun 1880 in Yazoo County, Mississippi.[451]
M. W. Bonney. Age 37. Living with her husband and son, C. W. Bonney. (image very faint)

• She appeared on the United States census on 19 Jun 1900 in Yazoo County, Mississippi.[452]
Matilda Bonny [Baney]. Age 57. Jul 1842. Living with her husband, James Bonny and his sister, Mary B. Fields. Married 34 years. Children: 4; Living: 1.

• She appeared on the United States census on 18 Apr 1910 in Yazoo County, Mississippi.[453]
Mattie Bonney. Age 69. Manager/ General farm. Head of household. Widow. Living with her son, Dr. Caleb W. Bonney and sister in-law, Mary B. Fields. Also in the household is an orphan, Alsy Smith, age 17. Children: 4; Living: 1.

Matilda married **James Madison Bonney,** son of **Dr. Caleb Dawley Bonney** and **Indiana Catherine Hall,** on 6 Nov 1866 in Yazoo County, Mississippi.[454] James was born on 7 Apr 1841 in Yazoo County, Mississippi,[455] died on 23 Feb 1910 in Yazoo

County, Mississippi[456] at age 68, and was buried in Feb 1910 in Yazoo County, Mississippi (Bonney Cemetery (AKA Churchill Plantation Cemetery)).[457]

General Notes:

*"William W. Wildy. the "Grandfather of Roswell," died in Yazoo County, Mississippi, on February 7, 1881, at the age of 71 years... C. D. Bonney, Jr., and his two brothers, John H. and **James**, all of Yazoo County, Mississippi, arrived back in Roswell on June 4, 1881. The Bonneys were the sons of Dr. Caleb D. Bonney, Sr., a wealthy doctor who had plantations in Yazoo County, Mississippi, and Shelby County, Kentucky... James Bonney was W. W. Wildy's son-in-law, married in 1866 to Mattie Wildy. He apparently came to inspect the land his wife had inherited upon the recent death of her father. He soon returned to Mississippi."[363]*

Noted events in his life were:

- He appeared on the United States census on 2 Aug 1850 in Shelby County, Kentucky.[458]
  Jas. Bonney. Age 9. Living with his parents.

- He appeared on the United States census on 30 Jul 1860 in Shelby County, Kentucky.[459]
  James M. Bonney. Age 19. Farmer. Living with his parents.

- He appeared on the United States census on 24 Jun 1870 in Yazoo County, Mississippi.[450]
  F. M. Bonney. Age 29. Farmer. Living with his wife, M. W. Bonney and daughters, Ella and Mary.

- He appeared on the United States census on 21 Jun 1880 in Yazoo County, Mississippi.[451]
  J. M. Bonney. Age 39. Farmer. Living with his wife, M. W. and son, C. W. Bonney. (image very faint)

- He appeared on the United States census on 19 Jun 1900 in Yazoo County, Mississippi.[452]
  Jas. M. Bonny (indexed as Baney). Age 59. Birth date: April 1841. Farmer. Living with his wife Matilda W. Bonny and sister, Mary B. Fields. Married 34 years.

- He served in the military as an Officer in the Confederate States of America from 1862 to 1865.[460]
  James Bonney enlisted in March 1862 for 3 years or the "war" in Satartia, Mississippi. He was listed as 3rd or 2nd Lt. Co. H, 29th Regiment of the Mississippi Volunteers, Walthal's Brigade on various Muster Rolls. Records from a Regimental Return dated June 1862 indicate that he was promoted from Orderly Sergeant to 2nd Lieutenant by General Bragg on June 22, 1862.

  On November 25, 1862 he was sent home from Murfreesboro, Tennessee on sick leave by Surgeon's order. There is some confusion regarding his whereabouts during this time period. Some reports indicate that he was captured at the battle of Murfreesboro or Stone's River and sent to prison in Nashville, then paroled due to ill health to go home. His name appears on a list of Prisoners of War who had been forwarded to Nashville. This list says he was captured on January 9, 1863 in Murfreesboro, Tennessee.

  He returned to the army and served as Captain of Company G. Later he commanded Company H during the Battle of Lookout Mountain, Georgia where he was captured again, November 24, 1863, and sent to prison at Johnson's Island, Ohio for eighteen months until the end of the war. "J. M. Binny (Bonney) appears on a list of soldiers killed, wounded or missing of Walthal's Brigade in the engagement on Lookout Mountain, Tenn. Nov. 24, 1863." This list was dated Dec. 18, 1863 "at camp near Dalton, Georgia." A notation on one CSA Muster Roll states that he was dropped from the rolls by April 1864. Jas. Bonney appears on an inspection report of Prisoners of War dated Aug. 19, 1864 in Atlanta, Georgia.

  There seems to be some Service Record cards mixed in with James Bonney's file or else he used an assumed name upon his return. The names of Monroe Bonner and Monroe Bonney are intermixed with the file of James M. Bonney. These detail his capture and imprisonment from Lookout Mountain; and eventual release from Louisville on June 12, 1865. A record of his Oath of Allegiance to the United States dated June 12, 1865 describes Monroe Bonney, 2nd Lt 29 Regt Miss Inf; Residence: Satartia, Miss; Age: 25; Complexion: Light; Hair: Light; Eyes: Blue; Height: 5' 8".

- He was involved in a court case in Apr 1886 in Yazoo County, Mississippi.[461]
  The court case involved a sale of land from J. M. Bonney to his mother, who immediately transferred title to the land to C. Wildy Bonney, a minor and James's son. The plaintiffs were claiming that the transfer was illegally shielding assets from their attempts to collect on a debt. The defendants prevailed. For genealogical purposes the suit names three generations of a family, mother, son and grandson.

Children from this marriage were:

200 F i. **Ella Bonney** was born on 16 Nov 1867 in Yazoo County, Mississippi,[462] died on 16 Jun 1869 in Yazoo County, Mississippi[369] at age 1, and was buried in Jun 1869 in Yazoo County, Mississippi (Wesley Chapel Cemetery).[463] She never married and had no children.

Noted events in her life were:
- She appeared on the United States census on 24 Jun 1870 in Yazoo County, Mississippi.[450] Ella Bonney. Age 1. Living with her parents and sister, Mary.

This might seem to contradict the date of death given in other records. However, by all accounts, she was alive on the 1st day of June 1870. Did those who recorded her death in the Family Bible miss it by exactly one year? --rch, 2012

201 F ii. **Mary Bonney** was born on 23 May 1869 in Yazoo County, Mississippi,[369] died on 24 Jun 1869 in Yazoo County, Mississippi,[369] and was buried in Jun 1869 in Yazoo County, Mississippi (Wesley Chapel Cemetery).[464] She never married and had no children.

Noted events in her life were:
- She appeared on the United States census on 24 Jun 1870 in Yazoo County, Mississippi.[450] Mary Bonney. Age 1/12. Living with her parents and sister, Ella. Birth month is given on this record as May.

Again we have conflicting dates between the Census record and the recorded date of death. --rch, 2012

202 M iii. **Dr. Caleb Wildy Bonney** was born on 25 Dec 1870 in Yazoo County, Mississippi,[465] died on 28 Dec 1964 in Yazoo County, Mississippi[466] at age 94, and was buried in Yazoo County, Mississippi (Bonney Cemetery (AKA Churchill Plantation Cemetery)).[467] He never married and had no children.

Noted events in his life were:
- He appeared on the United States census on 21 Jun 1880 in Yazoo County, Mississippi.[451] C. W. Bonney. Age 9. Living with his parents. (image very faint)

- He appeared on the United States census on 25 Jun 1900 in Tensas Parish, Louisiana.[468] C. Wildy Bonney. Age 29. Birth date: Dec. 1870. Physician. Single. Living alone.

- He appeared on the United States census on 19 Apr 1910 in Yazoo County, Mississippi.[453] Dr. Caleb W. Bonney. Age 39. Physician/ County & General farm. Living with his mother, Mattie Bonney and aunt, Mary B. Fields.

- He appeared on the United States census on 30 Jan 1920 in Yazoo County, Mississippi.[469] Wildy C. Bonney. Age 49. "Planter and Dr."/General farm. Head of household. Living with his cousin, Lilly Long. Address in 1920: Yazoo and Vicksburg Road.

- He appeared on the United States census on 25 Apr 1930 in Yazoo County, Mississippi.[470] Caleb W. Bonney. Age 59. Farmer/ General farm. Living with Lillian C. Long, age 48, divorced. Listed as a half-sister.

148. Sally Edith Wildy *(Laurena Matilda Hall [70], Samuel S. [13], William [3], John [1])* was born on 3 Nov 1848 in Yazoo County, Mississippi,[362] died on 20 Feb 1884 in Chaves County, New Mexico[363] at age 35, and was buried in Feb 1884 in Chaves County, New Mexico (South Side Cemetery).

Death Notes:
"Sallie Wildy Lea's health declined for several months in 1883- 84. She died on February 20, 1884, at the age of 34. "The hard, rough life and being far from a physician's care during her last illness was responsible for her early death," Ella Lea Dow said of her mother in 1936. Sallie's death was a great shock for the Capt.. Her stunned family buried her in the new South Side cemetery south of town. At the age of 42, Lea was widowed for the second time; and this time he had two small children dependent upon him."

Noted events in her life were:
- She appeared on the United States census on 14 Sep 1850 in Yazoo County, Mississippi.[337] Sally Wildy. Age 2. Living with her parents.

- She appeared on the United States census on 21 Aug 1860 in Yazoo County, Mississippi.[338]
  Sally Wildy. Age 12. Living with her parents.

- She appeared on the United States census on 2 Aug 1870 in Yazoo County, Mississippi.[339]
  Sallie Wildy. Age 21. At school. Living with her parents.

- She appeared on the United States census on 1 Jun 1880 in Lincoln County, New Mexico.[471]
  Sallie E. Lea. Age 30. Living with her husband, Jospeh C. Lea, family and boarders.

- She worked as a Boarding House Operator after 1881 in Chaves County, New Mexico.[363]
  She and her husband, Capt Lea, owned the old Smith and Wilburn Hotel built by Van C. Smith and operated it as a boarding house.

- She was described physically after 1881 in Chaves County, New Mexico.[472]
  "In her book [Buckboard Days], Sophie Alberding Poe describes Sallie Lea as "...a woman of medium height, with a mass of lovely brown hair coiled on top of her head. She had the graciousness typical of the women of the South." Sophie next met Ella Calfee, Capt. Lea's widowed sister. "Mrs. Calfee was very much a contrast to [Mrs. Lea], in appearance," she wrote. "Like her brother, the Captain, she was tall and angular. Both women wore long, full calico dresses reaching to the ground, and were much beruffled around the lower edge. They did not make the least pretense of being stylishly dressed. They had been in New Mexico so long that they had lost interest in 'prevailing styles.' They wore what seemed best suited to their needs." Mrs. Calfee and her two small sons, Frank and Edgar, occupied the upstairs room of the Lea residence; and the "gal tenderfoot" Sophie Alberding moved in with them. Mrs. Poe's description of her first meal at the Lea house provides some clues to what was going on in the community. The former Smith & Wilburn hotel, which had been a saloon and casino as well, was strictly a boarding house under Sallie Lea's supervision, with no liquor allowed. As long as she lived, no establishment selling liquor by the drink was permitted in Roswell. Some writers have claimed that Mrs. Lea had the liquor ban written into her deeds, but that seems to be more folklore than fact. "Capt. Lea, of course, keeps whisky in his store," Mrs. Poe writes, quoting her brother Fred, "for it's just as much a part of the supplies as sugar or flour or gunpowder. The cowboys wouldn't work if they couldn't look forward to a few drinks when they came to town. Capt. Lea sells it by the bottle or by the jug, but he won't allow them to drink it in the store...."

Sally married **Capt. Joseph Calloway Lea,** son of **Pleasant John Graves Lea** and **Lucinda Calloway,** on 20 Feb 1876 in Leflore County, Mississippi.[403] Joseph was born on 8 Nov 1841 in Bradley County, Tennessee,[352] died on 4 Feb 1904 in Chaves County, New Mexico[473] at age 62, and was buried in Feb 1904 in Chaves County, New Mexico.

Noted events in his life were:
- He served in the military a soldier in the CSA - 6th Missouri Regiment, Shelby's Brigade from 1861 to 1864.[352]
  "Although he reached the rank of colonel in 1864, he was known as "Capt. Lea" for the rest of his life."

- He worked as a Postmaster in 1879 in Roswell, Chaves County, New Mexico.[352]

- He appeared on the United States census on 1 Jun 1880 in Lincoln County, New Mexico.[471]
  Joseph Lea. Age 38. Stock Raiser. Living with his wife, Sallie E. Lea, and son, H. Wildy Lea; his widowed sister, Ella and her children; brother-in-law, Earnest L. Wildy and boarders. The occupations of the boarders ranged from a surveyor to sheep herders, farmers and stage drivers.

- He was elected as a member of Territorial House of Representatives in 1888 in Lincoln County, New Mexico.[474]

Children from this marriage were:

+ 203 M   i. **Harry Wildy Lea** was born on 3 Apr 1877 in Colfax County, New Mexico,[474] died on 19 Mar 1938 in Las Vegas County, New Mexico[475] at age 60, and was buried in Mar 1938 in Chaves County, New Mexico (South Park Cemetery).[476]

+ 204 F   ii. **Ellenor Laurena Lea** was born on 18 Mar 1881 in Roswell, Lincoln County, New Mexico,[474] died on 22 May 1962 in Roswell, Chaves County, New Mexico[477] at age 81, and was buried in May 1962 in Chaves County, New Mexico (South Park Cemetery).[478]

149. Ada Byron Wildy *(Laurena Matilda Hall [70], Samuel S. [13], William [3], John [1])* was born on 21 Mar 1849 in Yazoo County, Mississippi[364] and died on 29 Apr 1924 in Chaves County, New Mexico at age 75.

Noted events in her life were:

• She appeared on the United States census on 14 Sep 1850 in Yazoo County, Mississippi.[337]
Ada Wildy. Age 1. Living with her parents.

• She appeared on the United States census on 21 Aug 1860 in Yazoo County, Mississippi.[338]
Ada Wildy. Age 10. Living with her parents.

• She appeared on the United States census on 2 Aug 1870 in Yazoo County, Mississippi.[339]
Ada Wildy. Age 19. Living with her parents.

• She appeared on the United States census on 15 Jun 1880 in Yazoo County, Mississippi.[354]
Ada B. Holloma. Age 30. House keeping. Widow. Living with her daughter, Ellen in her father's household.

• She appeared on the United States census on 23 Apr 1910 in Chaves County, New Mexico.[479]
Ada B. Davis. Age 59. Living with her husband, George T. Davis and children. Married 2 times. Married 21 years. Children: 6; Living: 5. Address in 1910: 709 N. Washington.

• She appeared on the United States census on 9 Jan 1920 in Chaves County, New Mexico.[480]
Ada B. Davis. Age 68. Living with her husband, George T. Davis. Living next door to daughter's family, Mabel and Thomas H. Watts. Address in 1920: 907 West 11th St.

Ada married **William E. Holloman,** son of **Rev. John B. Holloman** and **Nancy H. Bruffey,** on 29 Apr 1874 in Yazoo County, Mississippi.[481] William was born on 16 May 1842 in Jasper County, Missouri,[482] died on 21 Oct 1875 in Yazoo County, Mississippi[367] at age 33, and was buried in Oct 1875 in Yazoo County, Mississippi (Wesley Chapel Cemetery).[483]

Noted events in his life were:
• He served in the military Sgt. CSA 46th Mississippi Infantry, Company E.[484]

The child from this marriage was:

+ 205 F   i.   **Helen Laurena Holloman** was born on 2 May 1875 in Yazoo County, Mississippi.[367]

Ada next married **William Douglas Edwards,** son of _____ _____ and _____ _____, on 19 Dec 1880 in Yazoo County, Mississippi.[485] William was born on 12 Jul 1840 in Hinds County, Mississippi.[486]

The child from this marriage was:

206 M   i.   **Earnest Edwards** was born on 29 Dec 1882 in Yazoo County, Mississippi.[363]

Ada next married **George Tennel Davis,** son of **Jesse Kincheloe Davis** and **Mary Eliza** _____, about 1888 in Chaves County, New Mexico.[486] George was born on 17 Mar 1851 in Gonzales County, Texas,[486] died on 12 Mar 1935 in Chaves County, New Mexico[367] at age 83, and was buried in Mar 1935 in Chaves County, New Mexico.

Noted events in his life were:

• He worked as a Blacksmith and Farmer after 1888 in Chaves County, New Mexico.[363]

• He appeared on the United States census on 23 Apr 1910 in Chaves County, New Mexico.[479]
George T. Davis. Age 59. Rancher/Stockman. Living with his wife, Ada B. and children. Married 1 time. Years married: 21. Address in 1910: 709 N. Washington.

• He appeared on the United States census on 9 Jan 1920 in Chaves County, New Mexico.[480]
George T. Davis. Age 68. Living with his wife, Ada. Living next door to daughter's family, Mabel and Thomas H. Watts.

Children from this marriage were:

+ 207 F   i.   **Mabel Davis** was born on 8 Jul 1889 in Chaves County, New Mexico[487] and died on 15 Dec 1939 in Chaves County, New Mexico[487] at age 50.

208 F   ii.   **Jessie Warren Davis** was born on 7 Oct 1890 in Chaves County, New Mexico[487] and died on 12 Aug 1921 in Eddy County, New Mexico[487] at age 30.

Noted events in her life were:
• She appeared on the United States census on 23 Apr 1910 in Chaves County, New Mexico.[479]
Jessie W. Davis. Age 19. Living with her parents.

209   F   iii.   **Ada Bell Davis** was born on 7 Nov 1893 in Chaves County, New Mexico,[487] died on 7 Jan 1969 in Eddy County, New Mexico[487] at age 75, and was buried in Jan 1969 in Eddy County, New Mexico (Hope Cemetery).

Noted events in her life were:
- She appeared on the United States census on 23 Apr 1910 in Chaves County, New Mexico.[479]
  Ada B. Davis. Age 17. Living with her parents.

210   F   iv.   **Ethel G. Davis** was born on 14 Nov 1895 in Chaves County, New Mexico,[487] died on 15 Mar 1972 in Eddy County, New Mexico[487] at age 76, and was buried in Mar 1972 in Eddy County, New Mexico (Hope Cemetery).

Noted events in her life were:
- She appeared on the United States census on 23 Apr 1910 in Chaves County, New Mexico.[479]
  Ethel G. Davis. Age 14. Living with her parents.

150. John Hall Wildy *(Laurena Matilda Hall [70], Samuel S. [13], William [3], John [1])* was born on 18 Oct 1853 in Yazoo County, Mississippi,[365] died on 5 Nov 1893 in Miami, Roberts County, Texas[363] at age 40, and was buried in Nov 1893 in Roberts County, Texas.

Death Notes:
"An article in the Eddy Argus on November 24, 1893, a reprint of an item from a Roswell newspaper, reported: "Last Sunday the sad news of the death of John H. Wildy reached his brother and sister here [Roswell]. He was killed at his ranch in the panhandle, by a horse falling with him." The brother and sister were Ernest L. Wildy and Ada Wildy Davis."

Noted events in his life were:
- He appeared on the United States census on 21 Aug 1860 in Yazoo County, Mississippi.[338]
  John Wildy. Age 7. Living with his parents.

- He appeared on the United States census on 2 Aug 1870 in Yazoo County, Mississippi.[339]
  John Wildy. Age 17. At school. Living with his parents.

- He appeared on the United States census on 21 Jun 1880 in Tulare County, California.[488]
  This could be the 1880 Census record for John H. Wildy of this family:
  J. H. Wildy. Age 25. Civil Engineer. Working for a railroad crew. Many members of the "household" are Chinese.

- He was educated at University of Mississippi in 1874 in Mississippi.[489]
  John Hall Wildy is listed in a book titled: <u>Announcements and Catalogue</u> by the University of Mississippi as a Civil Engineer living in Los Angeles, California.

- He attended school at Virginia Military Institute in 1874 in Lexington, Rockbridge County, Virginia.[490]
  ***"Wildy, John Hall**; Satartia, Yazoo Co., Miss.; 3 yrs.; Grad., U. of Miss.; Civil Engr., Los Angeles, Calif., Carson City, Nevada; Builder on the Western R. R.; Died in Miami, Fla., Nov. 5, 1893."*

The information here regarding his place of death could be incorrect as an extensive article states that he died in Miami, Texas. --rch

- He worked as a Civil Engineer and Cattle Rancher in California, Nevada, New Mexico and Texas.[491]
  The St. Augustine Ranch was at the eastern foot of the Organ Mts., just south of the White Sands. It was established by Thomas Bull at St. Augustine Spring just after the Mexican War. He sold the place to Warren T. Shedd of St. Louis, who made various improvements before selling the facility [in the late 1870's] to Benjamin Davies.

"Benjamin Davies [owner of the St. Augustine Ranch] died sometime in the late 1880's. This is where John H. Wildy enters the picture. He secured the position of administrator and manager of the ranch. Mrs. Davies had a daughter, Jessie, by a previous marriage, who later married Wildy. Wildy operated the San Augustine Ranch for just a few years because a relentless dry spell caused a great loss of cattle. Wildy took the rest of the cattle to the Texas Panhandle, where he met an untimely death."

Jessie Davies Wildy and her mother were unable to operate the San Augustine Ranch successfully, so they decided to sell it. It was purchased by William W. Cox. The ranch is said to be the place *"...where the famous gunfight took place in 1898 between Oliver Lee and Jim Gililland on one side and Pat Garrett and his deputies on the other."*
--

"Personal

*J. H. Wildy, one of our Donn Ana cattle barons, returned on Tuesday from Mexico, where he had gone to buy stock horses." --*Mesilla Valley Democrat

- His obituary was published in the Las Cruces Democrat on 15 Nov 1893 in Las Cruces, Dona Ana County, New Mexico.[492]
"Information from Miami, Texas reached here last Wednesday that Mr. J. H. Wildy had been thrown from his horse, and, after lingering several days, had died from injuries received."

John married **Jessie Davies,** daughter of **Unknown** and **Julia** _____, about 1889.[366]

151. Earnest Linwood Wildy *(Laurena Matilda Hall [70], Samuel S. [13], William [3], John [1])* was born on 29 Apr 1856 in Yazoo County, Mississippi[366] and died in May 1912 in Long Beach, Los Angeles County, California at age 56.

Noted events in his life were:

- He appeared on the United States census on 21 Aug 1860 in Yazoo County, Mississippi.[338]
Earnest Wildy. Age 5. Living with his parents.

- He appeared on the United States census on 2 Aug 1870 in Yazoo County, Mississippi.[339]
Earnest Wildy. Age 14. At school. Living with his parents.

- He appeared on the United States census on 1 Jun 1880 in Lincoln County, New Mexico.[471]
Earnest L. Wildy. Age 24. Clerk in store. Living in the household of his brother in-law, Joseph Lea.

- He appeared on the United States census on 29 Jun 1900 in Chaves County, New Mexico.[374]
Earnest L. Wildy. Age 44. Birth date: March 1856. Real Estate. Living with his wife and children: Douglas, Mamie and Harry. Years married: 17. His mother-in-law, Mary Hall also lives with them. Address in 1900: Missouri Avenue.

- He appeared on the United States census on 15 Apr 1910 in Los Angeles County, California.[493]
Earnest Wildy. Age 54. Real Estate Salesman. Living with his wife and children: Mary L., Harry H. and Leon R. Wildy. Married 27 years. Address in 1910: 2082 West 30th Street.

- He worked as a Real Estate Broker after 1890 in Chaves County, New Mexico.[363]
He was also elected to the Roswell Board of Trustees and served as Chairman of the Board from 1898 - 1899.

Earnest married **Willie Laurena Hall,** daughter of **William C. Hall** and **Mary E. Pace,** on 8 May 1883 in Warren County, Mississippi.[494] Willie was born on 14 Nov 1861 in Mississippi[366] and died on 22 May 1940 in Los Angeles County, California[376] at age 78.

General Notes:

"The steamer, State of California arrived early yesterday morning from San Francisco and way ports...The steamer took on considerable freight during the day, though citrus shipments are falling off to a marked extent, and sailed on time with the following passengers: ...Mrs. E. L. Wildy and Harry Wildy." -- The San Diego Union, *Sunday Morning, September 1st 1903*[495]

Noted events in her life were:

- She appeared on the United States census on 27 Jul 1870 in Warren County, Mississippi.[373]
W. E. Hall. Age 9. Living with her mother, M. E. Hall, age 36.

- She appeared on the United States census on 29 Jun 1900 in Chaves County, New Mexico.[374]
Willie H. Wildy. Age 38. Birth date: Nov 1861. Living with her husband, Earnest L. Wildy and children: Douglas, Mamie and Harry. Married 17 years. Children: 5; Living: 3. Her mother, Mary Hall is also listed in the household. Address in 1900: Missouri Avenue.

- She appeared on the United States census on 15 Apr 1910 in Los Angeles County, California.[493]
Willie Wildy. Age 48. Living with her husband and children: Mary L., Harry H. and Leon R.. Children: 6; 4 Living. Married 27 years. Address in 1910: 2082 West 30th Street.

- She appeared on the United States census on 10 Apr 1930 in Los Angeles County, California.[496]
Willie H. Wildy. Age 68. Widow. In the household is a lodger, Ismail Palafox. Address in 1930: 734 California Street.

- She appeared on the United States census on 24 Apr 1940 in Los Angeles County, California.[497]
Willie Wildy. Age 79. Widow. Resident at rural resthome.

- She had a residence in 1934 in Los Angeles County, California.[498]

Willie H. Wildy is listed as a registered voter in Los Angeles County, California in 1934. Her address is given: 425 S. Fremont Ave. She was a Democrat.

Children from this marriage were:

211 M   i. **Douglas Wildy** was born in Feb 1885 in Mississippi and died before 1910. He never married and had no children.

Noted events in his life were:
- He appeared on the United States census on 29 Jun 1900 in Chaves County, New Mexico.[374]
  Douglas Wildy. Age 15. Birth date: Feb 1885. At School. Living with his parents.

212 F   ii. **Mary L. Wildy** was born on 21 Feb 1887 in Mississippi and died on 29 Jul 1965 in Ventura County, California[499] at age 78. She never married and had no children.

Noted events in her life were:
- She appeared on the United States census on 29 Jun 1900 in Chaves County, New Mexico.[374]
  Mamie Wildy. Age 13. Birth date: Feb 1887. At school. Living with her parents.
- She appeared on the United States census on 15 Apr 1910 in Los Angeles County, California.[493]
  Mary L. Wildy. Age 20. Church organist. Living with her parents.
- She appeared on the United States census on 11 Apr 1930 in San Bernadino County, California.[500]
  Mary Wildy. Age 39. Inmate at Patton State Hospital. Laundress in the hospital.
- She appeared on the United States census on 10 Apr 1940 in Ventura County, California.[501]
  Mary Wildy. Age 53. Resident at the Camarillo State Mental Institution. Born in Mississippi.

+ 213 M   iii. **Harry Hill Wildy** was born on 5 Aug 1890 in Yazoo County, Mississippi[502] and died on 20 May 1978 in Los Angeles County, California[503] at age 87.

214 M   iv. **William Hall Wildy** was born on 13 Oct 1891 in Yazoo County, Mississippi,[369] died on 19 Sep 1892 in Yazoo County, Mississippi,[369] and was buried in Sep 1892 in Yazoo County, Mississippi (Wesley Chapel Cemetery).[504] He never married and had no children.

215 M   v. _____ **Wildy** was born about 1895 and died before 1900. He never married and had no children.

216 M   vi. **Leon Rudolph Wildy** was born on 25 Aug 1900 in New Mexico[505] and died on 6 Feb 1975 in Los Angeles County, California[506] at age 74. He never married and had no children.

Birth Notes:
1900 Census information may give his place of birth as New Mexico, not Mississippi. The record is hard to read. [rch 2008]

Noted events in his life were:
- He appeared on the United States census on 15 Apr 1910 in Los Angeles County, California.[493]
  Leon R. Wildy. Age 9. Living with his parents.
- He appeared on the United States census on 3 Apr 1930 in San Bernadino County, California.[507]
  Leon Wildy. Age 29. Inmate at Patton State Hospital.
- He appeared on the United States census on 10 Apr 1940 in Ventura County, California.[508]
  Leon Wildy. Age 40. Resident at Camarillo State Mental Hospital. Born in New Mexico.

154. Willie Laurena Hall *(William C.[71], Samuel S.[13], William[3], John[1])* was born on 14 Nov 1861 in Mississippi[366] and died on 22 May 1940 in Los Angeles County, California[376] at age 78.

General Notes:
"The steamer, State of California arrived early yesterday morning from San Francisco and way ports...The steamer took on considerable freight during the day, though citrus shipments are falling off to a marked extent, and sailed on time with the following passengers: ...Mrs. E. L. Wildy and Harry Wildy." -- The San Diego Union, Sunday Morning, September 1st 1903[495]

Noted events in her life were:
- She appeared on the United States census on 27 Jul 1870 in Warren County, Mississippi.[373]
  W. E. Hall. Age 9. Living with her mother, M. E. Hall, age 36.

- She appeared on the United States census on 29 Jun 1900 in Chaves County, New Mexico.[374]
  Willie H. Wildy. Age 38. Birth date: Nov 1861. Living with her husband, Earnest L. Wildy and children: Douglas, Mamie and Harry. Married 17 years. Children: 5; Living: 3. Her mother, Mary Hall is also listed in the household. Address in 1900: Missouri Avenue.

- She appeared on the United States census on 15 Apr 1910 in Los Angeles County, California.[493]
  Willie Wildy. Age 48. Living with her husband and children: Mary L., Harry H. and Leon R.. Children: 6; 4 Living. Married 27 years. Address in 1910: 2082 West 30th Street.

- She appeared on the United States census on 10 Apr 1930 in Los Angeles County, California.[496]
  Willie H. Wildy. Age 68. Widow. In the household is a lodger, Ismail Palafox. Address in 1930: 734 California Street.

- She appeared on the United States census on 24 Apr 1940 in Los Angeles County, California.[497]
  Willie Wildy. Age 79. Widow. Resident at rural resthome.

- She had a residence in 1934 in Los Angeles County, California.[498]
  Willie H. Wildy is listed as a registered voter in Los Angeles County, California in 1934. Her address is given: 425 S. Fremont Ave. She was a Democrat.

Willie married **Earnest Linwood Wildy,** son of **Maj. William W. Wildy** and **Laurena Matilda Hall,** on 8 May 1883 in Warren County, Mississippi.[494] Earnest was born on 29 Apr 1856 in Yazoo County, Mississippi[366] and died in May 1912 in Long Beach, Los Angeles County, California at age 56.

Noted events in his life were:
- He appeared on the United States census on 21 Aug 1860 in Yazoo County, Mississippi.[338]
  Earnest Wildy. Age 5. Living with his parents.

- He appeared on the United States census on 2 Aug 1870 in Yazoo County, Mississippi.[339]
  Earnest Wildy. Age 14. At school. Living with his parents.

- He appeared on the United States census on 1 Jun 1880 in Lincoln County, New Mexico.[471]
  Earnest L. Wildy. Age 24. Clerk in store. Living in the household of his brother in-law, Joseph Lea.

- He appeared on the United States census on 29 Jun 1900 in Chaves County, New Mexico.[374]
  Earnest L. Wildy. Age 44. Birth date: March 1856. Real Estate. Living with his wife and children: Douglas, Mamie and Harry. Years married: 17. His mother-in-law, Mary Hall also lives with them. Address in 1900: Missouri Avenue.

- He appeared on the United States census on 15 Apr 1910 in Los Angeles County, California.[493]
  Earnest Wildy. Age 54. Real Estate Salesman. Living with his wife and children: Mary L., Harry H. and Leon R. Wildy. Married 27 years. Address in 1910: 2082 West 30th Street.

- He worked as a Real Estate Broker after 1890 in Chaves County, New Mexico.[363]
  He was also elected to the Roswell Board of Trustees and served as Chairman of the Board from 1898 - 1899.

(Duplicate Line. See Person 151 on Page 96)

162. Tabitha Ann Russell *(William Ross Russell [79], Tabitha Hall [16], William [3], John [1])* was born on 13 Oct 1841 in Carroll County, Mississippi.[390]

Birth Notes:
Hand written in the Family Register of the William Ross Russell Family Bible: *"Tabitha Ann Rufsell Daughter of William and Elizabeth was Born the 13th day of October AD 1841."*

Noted events in her life were:
- She appeared on the United States census on 1 Oct 1850 in Carroll County, Mississippi.[387]
  Tobitha Russell. Age 8. Living with her father, William R. Russell and stepmother, Susan.

Tabitha married **Joseph Jamison,** son of _____ _____ and _____ _____, on 30 Oct 1859 in Carroll County, Mississippi.[119]

167. Thomas Shelton Russell *(William Ross Russell [79], Tabitha Hall [16], William [3], John [1])* was born on 20 Mar 1852 in Mississippi[400] and died on 31 Aug 1912 in Fort Worth, Tarrant County, Texas[401] at age 60.

Birth Notes:
Hand written in the Family Register of the William Ross Russell Family Bible: *"Thomas Shelton Russell was born 20th of March A.D. 1852 Son of Wm R. & Susan G. Russell"*

Hand written in the Family Register of the Thomas Benton Maddox Bible: *"Thomas S. Russell was born March 20th 1852 in Mississippi"*

Death Notes:
Hand written in the Family Register of the William Ross Russell Family Bible: *"Thomas Shelton Russell died Aug 31st 1912 Age 60"*

--

Hand written in the Family Register of the Thomas Benton Maddox Bible: *"Thomas S. Russell died Aug 31 / 1912 in Ft Worth at 1011 W. Weatherford St."*

Noted events in his life were:
• He appeared on the United States census on 18 Sep 1860 in Carroll County, Mississippi.[398]
Thomas Russell. Age 8. Living with his mother and step father.

• He appeared on the United States census on 9 Jul 1870 in Carroll County, Mississippi.[509]
Thomas Russell. Age 17. Works on farm. Living in the household of America Scrivner and her daughters. Relationship is unknown.

• He appeared on the United States census on 4 Jun 1880 in Tarrant County, Texas.[510]
Thos. S. Russell. Age 27. Farmer. Living with his wife, Sallie T. and daughter Bettie.

• He appeared on the United States census on 28 Jun 1900 in Tarrant County, Texas.[511]
Thomas Russel. Age 48. Birth date: March 1852. Dairyman. Living with his wife, Sarah and children: Claud, Hendley and Roxie.

• He appeared on the United States census on 15 Apr 1910 in Tarrant County, Texas.[512]
Thomas S. Russell. Age 58. Sexton at Cemetery. Living with his wife, Sallie and daughter, Roxie. Married 32 years. Address in 1910: 1317 Lake Avenue.

Thomas married **Sarah "Sallie" Thomas Maddox,** daughter of **Thomas Benton Maddox** and **Elizabeth "Bettie" L. Bernaugh,** on 17 Feb 1878 in Texas.[513] Sallie was born on 21 Oct 1858 in Missouri,[514] died on 15 Sep 1928 in Fort Worth, Tarrant County, Texas[515] at age 69, and was buried on 16 Sep 1928 in Tarrant County, Texas (East Oakwood Cemetery). She was usually called Sallie.

Marriage Notes:
Hand written in the Family Register of the Thomas Benton Maddox Bible: *"Thomas S. Russell and Sallie T. Maddox were married in Texas February 17th 1878"*

"Thomas Shelton Russell son of William Ross Russell and Susan Thomas Caperton married Sallie Thomas Maddox, daughter of Thomas B and Betty Burnaw Maddox on 17 February 1878." --from Wm. Ross Family Bible[514]

Birth Notes:
Hand written in the Family Register of the Thomas Benton Maddox Bible: *"Sarah Thomas Maddox was born October 21st 1858 in Mo"*

Death Notes:
Hand written in the Family Register of the William Ross Russell Family Bible: *"Sallie T Russell died Sept 15th 1928 age 69"*.

Hand written in the Family Register of the Thomas Benton Maddox Bible: *"Sallie T. Russell (nee Maddox) died September 15 - 1928 in Fort Worth, Texas"*

Noted events in her life were:
- She appeared on the United States census on 4 Jun 1880 in Tarrant County, Texas.[510]
  Sallie T. Russell. Age 22. Living with her husband, Thos. S. Russell and daughter Bettie.

- She appeared on the United States census on 28 Jun 1900 in Tarrant County, Texas.[511]
  Sarah Russel. Age 41. Birth date: Oct 1858. Living with her husband and children: Claud, Hendley and Roxie.

- She appeared on the United States census on 15 Apr 1910 in Tarrant County, Texas.[512]
  Sallie Russell. Age 51. Living with her husband, Thomas and daughter, Roxie. Married 32 years. Children: 9; Living: 7. Address in 1910: 1317 Lake Avenue.

Children from this marriage were:

217 F   i.   **Bettie Russell** was born about 1879 in Tarrant County, Texas.

                      Noted events in her life were:
- She appeared on the United States census on 4 Jun 1880 in Tarrant County, Texas.[510]
  Bettie Russell. Age 1. Living with her parents.

+ 218 M   ii.   **Claud Caperton Russell** was born on 22 Aug 1881 in Tarrant County, Texas,[516] died on 16 May 1965 in Tarrant County, Texas[517] at age 83, and was buried on 18 May 1965 in Tarrant County, Texas (Oakwood Cemetery).

+ 219 M   iii.   **Hendley Mathews Russell** was born on 2 Mar 1885 in Keller, Tarrant County, Texas,[518] died on 1 Apr 1951 in Tarrant County, Texas[519] at age 66, and was buried on 8 Apr 1951 in Tarrant County, Texas (Greenwood Cemetery).

220 F   iv.   **Roxie Russell** was born about Sep 1890 in Tarrant County, Texas.

                      Noted events in her life were:
- She appeared on the United States census on 28 Jun 1900 in Tarrant County, Texas.[511]
  Roxie Russel. Age 9. Living with her parents.

- She appeared on the United States census on 15 Apr 1910 in Tarrant County, Texas.[512]
  Roxie Russell. Age 19. Living with her parents.

176. Ada Beatrice Pierce *(Benjamin Franklin Pierce[89], Rhoda Hall[18], William[3], John[1])* was born on 2 Jun 1870 in Choctaw County, Mississippi and died on 8 Dec 1962 in Clinton, East Feliciana Parish, Louisiana[410] at age 92.

        Noted events in her life were:
- She appeared on the United States census on 18 Jun 1880 in Montgomery County, Mississippi.[407]
  Ada Pierce. Age 10. Living with her parents.

Ada married **William Madison Holmes,** son of _____ _____ and _____ _____, on 24 Dec 1887 in Montgomery County, Mississippi.[520] William was born on 24 Oct 1861 in Mississippi[521] and died in 1947 in Mississippi at age 86.

Descendants of John Hall (1735 - 1794)
of Bedford County, Virginia

Sixth Generation

182. Jessie Lena Hall *(John Andrew Houston [127], Joseph Marion [63], John [11], John, Jr. [2], John [1])* was born on 20 Oct 1884 in Lampasas County, Texas,[420] died on 22 Sep 1986 in Tom Green County, Texas[420] at age 101, and was buried in Sep 1986 in Tom Green County, Texas (Mereta Cemetery).[420]

Noted events in her life were:

- She appeared on the United States census on 30 Jun 1900 in Lampasas County, Texas.[414]
  Jessie E. Hall. Age 15. Birth date: Oct 1884. At school. Living with her father and siblings.

- She appeared on the United States census on 4 May 1910 in Tom Green County, Texas.[522]
  Jessie L. Jones. Age 25 (illegible). Living with her husband, Charley M. Jones and children: Oral I., Glades M., and Paul Jones. Married 8 years. Children 3; Living: 3.

- She appeared on the United States census on 18 Feb 1920 in Tom Green County, Texas.[523]
  Jessie L. Jones. Age 35. Living with her husband, Charles M. Jones and children: Oral I., Gladys M., Paul R., and T. H. Jones. Also in the household is her brother, Archie A. Hall. Address in 1920: San Angelo/Eden Road.

- She appeared on the United States census on 19 Apr 1930 in Tom Green County, Texas.[524]
  Jesse L. Jones. Age 45. Living with her husband, Charley M. Jones and son, T. H. Jones.

  Also in the household is a nephew [niece], Dorit [Dorothy] Smiley and niece, Margaret R. [Ruth] Smiley. The Smiley children are survivors of a tornado that killed the rest of the family (Charles Oscar and Belle Hall Smiley and 5 children.) on May 9, 1927 in Garland, Texas.

- She appeared on the United States census on 9 May 1940 in Tom Green County, Texas.[525]
  Jessie Jones. Age 55. Living with her husband, Charlie M. Jones.

  Also in the household is a niece, Margaret Smiley. Margaret Smiley is a daughter of sister, Belle Hall and a survivor of a tornado that killed the rest of the family, except her sister, Dorit on May 9, 1927 in Garland, Texas.

  The Jones family lived in the same house on April 1, 1935.

Jessie married **Charles Marion Jones,** son of _____ _____ and _____ _____, on 20 Jul 1902 in Lampasas County, Texas.[526] Charles was born on 24 Jul 1877 in Tennessee,[527] died on 11 May 1940 in Van Court, Tom Green County, Texas[528] at age 62, and was buried on 12 May 1940 in Tom Green County, Texas (Mereta Cemetery).[527]

Noted events in his life were:

- He appeared on the United States census on 4 May 1910 in Tom Green County, Texas.[522]
  Charley M. Hall. Age 32. Farmer/Gen Farm. Living with his wife, Jessie L. Jones and children: Oral I., Glades M., and Paul Jones. Married 8 years.

- He appeared on the United States census on 18 Feb 1920 in Tom Green County, Texas.[523]
  Charles M. Jones. Age 42. Farmer/General Farm. Living with his wife, Jessie L. Jones and children: Oral I., Gladys M., Paul R., and T. H. Jones. Also in the household is his brother-in-law, Archie A. Hall. Address in 1920: San Angelo/Eden Road.

- He appeared on the United States census on 19 Apr 1930 in Tom Green County, Texas.[524]
  Charley M. Jones. 52. Living with his wife, Jesse L. Jones and son, T. H. Jones. Also in the household is a nephew [niece], Dorit [Dorothy] Smiley and niece, Margaret R. [Ruth] Smiley. The Smiley children are survivors of a tornado that killed the rest of the family on May 9, 1927 in Garland, Texas.

- He appeared on the United States census on 9 May 1940 in Tom Green County, Texas.[525]
  Charlie M. Jones. Age 62. Farmer/Farm. Living with his wife, Jessie.

  Also in the household is a niece, Margaret Smiley. Margaret Smiley is a daughter of sister-in-law, Belle Hall and a survivor of a tornado that killed the rest of the family, except her sister, Dorit on May 9, 1927 in Garland, Texas.

  The Jones family lived in the same house on April 1, 1935.

184. Belle Hall (*John Andrew Houston* [127], *Joseph Marion* [63], *John* [11], *John, Jr.* [2], *John* [1]) was born on 30 Oct 1890 in Lampasas County, Texas,[421] died on 9 May 1927 in Garland, Dallas County, Texas[421] at age 36, and was buried in Garland, Dallas County, Texas (Mills Cemetery).[421] The cause of her death was was a result of injuries sustained from a tornado that killed 17 people in Garland, Texas.[421]

Burial Notes:
Tombstone:

"Inscription SMILEY Mother: Belle Hall, born October 30, 1890 Father: Chas Oscar, born March 17, 1890 Daughters: Lilath Merle, born June 20, 1914 Gretta May, born December 27, 1915 Charlena, born February 9, 1927 All Died May 9, 1927."

Noted events in her life were:
- She appeared on the United States census on 30 Jun 1900 in Lampasas County, Texas.[414]
  Bell Hall. Age 9. Birth date: Oct 1890. At school. Living with her father and siblings.

- She appeared on the United States census on 27 Apr 1910 in Burnet County, Texas.[426]
  Belle Hall. Age 19. Living with her father, John A. Hall and siblings.

- Her obituary was published in The Richardson Echo on 13 May 1927 in Richardson, Dallas County, Texas.[529]

Belle married **Charles Oscar Smiley,** son of **Henry Smiley** and **Amanda J. Hood,** about 1912 in Texas. Charles was born on 17 Nov 1890 in Tennessee,[530] died on 9 May 1927 in Garland, Dallas County, Texas[530] at age 36, and was buried in Garland, Dallas County, Texas (Mills Cemetery).[530] The cause of his death was was a result of injuries sustained from a tornado that killed 17 people in Garland, Texas.[530]

Noted events in his life were:
- His obituary was published in The Dallas Morning News on 11 May 1927 in Dallas, Dallas County, Texas.[531]

- His obituary was published in The Richardson Echo on 13 May 1927 in Richardson, Dallas County, Texas.[529]

185. Sweet Ora Hall (*John Andrew Houston* [127], *Joseph Marion* [63], *John* [11], *John, Jr.* [2], *John* [1]) was born on 14 May 1892 in Lampasas County, Texas,[422] died on 4 Dec 1977 in New York[422] at age 85, and was buried in Warren County, Virginia (Prospect Hill Cemetery).[423]

Noted events in her life were:
- She appeared on the United States census on 30 Jun 1900 in Lampasas County, Texas.[414]
  Sweet O. Hall. Age 8. Birth date: May 1892. At school. Living with her father and siblings.

- She appeared on the United States census on 27 Apr 1910 in Burnet County, Texas.[426]
  Ora Hall. Age 17. Living with her father, John A. Hall and siblings.

Sweet married **William Leonard MacAtee, Sr,** son of **George Washington MacAtee** and **Henrietta Maria Wight,** on 8 May 1915 in Houston, Harris County, Texas.[423] William was born on 20 Nov 1885 in Front Royal, Warren County, Virginia,[423] died on 16 Jun 1950 in Saint Petersburg, Pinellas County, Florida[423] at age 64, and was buried in Warren County, Virginia (Prospect Hill Cemetery).[423]

Noted events in his life were:
- His obituary was published on 22 Jun 1950 in Front Royal, Warren County, Virginia.[423]
  "Requiem Mass For L. W. MacAtee Held Here Tuesday
  A requiem mass was held in St. John's Catholic Church Tuesday morning at 10 o'clock for the late William Leonard MacAtee who died Friday, June the 16th at his home in St. Petersburg, Fla.

  He was the son of the late Mr. George MacAtee and Mrs. Nettie (Wight) MacAtee who lived at "Oakley," now the Johnson Nursing Home. Upon graduation from Eastern College, Front Royal, Va., Mr. MacAtee moved to Houston, Texas in 1902. He went to work for the Texas Company in 1912. He married Miss Ora Hall of Houston, Texas, in 1915, and in 1917 was transferred to the New York office of Texaco where he was stationed until 1948.

  Upon his retirement he moved to St. Petersburg, Fla. Mr. MacAtee's father and mother gave the land for the erection of the present St. John's Catholic Church in Front Royal. Mr. MacAtee and his brothers were among the first altar boys of

the church. He is survived by his wife, Mrs. Ora Hall MacAtee, a daughter, Miss Oralyn, of New York City, and a son, Richard. He is also survived by two sisters and a brother, Mrs. Nettie M. Kilbride, of Chicago, Ill., Mrs. Miriam M. Bryan, of Houston, Texas, and Claude MacAtee, of La Jolla, California.
Active pallbearers were Messrs Henry B. Weaver, George N. Buck, Alex Earle, Russell Corron, LeRoy Corron, and J. E. Mitchell, of Hagarstown, Md. Henry Weaver, George N. Buck, Je. E. Mitchel and Russell Corron were boyhood friends of Mr. MacAtee.

The honorary pallbearers were: John B. Flynn, Wiliiam Allen, John P. Dennis, Charles Jones, Ralph Glacel, Gus Martin, Stewart Smith, Robert Woods, Oscar Lassee, and Ross Hobby, all of New York City; Earl Goslee, Los Angeles, Calif.; Sheridan Denny, Seattle, Wash.; Gen. S. Gardner-Waller, Richmond, Va.; J. Johns, Tampa, Fla.; John Hardy, Norfolk, Va.; Medard Kerr, Houston, Texas; Frank Forsyth, Jr., Front Royal and Ralph Krass, Mt. Vernon, NY."

187. George Dewey Hall *(John Andrew Houston [127], Joseph Marion [63], John [11], John, Jr. [2], John [1])* was born on 5 Feb 1898 in Lampasas County, Texas,[427] died on 22 Dec 1946 in Edinburg, Hidalgo County, Texas[427] at age 48, and was buried on 25 Dec 1946 in Hidalgo County, Texas (Edinburg Cemetery).[427]

Noted events in his life were:
- He appeared on the United States census on 30 Jun 1900 in Lampasas County, Texas.[414]
  Dewey Hall. Age 2. Birth date: Feb 1898. Living with his father and siblings.

- He appeared on the United States census on 27 Apr 1910 in Burnet County, Texas.[426]
  Dewey Hall. Age 12. Living with his father, John A. Hall and siblings.

- He appeared on the United States census on 8 Apr 1930 in Hidalgo County, Texas.[532]
  Dewey Hall. Age 31. Mechanical Engineer - Machinery. Living with his wife, Ida and son, Dewey, Jr. Also in the household is a nephew, Dorit Smiley, age 9.

- He appeared on the United States census on 13 Apr 1940 in Hidalgo County, Texas.[533]
  Dewey Hall. Age. 41. Machinist Packing Plant. Steam Canning Plant. Living with his wife (2nd?), Louise. Address in 1940: 512 Sth 7th Street. Lived in the same place on April 1, 1935.

- He worked as a Mechanical Engineer in 1931 in Hidalgo County, Texas.[534]
  George Dewey Hall's occupation on his son's birth certificate (Allen Dee Arlyn Hall) was listed as a Mechanical Engineer. He was said to be 36 years old in 1931. Ida Adair was noted to be a school teacher.

- He worked as an Electrician - Mechanic - Auto Repair in 1946 in Hidalgo County, Texas.[427]
  His occupation was listed on his Death Certificate.

George married **Ida Mae Adair,** daughter of **Reuben Harvey Adair** and **Eula Wrenn,** about Feb 1920 in Texas. Ida was born about 1895 in Groesbeck, Limestone County, Texas and died on 15 Jun 1952 in Houston, Harris County, Texas[535] about age 57.

Noted events in her life were:
- She appeared on the United States census on 12 Jun 1900 in Limestone County, Texas.[536]
  Ida Adair. Age 5. Birth date: Jan 1895. Living with her parents and sisters.

- She appeared on the United States census on 22 Apr 1910 in Limestone County, Texas.[537]
  Ida M. Adair. Age 15. Farm laborer. Home farm. Living with her parents, Reuben H. and Eula Adair and sisters, Maggie F. and Mary H. Adair.

- She appeared on the United States census on 8 Jan 1920 in Cameron County, Texas.[538]
  Ida M. Adair. Age 23. Public School Teacher. Living with her parents.

- She appeared on the United States census on 8 Apr 1930 in Hidalgo County, Texas.[532]
  Ida Hall. Age 31. Teacher - Education. Living with her husband, Dewey and son, Dewey, Jr. Also in the household is a nephew, Dorit Smiley, age 9.

Children from this marriage were:

+ 221 M   i.   **George Dewey Hall, Jr.**[539] was born on 17 Dec 1921 in Edinburg, Hidalgo County, Texas,[540] died on 5 Aug 2012 in Bay City, Matagorda County, Texas[541] at age 90, and was buried on 10 Aug 2012 in Matagorda County, Texas (Cedarvale Cemetery).[542]

+ 222 M   ii.   **Allen Dee Arlyn Hall** was born on 4 Mar 1931 in Mercedes, Hidalgo County, Texas[534] and died on 31 Oct 2003 in Brownsville, Cameron County, Texas[543] at age 72.

George next married **Louise** _____, daughter of _____ _____ and _____ _____. Louise was born about 1909 in Arkansas. They had no children.

> **Noted events in her life were:**
> • She appeared on the United States census on 13 Apr 1940 in Hidalgo County, Texas.[533]
>
> Louise Hall. Age. 31. Living with her husband, Dewey Hall. Address in 1940: 512 Sth 7th Street. Lived in the same place on April 1, 1935.

188. Archie Andrew Hall (*John Andrew Houston [127], Joseph Marion [63], John [11], John, Jr. [2], John [1]*) was born on 16 Feb 1899 in Lampasas County, Texas,[428] died on 29 Jul 1960 in Crocket County, Texas[428] at age 61, and was buried on 31 Jul 1960 in Rankin County, Texas (Rankin Cemetery).[428]

> **Death Notes:**
> Archie A. Hall died on his residence/ranch located about 10 miles east of Iraan, Texas.
>
> **Noted events in his life were:**
> • He appeared on the United States census on 30 Jun 1900 in Lampasas County, Texas.[414]
> Jno. Hall. Age 1. Birth date: Feb 1899. Living with his father and siblings.
>
> • He appeared on the United States census on 27 Apr 1910 in Burnet County, Texas.[426]
> Archie A. Hall. Age 11. Living with his father, John A. Hall and siblings.
>
> • He appeared on the United States census on 18 Feb 1920 in Tom Green County, Texas.[544]
> Archie A. Hall. Age 20. Laborer. General Farm. Living with his sister, Jessie L. Jones and her family.

Archie married **Beulah Mae Bean,** daughter of _____ _____ and _____ _____, on 2 Sep 1923 in Tom Green County, Texas.[545] The marriage ended in divorce.

190. Edward G. Childress (*William Gordon Childress, Sr. [144], Laurena Matilda Hall [70], Samuel S. [13], William [3], John [1]*) was born about Jul 1872 in Yazoo County, Mississippi.

> **Noted events in his life were:**
> • He appeared on the United States census on 15 Jun 1880 in Yazoo County, Mississippi.[430]
> E. G. Childress. Age 7. Living with his parents.
>
> • He appeared on the United States census on 1 Jun 1900 in Yazoo County, Mississippi.[546]
> E. G. Childress. Age 27. Birth date: July 1872. Farmer. Living with his wife, Belle; children: Gordon and Geraldine and father, W. G. Childress. Married 8 years.
>
> • He appeared on the United States census on 15 Apr 1910 in Yazoo County, Mississippi.[547]
> E. G. Childress. Age 37. Cotton buyer through county. Living with wife, Belle and children: Gordon, Geraldine, Hellen and Flora Belle. Married 17 years.
>
> • He appeared on the United States census on 2 Jan 1920 in Yazoo County, Mississippi.[548]
> Edward G. Childress. Age 47. Farmer/ General farm. Living with his wife, Clara Belle and children: William G., Geraldine and Flora Bell. His brother and father are living several doors away.

Edward married **Clara Belle** _____, daughter of _____ _____ and _____ _____, about 1892 in New Mexico. Clara was born in Jul 1874 in Arizona.

> **Noted events in her life were:**
> • She appeared on the United States census on 1 Jun 1900 in Yazoo County, Mississippi.[546]
> Belle Childress. Age 25. Birth date: July 1874. Living with her husband, E. G. Childress and children. Married 8 years. Children: 2; Living: 2.
>
> • She appeared on the United States census on 15 Apr 1910 in Yazoo County, Mississippi.[547]
> Belle Childress. Age 36. Living with her husband, E. G. Childress and children: Gordon, Geraldine, Hellen and Flora Belle. Married 17 years. Childre: 4; Living: 4.

- She appeared on the United States census on 2 Jan 1920 in Yazoo County, Mississippi.[548]
Clara Belle Childress. Age 45. Living with her husband, Edward G. Childress and children: William G., Geraldine and Flora Bell.

Children from this marriage were:

223 M   i.   **Gordon Childress** was born in Nov 1892 in New Mexico.

       Noted events in his life were:
- He appeared on the United States census on 1 Jun 1900 in Yazoo County, Mississippi.[546]
Gordon Childress. Age 7. Birth date: Nov. 1892. Living with his parents.

- He appeared on the United States census on 15 Apr 1910 in Yazoo County, Mississippi.[547]
Gordon Childress. Age 16. Living with his parents, E. G. and Belle Childress and siblings: Geraldine, Hellen and Flora Belle. This Census record shows his birthplace as Mississippi.

- He appeared on the United States census on 2 Jan 1920 in Yazoo County, Mississippi.[549]
William G. Childress, 3rd. Age 26. Living with his parents.

224 F   ii.   **Geraldine Childress** was born in Dec 1896 in New Mexico.

       Noted events in her life were:
- She appeared on the United States census on 1 Jun 1900 in Yazoo County, Mississippi.[546]
Geraldine Childress. Age 3. Birth date: Dec 1896. Living with her parents.

- She appeared on the United States census on 15 Apr 1910 in Yazoo County, Mississippi.[547]
Geraldine Childress. Age 14. Living with her parents, E. G. and Belle Childress and siblings: Gordon, Hellen and Flora Belle. This Census record shows her birthplace as Mississippi.

- She appeared on the United States census on 2 Jan 1920 in Yazoo County, Mississippi.[549]
Geraldine Childress. Age 24. Living with her parents.

225 F   iii.   **Hellen Childress** was born about 1901 in Yazoo County, Mississippi.

       Noted events in her life were:
- She appeared on the United States census on 15 Apr 1910 in Yazoo County, Mississippi.[547]
Hellen Childress. Age 9. Living with her parents E. G. and Belle Childress and siblings: Gordon, Geraldine and Flora Belle.

226 F   iv.   **Flora Belle Childress** was born about 1906 in Yazoo County, Mississippi.

       Noted events in her life were:
- She appeared on the United States census on 15 Apr 1910 in Yazoo County, Mississippi.[547]
Flora Belle Childress. Age 4. Living with her parents, E. G. and Belle Childress and siblings: Gordon, Geraldine and Hellen.

- She appeared on the United States census on 2 Jan 1920 in Yazoo County, Mississippi.[549]
Flora Belle Childress. Age 14. Living with her parents.

191. Samuel Arthur Childress *(William Gordon Childress, Sr.* [144]*, Laurena Matilda Hall* [70]*, Samuel S.* [13]*, William* [3]*, John* [1]*)* was born on 18 Jul 1875 in Yazoo County, Mississippi.[550]

   Noted events in his life were:
- He appeared on the United States census on 15 Jun 1880 in Yazoo County, Mississippi.[430]
S. A. Childress. Age 5. Living with his parents.

- He appeared on the United States census on 16 Apr 1910 in Yazoo County, Mississippi.[432]
S. A. Childress. Age 34. Merchant at store. Head of household. Living with his wife, Flora and father, W. G. Childress. Married 5 years.

- He appeared on the United States census on 2 Jan 1920 in Yazoo County, Mississippi.[551]
Samuel A. Childress. Age 43. Merchant at General Store. Living with his wife, Flora B. and father, Wm. Gordon Childress, Sr.

- He appeared on the United States census on 29 Apr 1930 in Yazoo County, Mississippi.[552]
  Samuel A. Childress. Age 54. Retail merchant, dry goods store. Living with his wife, Flora B. Childress. Age at first marriage: 29.

Samuel married **Flora Mabel Bonney,** daughter of **Henry Clay Bonney** and **Alice Louise Bonney,** about 1905 in Mississippi. Flora was born on 3 Dec 1880 in Yazoo County, Mississippi[465] and died in Mar 1967 in Mississippi[553] at age 86. They had no children.

Noted events in her life were:
- She appeared on the United States census on 19 Jun 1900 in Yazoo County, Mississippi.[554]
  Flora Bonney. Age 19. Birth date: Dec 1880. Living with her parents and siblings.

- She appeared on the United States census on 16 Apr 1910 in Yazoo County, Mississippi.[432]
  Flora Childress. Age 29. Living with her husband, S. A. Childress. Also in the houeshold is W. G. Childress, her father-in-law.

- She appeared on the United States census on 2 Jan 1920 in Yazoo County, Mississippi.[551]
  Flora B. Childress. Age 39. Living with her husband, Samuel A. Childress and father-in-law, Wm. Gordon Childress, Sr.

- She appeared on the United States census on 29 Apr 1930 in Yazoo County, Mississippi.[552]
  Flora B. Childress. Age 49. Living with her husband, Samuel A. Childress. Age at first marriage: 24.

193. Lillie Childress *(William Gordon Childress, Sr.* [144]*, Laurena Matilda Hall* [70]*, Samuel S.* [13]*, William* [3]*, John* [1]*)* was born on 20 Jul 1879 in Yazoo County, Mississippi, died on 3 Mar 1971 in Yazoo County, Mississippi at age 91, and was buried in Yazoo County, Mississippi (Hart-Childress Cemetery).[437]

Noted events in her life were:
- She appeared on the United States census on 15 Jun 1880 in Yazoo County, Mississippi.[430]
  Lillie Childress. Age 1. Living with her parents.

- She appeared on the United States census on 7 Jun 1900 in Caddo Parish, Louisiana.[555]
  Lillie Long. Age 20. Birth date: Jul 1879. Boarder. Living with her husband, Lawrence W. Long. Married 2 years. Address in 1900: 616 Crockett Street.

- She appeared on the United States census on 26 Apr 1910 in Pulaski County, Arkansas.[556]
  Lillie Long. Age 30. Living with her husband, Lawrence W. Long and son, Lawrence W. Long, Jr.

- She appeared on the United States census on 30 Jan 1920 in Yazoo County, Mississippi.[469]
  Lilly Long. Age 40. House work. Cousin. Living with her cousin, Wildy C. Bonney. Address in 1920: Yazoo and Vicksburg Road.

- She appeared on the United States census on 25 Apr 1930 in Yazoo County, Mississippi.[470]
  Lillian C. Long. Age 48. Divorced. Living with Caleb W. Bonney. Listed as a half-sister.

Lillie married **Lawrence W. Long,** son of **L. H. Long** and **Anna B. Jackson,** about 1898 in Yazoo County, Mississippi. The marriage ended in divorce before 1920. Lawrence was born in Jul 1878 in Louisiana and died on 24 Mar 1928 in Tammany Parish, Louisiana[557] at age 49.

Noted events in his life were:
- He appeared on the United States census on 7 Jun 1900 in Caddo Parish, Louisiana.[555]
  Lawrence W. Long. Age 21. Birth date: Jul 1878. Salesman, dry goods. Boarder. Living with his wife, Lillie. Married 2 years. Address in 1900: 616 Crockett Street.

- He appeared on the United States census on 26 Apr 1910 in Pulaski County, Arkansas.[556]
  Lawrence W. Long. Age 32. Agent for Oats Co. Living with his wife, Lillie and son, Lawrence W. Long, Jr.

The child from this marriage was:
   227 M   i. **Dr. Lawrence Wilburn Long, Jr.** was born on 17 Mar 1902 in Hinds County, Mississippi,[558] died in Jul 1986[558] at age 84, and was buried in Yazoo County, Mississippi (Bonney Cemetery (AKA Churchill Plantation Cemetery)).[558]

Noted events in his life were:
- He appeared on the United States census on 26 Apr 1910 in Pulaski County, Arkansas.[556]
  Lawrence W. Long, Jr. Age 8. Living with his parents.

195. William Gordon Childress *(Samuel Hall Childress [145], Laurena Matilda Hall [70], Samuel S. [13], William [3], John [1])* was born on 11 Dec 1863 in Yazoo County, Mississippi,[445] died on 5 Mar 1944 in Yazoo County, Mississippi at age 80, and was buried in Mar 1944 in Yazoo County, Mississippi (Hart-Childress Cemetery).[446]

Noted events in his life were:
- He appeared on the United States census on 29 Jun 1870 in Yazoo County, Mississippi.[439]
  William Childress. Age 6. Living with his parents.

- He appeared on the United States census on 15 Jun 1880 in Yazoo County, Mississippi.[440]
  Willie Childress. Age 19. At home. Living with his father, S. H. Childress, stepmother, Lula and siblings: Minnie and Harry.

- He appeared on the United States census on 22 Jun 1900 in Yazoo County, Mississippi.[559]
  Will G. Childress. Age 36. Birth date: Dec 1863. Farmer. Living with his wife, Harriet E. Childress and children: Georgia R., Frankie, Sam H., Lacey, Rob, Ada A., Silah D., and Margaret E Childress. Number of years married: 16.

- He appeared on the United States census on 16 Apr 1910 in Yazoo County, Mississippi.[441]
  W. G. Childress (Indexed as Children). Age 46. Farm Manager. Widower. Living with his children: Frankie, Lacey, Sam, Lee, Ada, Cela Inez, and Margaret Childress. Also in the household is his father, Sam Childress; nephew, T. P. Carson, age 22 and housekeeper, Molly Rennolds.

William married **Elizabeth "Bettie" Harriet Perry,** daughter of _____ _____ and _____ _____, on 7 May 1884 in Yazoo County, Mississippi.[403] Bettie was born on 23 Jan 1865 in Mississippi, died on 18 Aug 1909 in Yazoo County, Mississippi at age 44, and was buried in Aug 1909 in Yazoo County, Mississippi (Hart-Childress Cemetery).[560] She was usually called Bettie.

Noted events in her life were:
- She appeared on the United States census on 22 Jun 1900 in Yazoo County, Mississippi.[559]
  Harriet E. Childress. Age 36. Birth date: Jan 1865. Living with her husband, Will G. Childress and children. Married 16 years. Children: 8; Living: 8.

Children from this marriage were:

228 F   i.   **Georgia Russell Childress** was born on 2 Mar 1885 in Yazoo County, Mississippi, died on 29 Nov 1903 in Yazoo County, Mississippi at age 18, and was buried in Yazoo County, Mississippi (Hart-Childress Cemetery).[561] She never married and had no children.

       Noted events in her life were:
       - She appeared on the United States census on 22 Jun 1900 in Yazoo County, Mississippi.[559]
        Georgia R. Childress. Age 15. Birth date: March 1885. At school. Living with her parents and siblings.

229 F   ii.   **Frankie Childress** was born about Jul 1887 in Yazoo County, Mississippi.

       Noted events in her life were:
       - She appeared on the United States census on 22 Jun 1900 in Yazoo County, Mississippi.[559]
        Frankie Childress. Age 12. Birth date: July 1887. Living with her parents and siblings.

       - She appeared on the United States census on 16 Apr 1910 in Yazoo County, Mississippi.[441]
        Frankie Childress. Age 22. Living with her father and siblings.

+ 230 M   iii.   **Samuel H. Childress** was born on 21 Dec 1888 in Yazoo County, Mississippi.[562]

231 M   iv.   **Lacey Childress** was born about Oct 1892 in Yazoo County, Mississippi.

       Noted events in his life were:
       - He appeared on the United States census on 22 Jun 1900 in Yazoo County, Mississippi.[559]
        Lacey Childress. Age 7. Birth date: Oct 1892. Living with his parents and siblings.

I cannot explain the close birth dates between Lacey and Robert Lee. There is an illegible note next to Lacey's name on this census. Second family? Adoption? --rch, 2012

- He appeared on the United States census on 16 Apr 1910 in Yazoo County, Mississippi.[441]
Lacey Childress. Age 17. Laborer/farm. Living with his father and siblings.

232 M   v. **Robert Lee Childress** was born on 31 Jan 1894 in Yazoo County, Mississippi, died on 14 Dec 1957 in Yazoo County, Mississippi at age 63, and was buried in Dec 1957 in Yazoo County, Mississippi (Hart-Childress Cemetery).[563]

Noted events in his life were:
- He appeared on the United States census on 22 Jun 1900 in Yazoo County, Mississippi.[559]
Rob Lee Childress. Age 7. Birth date: Jan 1893. Living with his parents and siblings. I cannot explain the close birth dates between Lacey and Robert Lee.

- He appeared on the United States census on 16 Apr 1910 in Yazoo County, Mississippi.[441]
Lee Childress. Age 17. Laborer/farm. Living with his father and siblings.

233 F   vi. **Ada A. Childress** was born about Dec 1895 in Yazoo County, Mississippi.

Noted events in her life were:
- She appeared on the United States census on 22 Jun 1900 in Yazoo County, Mississippi.[559]
Ada A. Childress. Age 4. Birth date: Dec 1895. Living with her parents.

- She appeared on the United States census on 16 Apr 1910 in Yazoo County, Mississippi.[441]
Ada Childress. Age 14. Living with her father and siblings.

234 F   vii. **Cela Inez Childress** was born about Apr 1898 in Mississippi.

Noted events in her life were:
- She appeared on the United States census on 22 Jun 1900 in Yazoo County, Mississippi.[559]
Selah I. Childress. Age 2. Birth date: April 1898. Living with her parents and siblings.

- She appeared on the United States census on 16 Apr 1910 in Yazoo County, Mississippi.[441]
Cela Inez Childress. Age 11. Living with her father and siblings.

235 F   viii. **Margaret E. Childress** was born about Mar 1900 in Yazoo County, Mississippi.

Noted events in her life were:
- She appeared on the United States census on 22 Jun 1900 in Yazoo County, Mississippi.[559]
Margaret E. Childress. Age 3/12. Birth date: March 1900. Living with her parents and siblings.

- She appeared on the United States census on 16 Apr 1910 in Yazoo County, Mississippi.[441]
Margaret Childress. Age 10. Living with her father and siblings.

196. Ada "Minnie" Childress (*Samuel Hall Childress* [145], *Laurena Matilda Hall* [70], *Samuel S.* [13], *William* [3], *John* [1]) was born on 27 Jun 1866 in Yazoo County, Mississippi, died on 26 Feb 1889 in Yazoo County, Mississippi at age 22, and was buried in Yazoo County, Mississippi (Hart-Childress Cemetery). She was usually called Minnie.

Noted events in her life were:
- She appeared on the United States census on 29 Jun 1870 in Yazoo County, Mississippi.[439]
Ada Childress. Age 3. Living with her parents and brothers: William and Robinson.

- She appeared on the United States census on 15 Jun 1880 in Yazoo County, Mississippi.[440]
Minnie Childress. Age 16. Living with her father, S. H. Childress and step mother, Lula.

Minnie married **James R. Lacey** _____, son of _____ _____ and _____ _____, on 9 Dec 1885 in Yazoo County, Mississippi.[403] They had no children.

203. Harry Wildy Lea (*Sally Edith Wildy* [148], *Laurena Matilda Hall* [70], *Samuel S.* [13], *William* [3], *John* [1]) was born on 3 Apr 1877 in Colfax County, New Mexico,[474] died on 19 Mar 1938 in Las Vegas County, New Mexico[475] at age 60, and was buried in Mar 1938 in Chaves County, New Mexico (South Park Cemetery).[476]

Medical Notes:

"Harry Wildy Lea was adjudged insane in 1905, and committed to the state institution for the insane, where he remained until his death on March 19, 1938. He was survived by his wife Alice Howard Lea and his daughter Annie Wildy Lea. Alice Howard Lea died intestate November 8, 1938, leaving as her only heir at law the defendant, who were formerly Annie Wildy Lea."[475]

Noted events in his life were:

• He appeared on the United States census on 1 Jun 1880 in Lincoln County, New Mexico.[471]
   H. Wildy Lea. Age 3. Living with his parents.

Harry married **Alice A. Howard,** daughter of _____ _____ and _____ _____. Alice was born about Mar 1878 in Tennessee and died on 8 Nov 1938 in New Mexico about age 60.

The child from this marriage was:

+ 236   F   i.   **Annie Wildy Lea** was born in New Mexico.

204. Ellenor Laurena Lea *(Sally Edith Wildy* [148]*, Laurena Matilda Hall* [70]*, Samuel S.* [13]*, William* [3]*, John* [1]*)* was born on 18 Mar 1881 in Roswell, Lincoln County, New Mexico,[474] died on 22 May 1962 in Roswell, Chaves County, New Mexico[477] at age 81, and was buried in May 1962 in Chaves County, New Mexico (South Park Cemetery).[478]

Birth Notes:
Find A Grave lists her birth date as May 18, 1881.

Noted events in her life were:

• She resided at the Horace K. Thurber family home after her mother died, in 1884 in San Jose, California.[474] Thurber and Lea were business partners in various ventures.

• She appeared on the United States census on 16 Apr 1910 in Chaves County, New Mexico.[564]
   Ella L. Bedell. Age 28. Living with her husband, Edgar Bedell, and daughter, Ellanor, age 5. Years married: 6. Children: 1; Living: 1.

Ellenor married **Edgar L. "Ted" Lucius Bedell,** son of _____ _____ and _____ _____, about 1904 in New Mexico. Ted was born about 1877 in Kansas. He was usually called Ted.

Noted events in his life were:

• He appeared on the United States census on 16 Apr 1910 in Chaves County, New Mexico.[564]
   Edgar L. Bedell. Age 33. Real Estate Salesman. Living with his wife Ella L. and daughter, Ellenor, age 5. Married 6 years.

Ellenor next married **Hiram Millet Dow,** son of **James Lesile "Les" Dow** and **Mary Molly Ann Neatherlin,**. Hiram was born on 21 Apr 1885 in Texas,[565] died in Mar 1969 in Roswell, Chaves County, New Mexico[565] at age 83, and was buried in Mar 1969 in Chaves County, New Mexico (South Park Cemetery).[565]

General Notes:

"Hiram graduated from the NM Military Institute in 1904 and received his law degree from Washington and Lee University in 1908, and was a former Mayor of Roswell. In 1936, Dow was elected lieutenant governor of the Democratic ticket with Governor Clyde Tingley and served one term. He became a distinguished attorney for the petroleum industry. He served many years a Civilian Aide to the Secretary of the Army and received many other honors and recognitions during his lifetime."[565]

205. Helen Laurena Holloman *(Ada Byron Wildy* [149]*, Laurena Matilda Hall* [70]*, Samuel S.* [13]*, William* [3]*, John* [1]*)* was born on 2 May 1875 in Yazoo County, Mississippi.[367]

Noted events in her life were:

• She appeared on the United States census on 15 Jun 1880 in Yazoo County, Mississippi.[354]
   Ellen Holoman. Age 5. Living with her mother, Ada B. Holloman and grandfather, W. W. Wildy.

Helen married **John C. Peck,** son of _____ _____ and _____ _____, in New Mexico. [363]

Noted events in his life were:
- He worked as a Sheriff about 1930 in Chaves County, New Mexico.[363]

207. Mabel Davis (*Ada Byron Wildy[149], Laurena Matilda Hall[70], Samuel S.[13], William[3], John[1]*) was born on 8 Jul 1889 in Chaves County, New Mexico[487] and died on 15 Dec 1939 in Chaves County, New Mexico[487] at age 50.

Noted events in her life were:
- She appeared on the United States census on 23 Apr 1910 in Chaves County, New Mexico.[479]
Mabel Davis. Age 20. Living with her parents.

- She appeared on the United States census on 9 Jan 1920 in Chaves County, New Mexico.[566]
Mabel Watts. Age 30. Living with his her husband, Thomas H. Watts and children: Mabel H. and Thomas H. Watts, Jr. Living next door to her parents. Address in 1920: 1108 North Union St.

Mabel married **Thomas H. Watts,** son of _____ _____ and _____ _____, in New Mexico. Thomas was born about 1869 in Kentucky.

Noted events in his life were:
- He appeared on the United States census on 9 Jan 1920 in Chaves County, New Mexico.[566]
Thomas H. Watts. Age 51. Solicitor/Canning factory. Living with his wife, Mabel and children: Mabel H. and Thomas H. Watts, Jr. Living next door to his wife's parents. Address in 1920: 1108 North Union St.

213. Harry Hill Wildy (*Earnest Linwood Wildy[151], Laurena Matilda Hall[70], Samuel S.[13], William[3], John[1]*) was born on 5 Aug 1890 in Yazoo County, Mississippi[502] and died on 20 May 1978 in Los Angeles County, California[503] at age 87.

Birth Notes:
1900 Census information may give a birth date of July 1890.

General Notes:
"The steamer, State of California arrived early yesterday morning from San Francisco and way ports...The steamer took on considerable freight during the day, though citrus shipments are falling off to a marked extent, and sailed on time with the following passengers: ...Mrs. E. L. Wildy and Harry Wildy." -- The San Diego Union, Sunday Morning, September 1st 1903[495]

Noted events in his life were:
- He appeared on the United States census on 29 Jun 1900 in Chaves County, New Mexico.[374]
Harry Wildy. Age 9. Birth date: Aug 1890. Living with his parents.

- He appeared on the United States census on 15 Apr 1910 in Los Angeles County, California.[493]
Harry H. Wildy. Age 19. Living with his parents.

- He resided at 4547 West 17th in 1924 in Los Angeles County, California.[567]
His occupation was listed as a surveyor on the Los Angeles County Voter Registration List of 1924.

- He appeared on the United States census on 9 Apr 1930 in Los Angeles County, California.[568]
H. H. Wildy. Age 39. Civil Engineer. Living with his wife "Mrs. H. H. Wildy". Married at age 31. Address in 1930: 4547 West 17th Street.

- He appeared on the United States census on 5 Apr 1940 in Los Angeles County, California.[569]
Harry H. Wildy. Age 49. Civil Engineer/ State of California. Living with his wife, Vivian R. Wildy. Lived in the same house on April 1, 1935. Address in 1940: 400 North Electric.

Harry married **Vivian Rose Dee,** daughter of **August Dee** and **Frances Peltz,** about 1921 in Los Angeles County, California. Vivian was born on 11 Sep 1885 in Minnesota and died on 23 Jan 1984 in Alhambra, Los Angeles, California[570] at age 98. They had no children.

Noted events in her life were:
- She appeared on the United States census on 8 Jun 1900 in Los Angeles County, California.[571]
Rose Dee. Age 14. Birth date: Sep 1885. At school. Living with her mother and brother Herman.

- She resided at 4547 West 17th in 1924 in Los Angeles County, California.[572]
Mrs. Vivian R. Wildy. Her occupation was listed as a housewife on the Los Angeles County Voter Registration List of 1924.

- She appeared on the United States census on 9 Apr 1930 in Los Angeles County, California.[568]
  Mrs. H. H. Wildy. Age 45. Living with her husband H. H. Wildy. Married at age 37. Address in 1930: 4547 West 17th Street.

- She appeared on the United States census on 5 Apr 1940 in Los Angeles County, California.[569]
  Vivian R. Wildy. Age 54. Living with her husband, Harry H. Wildy. Lived in the same house on April 1, 1935. Address in 1940: 400 North Electric.

218. Claud Caperton Russell *(Thomas Shelton Russell [167], William Ross Russell [79], Tabitha Hall [16], William [3], John [1])* was born on 22 Aug 1881 in Tarrant County, Texas,[516] died on 16 May 1965 in Tarrant County, Texas[517] at age 83, and was buried on 18 May 1965 in Tarrant County, Texas (Oakwood Cemetery).

Noted events in his life were:
- He appeared on the United States census on 28 Jun 1900 in Tarrant County, Texas.[511]
  Claud C. Russel. Age 18. Birth date: Aug 1881. Living with his parents.

- He appeared on the United States census in 1930 in Tarrant County, Texas.[573]
  Claude Russell. Age 48. Living with his wife, Josephine and daughter, Bernice. Also in the household is his mother-in-law, Francis Miller.

Claud married **Josephine Theadore Miller,** daughter of **Joe Miller** and **Frances Smith,** about 1922 in Texas. Josephine was born about 1884 in Texas, died on 22 Nov 1936 in Tarrant County, Texas about age 52, and was buried on 23 Nov 1936 in Tarrant County, Texas (Oakwood Cemetery).

Noted events in her life were:
- She appeared on the United States census in 1930 in Tarrant County, Texas.[574]
  Josephine Russell. Age 46. Living with her husband, Claud Russell and daughter, Bernice. Also in the household is her mother, Francis Miller.

219. Hendley Mathews Russell *(Thomas Shelton Russell [167], William Ross Russell [79], Tabitha Hall [16], William [3], John [1])* was born on 2 Mar 1885 in Keller, Tarrant County, Texas,[518] died on 1 Apr 1951 in Tarrant County, Texas[519] at age 66, and was buried on 8 Apr 1951 in Tarrant County, Texas (Greenwood Cemetery).

Birth Notes:
Hand written in the Family Register of the William Ross Russell Family Bible: *"Hendley Matthews son of Thomas S and Sallie T Russell was born Mar 2nd 1885"*

From the Family Record Section of the Hendley Matthews Russell Bible: GRAND PARENTS Father's Father: Thos. S. Russell, Born: When: _____, Where: _____, Died: When: 31 August 1912, Where: Fort Worth Texas; Father's Mother: Sallie T. Russell, Born: When: _____, Where: _____, Died: When: _____, Where: _____; Mother's Father: Born: When: 2 December 1837, Where: Somerville, AL, Died: When: 4 August 1908, Where: Dallas TX; Mother's Mother: Annie M. Spain, Born: When: 22 February 1842, Where: Nashville, TN, Died: When: 22 September 1922, Where: Dallas, TX; PARENTS Father: Hendley Russell, Born: When: 2 March 1885, Where: Keller, TX, Died: When: _____, Where: _____; Mother: Tula Russell, Born: When: 26 August 1882, Where: Palo Pinto, TX, Died: When: _____, Where: _____; CHILDREN Wade Aldredge Russell, Born: When: 22 December 1904, Where: No Fort Worth, Died: When: _____, Where: _____; Married: When: 22 February 1935 Annabel Goldthwaite.

Hand written in the Family Register of the Thomas Benton Maddox Bible: *"Hendley Matthews Russell was born March 2nd 1885"*

Noted events in his life were:
- He appeared on the United States census on 28 Jun 1900 in Tarrant County, Texas.[511]
  Hendley M. Russel. Age 15. Living with his parents.

Hendley married **Annie Lee "Tula" Spain,** daughter of **John Dent Spain** and **Annie Millicent Barclift,** on 2 Mar 1904 in Fort Worth, Tarrant County, Texas.[575] Tula was born on 26 Aug 1882 in Texas[576] and died about 1970 in Tarrant County, Texas about age 88. She was usually called Tula.

Marriage Notes:

Hendley Matthews Russell Bible Family Record: Annie Lee Spain and Hendley M. Russell Marriage Record

From the Marriage Certificate of Hendley M Russell and Tula Spain: "WHAT THEREFORE GOD HATH JOINED TOGETHER LET NOT MAN PUT ASUNDER. THIS IS TO CERTIFY THAT "Hendley M. Russell" AND "Tula Spain" WERE UNITED BY ME IN HOLY MATRIMONY AT "No. Fort Worth" ON THE "2nd" DAY OF "March" IN THE YEAR OF OUR LORD ONE THOUSAND "Nine" HUNDRED AND "Four" IN THE PRESENCE OF WITNESSES. SIGNED "J. J. Creed Methodist Minister" THEREFORE SHALL A MAN LEAVE HIS FATHER AND HIS MOTHER AND SHALL CLEAVE UNTO HIS WIFE AND THEY SHALL BE OF ONE FLESH.

Hand written in the Family Register of the William Ross Russell Bible: *"Hendley Matthews Russell second son of Thomas Shelton and Sallie Russell married Annie Lee Spain daughter of John and Annie Spain on March 2nd 1904."*

Hand written in the Marriage Register of the John Dent Spain Bible: *"Tula Spain of Ft. Worth Tarrant Co Tex and Hendley M. Russell of same County on 2nd of March 1904, at the home of the brides father & mother, by Rev. J. J. Creed."*[577]

Birth Notes:

Hand written in the Family Register of the John Dent Spain Bible: *"Annie L Spain, Daughter of John D. and Annie M. Spain, was born August - 26 - 1882."*

Seventh Generation

221. George Dewey Hall, Jr.[539] *(George Dewey* [187]*, John Andrew Houston* [127]*, Joseph Marion* [63]*, John* [11]*, John, Jr.* [2]*, John* [1]*)* was born on 17 Dec 1921 in Edinburg, Hidalgo County, Texas,[540] died on 5 Aug 2012 in Bay City, Matagorda County, Texas[541] at age 90, and was buried on 10 Aug 2012 in Matagorda County, Texas (Cedarvale Cemetery).[542]

> **Noted events in his life were:**
> - He appeared on the United States census on 8 Apr 1930 in Hidalgo County, Texas.[532]
>   Dewey Hall, Jr. Age 8. Living with his parents. Also in the household is a cousin, Dorit Smiley, age 9.
>
> - His obituary was published in the <u>The Bay City Tribune</u> on 7 Aug 2012 in Bay City, Matagorda County, Texas.[541]
>   *"George Dewey Hall, Jr.*
>   *Dec. 17, 1921*
>   *Aug. 5, 2012*
>   *George Dewey Hall, Jr., 90, was born in Edinburg, Texas to the late George Dewey Hill, Sr. and Ida Mae Adair Hall on December 17, 1921. He slipped the bonds of this earth on August 5, 2012.*
>   *He was raised in the Rio Grande Valley by his schoolteacher mother and graduated salutatorian at El Jardin High School in Brownsville, Texas in May 1939.*
>   *George served his country during World War II as a civil servant attached to the 8th Air Force at the Warrington Air Base in England and at air bases in San Antonio.*
>   *After the war, he met his wife, Brondelle Moseley in Brownsville where they began their 65-year-long romance.*
>   *Work took George to chemical plants in Texas and Mississippi and eventually to Bay City where he retired from Celanese. George was a member of the Sons of the American Revolution, Cradle of Texas Chapter.*
>   *He is survived by: his wife, Brondelle; son, Tim Hall and wife Susan; daughter, Ann Patterson; grandchildren, David Hall, Christopher Hall, Kristen Patterson, Stephanie and Sergio Perez, Jim Patterson and great-grandchildren, Mila and Penelope Perez.*
>   *Graveside services will be from 9 a.m. Friday, August 10, 2012 at Cedarvale Cemetery in Bay City with the Rev. Jeff Gantz officiating.*
>   *The family will receive friends and family at the Bay House on the Legacy Campus following the service.*
>   *Memorial donations may be made to the Bay City Public Library in his memory.*
>   *His grandchildren and fellow Cradle of Texas members will serve as honorary pallbearers.*
>   *Online condolences may be shared with the family by visiting www.taylorbros.net <http://www.taylorbros.net>.*
>   *Arrangements are with Taylor Bros. Funeral Home in Bay City, 979-245-4613."*

George married **Frances Brondell Moseley**,[539] daughter of **Elijah M. Moseley** and **Estelle Gregg**, about 1947 in Texas. Frances was born on 19 Oct 1929 in Cherokee County, Texas.[578]

Children from this marriage were:

+ 237 M   i.   **Timothy Elijah Hall**

+ 238 F   ii.   **Eleanor Ann Hall**

222. Allen Dee Arlyn Hall *(George Dewey* [187]*, John Andrew Houston* [127]*, Joseph Marion* [63]*, John* [11]*, John, Jr.* [2]*, John* [1]*)* was born on 4 Mar 1931 in Mercedes, Hidalgo County, Texas[534] and died on 31 Oct 2003 in Brownsville, Cameron County, Texas[543] at age 72.

> **Noted events in his life were:**
> - His obituary was published in the Brownsville Herald on 6 Dec 2003 in Brownsville, Cameron County, Texas.[543]
>   *"ALLEN D. HALL*
>   *Allen D. Hall, 72, of Brownsville, entered into eternal rest at his residence on Friday, October 31, 2003. He was born on March 4, 1931 in Relampago, Texas and lived in the Valley all his life.*
>
>   *He graduated from Brownsville High School and received the Associates Arts Degree from Texas Southmost College. He served in the U.S. Army during the Korean Conflict as a Sergeant. He came home and married his high school sweetheart, Elaine Denson. They had three children Johnny, Terry and Nadine. He has four grandchildren Steven, Andrew, Sarah and Willy. He also has a brother, George Hall, cousins Don and Pat Crow and Roni Rentfro. He also has a good friend, Jimmy Berry, who cared for him.*

Mr. Hall joined the Presbyterian Church in the 70?s and has served as a deacon or elder almost every year since. He was chairman of the Christian Education Committee, Evangelism Committee and sponsor of youth. He served on Presbyterian committees. He was director of the Bicycle Camp at John Knox Ranch for several years. Summer Place was where he worked on maintenance of buildings and equipment as well as being a summer camp counselor. He enjoyed working with the youth and their many activities. Church was his greatest interest and he was seldom absent unless he was on a camping trip.

Mr. Hall was a mechanic for Pan American Airways until they closed operations here in Brownsville. He was co-owner of an auto salvage yard and an insurance adjuster for most of his career.

His hobbies were bicycling, which he did almost every day ? Red, Julio, Jack and Tom Keller were his riding partners for many years. He enjoyed working on cars and tinkering around the house. He also enjoyed football games and the friends he attended those games with.

Memorial services will be held at 3 p.m. Monday, November 3, 2003 at the First Presbyterian Church, 434 Palm Blvd.

In lieu of flowers, memorial donations may be made to the Memorial Fund of the First Presbyterian Church, 435 Palm., Blvd., Brownsville, Texas 78520.

Arrangements have been entrusted to Darling-Mouser Funeral Home, 945 Palm Blvd., (956) 546-7111."

Allen married **Elaine Denson,** daughter of _____ _____ and _____ _____.

Children from this marriage were:

239   M   i.   **Johnny Hall**

240   M   ii. **Terry Hall**

241   F   iii. **Nadine Hall**

230. Samuel H. Childress *(William Gordon Childress [195], Samuel Hall Childress [145], Laurena Matilda Hall [70], Samuel S. [13], William [3], John [1])* was born on 21 Dec 1888 in Yazoo County, Mississippi.[562]

Noted events in his life were:

• He appeared on the United States census on 22 Jun 1900 in Yazoo County, Mississippi.[559]
Sam H. Childress. Age 11. Birth date: Dec 1888. Living with his parents and siblings.

• He appeared on the United States census on 16 Apr 1910 in Yazoo County, Mississippi.[441]
Sam Childress. Age 21. Salesman/retail store. Living with his father and siblings.

• He appeared on the United States census on 29 Apr 1930 in Yazoo County, Mississippi.[579]
Sam H. Childress. Age 41. Retail merchant, grocery store. Living with his wife, Eibel B. Childress and children: Sam H. Jr. (12) and Annie R. (4/12). Age at first marriage: 28.

Samuel married **Eibel B.** _____, daughter of _____ _____ and _____ _____, about 1917 in Mississippi. Eibel was born about 1891 in Mississippi.

Noted events in her life were:

• She appeared on the United States census on 29 Apr 1930 in Yazoo County, Mississippi.[579]
Eibel B. Childress. Age 39. Living with her husband, Sam H. Childress and children: Sam H. Jr. (12) and Annie R. (4/12). Age at first marriage: 26.

236. Annie Wildy Lea *(Harry Wildy Lea [203], Sally Edith Wildy [148], Laurena Matilda Hall [70], Samuel S. [13], William [3], John [1])* was born in New Mexico.

Annie married _____ **Garry,** son of _____ _____ and _____ _____.

Eighth Generation

237. Timothy Elijah Hall *(George Dewey, Jr.[221], George Dewey[187], John Andrew Houston[127], Joseph Marion[63], John[11], John, Jr.[2], John[1])*

Timothy married **Susan Jean Kuchembecker,** daughter of _____ _____ and _____ _____.

Children from this marriage were:

    242 M   i. **David Hall**

    243 M   ii. **Christopher Randle Hall**

238. Eleanor Ann Hall *(George Dewey, Jr.[221], George Dewey[187], John Andrew Houston[127], Joseph Marion[63], John[11], John, Jr.[2], John[1])*

Eleanor married _____ **Patterson,** son of _____ _____ and _____ _____.

Children from this marriage were:

    244 F   i. **Kristen Patterson**

    245 F   ii. **Stephanie Patterson**

    246 M   iii. **Jim Patterson**

Pedigree Chart for George Dewey Hall, Jr.

No. 1 on this chart is the same as no. 1 on chart no. 1

16 John Hall
b. Abt 1780
d. Bef Oct 1869
cont. 2

8 Joseph Marion Hall
b. 8 Aug 1833
p. Tennessee
m. 20 Apr 1853
p. Dent County, Missouri
d. 19 May 1905
p. McKinney, Collin County, Texas

17 Delilah Crawford
b. Abt 1799
d. Oct 1869
cont. 3

4 John Andrew Houston Hall
b. 31 Jan 1854
p. Lafayette County, Arkansas
m. 9 Jun 1881
p. Burnet County, Texas
d. 11 Feb 1943
p. San Angelo, Tom Green County, Texas

18 Bluford Estes
b. Abt 1801
d.
cont. 4

9 Mary "Polly" Ann Estes
b. 30 Sep 1834
p. Missouri
d. 20 Mar 1912
p. Collin County, Texas

19 Rebecca
b. Abt 1806
d.

2 George Dewey Hall
b. 5 Feb 1898
p. Lampasas County, Texas
m. Abt Feb 1920
p. Texas
d. 22 Dec 1946
p. Edinburg, Hidalgo County, Texas

20
b.
d.

10 Charles Bean
b. Abt 1830
p. Tennessee
m. 16 Jan 1853
p. Bartow County, Georgia
d.
p. Texas

21
b.
d.

5 Ora Bean
b. 19 Mar 1867
p. Texas
d. 22 Apr 1900
p. Lampasas County, Texas

22
b.
d.

11 Frances Turner
b. Abt 1838
p. Georgia
d.
p. Texas

23
b.
d.

1 George Dewey Hall, Jr.
b. 17 Dec 1921
p. Edinburg, Hidalgo County, Texas
m. Abt 1947
p. Texas
d. 5 Aug 2012
p. Bay City, Matagorda County, Texas
sp. Frances Brondell Moseley

24
b.
d.

12 Elisha Garland Adair
b. Abt 1811
p. Georgia
m.
p.
d.
p.

25
b.
d.

6 Reuben Harvey Adair
b. 26 Jan 1863
p. Prentiss County, Mississipppi
m. Abt 1888
p.
d. 3 Jun 1948
p. Brownsville, Cameron County, Texas

26
b.
d.

13 Mary F. Mchaffey
b.
p. Alabama
d. Bef 1880
p.

27
b.
d.

3 Ida Mae Adair
b. Abt 1895
p. Groesbeck, Limestone County, Texas
d. 15 Jun 1952
p. Houston, Harris County, Texas

28
b.
d.

14
b.
p.
m.
p.
d.
p.

29
b.
d.

7 Eula Wrenn
b. Jul 1868
p. Mississippi
d. 4 Dec 1945
p. Willacy County, Texas

30
b.
d.

15
b.
p.
d.
p.

31
b.
d.

Pedigree Chart for John Hall

No. 1 on this chart is the same as no. 16 on chart no. 1

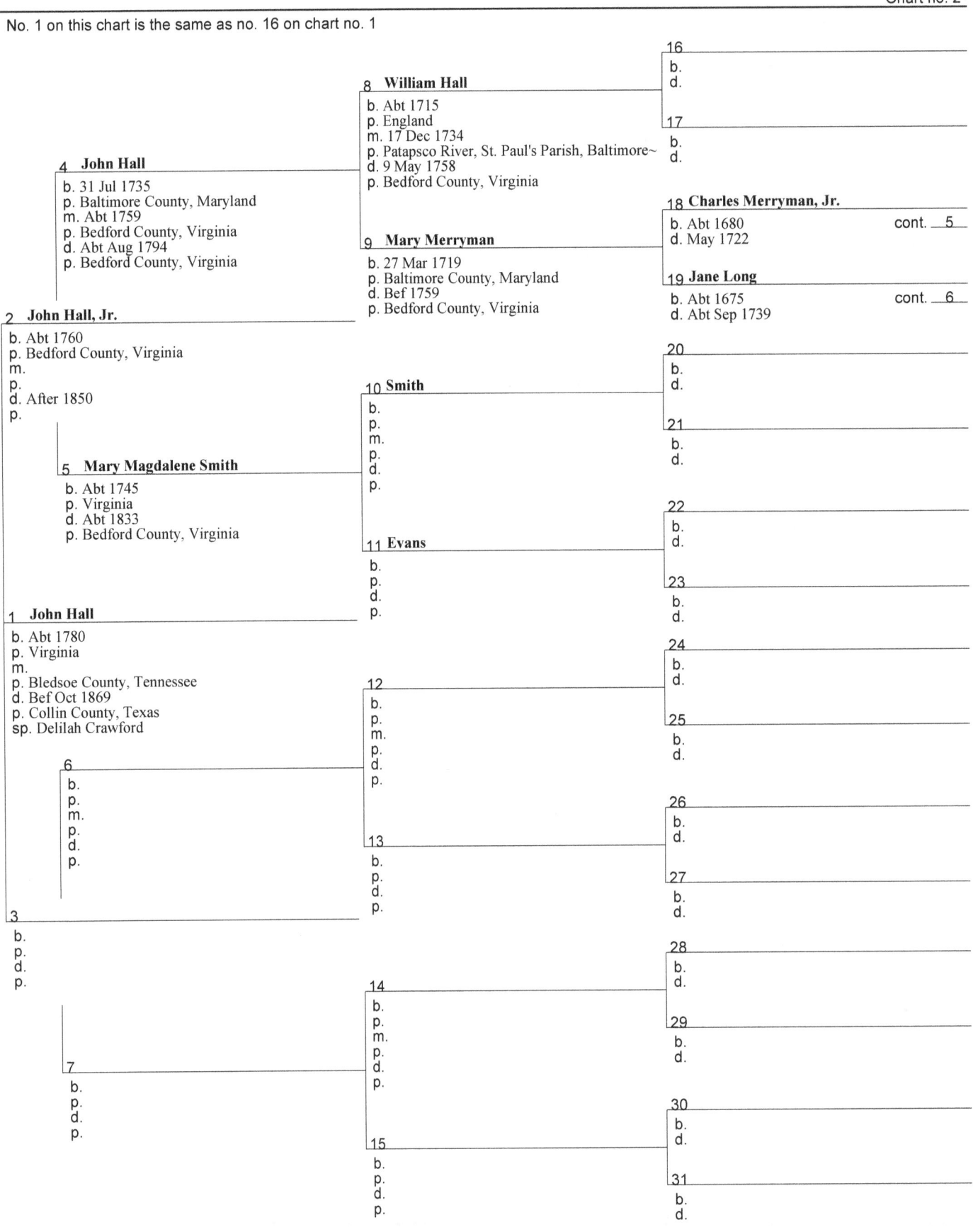

16
b.
d.

8 William Hall
b. Abt 1715
p. England
m. 17 Dec 1734
p. Patapsco River, St. Paul's Parish, Baltimore~
d. 9 May 1758
p. Bedford County, Virginia

17
b.
d.

4 John Hall
b. 31 Jul 1735
p. Baltimore County, Maryland
m. Abt 1759
p. Bedford County, Virginia
d. Abt Aug 1794
p. Bedford County, Virginia

18 Charles Merryman, Jr.
b. Abt 1680   cont. __5__
d. May 1722

9 Mary Merryman
b. 27 Mar 1719
p. Baltimore County, Maryland
d. Bef 1759
p. Bedford County, Virginia

19 Jane Long
b. Abt 1675   cont. __6__
d. Abt Sep 1739

2 John Hall, Jr.
b. Abt 1760
p. Bedford County, Virginia
m.
p.
d. After 1850
p.

20
b.
d.

10 Smith
b.
p.
m.
p.
d.
p.

21
b.
d.

5 Mary Magdalene Smith
b. Abt 1745
p. Virginia
d. Abt 1833
p. Bedford County, Virginia

22
b.
d.

11 Evans
b.
p.
d.
p.

23
b.
d.

1 John Hall
b. Abt 1780
p. Virginia
m.
p. Bledsoe County, Tennessee
d. Bef Oct 1869
p. Collin County, Texas
sp. Delilah Crawford

24
b.
d.

12
b.
p.
m.
p.
d.
p.

25
b.
d.

6
b.
p.
m.
p.
d.
p.

26
b.
d.

13
b.
p.
d.
p.

27
b.
d.

3
b.
p.
d.
p.

28
b.
d.

14
b.
p.
m.
p.
d.
p.

29
b.
d.

7
b.
p.
d.
p.

30
b.
d.

15
b.
p.
d.
p.

31
b.
d.

Pedigree Chart for Delilah Crawford

No. 1 on this chart is the same as no. 17 on chart no. 1

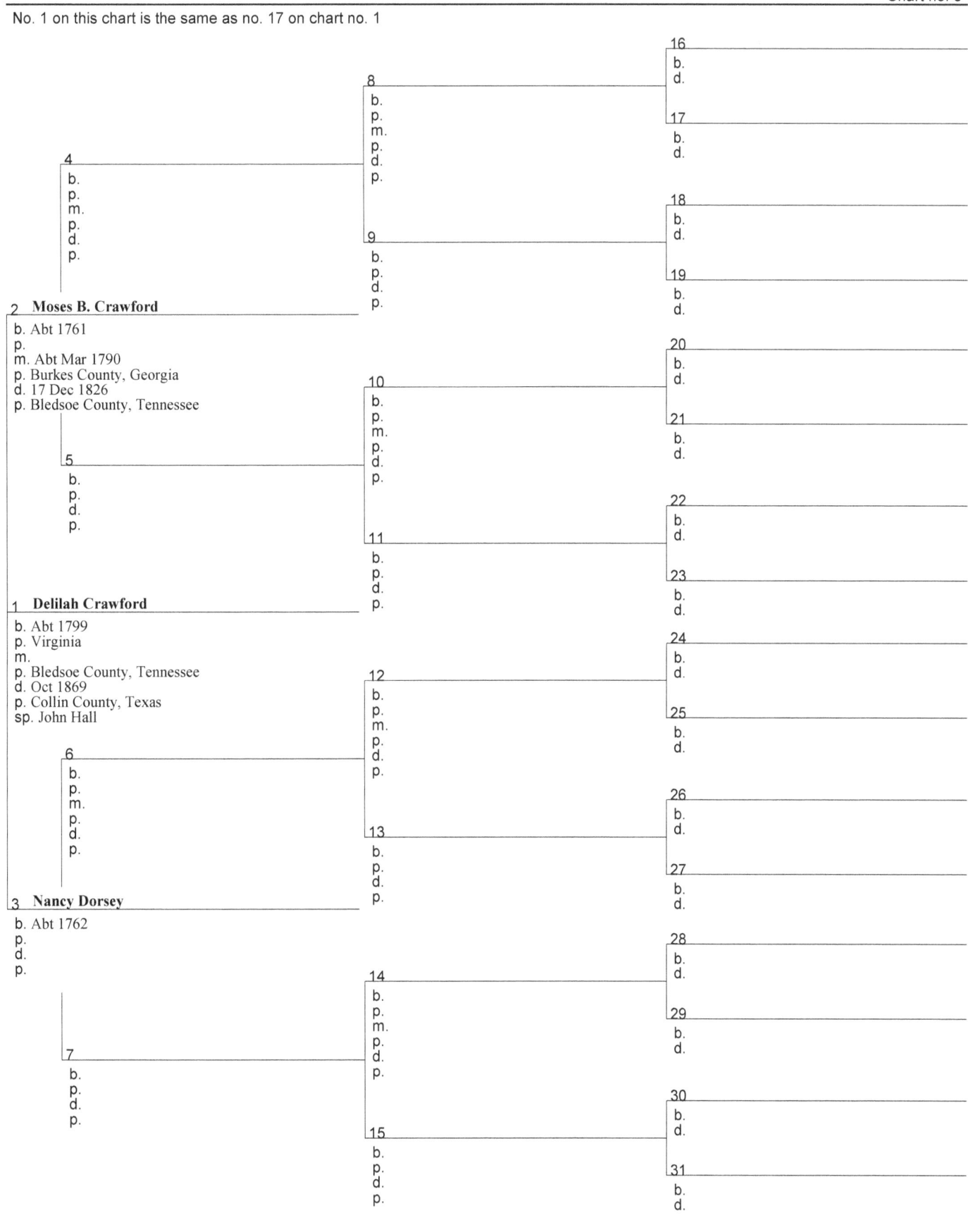

16
b.
d.

8
b.
p.
m.
p.
d.
p.

17
b.
d.

4
b.
p.
m.
p.
d.
p.

18
b.
d.

9
b.
p.
d.
p.

19
b.
d.

2 **Moses B. Crawford**
b. Abt 1761
p.
m. Abt Mar 1790
p. Burkes County, Georgia
d. 17 Dec 1826
p. Bledsoe County, Tennessee

20
b.
d.

10
b.
p.
m.
p.
d.
p.

21
b.
d.

5
b.
p.
d.
p.

22
b.
d.

11
b.
p.
d.
p.

23
b.
d.

1 **Delilah Crawford**
b. Abt 1799
p. Virginia
m.
p. Bledsoe County, Tennessee
d. Oct 1869
p. Collin County, Texas
sp. John Hall

24
b.
d.

12
b.
p.
m.
p.
d.
p.

25
b.
d.

6
b.
p.
m.
p.
d.
p.

26
b.
d.

13
b.
p.
d.
p.

27
b.
d.

3 **Nancy Dorsey**
b. Abt 1762
p.
d.
p.

28
b.
d.

14
b.
p.
m.
p.
d.
p.

29
b.
d.

7
b.
p.
d.
p.

30
b.
d.

15
b.
p.
d.
p.

31
b.
d.

Pedigree Chart for Bluford Estes

No. 1 on this chart is the same as no. 18 on chart no. 1

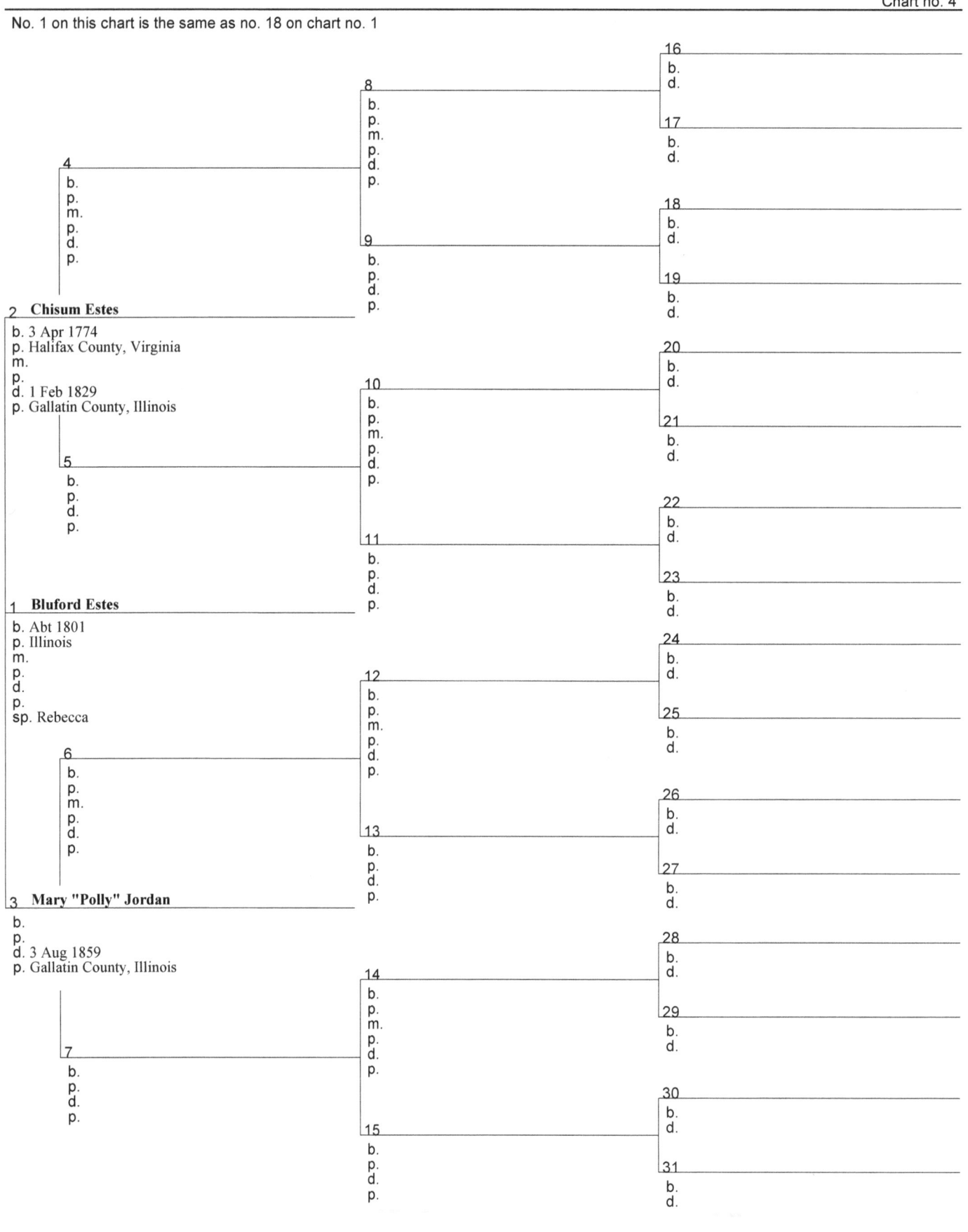

16
b.
d.

8
b.
p.
m.
p.
d.
p.

17
b.
d.

4
b.
p.
m.
p.
d.
p.

18
b.
d.

9
b.
p.
d.
p.

19
b.
d.

2   Chisum Estes
b. 3 Apr 1774
p. Halifax County, Virginia
m.
p.
d. 1 Feb 1829
p. Gallatin County, Illinois

20
b.
d.

10
b.
p.
m.
p.
d.
p.

21
b.
d.

5
b.
p.
d.
p.

22
b.
d.

11
b.
p.
d.
p.

23
b.
d.

1   Bluford Estes
b. Abt 1801
p. Illinois
m.
p.
d.
p.
sp. Rebecca

24
b.
d.

12
b.
p.
m.
p.
d.
p.

25
b.
d.

6
b.
p.
m.
p.
d.
p.

26
b.
d.

13
b.
p.
d.
p.

27
b.
d.

3   Mary "Polly" Jordan
b.
p.
d. 3 Aug 1859
p. Gallatin County, Illinois

28
b.
d.

14
b.
p.
m.
p.
d.
p.

29
b.
d.

7
b.
p.
d.
p.

30
b.
d.

15
b.
p.
d.
p.

31
b.
d.

Pedigree Chart for Charles Merryman, Jr.

No. 1 on this chart is the same as no. 18 on chart no. 2

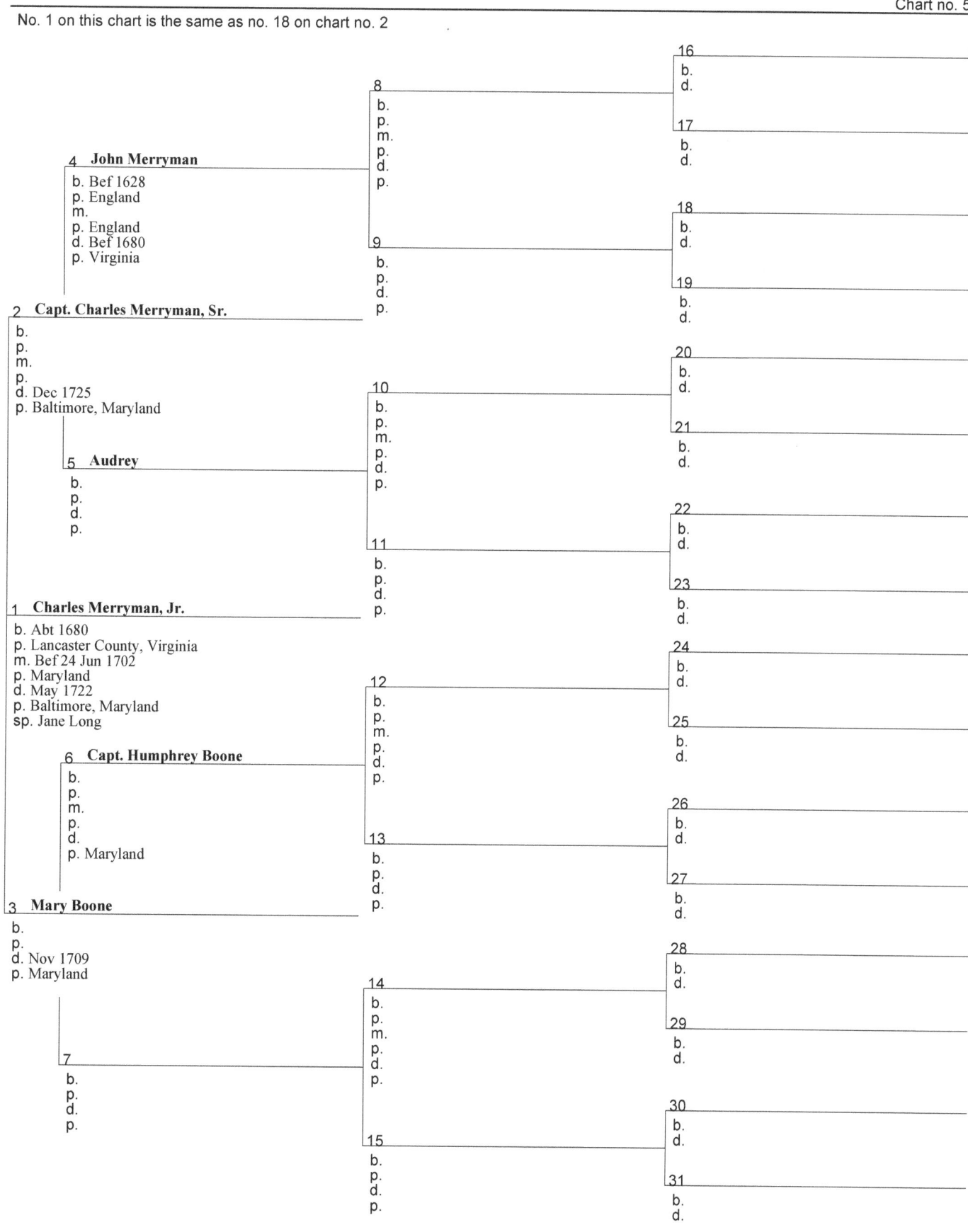

4   John Merryman
b. Bef 1628
p. England
m.
p. England
d. Bef 1680
p. Virginia

2 Capt. Charles Merryman, Sr.
b.
p.
m.
p.
d. Dec 1725
p. Baltimore, Maryland

5   Audrey
b.
p.
d.
p.

1   Charles Merryman, Jr.
b. Abt 1680
p. Lancaster County, Virginia
m. Bef 24 Jun 1702
p. Maryland
d. May 1722
p. Baltimore, Maryland
sp. Jane Long

6   Capt. Humphrey Boone
b.
p.
m.
p.
d.
p. Maryland

3   Mary Boone
b.
p.
d. Nov 1709
p. Maryland

7
b.
p.
d.
p.

8
b.
p.
m.
p.
d.
p.

9
b.
p.
d.
p.

10
b.
p.
m.
p.
d.
p.

11
b.
p.
d.
p.

12
b.
p.
m.
p.
d.
p.

13
b.
p.
d.
p.

14
b.
p.
m.
p.
d.
p.

15
b.
p.
d.
p.

16
b.
d.

17
b.
d.

18
b.
d.

19
b.
d.

20
b.
d.

21
b.
d.

22
b.
d.

23
b.
d.

24
b.
d.

25
b.
d.

26
b.
d.

27
b.
d.

28
b.
d.

29
b.
d.

30
b.
d.

31
b.
d.

Pedigree Chart for Jane Long

No. 1 on this chart is the same as no. 19 on chart no. 2

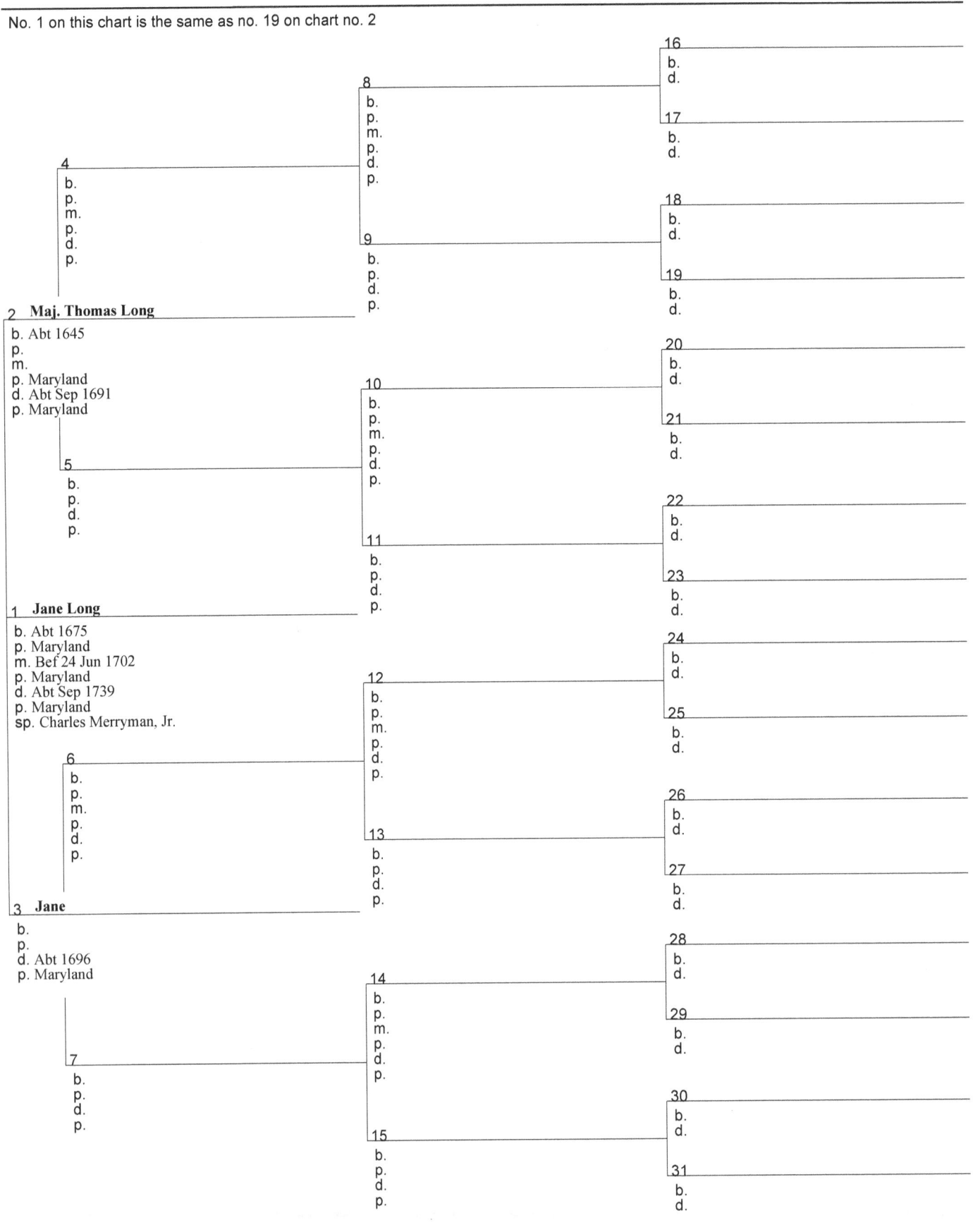

16
b.
d.

8
b.
p.
m.
p.
d.
p.

17
b.
d.

4
b.
p.
m.
p.
d.
p.

18
b.
d.

9
b.
p.
d.
p.

19
b.
d.

2   **Maj. Thomas Long**

b. Abt 1645
p.
m.
p. Maryland
d. Abt Sep 1691
p. Maryland

20
b.
d.

10
b.
p.
m.
p.
d.
p.

21
b.
d.

5
b.
p.
d.
p.

22
b.
d.

11
b.
p.
d.
p.

23
b.
d.

1   **Jane Long**

b. Abt 1675
p. Maryland
m. Bef 24 Jun 1702
p. Maryland
d. Abt Sep 1739
p. Maryland
sp. Charles Merryman, Jr.

24
b.
d.

12
b.
p.
m.
p.
d.
p.

25
b.
d.

6
b.
p.
m.
p.
d.
p.

26
b.
d.

13
b.
p.
d.
p.

27
b.
d.

3   **Jane**

b.
p.
d. Abt 1696
p. Maryland

28
b.
d.

14
b.
p.
m.
p.
d.
p.

29
b.
d.

7
b.
p.
d.
p.

30
b.
d.

15
b.
p.
d.
p.

31
b.
d.

Descendants of Hezekiah Hall (c. 1740 - 1811)
of Bedford County, Virginia

First Generation

1. Hezekiah Hall, son of **William Hall** and **Mary Merryman,** was born about 1740 in Baltimore County, Maryland[24] and died about Jul 1811 in Bedford County, Virginia[25] about age 71.

Birth Notes:
William and Mary (Merryman) Hall did not move to Lunenburg, Virginia before 1747. It is presumed that Hezekiah was born in Maryland.--rch 2010

Noted events in his life were:
- He served in the military militia about 1756 in Lunenburg County, Virginia.[26]
  From: <u>Hening's Statutes</u>, Volume 7
  pages 21-22 - Act of Assembly for the State of Virginia, Mar 1756: *"Payment for services rendered for the defence and protection of the frontiers of the colony against the incursions and depredations of the French and their Indian allies..."*

  September 1758, page 225 - Lunenburg County: Hezekiah and Aquilla Hall, £4 5s. each

- He owned land in Jan 1762 in Bedford County, Virginia.[27]
  Hezekiah purchased 200 acres of land on Back Creek in January, 1762. The land was purchased for 100 pounds from a land speculator named, John Hall who had acquired it in 1758. Hezekiah's brother, John Hall, witnessed the transaction and guaranteed the payments. Witnesses to the transaction were: Thos. Christian, John Callaway, William Verdeman, William Callaway and Henry Snow.

  Recorded Bedford Deed Book A-1 1754-1762; March 23, 1762; Page 535.

  When Campbell County was formed from Bedford in 1782, Back Creek was part of the diving line. Hezekiah's land fell in both counties.

- He signed a will on 9 Mar 1811 in Bedford County, Virginia.[28]
  "The Will is a short, terse document. Keziah, his wife, received one-third of the land, 170 acres. For Samuel, James, Abner and Keziah, his daughter, this amounted to a little over 60 acres for each of them. The older children, William, Thomas, Elisha, Sarah and Tabitha a token bequest - five shillings each." --Carrol Carmen Hall

"Will of Hezekiah Hall
I, Hezekiah Hall of Bedford County do hereby make this my last will and testament in manner and form following, that is to say, I desire that all my Just debts be first paid. I lend one third of my estate both real and personal to my wife Kiziah Hall during her natural life, and after her decease, I give the same to my four first mentioned children equally to be divided among them and to be enjoyed forever. Item, I give unto Samuel Hall, James Hall, <u>Abner Hall</u> and Kiziah Hall which are my beloved sons and daughter, all my estate both real and personalty not otherwise disposed of. Item, I give unto William Hall five shillings. Item, I give unto Sarah Smith my daughter five shillings. Item, I give unto Thomas Hall five shillings, Item, I give unto Elisha Hall five shillings. Item, I given unto Tabitha Dalton my daughter five shillings which I give to the, their heirs, executors, administrators and assigns forever. I do hereby constitute my friends Jesse Leftwich, Burwel Lee and Ralph Smith executors of this my last will and testament hereby revoking all other or former wills or testaments by me heretofore made. In Witness whereof I have set my hand and seal this ninth day of March one thousand eight hundred and eleven.

Hezekiah Hall {seal}
Signed sealed in the presence of
John Overstreet
Francis {X} his mark Wood
Littleberry {X} his mark Dixon

At a court held for Bedford County at the courthouse the 22nd day of July, 1811.
This last will and testament of Hezekiah Hall, dec'd, was exhibited in Court and proven by the oaths of Francis Wood and Littleberry Dixon subscribing witnesses thereto and ordered to be recorded. And at _____ held for said County at the Courthouse the 26th day of August following - on the motion of Burwell Lee one of the executors therein mentioned certificate is granted him for obtaining a probate thereof in due form, liberty being reserved the other executors to join in the probate when they shall think fit.

Teste,
J. Steptoe, C.B.C.
Clerk Bedford County"

- He had an estate probated in 1813 in Pittsylvania County, Virginia.[28]
  In 1813 a suit was filed in Pittsylvania County by Litterbery Dixon to become the Executor. In the same year the suit was dismissed and Burwel Lee was retained. Land in the estate was divided by court order in March 1813.

Hezekiah married **Keziah Smith,** daughter of _____ _____ and _____ _____, about 1774 in Bedford County, Virginia.[29] Keziah was born about 1750 in Virginia[29] and died about 1820 in Lawrence County, Ohio[29] about age 70.

Marriage Notes:
Some sources suggest that Keziah and Mary Magdalene Smith, wife of John, are sisters and daughters of Gideon Smith. Some sources suggest that Keziah may have married a Banks first. These issues are presently unresolved. --rch 2011

Noted events in her life were:
- She had a residence in 1815 in Ohio.[30]
  Widow Hall who owned land in Bedford County, Virginia noted on the 1815 Land Tax that her principal residence was in Ohio.

Children from this marriage were:

+ 2 M   i.   **William Hall** was born on 9 Jan 1775 in Bedford County, Virginia[29] and died on 11 Aug 1847 in Lawrence County, Ohio[29] at age 72.

+ 3 M   ii. **Thomas Hall** was born about 1781 in Bedford County, Virginia[29] and died about 1815 in Bedford County, Virginia[29] about age 34.

+ 4 M   iii. **Elisha Hall** was born on 30 Jul 1783 in Bedford County, Virginia,[580] died on 22 Sep 1838 in Sangamon County, Illinois[580] at age 55, and was buried in 1838 in Illinois.

+ 5 F   iv. **Sarah Hall** was born about 1784 in Bedford County, Virginia[29] and died about 1824 in Ohio[29] about age 40.

+ 6 F   v.   **Tabitha Hall** was born about 1788 in Bedford County, Virginia[29] and died after 1839 in Sumner County, Tennessee.

+ 7 M   vi. **Samuel Hall** was born about 1790 in Bedford County, Virginia[29] and died about 1863 in Van Buren County, Iowa[29] about age 73.

+ 8 M   vii. **James Hall** was born about 1791 in Bedford County, Virginia[29] and died about 1850 in Illinois[29] about age 59.

+ 9 M   viii. **Abner Hall** was born about 1795 in Bedford County, Virginia[29] and died on 10 Apr 1843 in Sangamon County, Illinois[581] about age 48.

+ 10 F   ix. **Keziah "Kitty" Hall** was born about 1797 in Bedford County, Virginia[29] and died about 1825 in Ohio[29] about age 28.

Descendants of Hezekiah Hall (c. 1740 - 1811)
of Bedford County, Virginia

Second Generation

2. William Hall *(Hezekiah [1])* was born on 9 Jan 1775 in Bedford County, Virginia[29] and died on 11 Aug 1847 in Lawrence County, Ohio[29] at age 72.

William married **Nancy Dixon,** daughter of _____ _____ and _____ _____, on 7 Mar 1802 in Bedford County, Virginia.[582] Nancy was born about 1785 in Virginia and died on 1 Sep 1857 in Lawrence County, Ohio about age 72.

> **Noted events in her life were:**
> • She appeared on the United States census on 10 Sep 1850 in Lawrence County, Ohio.[583]
> This may be the census record for Nancy Dixon Hall, widow of William Hall.
> --
> Nancy Hall. Age 64. Living in the household of her son, William H. Hall and his wife, Elizabeth and children.

3. Thomas Hall *(Hezekiah [1])* was born about 1781 in Bedford County, Virginia[29] and died about 1815 in Bedford County, Virginia[29] about age 34.

Thomas married **Elizabeth Radford,** daughter of _____ **Radford** and **Polly** _____, on 18 Nov 1809 in Bedford County, Virginia.[584]

The child from this marriage was:

+ 11 M   i.   **Wesley Hall** was born about 1811 in Bedford County, Virginia,[585] died about 1893 in Menard County, Illinois[585] about age 82, and was buried in Menard County, Illinois (Walnut Ridge Cemetery).[585]

4. Elisha Hall *(Hezekiah [1])* was born on 30 Jul 1783 in Bedford County, Virginia,[580] died on 22 Sep 1838 in Sangamon County, Illinois[580] at age 55, and was buried in 1838 in Illinois.

> **Noted events in his life were:**
> • He appeared on the United States census in 1820 in Lawrence County, Ohio.[586]
> Elisha Hall. Head of household. Presumably the oldest male in the household.
> Males: <10 - 3; 26< 45 - 1; Females: <10 - 3; 26< 45- 1; Foreigners not naturalized: 1.
>
> Next name on the list is John Overstreet, Jr., his brother-in-law.
>
> • He appeared on the United States census in 1830 in Sangamon County, Illinois.[587]
> Elisha Hall. Head of household. Presumably the oldest male.
> Males <5, (4); 5 to 10, (1); 10 to 15, (1); 15 to 20, (1); 40 to 50, (1).
> Females 5 to 10, (2); 15 to 20, (1); 30 to 40, (1).
> Living next door to his brothers, James and Abner Hall
>
> • He had an estate probated from 1838 to 1841 in Sangamon County, Illinois.[588]
> Nancy Hall, Administrator of Elisha Hall, deceased submitted a legal notice to the <u>Sangamon Journal</u>, Nov. 17, 1838:
> *"Notice that Nancy Hall, Administrator of Elisha Hall, deceased will attend before the Probate Justice of said county at his office in Springfield on the first Monday of January next, to receive and adjust all claims against said estate. All persons indebted to said estate are requested to make immediate payment. Athens, Nov. 6, 1838"*

Elisha married **Nancy Overstreet,** daughter of **John Overstreet, Sr.** and **Nancy Dabney,** on 17 Jul 1811 in Bedford County, Virginia.[589] Nancy was born about 1794 in Virginia, died on 9 May 1862 in Menard County, Illinois[590] about age 68, and was buried in 1862 in Illinois.

> **Noted events in her life were:**
> • She appeared on the United States census in 1820 in Lawrence County, Ohio.[586]
> Nancy Hall. Presumably the oldest female in the household of her husband, Elisha Hall.
> Males: <10 - 3; 26< 45 - 1; Females: <10 - 3; 26< 45- 1; Foreigners not naturalized: 1.
>
> Next name on the list is John Overstreet, Jr., her brother.
>
> • She appeared on the United States census in 1830 in Sangamon County, Illinois.[587]

Nancy Hall. Presumably the oldest female in the Elisha Hall household.
Males <5, (4); 5 to 10, (1); 10 to 15, (1); 15 to 20, (1); 40 to 50, (1).
Females 5 to 10, (2); 15 to 20, (1); 30 to 40, (1).

• She appeared on the United States census on 5 Sep 1850 in Menard County, Illinois.[591]
Nancy Hall. Age 60. Apparently a widow. Living with her children and grandchildren(?): P. (age 30), Dabney (age 21), Wm. (age 19), F. (age 15), N. J. (age 11), W. (age 5), Virginia (Hall?) Pierce (age 17) and Virginia's husband, George Pierce.
--
It would seem likely that W. is a grandchild of Nancy. I cannot tell from this record.

• She appeared on the United States census on 10 Sep 1860 in Menard County, Illinois.[592]
Nancy Hall. Age 65. Living in the household of Oliver and Nancy J. Pierce. Next door is the Joseph B. Ayers family.

Children from this marriage were:

+ 12 F   i. **Adelia Hall** was born on 31 May 1812 in Bedford County, Virginia[588] and died before 1850 in Menard County, Illinois.

+ 13 F   ii. **Keziah Hall** was born on 15 Apr 1813 in Lawrence County, Ohio.[588]

+ 14 M   iii. **Joel Wesley Hall** was born on 4 Nov 1814 in Lawrence County, Ohio[588] and died on 17 Nov 1853 at age 39.

+ 15 M   iv. **John Nelson Hall** was born on 10 Jun 1816 in Lawrence County, Ohio[593] and died on 25 Oct 1902 in Menard County, Illinois[594] at age 86.

+ 16 M   v. **James Pembrook Hall** was born on 1 Jul 1818 in Lawrence County, Ohio,[595] died on 11 Oct 1892 in Menard County, Illinois[595] at age 74, and was buried in Oct 1892 in Menard County, Illinois (Walnut Ridge Cemetery).[595]

+ 17 F   vi. **Lucinda Hall** was born on 28 Apr 1820 in Lawrence County, Ohio.[588]

+ 18 F   vii. **Sarah Hall** was born on 17 Mar 1822 in Lawrence County, Ohio.[588]

+ 19 M   viii. **Elisha Banks Hall** was born on 25 Oct 1824 in Lawrence County, Ohio[588] and died in 1902 at age 78.

+ 20 M   ix. **George Hall** was born on 18 May 1826 in Lawrence County, Ohio.[588]

+ 21 M   x. **Dabney Hall** was born on 5 Nov 1828 in Sangamon County, Illinois,[588] died on 18 Apr 1874 in Menard County, Illinois at age 45, and was buried in Apr 1874 in Menard County, Illinois (West Cemetery).

    22 M   xi. **William M. Hall** was born on 21 Oct 1830 in Sangamon County, Illinois,[588] died on 23 Jul 1864 at age 33, and was buried in Jul 1864 in Menard County, Illinois (Old West Cemetery).[596]

        Noted events in his life were:
        • He appeared on the United States census on 5 Sep 1850 in Menard County, Illinois.[597]
        Wm. Hall. Age 19. Farmer. Living with his mother, Nancy and siblings.

+ 23 F   xii. **Virginia Hall** was born on 19 Jun 1833 in Sangamon County, Illinois[588] and died on 21 Jun 1925 in Illinois at age 92.

+ 24 F   xiii. **Tabitha Hall** was born on 13 Mar 1835 in Sangamon County, Illinois.[588]

    25 F   xiv. **Susannah Rogers Hall** was born on 23 Mar 1837 in Sangamon County, Illinois.[588]

+ 26 F   xv. **Nancy Jane Hall** was born on 1 Feb 1838 in Sangamon County, Illinois.[588]

5. Sarah Hall (*Hezekiah* [1]) was born about 1784 in Bedford County, Virginia[29] and died about 1824 in Ohio[29] about age 40.

Noted events in her life were:
• She appeared on the United States census in 1820 in Lawrence County, Ohio.[598]
Sarah Smith. Presumably the oldest female in the household of her husband, Augustine Smith.
Males: <10 - 1; 10 <16 - 1; 16 <18 - 1; 16 <26 - 2; 26 <45 - 1; Females: <10 - 2; 10 <16 - 1; 16 <26 - 1; 26< 45 - 1.

Sarah married **Augustine Smith,** son of **John Smith** and **Unknown,** on 26 Feb 1800 in Bedford County, Virginia.[599] Augustine was born in Virginia.

Noted events in his life were:
- He appeared on the United States census in 1820 in Lawrence County, Ohio.[600]
  Augustine Smith. Head of household. Presumably the oldest male in the household.
  Males: <10 - 1; 10 <16 - 1; 16 <18 - 1; 16 <26 - 2; 26 <45 - 1; Females: <10 - 2; 10 <16 - 1; 16 <26 - 1; 26< 45- 1.

6. Tabitha Hall *(Hezekiah ¹)* was born about 1788 in Bedford County, Virginia[29] and died after 1839 in Sumner County, Tennessee.

Tabitha married **Robert Calvin Dalton,** son of **Robert Dalton** and **Unknown,** on 8 Apr 1806 in Bedford County, Virginia.[29] Robert was born about 1780 in Virginia.

General Notes:
Robert Dalton's grandfather, Timothy Dalton was a deponent in the judicial proceedings investigation the death of William Hall, grandfather of Tabitha Hall, his wife.

7. Samuel Hall *(Hezekiah ¹)* was born about 1790 in Bedford County, Virginia[29] and died about 1863 in Van Buren County, Iowa[29] about age 73.

Noted events in his life were:
- He had a residence in 1815 in Ohio.[30]
  Samuel Hall who owned land in Bedford County, Virginia noted on the 1815 Land Tax that his principal residence was in Ohio.

- He appeared on the United States census in 1820 in Lawrence County, Ohio.[601]
  Sam'l Hall. Head of household. Presumably the oldest male in the household.
  Males: <10 - 3; 26 <45 - 1; Females: <10 - 1; 26 <45 - 1.

On the same page are Abner Hall, John Neal and John Overstreet families.

- He appeared on the United States census on 22 Oct 1850 in Van Buren County, Iowa.[602]
  Samuel Hall. Age 60. Farmer. Living with his children: Eliza (age 35), Townsend (age 33), Elizabeth (age 31), Sarah Bryan (age 29), Wm. Hall (age 27). Next appears to be Wm.'s wife, Levi (age 28) and their children: Eliza (age 10), John (age 9), Nancy (age 9), Nancy (age 7), Sarah (age 7). Then Rebecca Bryan (age 2; Sarah's child?) is listed; and perhaps another married daughter (of Samuel), Lydia A. Lovel (age 20).

- He appeared on the Iowa State census in 1856 in Van Buren County, Iowa.[603]
  Samuel Hall. Age 66. Farmer. Born in Virginia. Widowed. Also in household is Sarah Davis (age 17), Ohio.

- He appeared on the United States census on 4 Jun 1860 in Van Buren County, Iowa.[604]
  Saml. Hall. Age 70. Farmer. Cannot read or write. Also in the household is Sarah A. Hall, age 17, housekeeper. Next door is his son, Elsey and wife, Ruth and children.

Samuel married **Jane Smith,** daughter of _____ _____ and _____ _____, on 4 Feb 1813 in Gallia County, Ohio.[29] Jane died before 1850 in Iowa.

Noted events in her life were:
- She appeared on the United States census in 1820 in Lawrence County, Ohio.[601]
  Jane Hall. Presumably the oldest female in the household of her husband, Sam'l Hall.
  Males: <10 - 3; 26 <45 - 1; Females: <10 - 1; 26 <45 - 1.

On the same page are Abner Hall, John Neal and John Overstreet families.

8. James Hall *(Hezekiah ¹)* was born about 1791 in Bedford County, Virginia[29] and died about 1850 in Illinois[29] about age 59.

Noted events in his life were:
- He appeared on the United States census in 1830 in Sangamon County, Illinois.[605]
  James Hall. Head of household.
  Males: 30 to 40, (1).
  Females: <5, (2); 5 to 10, (4); 10 to 15, (1); 30 to 40, (1).

Living next door to his brothers, Elisha and Abner Hall

James married **Eleanor Swearingen,** daughter of _____ _____ and _____ _____, about 1815 in Ohio.[29] Eleanor was born about 1793 in Bedford County, Virginia and died after 1850 in Illinois.

Noted events in her life were:
- She appeared on the United States census in 1830 in Sangamon County, Illinois.[605]
  Eleanor Hall. Presumably the oldest female in the household of James Hall.
  Males: 30 to 40, (1).
  Females: <5, (2); 5 to 10, (4); 10 to 15, (1); 30 to 40, (1).
  Living next door to his brothers, Elisha and Abner Hall

- She appeared on the United States census on 23 Aug 1850 in Menard County, Illinois.[606]
  Eleanor Hall. Age 57. Living with her children: Minerva (19), John (17), S. M. (12), James (10). Also in the household is [illegible] Swearingen (23), perhaps a niece?

Children from this marriage were:

27 F i. **Minerva Hall** was born in 1831 in Illinois.

Noted events in her life were:
- She appeared on the United States census on 23 Aug 1850 in Menard County, Illinois.[607]
  Minerva Hall. Age 19. Living with her mother, Eleanor Hall and siblings.

28 M ii. **John Hall** was born about 1833 in Illinois.

Noted events in his life were:
- He appeared on the United States census on 23 Aug 1850 in Menard County, Illinois.[608]
  John Hall. Age 17. Living with his mother, Eleanor Hall and siblings.

29 F iii. **S. M. Hall** was born about 1838 in Illinois.

Noted events in her life were:
- She appeared on the United States census on 23 Aug 1850 in Menard County, Illinois.[609]
  S. M. Hall. Age 12. Living with her mother, Eleanor Hall and siblings.

30 M iv. **James Hall** was born about 1840 in Illinois.

Noted events in his life were:
- He appeared on the United States census on 23 Aug 1850 in Menard County, Illinois.[610]
  James Hall. Age 10. Living with his mother, Eleanor Hall and siblings.

9. Abner Hall *(Hezekiah [1])* was born about 1795 in Bedford County, Virginia[29] and died on 10 Apr 1843 in Sangamon County, Illinois[581] about age 48.

Death Notes:
Some sources say 10 April 1845.

Noted events in his life were:
- He had a residence in 1815 in Ohio.[30]
  Abner Hall who owned land in Bedford County, Virginia noted on the 1815 Land Tax that his principal residence was in Ohio.

- He appeared on the United States census in 1820 in Lawrence County, Ohio.[611]
  Abahan Hall. Head of household. Presumably the oldest male in the household.
  Males: <10 - 2; 10 <16 - 3; 16 <26 - 1; Females: <10 - 1; 16 <26 - 1.

  On the same page are Sam'l. Hall, John Neal and John Overstreet families.

- He appeared on the United States census in 1830 in Sangamon County, Illinois.[612]
  Abner Hall. Head of household. Presumably the oldest male in the household.
  Males: <5, (1); 5 to 10, (1); 15 to 20, (1); 30 to 40, (1).

Females: <5, (1); 5 to 10, (2); 10 to 15, (1); 30 to 40, (1).
Living next door to his brothers, Elisha and James Hall

- He owned land in 1837 in Springfield, Sangamon County, Illinois.[613]
"As tenants in common" with Joseph B. Ayres, he purchased 27.84 acres on 18 March 1837.

Abner married **Jane Overstreet,** daughter of **John Overstreet, Sr.** and **Nancy Dabney,** about 1814 in Bedford County, Virginia.[29] Jane was born about 1793 in Virginia and died after 1850 in Illinois.

Noted events in her life were:
- She appeared on the United States census in 1820 in Lawrence County, Ohio.[611]
Jane Hall. Presumably the oldest female in the household of her husband, Abner Hall.
Males: <10 - 2; 10 <16 - 3; 16 <26 - 1; Females: <10 - 1; 16 <26 - 1.

  On the same page are Sam'l. Hall, John Neal and John Overstreet families.

- She appeared on the United States census in 1830 in Sangamon County, Illinois.[612]
Jane Hall. Presumably the oldest female in the Abner Hall household.
Males: <5, (1); 5 to 10, (1); 15 to 20, (1); 30 to 40, (1).
Females: <5, (1); 5 to 10, (2); 10 to 15, (1); 30 to 40, (1).
Living next door to his brothers, Elisha and James Hall

- She appeared on the United States census on 23 Aug 1850 in Menard County, Illinois.[614]
Jenny Hall. Age 57. Living with two children: And (21), Mary (15). The A. B. Hall family and daughter also live in the household. Matilda Clarke and family are living next door.

Children from this marriage were:
+ 31 M   i.   **James Wesley Hall** was born about 1814 in Lawrence County, Ohio,[615] died about 1868 in Menard County, Illinois[616] about age 54, and was buried in Menard County, Illinois (Old West Cemetery).[615]

   32 M   ii.   **Elisha Hall**.

+ 33 F   iii.   **Catharine Hall** was born on 7 Apr 1817 in Lawrence County, Ohio,[617] died on 5 Jul 1900 in Menard County, Illinois[617] at age 83, and was buried in Jul 1900 in Menard County, Illinois (West Cemetery).[617]

+ 34 M   iv.   **Abner Banks Hall** was born about 1820 in Lawrence County, Ohio,[618] died on 28 Sep 1896 in Menard County, Illinois[618] about age 76, and was buried on 29 Sep 1896 in Menard County, Illinois (West Cemetery).[619]

+ 35 F   v.   **Matilda Hall** was born about 1828 in Illinois.

10. Keziah "Kitty" Hall *(Hezekiah [1])* was born about 1797 in Bedford County, Virginia[29] and died about 1825 in Ohio[29] about age 28. She was usually called Kitty.

Noted events in her life were:
- She had a residence in 1815 in Ohio.[30]
"Kitty" Hall who owned land in Bedford County, Virginia noted on the 1815 Land Tax that her principal residence was in Ohio.

- She appeared on the United States census in 1820 in Lawrence County, Ohio.[620]
Keziah Neal. Presumably the oldest female in the household of her husband, John Neal.
Males: <10 - 2; 26 <45 - 1; Females: <10 - 1; 10 <16 - 1; 16 <26 - 1.

  On the same page are Overstreet and Hall families.

Kitty married **John Neal,** son of _____ _____ and _____ _____, on 28 Jan 1814 in Gallia County, Ohio.[29]

Noted events in his life were:
- He appeared on the United States census in 1820 in Lawrence County, Ohio.[620]
John Neal. Head of household. Presumably the oldest male in the household.
Males: <10 - 2; 26 <45 - 1; Females: <10 - 1; 10 <16 - 1; 16 <26 - 1.

Descendants of Hezekiah Hall (c. 1740 - 1811)
of Bedford County, Virginia

On the same page are Overstreet and Hall families.

Descendants of Hezekiah Hall (c. 1740 - 1811) of Bedford County, Virginia

Third Generation

11. Wesley Hall *(Thomas[3], Hezekiah[1])* was born about 1811 in Bedford County, Virginia,[585] died about 1893 in Menard County, Illinois[585] about age 82, and was buried in Menard County, Illinois (Walnut Ridge Cemetery).[585]

> **Noted events in his life were:**
> - He appeared on the United States census on 20 Sep 1850 in Menard County, Illinois.[621]
>   Wesley Hall. Age 38. Farmer. Living with his wife, Nancy and children: Aug, C. W., B. H., and L. E. Hall. Also in the household is Sarah Ferguson, age 55. Presumably, she is Nancy's mother.
>
> - He appeared on the State of Illinois census in 1855 in Menard County, Illinois.[622]
>   Westley Hall. Head of household. 7 in household.
>
> - He appeared on the United States census on 21 Jun 1880 in Menard County, Illinois.[623]
>   Wesley Hall. Age 69. Farmer. Living with his wife, Nancy Hall and children: John T., Thomas H., Ann E. and Lena F. Hall.

Wesley married **Nancy Ferguson,** daughter of **Unknown** and **Sarah** _____, about 1838.[624] Nancy was born on 9 Feb 1821 in Kentucky,[624] died on 23 Jan 1904 in Menard County, Illinois[624] at age 82, and was buried in Menard County, Illinois (Walnut Ridge Cemetery).[624]

> **Noted events in her life were:**
> - She appeared on the United States census on 20 Sep 1850 in Menard County, Illinois.[621]
>   Nancy Hall. Age 28. Living with her husband, Wesley and children: Aug, C. W., B. H., and L. E. Hall. Also in the household is Sarah Ferguson, age 55. Presumably, she is Nancy's mother.
>
> - She appeared on the United States census on 21 Jun 1880 in Menard County, Illinois.[623]
>   Nancy Hall. Age 59. Keeping house. Living with her husband, Wesley Hall and children: John T., Thomas H., Ann E. and Lena F. Hall.
>
> - She appeared on the United States census on 1 Jun 1900 in Menard County, Illinois.[625]
>   Mancy H. Hall. Age 79. Birth date: Feb 1821. Widow. Living with her son, Thomas H. Hall. Children: 6; Living: 4.

12. Adelia Hall *(Elisha[4], Hezekiah[1])* was born on 31 May 1812 in Bedford County, Virginia[588] and died before 1850 in Menard County, Illinois.

Adelia married **John Hide,** son of _____ _____ and _____ _____, in Sangamon County, Illinois. John was born about 1813 in Kentucky.

13. Keziah Hall *(Elisha[4], Hezekiah[1])* was born on 15 Apr 1813 in Lawrence County, Ohio.[588]

Keziah married _____ **Jordan,** son of _____ _____ and _____ _____, in Sangamon County, Illinois.

14. Joel Wesley Hall *(Elisha[4], Hezekiah[1])* was born on 4 Nov 1814 in Lawrence County, Ohio[588] and died on 17 Nov 1853 at age 39.

Joel married _____ **Ferguson,** daughter of _____ _____ and _____ _____, on 12 Dec 1840 in Menard County, Illinois.

15. John Nelson Hall *(Elisha[4], Hezekiah[1])* was born on 10 Jun 1816 in Lawrence County, Ohio[593] and died on 25 Oct 1902 in Menard County, Illinois[594] at age 86.

> **Noted events in his life were:**
> - He appeared on the United States census on 27 Aug 1850 in Menard County, Illinois.[626]
>   Nelson Hall. Age 32. Farmer. Living with his wife, Sarah and children: Thomas (7), A. E. (6), Abram (4), Wm. E. (2), C. A. (6/12). Nearby is the Joseph Ayres family.
>
> - He appeared on the United States census on 7 Jun 1900 in Menard County, Illinois.[627]
>   John N. Hall. Age 83. Birth date: Jun 1816. Farmer. Widower. Living with his daughters: Delia A.(37), Ella M. (30) and grandson: Eugene Primm (18).

John married **Sarah Parker,** daughter of _____ _____ and _____ _____, on 4 Apr 1842 in Menard County, Illinois.[628] Sarah was born on 4 Nov 1824 in Illinois[594] and died on 10 Mar 1890 in Menard County, Illinois[594] at age 65.

> **Noted events in her life were:**
> • She appeared on the United States census on 27 Aug 1850 in Menard County, Illinois.[626]
> Sarah Hall. Age 26. Living with her husband, Nelson Hall and children: Thomas (7), A. E. (6), Abram (4), Wm. E. (2), C. A. (6/12). Nearby is the Joseph Ayres family.

16. James Pembrook Hall *(Elisha [4], Hezekiah [1])* was born on 1 Jul 1818 in Lawrence County, Ohio,[595] died on 11 Oct 1892 in Menard County, Illinois[595] at age 74, and was buried in Oct 1892 in Menard County, Illinois (Walnut Ridge Cemetery).[595]

> **Noted events in his life were:**
> • He appeared on the United States census on 5 Sep 1850 in Menard County, Illinois.[591]
> P. Hall. Age 30. Farm laborer. Living with his mother, Nancy Hall and siblings.

James married **Mary Jane Pierce,** daughter of **Charles Robertson Pierce** and **Malinda Anderson,** on 24 Dec 1850 in Menard County, Illinois.[595] Mary was born on 16 Jul 1830 in Illinois,[629] died on 21 Sep 1905 in Menard County, Illinois[629] at age 75, and was buried in Sep 1905 in Menard County, Illinois (Walnut Ridge Cemetery).[629]

17. Lucinda Hall *(Elisha [4], Hezekiah [1])* was born on 28 Apr 1820 in Lawrence County, Ohio.[588]

Lucinda married _____ **Primm,** son of _____ _____ and _____ _____, on 18 Jun 1839 in Menard County, Illinois.

18. Sarah Hall *(Elisha [4], Hezekiah [1])* was born on 17 Mar 1822 in Lawrence County, Ohio.[588]

Sarah married _____ **Patterson,** son of _____ _____ and _____ _____, about 1840 in Menard County, Illinois.

19. Elisha Banks Hall *(Elisha [4], Hezekiah [1])* was born on 25 Oct 1824 in Lawrence County, Ohio[588] and died in 1902 at age 78.

Elisha married _____ **Parker,** daughter of _____ _____ and _____ _____, in Menard County, Illinois.

20. George Hall *(Elisha [4], Hezekiah [1])* was born on 18 May 1826 in Lawrence County, Ohio.[588]

George married _____ **Short,** daughter of _____ _____ and _____ _____, in Menard County, Illinois.

21. Dabney Hall *(Elisha [4], Hezekiah [1])* was born on 5 Nov 1828 in Sangamon County, Illinois,[588] died on 18 Apr 1874 in Menard County, Illinois at age 45, and was buried in Apr 1874 in Menard County, Illinois (West Cemetery).

> **Noted events in his life were:**
> • He appeared on the United States census on 5 Sep 1850 in Menard County, Illinois.[591]
> Dabney Hall. Age 21. Farm Laborer. Living with his mother, Nancy and siblings.
>
> • He appeared on the United States census on 3 Aug 1870 in Mason County, Illinois.[630]
> Dabney Hall. Age 43. Saloon Keeper. Living with his wife, Tobetha and children: Julius M. and Edwin. Also in the household are twins Cynthia and John Simms, age 14.
>
> • He served in the military a PVT (Farrier) in Co K, 106th Illinois Infantry from 1862 to 1865.[631]

Dabney married **Tobetha Short,** daughter of _____ _____ and _____ _____, about 1865 in Menard County, Illinois. Tobetha was born about 1838 in Illinois.

> **Noted events in her life were:**
> • She appeared on the United States census on 3 Aug 1870 in Mason County, Illinois.[632]
> Tobtha Hall. Age 32. Keep House. Living with her husband, Dabney Hall and children: Julius M. and Edwin. Also in the household are twins Cynthia and John Simms, age 14.

23. Virginia Hall *(Elisha [4], Hezekiah [1])* was born on 19 Jun 1833 in Sangamon County, Illinois[588] and died on 21 Jun 1925 in Illinois at age 92.

> **Noted events in her life were:**
> - She appeared on the United States census on 5 Sep 1850 in Menard County, Illinois.[633]
> Virginia Pierce. Age 17. Living with her mother, Nancy Hall; siblings and husband, George Pierce.
>
> - She appeared on the United States census on 2 Jun 1880 in Brown County, Kansas.[634]
> Virginia Pierce. Age 47. Keeping house. Living with her husband, George Pierce and daughter, Della (age 21).

Virginia married **George Pierce,** son of **Charles Robertson Pierce** and **Malinda Anderson,** about 1850 in Menard County, Illinois. George was born about 1829 in Illinois.

> **Noted events in his life were:**
> - He appeared on the United States census on 5 Sep 1850 in Menard County, Illinois.[635]
> George Pierce. Age 21. Farmer. Living with his wife, Virginia and her mother and family.
>
> - He appeared on the United States census on 2 Jun 1880 in Brown County, Kansas.[636]
> George Pierce. Age 51. Farmer. Living with his wife, Virginia and daughter, Della (age 21).

24. Tabitha Hall *(Elisha [4], Hezekiah [1])* was born on 13 Mar 1835 in Sangamon County, Illinois.[588]

Tabitha married _____ **Logue,** son of _____ _____ and _____ _____, in Menard County, Illinois.

26. Nancy Jane Hall *(Elisha [4], Hezekiah [1])* was born on 1 Feb 1838 in Sangamon County, Illinois.[588]

> **Noted events in her life were:**
> - She appeared on the United States census on 5 Sep 1850 in Menard County, Illinois.[637]
> N. J. Hall. Age 11. Living with her mother, Nancy and siblings.
>
> - She appeared on the United States census on 10 Sep 1860 in Menard County, Illinois.[592]
> Nancy J. Pierce. Age 22. Living with her husband, Oliver and her daughter, Rosella. Also in the household is her mother, Nancy Hall. Next door is the Joseph B. Ayers family.

Nancy married **Oliver Perry Pierce,** son of **Charles Robertson Pierce** and **Malinda Anderson,** on 12 Mar 1857 in Menard County, Illinois.[638] Oliver was born on 15 Feb 1836 in Sangamon County, Illinois and died on 7 Jan 1927 in Cowley County, Kansas at age 90.

> **Noted events in his life were:**
> - He appeared on the United States census on 10 Sep 1860 in Menard County, Illinois.[639]
> Oliver Pierce. Age 23. Farmer. Living with his wife, Nancy J. Pierce and daughter, Rosella. Also in the household is: Nancy Hall, his mother-in-law. Next door is the Joseph B. Ayers family.

The child from this marriage was:

> 36　F　　i.　**Rosella Pierce** was born about 1859 in Menard County, Illinois.
>
> > **Noted events in her life were:**
> > - She appeared on the United States census on 10 Sep 1860 in Menard County, Illinois.[592]
> > Rosella Pierce. Age 1. Living with her parents.

Descendants of Hezekiah Hall (c. 1740 - 1811) of Bedford County, Virginia

31. James Wesley Hall (*Abner⁹, Hezekiah¹*) was born about 1814 in Lawrence County, Ohio,[615] died about 1868 in Menard County, Illinois[616] about age 54, and was buried in Menard County, Illinois (Old West Cemetery).[615]

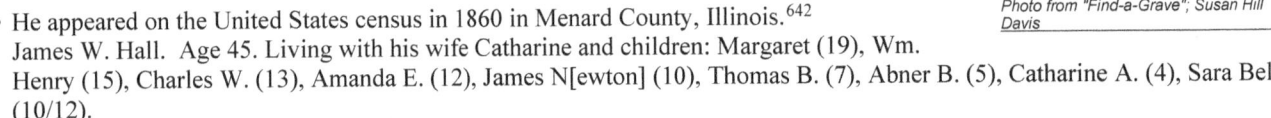

James Wesley Hall
Photo from "Find-a-Grave"; Susan Hill Davis

Noted events in his life were:

- He appeared on the United States census in 1840 in Sangamon County, Illinois.[640]
  James W. Hall. Males: (20-29) 1; Females: (>5) 3; (20-29) 1. Employed in agriculture (1). Slaves: 0

- He appeared on the United States census on 27 Aug 1850 in Menard County, Illinois.[641]
  James Hall. Age 35. Brick Mason. Living with his wife, Catharine and children: M. F. (13), S. M. (11), E. J. (9), Wm. H. (7), C. W. (3), A. E. (1), J. N. (6/12)

- He appeared on the United States census in 1860 in Menard County, Illinois.[642]
  James W. Hall. Age 45. Living with his wife Catharine and children: Margaret (19), Wm. Henry (15), Charles W. (13), Amanda E. (12), James N[ewton] (10), Thomas B. (7), Abner B. (5), Catharine A. (4), Sara Bell (10/12).

James married **Catharine Claypoole**, daughter of _____ _____ and _____ _____, about 1837 in Illinois. Catharine was born about 1819 in Ohio, died on 3 Jun 1872 in Illinois[643] about age 53, and was buried in Illinois.

Noted events in her life were:

- She appeared on the United States census in 1840 in Sangamon County, Illinois.[640]
  Presumably the oldest female in the household of James W. Hall.

- She appeared on the United States census on 27 Aug 1850 in Menard County, Illinois.[644]
  Catharine Hall. Age 30. Living with her husband, James Hall and children: M. F. (13), S. M. (11), E. J. (9), Wm. H. (7), C. W. (3), A. E. (1), J. N. (6/12)

- She appeared on the United States census in 1860 in Menard County, Illinois.[645]
  Catharine Hall. Age 43. Living with her husband, James W. Hall and children: Margaret (19), Wm. Henry (15), Charles W. (13), Amanda E. (12), James N[ewton]. (10), Thomas B. (7), Abner B. (5), Catharine A. (4), Sara Bell (10/12).

33. Catharine Hall (*Abner⁹, Hezekiah¹*) was born on 7 Apr 1817 in Lawrence County, Ohio,[617] died on 5 Jul 1900 in Menard County, Illinois[617] at age 83, and was buried in Jul 1900 in Menard County, Illinois (West Cemetery).[617]

Noted events in her life were:

- She appeared on the United States census on 27 Aug 1850 in Menard County, Illinois.[646]
  Catharine Ayres. Age 32. Living with her husband, Joseph Ayres and children: Mary (13), Ann (10), Wm. (8), James (6) and Arminda (2).

- She appeared on the United States census on 10 Sep 1860 in Menard County, Illinois.[647]
  Catharine Ayres. Age 43. Living with her husband, Jas. B. Ayres and children: Mary (23), William B. (18), James K. T. (15), Alice (6). Also in the household is Mary F. Ward (21). Nancy Hall lives next door.

- She appeared on the United States census on 24 Jul 1870 in Menard County, Illinois.[648]
  Cathrine Ayres. Age 56. Keeping house. Living with her husband, Joseph Ayres and a niece(?), Ada Clark (16).

Catharine married **Joseph B. Ayers**, son of _____ _____ and _____ _____, on 22 Feb 1832 in Sangamon County, Illinois.[649] Joseph was born on 13 Dec 1807 in Monmouth County, New Jersey, died on 16 Jan 1880 in Menard County, Illinois[650] at age 72, and was buried in Jan 1880 in Menard County, Illinois (West Cemetery).[651] The cause of his death was heart disease.

Noted events in his life were:

- He owned land in 1837 in Springfield, Sangamon County, Illinois.[652]
  "As tenants in common" with Abner Hall, he purchased 27.84 acres on 18 March 1837.

- He appeared on the United States census on 27 Aug 1850 in Menard County, Illinois.[646]
  Joseph Ayres. Age 42. Farmer. Living with his wife, Catharine and children: Mary (13), Ann (10), Wm. (8), James (6) and Arminda (2).

- He appeared on the United States census on 10 Sep 1860 in Menard County, Illinois.[647]

Jas. B. Ayres. Age 52. Farmer. Living with his wife, Catharine and children: Mary (23), William B. (18), James K. T. (15), Alice (6). Also in the household is Mary F. Ward (21).

- He appeared on the United States census on 24 Jul 1870 in Menard County, Illinois.[648]
Joseph Ayres. Age 65. Farmer. Living with his wife, Catharine and a niece(?), Ada Clark (16).

34. Abner Banks Hall *(Abner [9], Hezekiah [1])* was born about 1820 in Lawrence County, Ohio,[618] died on 28 Sep 1896 in Menard County, Illinois[618] about age 76, and was buried on 29 Sep 1896 in Menard County, Illinois (West Cemetery).[619]

Noted events in his life were:
- He appeared on the United States census on 23 Aug 1850 in Menard County, Illinois.[653]
A. B. Hall. Age 28. Living with his wife, F. J. Hall and son, Edward (2) in the household of his mother, Jenny Hall.

- His obituary was published about Oct 1896 in Menard County, Illinois.[618]
"ABNER BANKS HALL
(unknown newspaper)

Death of an Old Settler
One by one the pioneers of Athens and Menard county are being gathered to their fathers. The ties that bind them to earth are being severed and it will not be many years until all that is left of them will be in the memory of their successors on the stage of action. This week we are called upon to chronicle the decease of one of the old land marks whose well-known face has been familiar to the successive generations of Athens since the first settlement of this community - A. B. Hall
Abner Banks Hall was the son of Abner and Jane (Overstreet) Hall and was born in Lawrence county, Ohio in 1820. He came with his father's family to Illinois about 1825, and located a short distance north of the present city of Athens, on a piece of land afterward known as the Tice farm, now the property of H. C. Rogers. Later they located on what is now a part of this city. His father was one of the first merchants of Athens, forming a partnership with his brother, Elisha Hall in 1833. The deceased has resided here since that time and has been permitted to behold the most wonderful century of the world's history.
During his life the rugged wilderness has been transformed into the blooming garden spot of the world. The packhorse and stage coach have given way to the vestibuled train. The primitive methods of communication have been supplanted by the telegraph and telephone. The rising generation can scarcely grasp the greatness of the changes that have been wrought within the span of his life.
Mr. Hall was united in marriage with Miss Jeanette Francis about 1844. Several children were born to them, three of whom with their mother are still living: Mrs. Ida Croft, of Irish Grove, Calvin F. Hall and Mrs. Abbie Parrish, of this city. He is survived by two sisters, Mrs. Catherine Ayers and Mrs. Matilda Clark, who are all that remain of a family of ten.
His death occurred at the home of his daughter, Mrs. Parrish, at 12:05 a.m. Tuesday, Sept. 28, 1896, after a two weeks illness. He made no profession of religion during his life until during his last illness. He assured his family and friends that he was ready and willing to die.
Funeral services were held at the Presbyterian church on Wednesday at 10 o'clock a.m., conducted by the pastor Rev. D. G. Carson, after which his mortal remains were laid to rest in the beautiful West Cemetery, the cite of which was donated by his father to the public for a burying ground."

Transcribed by: Matthew <mailto:Rlferricks2@aol.com>

Abner married **Jeanette Francis,** daughter of _____ _____ and _____ _____, about 1844 in Illinois. Jeanette was born about 1826 in Connecticut, died after 1896 in Illinois, and was buried in Menard County, Illinois (West Cemetery).[654]

Noted events in her life were:
- She appeared on the United States census on 23 Aug 1850 in Menard County, Illinois.[655]
F. J. Hall. Age 24. Living with her husband, A. B. Hall and son, Edward (2) in the household of her mother-in-law, Jenny Hall.

35. Matilda Hall *(Abner [9], Hezekiah [1])* was born about 1828 in Illinois.

Noted events in her life were:
- She appeared on the United States census on 23 Aug 1850 in Menard County, Illinois.[656]
Matilda Clarke. Age 22. Living with her husband, [illegible] Clarke and children: A. (5), [illegible] (6/12). Her mother,

Jenny Hall and brother, A. B. Hall live next door.

Matilda married **C. Clark,** son of _____ _____ and _____ _____, about 1845 in Illinois. C. was born about 1821 in Illinois.

Noted events in his life were:

- He appeared on the United States census on 23 Aug 1850 in Menard County, Illinois.[656]
  [illegible] Clarke. Age 29. Brick maker. Living with his wife, Matilda Clarke and children: A. (5), [illegible] (6/12).

Descendants of Elisha Hall
of Bedford County, Virginia

First Generation

1. Elisha Hall, son of **William Hall** and **Mary Merryman,** was born before 1748 in Lunenburg County, Virginia.

Noted events in his life were:
- He was involved in a court case about his apprenticeship to Jeremiah Early about 1762 in Bedford County, Virginia.[31] Elisha sought to obtain his release.

- He was involved in a court case about regarding his apprenticeship in Jul 1766 in Bedford County, Virginia.[32] Elisha was bound over to a new "master", "Donathan".

Elisha married **Caroline Estes,** daughter of _____ _____ and _____ _____, about 1774 in Virginia.

Children from this marriage were:

+ 2 M   i.   **Elisha Hall** was born about 1775 in Bedford County, Virginia[657] and died on 28 Feb 1851 in Clinton County, Missouri[658] about age 76.

+ 3 M   ii.   **Jerimiah S. Hall** was born on 24 Jun 1783 in Virginia,[659] died on 30 Oct 1859 in Clinton County, Missouri[659] at age 76, and was buried in Clinton County, Missouri (Pleasant Hill Primitive Baptist Church Cemetery).

   4 M   iii.   **James Hall**.

Descendants of Elisha Hall
of Bedford County, Virginia

Second Generation

2. Elisha Hall *(Elisha [1])* was born about 1775 in Bedford County, Virginia[657] and died on 28 Feb 1851 in Clinton County, Missouri[658] about age 76.

> **Noted events in his life were:**
> - He served in the military as a soldier in the War of 1812 in New Orleans, Orleans Parish, Louisiana.[660]
>   It is said that he was one of Andrew Jackson's body guards.
>
> - He appeared on the United States census in 1840 in Clay County, Missouri.[661]
>   Elisha Hall. Age: 60 <70 - 1. The only individual listed in the household.
>
> - He appeared on the United States census on 24 Oct 1850 in Clinton County, Missouri.[662]
>   Elisha Hall. Age 78. Living in his daughter's household, Jefferson and Mary Ann Fry.

Elisha married **Alice "Alsey" DePriest,** daughter of **William DePriest** and **Alsie Annie Elliott,** on 8 Apr 1795 in Madison County, Kentucky.[663] Alsey was born about 1773 in Virginia and died before 1840 in Missouri. She was usually called Alsey.

> **Marriage Notes:**
> Some reports state they were married in Knoxville, Tennessee. --rch

Children from this marriage were:

+ 5 M i. **William Hall** was born on 28 Dec 1795 in Virginia[660] and died on 23 Oct 1848 in Clinton County, Missouri[660] at age 52.

+ 6 M ii. **James Elliott Hall** was born on 6 Jan 1798 in Madison County, Kentucky[657] and died on 2 Jun 1870 in Marion County, Oregon[664] at age 72.

+ 7 M iii. **John DePriest Hall** was born on 23 Apr 1800 in Kentucky[665] and died on 1 Mar 1865 in Liberty, Clay County, Missouri[665] at age 64.

+ 8 M iv. **Samuel C. Hall** was born on 28 Jul 1802 in Kentucky[664] and died on 16 Dec 1868 in Lake County, California[664] at age 66.

+ 9 F v. **Elizabeth "Betsy" A. Hall** was born on 23 Nov 1804 in Missouri[660] and died after 1860 in Missouri.[664]

+ 10 M vi. **Jerimiah Hall** was born on 10 Aug 1807 in Virginia[660] and died in Mar 1838 in Clay County, Missouri[657] at age 30.

+ 11 M vii. **George C. Hall** was born on 29 Aug 1810[657] and died about 1840 in Clay County, Missouri[664] about age 30.

+ 12 M viii. **David Madison Hall** was born on 21 May 1812 in Tennessee[657] and died on 3 Aug 1880 in Marion County, Oregon[664] at age 68.

+ 13 F ix. **Mary Ann Hall** was born about 1814 in Tennessee[660] and died on 28 Apr 1895 in Douglas County, Colorado[657] about age 81.

14 F x. **Polly Hall** was born about 1816.[660]

15 F xi. **Adaline Hall** was born on 1 Jun 1821.[660]

3. Jerimiah S. Hall *(Elisha [1])* was born on 24 Jun 1783 in Virginia,[659] died on 30 Oct 1859 in Clinton County, Missouri[659] at age 76, and was buried in Clinton County, Missouri (Pleasant Hill Primitive Baptist Church Cemetery).

> **General Notes:**
> *"Jeremiah S. Hall and his wife, Sarah (Cochran) Hall, were among the earliest settlers of Clay County in western Missouri. He was born in Virginia and she in North Carolina. We know almost nothing of their family origins. They probably came as children or young adults to Kentucky, where they married, apparently in Madison County on September 12, 1807. At that date, he would have been about 24 years old; she about 21.*
>
> *The family moved to Bedford County, Tennessee by 1811 (according to a county tax list) and on to Missouri, first to Boone County about 1818, and then to Clay County, where Jeremiah Hall purchased land from the government beginning in June 1823. These migrations were shared by the family of Elisha (sometimes recorded as Elijah) Hall (born about 1773). Due to the similarity in their histories and in the first names among their children, it seems very likely that Jeremiah and Elisha were*

brothers. This agrees with a single, unverified source which indicates that Jeremiah's father may have been an Elisha Hall who had two sons named Elisha and Jeremiah, both of whom migrated to Missouri. Jeremiah and Sarah lived and farmed east of Liberty, near the old Stockdale crossroads, for many years. They were apparently successful in farming, as the size and value of their holdings increased over the years. Sometime after 1850 they moved to Clinton County where several of their children were living.

Jeremiah died in Clinton County in 1859. In 1860, Sarah was living with her son Andrew in Clinton County. Andrew died in 1863 and she probably lived with other of her children in Clinton County until her own death in 1867. Jeremiah and Sarah share a tombstone in the Pleasant Hill Cemetery in southwestern Clinton County that is unusual in that it is a single block about two feet square and four feet high. It stands solid and erect over many newer stones that have toppled." --Find A Grave.com[666]

Noted events in his life were:

- He appeared on the United States census in 1830 in Clay County, Missouri.[667]
  Jeremiah Hall, Sr. Head of household. Presumably the oldest male listed.
  Males: 15 <20 - 3; 40 <50 - 1. Females: 5 <10 - 3; 40 <50 - 1.

- He appeared on the United States census on 29 Aug 1850 in Clay County, Missouri.[668]
  Jerimiah Hall. Age 67. Farmer. Living with his wife, Sally and children: Andrew N., (age 23), America (age 24). Also in the household is America C. Dunigan (age 3).

Jerimiah married **Sarah Cochran,** daughter of _____ _____ and _____ _____, on 12 Sep 1807 in Madison County, Kentucky.[659] Sarah was born about 1787 in North Carolina, died on 2 May 1867 in Clinton County, Missouri[669] about age 80, and was buried in May 1867 in Clinton County, Missouri (Pleasant Hill Primitive Baptist Church Cemetery).

Noted events in her life were:

- She appeared on the United States census in 1830 in Clay County, Missouri.[667]
  Sarah Hall. Presumably the oldest female listed in the household of her husband, Jeremiah Hall, Sr.
  Males: 15 <20 - 3; 40 <50 - 1. Females: 5 <10 - 3; 40 <50 - 1.

- She appeared on the United States census on 29 Aug 1850 in Clay County, Missouri.[668]
  Sally Hall. Age 63. Living with her husband, Jerimiah and children: Andrew N., (age 23), America (age 24). Also in the household is America C. Dunigan (age 3).

Descendants of Elisha Hall
of Bedford County, Virginia

Third Generation

5. William Hall *(Elisha², Elisha¹)* was born on 28 Dec 1795 in Virginia[660] and died on 23 Oct 1848 in Clinton County, Missouri[660] at age 52.

Noted events in his life were:
- He appeared on the United States census in 1830 in Clay County, Missouri.[670]
William Hall. Head of household.
Presumably the oldest male listed and the son of Elisha and Alice Hall.
Males: <5 - 2; 5 <10 - 2; 20 <30 - 1. Females: <5 - 1; 20 <30 - 1.

- He appeared on the United States census in 1840 in Clay County, Missouri.[671]
Wm. Hall. Head of family.
Presumably the male aged 40-50.
Males: <5 (1), 10 -15 (2), 15 -20 (1), 40 -50 (1); Females: <5 (1), 5 -10 (1), 10 -15 (1), 30 -40 (1).
His brother James E. Hall and brother in -law, Thomas Fry live close by (same page).

William married **Sarah Estes,** daughter of **Littleberry Estes** and **Unknown,** on 9 Dec 1819 in Clay County, Missouri.[672] Sarah was born on 21 Jun 1804 in Kentucky[664] and died on 24 Dec 1856 in Clay County, Missouri[664] at age 52.

Noted events in her life were:
- She appeared on the United States census in 1830 in Clay County, Missouri.[670]
Sarah Hall. Presumably the oldest female listed in the household of her husband, William Hall.
Males: <5 - 2; 5 <10 - 2; 20 <30 - 1. Females: <5 - 1; 20 <30 - 1.

- She appeared on the United States census on 24 Oct 1850 in Clinton County, Missouri.[673]
Mrs. Hall. Age 45. Apparently a widow. Living with her children: Rich (age 21), M (age 17), Adiline (age 12), George (age 10), John (age 8) and Antone (age 4).

- She had an estate probated in Clinton County, Missouri.[672]
Littleberry G. Hall was the administrator of the estate. Jefferson Fry posted security.

Children from this marriage were:

16 M   i.   **Richmond Hall** was born on 1 Oct 1820 in Clay County, Missouri.[672]

17 M   ii. **Elisha Estes Hall** was born on 19 Feb 1822 in Clay County, Missouri.[672]

+ 18 M iii. **Little Berry Green Hall** was born on 17 Aug 1823 in Saline County, Missouri[672] and died on 16 Feb 1897 in Rouge River Valley, Oregon[672] at age 73.

19 M   iv. **William Wallace Hall** was born on 8 Jun 1825 in Missouri[672] and died in Dec 1862[672] at age 37.

            Noted events in his life were:
            - He appeared on the United States census on 1 Nov 1850 in Tarrant County, Texas.[674]
              Wm. W. Hall. Age 24. Farmer. Living with his brother, Little B. Hall. Perhaps in a boarding house.

+ 20 F   v.   **Leticia Ann Hall** was born on 28 Apr 1827.[672]

21 M   vi. **Rice Davenport Hall** was born on 9 Apr 1829 in Missouri[672] and died on 27 Oct 1852[672] at age 23.

            Noted events in his life were:
            - He appeared on the United States census on 24 Oct 1850 in Clinton County, Missouri.[673]
              Rich Hall. Age 21. Farmer. Living with his mother and siblings.

22 M vii. **Payton Ashby Hall** was born on 8 Jan 1831 in Clay County, Missouri.[672]

23 F viii. **Maryetta DePriest Hall** was born on 14 Feb 1833 in Missouri.[672]

            Noted events in her life were:
            - She appeared on the United States census on 24 Oct 1850 in Clinton County, Missouri.[673]
              M. Hall. Age 17. Living with her mother and siblings.

24   M   ix.   **James Marion Hall** was born on 28 Nov 1834.[672]

25   M   x.   **George Washington Hall** was born on 17 Feb 1836.[672]

26   F   xi.   **Adaline Hall** was born on 18 Mar 1837 in Missouri[672] and died on 18 Nov 1852 in Missouri[672] at age 15. She never married and had no children.

         Noted events in her life were:
- She appeared on the United States census on 24 Oct 1850 in Clinton County, Missouri.[673] Adiline Hall. Age 12. Living with her mother and siblings.

27   M   xii.   **George French Hall** was born on 8 Oct 1839 in Missouri.[672]

         Noted events in his life were:
- He appeared on the United States census on 24 Oct 1850 in Clinton County, Missouri.[673] George Hall. Age 10. Living with his mother and siblings.

28   M   xiii.   **John Riley Hall** was born on 29 Nov 1841 in Missouri.[672]

         Noted events in his life were:
- He appeared on the United States census on 24 Oct 1850 in Clinton County, Missouri.[673] John Hall. Age 8. Living with his mother and siblings.

+ 29   M   xiv.   **Antoine Elisha Hall** was born on 21 May 1846 in Clay County, Missouri.[672]

6. James Elliott Hall *(Elisha ², Elisha ¹)* was born on 6 Jan 1798 in Madison County, Kentucky[657] and died on 2 Jun 1870 in Marion County, Oregon[664] at age 72.

      Noted events in his life were:
- He appeared on the United States census in 1830 in Clay County, Missouri.[675]
  James E. Hall. Head of household. Presumably the oldest male listed.
  Males: <5 - 1; 20 <30 - 1. Females: <5 - 1; 5 <10 - 1; 10 <15 -1; 20 <30 - 1.

- He appeared on the United States census in 1840 in Clay County, Missouri.[676]
  Jame[s] E. Hall. Head of family.
  Presumably the oldest male aged 40 -50.
  Males: <5 (2), 10 -15 (1), 20 -30 (1), 30 -40 (1), 40 -50 (1); Females: 5 -10 (3), 10 -15 (1), 15 -20 (1), 20 -30 (1), 30 -40 (1). Looks like multiple families in the household. His brother, Wm. Hall and brother in -law, Thomas Fry live close by (sames page). --rch

- He appeared on the United States census on 27 Dec 1850 in Marion County, Oregon.[677]
  James E. Hall. Age 55. Farmer. Living with his wife, Synthia and children: Albert, James, America, William and Ellen. All children except Ellen were born in Missouri.

James married **Cynthia Ann Groom,** daughter of _____ _____ and _____ _____, on 27 Jul 1824 in Clay County, Missouri.[664] Cynthia was born on 2 Oct 1804 in Clark County, Kentucky[664] and died on 20 Jun 1897 in Marion County, Oregon[664] at age 92.

      Noted events in her life were:
- She appeared on the United States census in 1830 in Clay County, Missouri.[675]
  Cynthia Hall. Presumably the oldest female listed in the household of her husband, James E. Hall.
  Males: <5 - 1; 20 <30 - 1. Females: <5 - 1; 5 <10 - 1; 10 <15 -1; 20 <30 - 1.

- She appeared on the United States census on 27 Dec 1850 in Marion County, Oregon.[677]
  Synthia Hall. Age 46. Living with her husband, James E. Hall and children: Albert, James, America, William and Ellen. All children except Ellen were born in Missouri.

7. John DePriest Hall *(Elisha ², Elisha ¹)* was born on 23 Apr 1800 in Kentucky[665] and died on 1 Mar 1865 in Liberty, Clay County, Missouri[665] at age 64.

Descendants of Elisha Hall
of Bedford County, Virginia

Noted events in his life were:
- He appeared on the United States census in 1830 in Clay County, Missouri.[678]
  John D. Hall. Head of household. Presumably the oldest male listed.
  Males: <5 - 1; 20 <30 - 1. Females: <5 - 1; 20 <30 - 1.

- He appeared on the United States census on 2 Sep 1850 in Clay County, Missouri.[679]
  John D. Hall. Age 50. Farmer. Living with his wife, Eliza and children from three families: Mary E., Sarah, Adeliah, Elisha, George W., Jerimiah, Adaline, John, Alice; Robert C. Nutter, Downing J. Nutter, James S. Nutter, Sarah L. Nutter.

- He appeared on the United States census on 16 Jun 1860 in Clay County, Missouri.[680]
  John D. Hall. Age 60. Farmer. Living with his wife, Eliza and children from three families: Elish(23), George(21), Jerimiah(19), John(17), Adda(19), Alice(9); Allen(7), Gertrude(5), Lycurgus(4), Robert(1), Lucinda (17).

John married **Nancy Duncan,** daughter of **James Duncan** and **Nancy Musick Duncan,** on 28 Dec 1826 in Clay County, Missouri.[681] Nancy was born on 2 Dec 1811 in Bourbon County, Kentucky[664] and died about 1847 in Clay County, Missouri[682] about age 36.

Noted events in her life were:
- She appeared on the United States census in 1830 in Clay County, Missouri.[678]
  Nancy Hall. Presumably the oldest female listed in the household of her husband, John D. Hall.
  Males: <5 - 1; 20 <30 - 1. Females: <5 - 1; 20 <30 - 1.

Children from this marriage were:

30 M   i.   **James Duncan Hall** was born before 1830 in Missouri and died about 1847 in Mexico.[681] He never married and had no children.

+ 31 F   ii.   **Bellidera Hall** was born before 1830 in Missouri.

+ 32 F   iii.   **Mary Ellen Hall** was born about 1831 in Clay County, Missouri.[682]

+ 33 F   iv.   **Adeliah Hall** was born about 1832 in Clay County, Missouri.[682]

+ 34 F   v.   **Sarah Elizabeth Hall** was born about 1833 in Clay County, Missouri.[682]

35 M   vi.   **Elisha Hall**[681] was born about 1836 in Clay County, Missouri[682] and died about 1924[682] about age 88.

     Noted events in his life were:
     - He appeared on the United States census on 2 Sep 1850 in Clay County, Missouri.[679]
       Elisha Hall. Age 14. Living with his parents and siblings.

     - He appeared on the United States census on 16 Jun 1860 in Clay County, Missouri.[683]
       Elish Hall. Age 23. Living with his parents and siblings.

+ 36 M   vii.   **George W. Hall**[681] was born about 1838 in Clay County, Missouri[682] and died about 1893[682] about age 55.

37 M   viii.   **Jerimiah Hall**[681] was born about 1840 in Clay County, Missouri.[682]

     Noted events in his life were:
     - He appeared on the United States census on 2 Sep 1850 in Clay County, Missouri.[679]
       Jerimiah Hall. Age 11. Living with his father and siblings.

     - He appeared on the United States census on 16 Jun 1860 in Clay County, Missouri.[683]
       Jerimiah Hall. Age 19. Living with his parents and siblings.

+ 38 F   ix.   **Adaline Hall** was born about 1841 in Clay County, Missouri.[682]

+ 39 M   x.   **John Calvin Hall**[681] was born about 1843 in Clay County, Missouri.[681]

John next married **Eliza Adkins,** daughter of _____ _____ and _____ _____, on 2 Jul 1848 in Clay County, Missouri.[681] Eliza was born about 1817 in Kentucky[682] and died about 1899[682] about age 82.

Noted events in her life were:
- She appeared on the United States census on 16 Jun 1860 in Clay County, Missouri.[683]
  Eliza Hall. Age 43. Living with her husband, John and children from three families: Elish(23), George(21), Jerimiah(19),

John(17), Adda(19); Alice(9), Allen(7), Gertrude(5), Lycurgus(4), Robert(1); Lucinda (17)

Children from this marriage were:

+ 40 F   i.   **Alice Hall** was born about 1849 in Clay County, Missouri.[683]

+ 41 M   ii.   **Allen Hall** was born about 1853 in Clay County, Missouri[681] and died about 1889 in Clay County, Missouri[681] about age 36.

   42 F   iii.   **Gertrude Hall** was born about 1855 in Clay County, Missouri and died about 1869[684] about age 14.

       Noted events in her life were:
       • She appeared on the United States census on 16 Jun 1860 in Clay County, Missouri.[683]
       Gertrude Hall. Age 5. Living with her parents and siblings.

   43 M   iv.   **Kirk Hall**[684] was born about 1856 in Clay County, Missouri[682] and died about 1923[682] about age 67. Another name for Kirk was Lycurgus.

       Noted events in his life were:
       • He appeared on the United States census on 16 Jun 1860 in Clay County, Missouri.[683]
       Lycurgus Hall. Age 4. Living with his parents and siblings.

   44 M   v.   **Robert Emmet Hall** was born about 1859 in Clay County, Missouri[684] and died about 1869[684] about age 10.

       Noted events in his life were:
       • He appeared on the United States census on 16 Jun 1860 in Clay County, Missouri.[683]
       Robert Hall. Age 1. Living with his parents and siblings.

   45 F   vi.   **Anna W. Hall** was born about 1863 in Clay County, Missouri[682] and died about 1953[682] about age 90.

       Research Notes:
       The Estes Genealogy does not show an "Anna W." as a daughter of John DePriest Hall.

8. Samuel C. Hall *(Elisha² , Elisha¹)* was born on 28 Jul 1802 in Kentucky[664] and died on 16 Dec 1868 in Lake County, California[664] at age 66.

       Noted events in his life were:
       • He appeared on the United States census in 1830 in Clay County, Missouri.[685]
       Samuel Hall. Head of household. Presumably the oldest male listed.
       Males: <5 - 1; 20 <30 - 1. Females: <5 - 2; 20 <30 - 1.

Samuel married **Agnes Estes,** daughter of **Joel Estes, Jr.** and **Rachel Ward,** on 17 May 1825 in Clay County, Missouri.[660] Agnes was born on 24 Dec 1808 in Cabell County, Virginia[686] and died about 1890 in Clay County, Missouri[686] about age 82.

       Noted events in her life were:
       • She appeared on the United States census in 1830 in Clay County, Missouri.[685]
       Agnes Hall. Presumably the oldest female listed in the household of her husband, Samuel Hall.
       Males: <5 - 1; 20 <30 - 1. Females: <5 - 2; 20 <30 - 1.

The child from this marriage was:

   46 M   i.   **Frank Hall.**

9. Elizabeth "Betsy" A. Hall *(Elisha² , Elisha¹)* was born on 23 Nov 1804 in Missouri[660] and died after 1860 in Missouri.[664] She was usually called Betsy.

       Birth Notes:
       The 1860 United States Federal Census shows her birthplace as North Carolina. --rch

       Noted events in her life were:
       • She appeared on the United States census on 19 Aug 1850 in Clay County, Missouri.[687]
       Elizabeth Fry. Age 34. Living with her husband, Thomas Fry and children: Oliver, Lewis, M.J., Thomas, Ann and N.C. Fry.

- She appeared on the United States census on 18 Jul 1860 in Clay County, Missouri.[688]
  Elizabeth Fry. Age 45. Living with her husband, Thos. Fry, and children: Lewis, Mary, Thomas, Elizabeth, Nancy, Lucy and Allen Fry.

Betsy married **Thomas Fry,** son of **Isaac Fry** and **Unknown,** on 17 Jul 1823 in Clay County, Missouri.[689] Thomas was born on 27 Jul 1804 in Kentucky[664] and died on 31 Jan 1888[664] at age 83.

Noted events in his life were:
- He appeared on the United States census in 1840 in Clay County, Missouri.[690]
  Thomas Fry. Head of family.
  Presumably the oldest male aged 30 -40.
  Males: <5 (1), 5 -10 (1), 10 -15 (1), 15 -20 (1), 30 -40 (1); Females: 10 -15 (1), 20 -30 (1).
  His brother's in -law James E. Hall and Wm. Hall live close by (on same page). --rch

- He appeared on the United States census on 19 Aug 1850 in Clay County, Missouri.[687]
  Thomas Fry. Age 46. Farmer. Living with his wife, Elizabeth and children: Oliver, Lewis, M.J., Thomas, Ann and N.C. Fry.

- He appeared on the United States census on 18 Jul 1860 in Clay County, Missouri.[688]
  Thos. Fry. Age 56. Farmer. Living with his wife, Elizabeth and children: Lewis, Mary, Thomas, Elizabeth, Nancy, Lucy and Allen Fry.

10. Jerimiah Hall *(Elisha*[2]*, Elisha*[1]*)* was born on 10 Aug 1807 in Virginia[660] and died in Mar 1838 in Clay County, Missouri[657] at age 30.

Jerimiah married **Eleanor Duncan,** daughter of _____ _____ and _____ _____, on 23 Apr 1835 in Clay County, Missouri.[660] Eleanor was born on 11 Sep 1818 in Bourbon County, Kentucky.[664] They had no children.

11. George C. Hall *(Elisha*[2]*, Elisha*[1]*)* was born on 29 Aug 1810[657] and died about 1840 in Clay County, Missouri[664] about age 30.

George married **Elizabeth C. Hall,** daughter of _____ _____ and _____ _____, on 21 Nov 1829 in Clay County, Missouri.[664]

12. David Madison Hall *(Elisha*[2]*, Elisha*[1]*)* was born on 21 May 1812 in Tennessee[657] and died on 3 Aug 1880 in Marion County, Oregon[664] at age 68.

Noted events in his life were:
- He appeared on the United States census on 7 Oct 1850 in Daviess County, Missouri.[691]
  David M. Hall. Age 37. Carpenter. Living with his wife, Lucy and children: Willard (age 8), Thomas (age 7), Rebecca (age 5), Caroline (age 1). Living in his father-in-law's household, Porterfield Tolin.

David married **Amanda Vanlandingham,** daughter of _____ _____ and _____ _____, on 12 Nov 1834 in Ray County, Missouri.[664]

David next married **Lucy L. "Aunty Lucy" Tolin,** daughter of **Porterfield Tolin** and **Rebecca _____,** on 18 Jan 1842 in Daviess County, Missouri.[664] Aunty Lucy was born on 17 Jan 1827 in Lexington County, Kentucky[664] and died on 18 Feb 1897 in Marion County, Oregon[664] at age 70. She was usually called Aunty Lucy.

Noted events in her life were:
- She appeared on the United States census on 7 Oct 1850 in Daviess County, Missouri.[691]
  Lucy Hall. Age 23. Living with her husband, David M. Hall and children: Willard (age 8), Thomas (age 7), Rebecca (age 5), Caroline (age 1). Living in her father's household, Porterfield Tolin.

13. Mary Ann Hall *(Elisha*[2]*, Elisha*[1]*)* was born about 1814 in Tennessee[660] and died on 28 Apr 1895 in Douglas County, Colorado[657] about age 81.

Noted events in her life were:
- She appeared on the United States census on 24 Oct 1850 in Clinton County, Missouri.[692]
  Mary Ann Fry. Age 35. Living with her husband, Jefferson and children: William (age 18), S. (age 17), Thomas (age 14),

Adiline (age 10), George (age 7), P. (age 5), L. (age 5) and Chas. (age 1). Also in the household is her father, Elisha Hall.

Mary married **Jefferson Fry,** son of **Isaac Fry** and **Unknown,** on 3 Aug 1830 in Clay County, Missouri.[660] Jefferson was born on 28 Nov 1806 in Kentucky[664] and died on 6 Sep 1888 in Douglas County, Colorado[664] at age 81.

Noted events in his life were:
- He appeared on the United States census on 24 Oct 1850 in Clinton County, Missouri.[692]
  Jefferson Fry. Age 42. Farmer. Living with his wife, Mary Ann and children: William (age 18), S. (age 17), Thomas (age 14), Adiline (age 10), George (age 7), P. [Paulina] (age 5), L. [Louvina] (age 5) and Chas. (age 1). Also in the household is his father-in-law, Elisha Hall.

Descendants of Elisha Hall
of Bedford County, Virginia

Fourth Generation

18. Little Berry Green Hall *(William⁵, Elisha², Elisha¹)* was born on 17 Aug 1823 in Saline County, Missouri[672] and died on 16 Feb 1897 in Rouge River Valley, Oregon[672] at age 73.

    Noted events in his life were:
- He appeared on the United States census on 1 Nov 1850 in Tarrant County, Texas.[693]
  Little B. Hall. Age 26. Black Smith. Living with his brother, Wm. W. Hall. Perhaps in a boarding house.

- He appeared on the United States census on 1 Jun 1880 in Josephine County, Oregon.[694]
  Little B. G. Hall. Age 56. Farmer. Living with his wife, Lucy A. Says his parents were born in Kentucky. Next door is Thomas J. Hall (age 36) and his wife, Elizabeth (age 36) and children. Probably, Little B. G. Hall's son.

Little married **Lucy Ann Jones,** daughter of _____ _____ and _____ _____, on 6 Sep 1855 in Clay County, Missouri.[672] Lucy was born about 1827 in Kentucky,[672] died on 20 Jan 1899 in Plattsburg, Missouri[672] about age 72, and was buried in Plattsburg, Missouri (Pleasant Hill Church Cemetery).[672]

    Noted events in her life were:
- She appeared on the United States census on 1 Jun 1880 in Josephine County, Oregon.[695]
  Lucy A. Hall. Age 50. Keeping House. Living with her husband, Little B. G. Hall. Says her parents were born in Kentucky.

20. Leticia Ann Hall *(William⁵, Elisha², Elisha¹)* was born on 28 Apr 1827.[672]

Leticia married **J. C. Garner,** son of _____ _____ and _____ _____.

    The child from this marriage was:
- 47 F i. **Amanda Garner** was born on 28 Feb 1849 in Clay County, Missouri[672] and died on 1 Mar 1888 in Clay County, Missouri[672] at age 39.

29. Antoine Elisha Hall *(William⁵, Elisha², Elisha¹)* was born on 21 May 1846 in Clay County, Missouri.[672]

    Noted events in his life were:
- He appeared on the United States census on 24 Oct 1850 in Clinton County, Missouri.[673]
  Antone Hall. Age 4. Living with his mother and siblings.

Antoine married **Rebecca E. Groom,** daughter of _____ _____ and _____ _____, on 13 Jan 1872 in Clay County, Missouri.[672]

31. Bellidera Hall *(John DePriest⁷, Elisha², Elisha¹)* was born before 1830 in Missouri.

    Research Notes:
Bellidera Hall is not listed in The Grandfather's - Hall-Overstreet manuscript.

Bellidera married **Daniel Stout,** son of _____ _____ and _____ _____, on 2 Mar 1847 in Clay County, Missouri.[681]

    Research Notes:
Daniel Stout is not listed in The Grandfather's - Hall-Overstreet manuscript.

32. Mary Ellen Hall *(John DePriest⁷, Elisha², Elisha¹)* was born about 1831 in Clay County, Missouri.[682]

    Noted events in her life were:
- She appeared on the United States census on 2 Sep 1850 in Clay County, Missouri.[679]
  Mary E. Hall. Age 19. Living with her father and siblings.

Mary married **Thomas Duncan,** son of _____ _____ and _____ _____, in Missouri. [684] Thomas was born on 27 Apr 1824 in Glasgow, Kentucky[684] and died on 29 Oct 1915 in Excelsior Springs, Missouri[681] at age 91.

The child from this marriage was:

+ 48 M   i.   **Joseph Thomas Duncan** was born on 3 Jan 1856 in Smithville, Missouri[681] and died on 26 Oct 1933 in Perkinsville, Arizona[681] at age 77.

33. Adeliah Hall *(John DePriest[7], Elisha[2], Elisha[1])* was born about 1832 in Clay County, Missouri.[682]

> **Noted events in her life were:**
> - She appeared on the United States census on 2 Sep 1850 in Clay County, Missouri.[679]
> Adelia Hall. Age 16. Living with her father and siblings.

Adeliah married **Elijah Ecton**, son of _____ _____ and _____ _____, after 1850 in Clay County, Missouri.[696] Elijah was born about 1826 in Kentucky.

> **Noted events in his life were:**
> - He appeared on the United States census on 2 Sep 1850 in Clay County, Missouri.[697]
> Alijah Ecton. Age 24. Farmer. Living with his wife Luticia and son, James T.

34. Sarah Elizabeth Hall *(John DePriest[7], Elisha[2], Elisha[1])* was born about 1833 in Clay County, Missouri.[682]

> **Noted events in her life were:**
> - She appeared on the United States census on 2 Sep 1850 in Clay County, Missouri.[679]
> Sarah Hall. Age 17. Living with her father and siblings.

Sarah married **John Henry Mosby**, son of **Wade Mosby** and **Rebecca Shouse**, on 6 Feb 1855 in Clay County, Missouri.[698]

Children from this marriage were:

+ 49 F   i.   **Etta Mosby** was born on 29 Jan 1864 in Clay County, Missouri[684] and died on 27 Oct 1949 in Houston, Harris County, Texas[684] at age 85.

+ 50 F   ii.   **Gertrude Mosby**.

+ 51 F   iii.   **Ida Mosby** was born on 27 Mar 1866 in Liberty, Clay County, Missouri,[699] died on 15 May 1940 in Houston, Harris County, Texas[700] at age 74, and was buried in May 1940 in Kansas City, Jackson County, Missouri.

36. George W. Hall[681] *(John DePriest[7], Elisha[2], Elisha[1])* was born about 1838 in Clay County, Missouri[682] and died about 1893[682] about age 55.

> **Noted events in his life were:**
> - He appeared on the United States census on 2 Sep 1850 in Clay County, Missouri.[679]
> George W. Hall. Age 12. Living with his father and siblings.
>
> - He appeared on the United States census on 16 Jun 1860 in Clay County, Missouri.[683]
> George Hall. Age 21. Living with his parents and siblings.

George married _____ **Hancock**,[682] daughter of _____ _____ and _____ _____.

38. Adaline Hall *(John DePriest[7], Elisha[2], Elisha[1])* was born about 1841 in Clay County, Missouri.[682]

> **Noted events in her life were:**
> - She appeared on the United States census on 2 Sep 1850 in Clay County, Missouri.[679]
> Adaline Hall. Age 8. Living with her father and siblings.
>
> - She appeared on the United States census on 16 Jun 1860 in Clay County, Missouri.[683]
> Adda Hall. Age 19. Living with her parents and siblings.

Adaline married **Samuel Hardwick**, son of _____ _____ and _____ _____, on 27 Dec 1860 in Clay County, Missouri.[681] Samuel was born on 8 Sep 1833 in Clay County, Missouri.[681]

Descendants of Elisha Hall
of Bedford County, Virginia

Noted events in his life were:
- He worked as an Attorney in Clay County, Missouri.[681]

39. John Calvin Hall[681] *(John DePriest*[7]*, Elisha*[2]*, Elisha*[1]*)* was born about 1843 in Clay County, Missouri.[681]

Noted events in his life were:
- He appeared on the United States census on 2 Sep 1850 in Clay County, Missouri.[679]
John Hall. Age 7. Living with his father and siblings.

- He appeared on the United States census on 16 Jun 1860 in Clay County, Missouri.[683]
John Hall. Age 17. Living with his parents and siblings.

John married _____ **Stewart,** daughter of _____ _____ and _____ _____.

40. Alice Hall *(John DePriest*[7]*, Elisha*[2]*, Elisha*[1]*)* was born about 1849 in Clay County, Missouri.[683]

Research Notes:
"The Grandfathers - Hall-Overstreet Families" lists Alice Hall as a daughter of John DePriest Hall and Nancy Duncan not Eliza Nutter.

Noted events in her life were:
- She appeared on the United States census on 2 Sep 1850 in Clay County, Missouri.[679]
Alice Hall. Age 1. Living with her parents and 1/2 siblings.

- She appeared on the United States census on 16 Jun 1860 in Clay County, Missouri.[683]
Alice Hall. Age 9. Living with her parents and siblings.

Alice married **Thomas Jenkins,** son of _____ _____ and _____ _____.

41. Allen Hall *(John DePriest*[7]*, Elisha*[2]*, Elisha*[1]*)* was born about 1853 in Clay County, Missouri[681] and died about 1889 in Clay County, Missouri[681] about age 36.

Noted events in his life were:
- He appeared on the United States census on 16 Jun 1860 in Clay County, Missouri.[683]
Allen Hall. Age 7. Living with his parents and siblings.

Allen married someone. _____ _____

His child was:

   52 M   i. **Dr. Frank DePriest Hall**.

Fifth Generation

48. Joseph Thomas Duncan *(Mary Ellen Hall[32], John DePriest[7], Elisha[2], Elisha[1])* was born on 3 Jan 1856 in Smithville, Missouri[681] and died on 26 Oct 1933 in Perkinsville, Arizona[681] at age 77.

Joseph married **Josephine Cowdery,** daughter of **Jacob Edwin Cowdery** and **Louisa Lucette Waterman,**.

The child from this marriage was:

+ 53 F i. **Evelyn Duncan** was born on 12 Feb 1894 in Clay County, Missouri.[681]

49. Etta Mosby *(Sarah Elizabeth Hall[34], John DePriest[7], Elisha[2], Elisha[1])* was born on 29 Jan 1864 in Clay County, Missouri[684] and died on 27 Oct 1949 in Houston, Harris County, Texas[684] at age 85.

Etta married **Elisha Tapp Estes,** son of _____ _____ and _____ _____.

50. Gertrude Mosby *(Sarah Elizabeth Hall[34], John DePriest[7], Elisha[2], Elisha[1]).*

Gertrude married **Charles A. Evans,**[684] son of _____ _____ and _____ _____.

Noted events in his life were:
• He had a residence in 1940 in Los Angeles County, California.[684]

51. Ida Mosby *(Sarah Elizabeth Hall[34], John DePriest[7], Elisha[2], Elisha[1])* was born on 27 Mar 1866 in Liberty, Clay County, Missouri,[699] died on 15 May 1940 in Houston, Harris County, Texas[700] at age 74, and was buried in May 1940 in Kansas City, Jackson County, Missouri.

Ida married **S. E. Campbell,** son of _____ _____ and _____ _____.

Descendants of Elisha Hall
of Bedford County, Virginia

Sixth Generation

53. Evelyn Duncan *(Joseph Thomas Duncan [48], Mary Ellen Hall [32], John DePriest [7], Elisha [2], Elisha [1])* was born on 12 Feb 1894 in Clay County, Missouri.[681]

Evelyn married **Marion Nicholas Perkins,** son of **Marion Alexander Perkins** and **Harriet Ann York,**. Marion was born on 21 Aug 1887.[681]

Source Citations

1. The Church of Jesus Christ of Latter-day Saints, "Ancestral File," database,*FamilySearch* (http://www.familysearch.org : accessed 28 Jul 2009), William Hall (AFN: D189-47) and Mary Merryman (AFN: 56V2-ZJ) family group record; submission no. AF86-000886, Edwin C. Merryman, Ocean City, New Jersey. .... Carrol Carmen Hall,*The Grandfathers, The Hall and Overstreet Families* , 2 Volumes (Springfield, Illinois: Illinois Ancestors.org - Menard County (http://www.illinoisancestors.org/menard/), 1981-2007).

2. Maud Carter Clement,*The History of Pittsylvania County, Virginia* (Lynchburg, Virginia: J. P. Bell Company, 1929), pages 65-87. .... Thomas K. Cartmell, *Shenandoah Valley pioneers and their descendants; a history of Frederick County, Virginia, from its formation in 1738 to 1908* (Winchester, Virgtinia, Eddy Press Corp., 1909; reprint, Westminister, Maryland: Heritage Books, Inc, 1989; 2007), page 72. .... William L. McDowell Jr., editor, *Documents Related to Indian Affairs, 1754-1765* (Columbia, South Carolina: University of South Carolina Press, 1970), 464; Includes full transcript of Mayes Ferry Deposition - 1758 .... Timothy Dalton (Bedford, Virginia) to George Washington, Letter/ Sworn Testimony/Affidavit on Indian Raid, May 9, 1758; digital images, The Library of Congress, "George Washington Papers at the Library of Congress, 1741-1799: Series 4. General Correspondence. 1697-1799," *American Memory* (http://memory.loc.gov/cgi-bin/ampage?collId=mgw4&fileName=gwpage031.db&recNum=444 : accessed 31 Mar 2010);
Sent by President Blair to George Washington. Witnessed by Robert Baber.
Published by the Society of the Colonial Dames of America. Edited by Stanislaus Murray Hamilton. .... William Callaway (Bedford, Virginia) to George Washington, Letter, May 15 1758; digital images, The Library of Congress, "George Washington Papers at the Library of Congress,*American Memory* (http://memory.loc.gov/cgi-bin/ampage?collId=mgw4&fileName=gwpage031.db&recNum=487 : accessed 31 Mar 2010).

3. Timothy Dalton (Bedford, Virginia) to George Washington, Letter/ Sworn Testimony/Affidavit on Indian Raid, May 9, 1758; digital images, The Library of Congress, "George Washington Papers at the Library of Congress, 1741-1799: Series 4. General Correspondence. 1697-1799,"*American Memory* (http://memory.loc.gov/cgi-bin/ampage?collId=mgw4&fileName=gwpage031.db&recNum=444 : accessed 31 Mar 2010);
Sent by President Blair to George Washington. Witnessed by Robert Baber.
Published by the Society of the Colonial Dames of America. Edited by Stanislaus Murray Hamilton. .... William Callaway (Bedford, Virginia) to George Washington, Letter, May 15 1758; digital images, The Library of Congress, "George Washington Papers at the Library of Congress,*American Memory* (http://memory.loc.gov/cgi-bin/ampage?collId=mgw4&fileName=gwpage031.db&recNum=487 : accessed 31 Mar 2010).

4. Paul Clements,*A Past Remembered Volume I* (Nashville, Tennessee: Clearview Press, 1987), 172. .... Carrol Carmen Hall,*The Grandfathers, The Hall and Overstreet Families* , 2 Volumes (Springfield, Illinois: Illinois Ancestors.org - Menard County (http://www.illinoisancestors.org/menard/), 1981-2007), Section I; Chapter 2; Page 13; Citing: Letters of Mrs. Eleanor Hodgkins, deceased of Ft. Worth, Texas .... Justin Sanders to Ronald C. Hall, e-mail, March 31, 2010, "RE: William Callaway Letter, 1758"; privately held by Hall, Fort Worth, Texas;
*"Ronald,
By dashing off a quick reply this morning I did not fully explain my interest in the John Hall found on the 1748 Lunenburg tax list. Obviously he is too old to be John, s/o William. Since our John is reportedly the oldest son of William, if the English naming tradition was followed he was probably named after his paternal grandfather, making the unknown father of William: John. The Lunenburg John of 1748 is of the right age range to be William's brother. That the two are both found on the south side of the James is something that can't be overlooked. If we are able to find information regarding the family group of the 1748 John, and if he is truly William's brother his firstborn son should be John Jr., or John III as the case may be. Should that scenario prove correct, we will have pinpointed William's father and widened his family group.*

If the Halls are truly English, and if they came to the colonies in 1725, I am skeptical about the claim that they entered the new world via the Penn Colony. I think it far more likely that they entered through the Chesapeake region somewhere. If so, they might be found on passenger manifests. Justin."

5. John David Davis, *Baltimore County, Maryland Deed Records: 1727-1757* (Heritage Books, 1997), Volume 2 of Baltimore County, Maryland Deed Records, 2: 143-144; digital images - preview,*Google Books* (http://books.google.com/ : downloaded 3 Nov 2009). .... John David Davis, *Baltimore County, Maryland Deed Records: 1727-1757* (Heritage Books, 1997), Volume 2 of Baltimore County, Maryland Deed Records, 2: 216, 236; digital images - preview,*Google Books* (http://books.google.com/ : downloaded 6 Mar 2010). .... Shawn Martin, "Choate's Fancy,"*Choate-L Archives*, mailing list, February 28, 2002 (http://archiver.rootsweb.ancestry.com/th/index/CHOATE : accessed 25 Dec 2009); http://archiver.rootsweb.ancestry.com/th/read/CHOATE/2002-02/1014905874

6. Nancy Schmitt, "Re: Joseph Cross Sr and Brood,"*CROSS-L Archives*, mailing list, 2 Oct 2002 (http://archiver.rootsweb.ancestry.com/th/read/CROSS/ : accessed 7 Feb 2010); http://archiver.rootsweb.ancestry.com/th/read/CROSS/2002-10/1033561576 .... William B. Marye, "The Old Indian Road,"*Maryland Historical Magazine, Volume 15*, 1920, pages 345-346; digital images, Google Books, *Google Boooks.com* (http://books.google.com/books?id=yvUMAAAAYAAJ&dq=%22William+Hall%22,+Patapsco+River, +Maryland&source=gbs_navlinks_s : accessed 6 Mar 2010); Citing: Baltimore County Land Records .... Robert William Barnes*Baltimore County Families, 1659-1759* (Baltimore, Maryland: Genealogical Publisher Company, 1989), 161.

7. Robert William Barnes,*Baltimore County Families, 1659-1759* (Baltimore, Maryland: Genealogical Publisher Company, 1989), 296; "may be William Hall, weaver, who with wife, Mary, sold 50 acres of Level Bottom to William Cross on August 4, 1746; probably the William who was listed in 1750 as owner of part of Pleasant Meadows and 50 acres of Hall's Range."; This source groups him with the family of Henry Hall of Baltimore County, Maryland.

8. Landon C. Bell,*Sunlight on the South Side - Lists of Tithes Lunenburg County, Virginia 1748-1783* (Philadelphia, Pennsylvania: George S. Ferguson Co., 1931, Baltimore, MD.: Genealogical Publishing Co., Inc., Reprinted for Clearfield Company, Inc. 1974, 1991), Page 81-86; Found on-line at: http://files.usgwarchives.net/va/lunenburg/census/sun002.txt;
In the 22nd year of George II, October, 1748,[66] an act was passed covering the subject of tithables, and repealing the above noticed act of 4th Queen Anne, and 12th George II, to be in force "from and immediately after the tenth day of June, which shall be in the year of our Lord, one thousand seven hundred and fifty-one." This law defined tithables as "all male persons of the age of sixteen years and upwards, and all Negroes, mulatto, and Indian women of the same age, except Indians tributary to this government and all wives of free Negroes, mulattoes, and Indians, except as before excepted," and "excepting such only as the county court, for charitable reasons appearing to them, shall think fit to excuse." New laws were inacted in 1777.
--
Partial lists from this book are also posted on the Internet, transcribed by Thomas Walter Duda.

9. Landon C. Bell,*Sunlight on the South Side - Lists of Tithes Lunenburg County, Virginia 1748-1783* (Philadelphia, Pennsylvania: George S. Ferguson Co., 1931, Baltimore, MD.: Genealogical Publishing Co., Inc., Reprinted for Clearfield Company, Inc. 1974, 1991), Pages 86-98; Also found

on-line at: http://files.usgwarchives.net/va/lunenburg/census/sun003.txt

10. Landon C. Bell, *Sunlight on the South Side - Lists of Tithes Lunenburg County, Virginia 1748-1783* (Philadelphia, Pennsylvania: George S. Ferguson Co., 1931, Baltimore, MD.: Genealogical Publishing Co., Inc., Reprinted for Clearfield Company, Inc. 1974, 1991), Page 135; Also found on-line at: http://files.usgwarchives.net/va/lunenburg/census/sun004.txt

11. Landon C. Bell, *Sunlight on the South Side - Lists of Tithes Lunenburg County, Virginia 1748-1783* (Philadelphia, Pennsylvania: George S. Ferguson Co., 1931, Baltimore, MD.: Genealogical Publishing Co., Inc., Reprinted for Clearfield Company, Inc. 1974, 1991), Page 183-208; Also found on-line at: http://files.usgwarchives.net/va/lunenburg/census/sun006.txt

12. Chilton, Ann, *Bedford County, Virginia Will Book 1 & Will Book 2,* Signal Mountain, TN: Mountain Press, 1988, page 7. .... Virginia. Bedford. County Clerk, *Bedford County, Virginia Order Book 1, 1754-1761,* Miami Beach, Florida: T. L. C. Genealogy, c2000, page 230. .... Virginia. Bedford. County Clerk, *Bedford County, Virginia Order Book 1, 1754-1761,* Miami Beach, Florida: T. L. C. Genealogy, c2000, page 162. .... Ann Chilton, *Bedford Co., Virginia Deed Book A-1 1754-1762* (Signal Mountain, Tennessee: Mountain Press, 1987), page 13.

13. The Church of Jesus Christ of Latter-day Saints [LDS], "International Genealogical Index," database *FamilySearch* (http://www.familysearch.org : accessed 28 Jul 2009), North America Region, entry for William Hall and Mary Merryman, married 17 Dec 1734 , Potapsco River St Pauls Church, Baltimore, Maryland, USA; citing FHL microfilm 1,235,239 (Patron Ordinance Submission Sheets 1969-1991), batch no. 7109715; sheet 40. .... Isabelle Board Obert, *The Board Family Chronicle: from Maryland to Bedford County, Virginia* (Baltimore, Maryland: I. B. Obert, 1997; Digitized 2007 Google Books), Page 119. .... Robert Barnes and Thomas L. Hollowak, *Maryland Genealogies : a consolidation of articles from the Maryland historical magazine*, 2 volumes (Baltimore, Maryland: Genealogical Publishing Co., 1980), Vol. 2: Culver, Francis B., "Merryman Family", page 212. .... Robert William Barnes, *Baltimore County Families, 1659-1759* (Baltimore, Maryland: Genealogical Publisher Company, 1989), 296, 444.

14. Francis B. Culver, "Merryman Family," *Maryland Historical Magazine*, March Vol. 10, 1915; page 180; Maryland Historical Magazine, by William Hand Browne, Louis Henry Dielman, Maryland Historical Society, Published by Maryland Historical Society., 1915, Original from the University of Virginia, Digitized Sep 7, 2007

15. Isabelle Board Obert, *The Board Family Chronicle: from Maryland to Bedford County, Virginia* (Baltimore, Maryland: I. B. Obert, 1997; Digitized 2007 Google Books), Page 119.

16. Robert William Barnes, *Baltimore County Families, 1659-1759* (Baltimore, Maryland: Genealogical Publisher Company, 1989), 295-296.

17. The Church of Jesus Christ of Latter-day Saints, "FamilySearch - Maryland Births and Christenings, 1650-1995," database *FamilySearch* (http://new.familysearch.org : accessed 18 Sep 2011), entry for John Hall; citing church records, FHL Film # 13696. .... Robert William Barnes, *Baltimore County Families, 1659-1759* (Baltimore, Maryland: Genealogical Publisher Company, 1989), 296.

18. Freddie Spradlin, "Military-French & Indian War: Providers of Provisions for Militia," database *USGenWeb Archives* (http://files.usgwarchives.net/va/bedford/military/frenchindian/fiwbedf.txt : accessed 15 Dec 2009), John Hall, Archibald Campbell and others.

19. Carrol Carmen Hall, *The Grandfathers, The Hall and Overstreet Families* , 2 Volumes (Springfield, Illinois: Illinois Ancestors.org - Menard County (http://www.illinoisancestors.org/menard/), 1981-2007), Section 1, Chapter 3, page 19; citing: Bedford County, Virginia Will Book B, page 140

20. Chilton, Ann, *Bedford County, Virginia Will Book 1 & Will Book 2,* Signal Mountain, TN: Mountain Press, 1988, page 85.

21. Carrol Carmen Hall, *The Grandfathers, The Hall and Overstreet Families* , 2 Volumes (Springfield, Illinois: Illinois Ancestors.org - Menard County (http://www.illinoisancestors.org/menard/), 1981-2007), Section VI, Chapter 21: 225.

22. 1830 U.S. census, Bedford, Virginia, p. 173, line 26, Elisha Hall; digital images, *Ancestry.com* (www.ancestry.com/ : accessed 5 Apr 2010); citing National Archives and Records Administration microfilm M19, roll M19- 194; Family History Film: 0029673.

23. Robert William Barnes, *Baltimore County Families, 1659-1759* (Baltimore, Maryland: Genealogical Publisher Company, 1989), 296.

24. Carrol Carmen Hall, *The Grandfathers, The Hall and Overstreet Families* , 2 Volumes (Springfield, Illinois: Illinois Ancestors.org - Menard County (http://www.illinoisancestors.org/menard/), 1981-2007), Section 1, Chapter 3: Page 28.

25. Carrol Carmen Hall, *The Grandfathers, The Hall and Overstreet Families* , 2 Volumes (Springfield, Illinois: Illinois Ancestors.org - Menard County (http://www.illinoisancestors.org/menard/), 1981-2007), Section 1, Chapter 3:28; Chapter 4:31.

26. William Fletcher Boogher, *Gleanings of Virginia History: An historical and genealogical collection, largely from original sources* (Washington, D. C.: W. F. Boogher, 1903; Digitized February 10, 2009), pages 76, 92. .... William Waller Hening, *The Statutes at Large, a collection of all the laws of Virginia*, 7 Volumes (Richmond, Virginia: Franklin Press, 1820), VII: 225.

27. Carrol Carmen Hall, *The Grandfathers, The Hall and Overstreet Families* , 2 Volumes (Springfield, Illinois: Illinois Ancestors.org - Menard County (http://www.illinoisancestors.org/menard/), 1981-2007), Section 1, Chapter 4, Page 31. .... Ann Chilton, *Bedford Co., Virginia Deed Book A-1 1754-1762* (Signal Mountain, Tennessee: Mountain Press, 1987), 14.

28. Carrol Carmen Hall, *The Grandfathers, The Hall and Overstreet Families* , 2 Volumes (Springfield, Illinois: Illinois Ancestors.org - Menard County (http://www.illinoisancestors.org/menard/), 1981-2007), Section 1, Chapter 4, Page 31.

29. Carrol Carmen Hall, *The Grandfathers, The Hall and Overstreet Families* , 2 Volumes (Springfield, Illinois: Illinois Ancestors.org - Menard County (http://www.illinoisancestors.org/menard/), 1981-2007), Section 1, Chapter 4: Page 31.

30. Roger G. Ward, "Hail Ye Also From Virginia?," *Virginia Genealogical Society Quarterly*, May 1999; Vol. 37; No. 2, 128.

Source Citations

31. Carrol Carmen Hall, *The Grandfathers, The Hall and Overstreet Families* , 2 Volumes (Springfield, Illinois: Illinois Ancestors.org - Menard County (http://www.illinoisancestors.org/menard/), 1981-2007), Section 6; Chapter 20; page 222; Citing Bedford County, Virginia - Order Book 2, 1761-62, page 1

32. Carrol Carmen Hall, *The Grandfathers, The Hall and Overstreet Families* , 2 Volumes (Springfield, Illinois: Illinois Ancestors.org - Menard County (http://www.illinoisancestors.org/menard/), 1981-2007), Section 6; Chapter 20; page 222; Citing Bedford County, Virginia - Order Book 3, July 1766, page 327

33. Lucas, Jr., Rev. Silas Emmett, ed,*Obituaries from Early Tennessee Newspapers 1794 - 1851* (Easley, South Carolina: Southern Historical Press, 1978), p. 157. .... "Obituary - Charles M. Hall," *(Nashville) National Banner and Nashville Whig*, October 14, 1826, p. 4.

34. The Historical Committee of the Bicentennial Commission of Campbell County, Virginia,*Lest it be Forgotten - A Scrapbook of Campbell County, Virginia* (Virginia: Alta Vista Printing Co., 1976), page 107. .... John H. Gwathmey,*Historical Register of Virginians in the Revolution 1775-1783* (Baltimore, Maryland: Genealogical Publishing Co., Inc., 1987), page 338. .... Charles Hall, muster rolls of Co. Willis, and payrolls of: 2nd Regiment Virginia - C.L., October 1777 - March 1778; NARA - Publication Number M246; Record Group 93; digital images, Footnote.com, "Revolutionary War Rolls, 1775-1783," *Footnote.com* (www.Footnote.com/ : accessed 10 Feb 2009). .... Valley Forge National Historical Park, "Muster Roll Data Sheet," database,*Valley Forge Legacy* (http://valleyforgemusterroll.org/ : accessed 25 Nov 2008), Charles Hall; citing 2nd Virginia Regiment. .... Carl Rhodes/Rhodes Family.org database,*William Rhodes and his Descendants "1745 to 1825"* (http://wm.rhodesfamily.org/Wm2ndVA.htm : accessed 9 Jan 2009), 2nd Regiment Virginia history. .... USHistory.org/ database*Historic Valley Forge - Who Served Here? Physicians, Surgeons and Mates with Washington at Valley Forge* (http://www.ushistory.org/valleyforge/served/surgeons.html : accessed 9 Jan 2009), Physicians, Surgeons and Mates with Washington at Valley Forge; citing: Weedon's Valley Forge Orderly Book, Charles William Heathcote, The Picket Post, January 1948, published by The Valley Forge Historical Society. .... Virginia. Virginia, Auditor of Public Accounts, "Virginia, Auditor of Public Accounts 1776-1928 - Court Booklets, indexes and lists, 1781-1783," database,*Library of Virginia Catalog* (http://lva1.hosted.exlibrisgroup.com/ : accessed 9 Jan 2009), Charles Hall of Bedford County; citing Revolutionary War Public Service Claims. .... Bedford, Virginia, Revolutionary War - Public Service Claims Bedford County Lists 1: 4,5, Charls Hall, September 11-12, 1781; Virginia State Library; JR 3280 JR 3280; Filmed by the Genealogical Society; Salt Lake City, Utah; March 30, 1954 .... Campbell, Virginia, Circuit Court Order Books and General Index Volume 2, 1785-1786: Page 369, Charles Hall, 6 July 1786; FHL microfilm 1,907,169. .... Carrol Carmen Hall,*The Grandfathers, The Hall and Overstreet Families* , 2 Volumes (Springfield, Illinois: Illinois Ancestors.org - Menard County (http://www.illinoisancestors.org/menard/), 1981-2007), Vol. 1: Section 11, Chapter 8, page 73.

35. Campbell, Virginia, Deed Books 1782-1896, Deed Book 4, 1796-1799: Pages 272-279, Samuel Hunter to Charles M. Hall, 11 September 1797; FHL microfilm 0,031,023; This property had been the residence of Alexander Hunter, father of Samuel Hunter. He had reserved this property for himself during his lifetime, "after giving to his several sons their respective portions of land...".

36. Chilton, Ann, *Bedford County, Virginia Will Book 1 & Will Book 2,* Signal Mountain, TN: Mountain Press, 1988, page 42. .... Harold Helm, "MOSES HELM family," *HELM-L Archives*, mailing list, 21 Jun 1996 (http://archiver.rootsweb.ancestry.com/th/read/HELM/1996-06/0835342679 : accessed 5 Feb 2010); Citing the family bible of Moses Helm.

37. Campbell, Virginia, "1785 Campbell County, Virginia Personal Property Tax List,"; New River Notes, Saltville; Weaver, Jeffrey C., transcriber; July 23, 1998; http://www.newrivernotes.com/va/camp1785.htm

38. Campbell, Virginia, Circuit Court Order Books and General Index Vol. 2 1785-1786: 299-300, Trial of George, a Negroe Slave owned by Charles Hall, 10 January 1786; FHL microfilm.

39. TLC Genealogy,*Campbell County, Virginia Deeds, 1784-1790* (Miami, Florida: TLC Genealogy, 1991), Page 31; Campbell County was divided into two districts: North and South. Some books are missing or damaged. .... Campbell, Virginia, Deed Books 1782-1896, Deed Book 2: 191, Andre Turner to Charles Hall, 1 February 1787; FHL microfilm 0,031,020. .... Campbell, Virginia, Deed Books 1782-1896, Deed Book 4: 251, 297, Charles M. Hall, Thomas Ogelsby, Martha Ogelsby to John M. Walker and Charles M. Hall to James McAllister, 11 Sep 1797 and 9 Oct 1797; FHL microfilm 0,031,023.

40. Virginia State Library,*Report of the Virginia State Library, Volumes 13-14* (1917; reprint, Richmond, Virginia: State of Virginia, Google Books, Digitized 2009), page 39, 41, 265. .... Don Chesnut, "Chronology of Robert Benge, aka Chief Bench "; report, 1997; Don Chesnut's Homepage; http://donchesnut.com/genealogy/pages/bobbenge.htm

41. Campbell, Virginia, Deed Books 1782-1896, No. 4 - 1796-1799: page 251, Hall and Oglesby to Walker, 11 September 1797; FHL microfilm # 0031023. .... Campbell, Virginia, Deed Books 1782-1896, Vol. 4: pages 270-272, Samuel Hunter to Charles M. Hall, 11 Sept 1797; FHL microfilm 0,031,023. .... Victor Oglesby to Ronald C. Hall, e-mail, 3 February 2009 and 1 March 2009, "Thomas Oglesby, Martha Oglesby, Charles M. Hall to John M. Walker - Bill of Sale"; privately held by Hall, Ft. Worth, Texas. .... Campbell, Virginia, Chancery Court Records Index Index No. 1798-014, Charles Hall v. Heirs of Walter West, 1798; digital images, Library of Virginia,*Virginia Memory - Library of Virginia* (http://www.lva.virginia.gov/ : accessed 9 Nov 2009).

42. Campbell, Virginia, 1797 - 1812 Tax Book, entry for Charles Hall; FHL microfilm Reel 212; Film # 1907190.

43. Campbell, Virginia, Circuit Court Order Books and General Index Vol. 6: 3 of Index, Deed, Hall to Walker, October 1797; FHL microfilm 1,907,169, item Reel 185. .... Jeffrey M. O'Dell, "Frederick County, Virginia Poor Farm," p. page 8; report to Hugh C. Miller, July 6 1993; National Register of Historic Places, United States Department of Interior - National Park Service, Washington; Document on-line: http://www.dhr.virginia.gov/registers/Counties/Frederick/034-0099_Frederick_County_Poor_Farm_1993_Final_Nomination.pdf .... James D. Watkinson, "Rogues, Vagabonds, and Fit Objects - The Treatment of the Poor in Antebellum Virginia,"*Virginia Cavalcade*, Winter 2000; See: http://www.poorhousestory.com/VA_Rogues_17.htm; A quarterly magazine published by the Library of Virginia. .... Campbell, Virginia, Circuit Court Order Books and General Index Vol. 6: 148, Jno. M. Walker appointed Overseer of the Poor, September 1798; FHL microfilm 1,907,169. .... Campbell, Virginia, Deed Books 1782-1896, Deed Book 4: 311, Charles M. Hall to John M. Walker; Power of Attorney, 9 October 1797; FHL microfilm 0,031,023. .... Whitten, Joida, *Abstracts of Bedford County, Virginia Wills, Inventories and Accounts 1754-1787,* Dallas, Texas: Taylor Publishing Co., 1968, Page 111. .... Eddlemon, Sherida K,*Genealogical Abstracts from Tennessee Newspapers 1803-1812* (Bowie, Maryland: Heritage Books, 1989), page 233. .... Marsh, Helen C. and Marsh, Timothy R,*Davidson County, Tennessee Wills & Inventories Volume One 1783-1816* (Greenville,

Source Citations

South Carolina: Southern Historical Press, Inc., 1990), page 138. .... Helen C. Marsh and Timothy R Marsh,*Land and Deed Genealogy of Davidson County, Tennessee* (Greenville, South Carolina: Southern Historical Press, 1992), 4: 138. .... Harold D. Moser and Shannon Macpherson, editors, *The Papers of Andrew Jackson Vol. II 1804-1813* (Knoxville, Tennessee: University of Tennessee Press, 1984), 529, 564.

44. Leona Taylor Aiken,*Donelson, Tennessee It's History and Landmarks* (Kingsport, Tennessee: Kingsport Press, Inc., 1968), 69, 218-219. .... The Nashville Room - The Public Library of Nashville - Davidson County,*Nashville Families & Homes* (Nashville, Tennessee: Williams Printing Co., 1983), page 111. .... James A. Hoobler, *A Guide to Historic Nashville, Tennessee* (Charleston, South Carolina: The History Press, 2008), page 23. .... U. S. Department of the Interior - National Park Service, "National Register of Historic Places; Notification of Pending Nominations and Related Actions," database(http://edocket.access.gpo.gov/2010/2010-4451.htm : accessed 7 Mar 2010), Hall-Harding-McCampbell House, 305 Kent Rd., Nashville, 10000141.

45. Wells, Carol,*Davidson County, Tennessee County Court Minutes 1792-1799* (Bowie, MD.: Heritage Books, Inc., 1991), p.118. As recorded on page 314, July 12, 1802.

46. "Ansearchin' News" (Quarterly Journal, Memphis, Tennessee, 1954-2008), p. Winter 1979, Vol. 26, No. 4, Page 164; digital images, Tennessee Genealogical Society, "DAVIDSON COUNTY TENNESSEE 1812 TAX LIST,"*Welcome to the Ansearchin' News Archives* (http://www.tngs.org/ : accessed 9 Mar 2010). .... Edythe Johns Rucker Whitley,*Pioneers of Davidson County, Tennessee* (Baltimore, Maryland: Genealogical Publishing Co., Inc., 1979), p. 19-20; The source document she drew on for a listing of soldiers in Captain Thomas's Militia may have been a tax list rather than a roster of soldiers. He was in Capt. Thomas's District. .... Jane Henry Thomas and J. G. M. Ramsey contributor,*Old Days in Nashville* (1897; reprint, Nashville, Tennessee: Charles Elder, 196?), 32-33; Reprint of the 1897 ed., to which is added an historical sketch of Nashville as of 1854, by J. G. M. Ramsey.

47. Prof. W. W. Clayton,*History of Davidson County, Tennessee* (Philadelphia, Pennsylvania: J. W. Lewis & Co., 1880), page 368; Transcript on-line: http://freepages.history.rootsweb.ancestry.com/~nashvillearchives/civildistricts.html. On-line document: http://www.tngenweb.org/records/davidson/history/clayton/367-376-PT_3_Dist.pdf

48. 1820 U.S. census, Davidson, Tennessee population schedule, Nashville, p. 96, line 47, Charles M. Hall; digital images,*Ancestry.com* (www.ancestry.com/ : accessed 10 Nov 2012); citing National Archives and Records Administration microfilm M33, roll 122.

49. "Obituary - Charles M. Hall," *(Nashville) National Banner and Nashville Whig*, October 14, 1826, p. 4.

50. *Davidson County, Tennessee - County Court Minutes 1824-1826* (Nashville, TN: Davidson County, Tennessee, County Clerk), page 557-558. .... Tennessee. Davidson. County Clerk,*Davidson County, Tennessee - Will Book Vol. 9,* Nashville, TN:, 19-20 March1827, page 98, 103. .... Tennessee. Davidson. County Clerk,*Davidson County, Tennessee - Minutes of the Circuit Court - Vol. G 1828-1831,* Nashville, TN:, 8 Dec 1828, page 12-13. This case documents a dispute among the heirs regarding the division of property of the estate of Charles M. Hall, deceased. Nancy B. Hall, widow, is the administrator of the estate. Other heirs listed: Charles M. Hall, Aristin L. Hall, Eliza Ann Hall (children of Nancy), and John B. Hall, William Hall, Charles M. Cross, trustee for Nancy C. Neely, Charles M. Cross, trustee for Elizabeth Shropshire, Maclin Cross and Polly, his wife. .... Tennessee. Davidson. County Clerk,*Davidson County, Tennessee - Minutes of the Circuit Court - Vol. G 1828-1831,* Nashville, TN:, June 3, 1829, pages 108-110. .... Tennessee. Davidson. County Clerk,*Davidson County, Tennessee - Minutes of the Circuit Court - Vol. G 1828-1831,* Nashville, TN:, November term 1830, page 381. .... Smith, Mary Sue,*Davidson County, Tennessee Deed Book "P"* (Bowie, Maryland: Heritage Books, Inc., 1997), page 95, 96.

51. Yazoo, Mississippi, Chancery Court - Probate Cases 1841-1873, Box 130, Charles M. Hall; FHL microfilm #2438942, item 1. .... Yazoo, Mississippi, Probate Minute Book Vol. A 1834-1838 p. 493, Estate of Charles M. Hall; John B. Hall, Administrator; FHL microfilm 0,885,171.

52. Edythe Rucker Whitley,*Membership Roster and Soldiers of the Tennessee Society of the Daughters of the American Revolution 1960-1970* (Tennessee: The Tennessee Society of the Daughters of the American Revolution, 1970), Page 240; Submitted by Grace Ruth Spencer Fassnacht (Mrs. Fred E.) No. 502220, Member of the Tennessee Society of the Daughters of the American Revolution .... "Ansearchin' News" (Quarterly Journal, Memphis, Tennessee, 1954-2008), p. Fall 1874, Vol. 31, No. 3, Page 106-108; digital images, Tennessee Genealogical Society, "The File Box, by Jerry Blair," *Welcome to the Ansearchin' News Archives* (http://www.tngs.org/ : accessed 9 Mar 2010).

53. Edythe Rucker Whitley,*Membership Roster and Soldiers of the Tennessee Society of the Daughters of the American Revolution 1960-1970* (Tennessee: The Tennessee Society of the Daughters of the American Revolution, 1970), Page 240. .... The Church of Jesus Christ of Latter-day Saints, "Pedigree Resource File," database,*FamilySearch* (http://www.familysearch.org : accessed 22 May 2009), entry for Agnes Campbell (PIN 3222966); submitted by Bill Campbell, Central City, Nebraska. .... Grace Spencer Fassnacht,*Campbell Kith and Kin: Campbell Kith and Kin: Descendants of Archibald Campbell and Elizabeth Baker, Who Came from Campbell County, Virginia, to Knox County, Tennessee, 1796.* (Chattanooga, Tennessee: n.p., 1983), 12; This book asserts that Archibald Campbell was born in Pennsylvania or Virginia ca. 1730 and that he married Elizabeth Baker ca. 1755. Some of their descendants are traced.

54. Whitten, Joida, *Abstracts of Bedford County, Virginia Wills, Inventories and Accounts 1754-1787,* Dallas, Texas: Taylor Publishing Co., 1968, Page 111. Will of John Beard. .... Knox County, Tennessee, Wills Vol. 0-3 July 1792-1824 Vol. 0-3, April Session 1802, Microfilm Roll #155: Page 30-31, Archibald Campbell Will - 8 September 1801; Dallas Public Library - J. Eric Jonsson, Dallas.

55. Tennessee. Davidson. County Clerk,*Davidson County, Tennessee - Marriage Book 1,* Nashville, TN:, page 100. .... Edythe Rucker Whitley compiler, *Marriages of Davidson County, Tennessee 1789-1847* (Baltimore, Maryland: Genealogical Publishing Co, 1981), page 23.

56. Eddlemon, Sherida K,*Genealogical Abstracts from Tennessee Newspapers 1803-1812* (Bowie, Maryland: Heritage Books, 1989), page 195.

57. Marsh, Helen C. and Marsh, Timothy R,*Davidson County, Tennessee Wills & Inventories Volume One 1783-1816* (Greenville, South Carolina: Southern Historical Press, Inc., 1990), Page 187. ....*(Nashville) Impartial Review and Cumberland Repository*, October 25, 1806.

58. Eddlemon, Sherida K,*Genealogical Abstracts from Tennessee Newspapers 1803-1812* (Bowie, Maryland: Heritage Books, 1989), page 195. Taken from "The Democratic Clarion and Tennessee Gazette", October 22, 1811, Vol. III, No. CXCIII.

59. Tennessee. Davidson. County Clerk,*Davidson County, Tennessee - Marriage Book 1,* Nashville, TN:, page 171. .... Edythe Rucker Whitley compiler, *Marriages of Davidson County, Tennessee 1789-1847* (Baltimore, Maryland: Genealogical Publishing Co, 1981), page 39. .... Jeanette Tillotson Acklen compiler,*Tennessee Records*, 2 volumes (Nashville, Tennessee: Cullom & Ghertner Co., 1933), Vol. 2 - Bible records and marriage bonds: 130, Steele Family.

60. Tennessee. Davidson. County Clerk,*Davidson County, Tennessee - Minutes of the Circuit Court - Vol. G 1828-1831,* Nashville, TN:, page 211. November Term 1829 - 14 Jan 1830 - The Court notices that Nancy B. Hall has died. No one denied it. .... Tennessee. Davidson. County Clerk, *Davidson County, Tennessee - Will Book Vol. 9,* Nashville, TN:, page 409. See record of 23 Dec 1829
Recorded 9 March 1830 - Inventory of the Estate of Nancy B. Hall, deceased. Property includes: 6 negros, 39 acres of land, 2 horses, 4 head of cattle, 15 geese, 3 spinning wheels, more...
Samuel Steele is administrator of the estate.
30 January 1830 - Sale of Inventory. Buyers include: Hugh Hayes, Samuel Steele, Ellendor Cason, Thomas Gleaves, William H. Williams.

61. Jeanette Tillotson Acklen compiler,*Tennessee Records*, 2 volumes (Nashville, Tennessee: Cullom & Ghertner Co., 1933), Vol. 2 - Bible records and marriage bonds: 130.

62. George W. Glass,*Glass Family Notes - Volume I* (Houston, Texas: n.p., n.d.), Collins - Glass Connection; Cites: "The Red River Iron Works: A Narrative of the Rise and Decline of a Basic Industry in Eastern Central Kentucky (1787-1830)" by Willard Rouse Jillson (Frankfort, Ky.: Roberts Printing Company, 1964. p. 30 Map, illustrations; Report, Research Notes, Copies and Transcripts of Original Records

63. Carrol Carmen Hall,*The Grandfathers, The Hall and Overstreet Families* , 2 Volumes (Springfield, Illinois: Illinois Ancestors.org - Menard County (http://www.illinoisancestors.org/menard/), 1981-2007), Section 6; Chapter 20; page 222; Citing Bedford County, Virginia - Order Book 3, July 1766, pages 262, 274, 327 .... Florence Houston and Laura Blaine,*Maxwell history and genealogy* (Indianapolis, Indiana: Press of C.E. Pauley, Indianapolis Engraving Co., 1916), Page 224. .... Russell Maas,*Bullock Genealogy* (http://bullockgenealogy.net/index.html : accessed 21 Sep 2011), Robert Clark (1738-1810);
From records of Capt. Robert G. Nicol, USN (Ret.) captnicol@comcast.net
Ruth Clark Dann, a descendant provides the following:

"Robert Clark Sr. was born June 13, 1738 in Louisa Co. (now Albemarle), Virginia. He was married in Albemarle Co. to Susannah Henderson, daughter of John and Frances (Goode) Henderson. He sold his property on Ivy Creek in Albemarle Co. in 1766 and moved to Bedford Co. (now Campbell), and in 1779 moved to Kentucky, settling on the Kentucky River in the Bush Settlement (now Clark Co.), Kentucky near the present site of the Old Providence Church, where he raised his family."

From DAR Vol. 115, page 105, # 114340(Ancestry.com):
Robert Clark 1738-99 Served as Captain in the Bedford Co., VA Militia 1785, removed to KY, where in 1794 he was made judge of Clark Co., he was born in Louisa Co., VA and died Clark Co., KY.
Event: Milit_Serv BETWEEN 1776 AND 1783
Note:
Captain of militia from Old Liberty (Bedford County), Virginia, during the Revolution.

From records of Vickie Beard Thompson <Familyquest1958@yahoo.com>
"Our Quaker Friends of Ye Olden Time" book #975.5 B413q

He was the first manufacturer of iron in Kentucky.

Individual Land Owners in the Bush Settlement in Clark County, Kentucky in 1780, included Robert Clark Sr.

Note: Robert and Susan moved to Bedford Co., VA in 1765, removed to KY 1779 and settled near the Kentucky River in Clark Co., KY.
Death: 10 APR 1810 Clark Co.,KY
Burial: Clark Family Cem, Winchester, Clark, Kentucky

64. Cecil D. Mc Donald Jr., "Augusta County, VA Marriages 1700-1799," database,*USGenWeb Archives* (http://files.usgwarchives.org/va/augusta/vitals/marriages/1700-99.txt : accessed 20 Sep 2011), William Hall m. Rebecca Braford. .... Debie Cox, Nashville, Tennessee to Ronald Hall, e-mail, September 7, 2011, "Hall Family"; privately held by Hall, Fort Worth, Texas; See her Blog: http://debieoeser.blogspot.com/2011/09/charles-m-hall-of-davidson-county.html .... Lyman Chalkley*Chronicles of the Scot-Irish Settlement of Virginia, extracted from the original court records of Augusta County, 1745-1800 – Augusta County (Va.)*, 3 Volumes (Roselyn, Virginia: National Society of the Daughters of the American Revolution, 1912), 1: 388;
November 1788 (A to C).
Wm. Hall and wife, Rebecca, administrators of Robert Brafford, deceased, vs. Samuel Brafford. Rebecca married Wm. after 1st May 1786. Writ, 30th August 1787.

65. Sandra Ferguson, "Re: Buchanan, Alexander,"*PA-OLD-CHESTER-L Archives*, mailing list, 28 Sep 2001 (http://archiver.rootsweb.ancestry.com/th/index/PA-OLD-CHESTER/ : accessed 21 Sep 2011).

66. Debie Cox, Nashville, Tennessee to Ronald Hall, e-mail, September 7, 2011, "Hall Family"; privately held by Hall, Fort Worth, Texas.

67. Carrol Carmen Hall,*The Grandfathers, The Hall and Overstreet Families* , 2 Volumes (Springfield, Illinois: Illinois Ancestors.org - Menard County (http://www.illinoisancestors.org/menard/), 1981-2007), Section 6; Chapter 20; page 222; Citing Bedford County, Virginia - Order Book, August 1768

68. Ancestry.com, *Historical Sketch of Bedford County, Virginia, 1753-1907* (Provo, Utah: The Generations Network, Inc., 2005), 44.

69. Carrol Carmen Hall,*The Grandfathers, The Hall and Overstreet Families* , 2 Volumes (Springfield, Illinois: Illinois Ancestors.org - Menard County (http://www.illinoisancestors.org/menard/), 1981-2007), Section 6; Chapter 20; page 222; Citing Bedford County, Virginia - Order Books, 1763 -

1771.

70. Carrol Carmen Hall, *The Grandfathers, The Hall and Overstreet Families* , 2 Volumes (Springfield, Illinois: Illinois Ancestors.org - Menard County (http://www.illinoisancestors.org/menard/), 1981-2007), Section 2, Chapter 21: Page 225.

71. *Yazoo County, Mississippi - Probate Records* (Yazoo City, Mississippi, Yazoo County, Mississippi, County Clerk), Book A, page 30.

72. Carrol Carmen Hall, *The Grandfathers, The Hall and Overstreet Families* , 2 Volumes (Springfield, Illinois: Illinois Ancestors.org - Menard County (http://www.illinoisancestors.org/menard/), 1981-2007), Section I, Chapter 3: 19.

73. Carrol Carmen Hall, *The Grandfathers, The Hall and Overstreet Families* , 2 Volumes (Springfield, Illinois: Illinois Ancestors.org - Menard County (http://www.illinoisancestors.org/menard/), 1981-2007), Section 1, Chapter 3: Page 19.

74. Carrol Carmen Hall, *The Grandfathers, The Hall and Overstreet Families* , 2 Volumes (Springfield, Illinois: Illinois Ancestors.org - Menard County (http://www.illinoisancestors.org/menard/), 1981-2007), Section 2, Chapter 21: Page 225. .... Bedford, Virginia, Chancery Court Index No. 1855-052, Mathew Hall v. Admin. Hezikiah Hall, Sept 1851; digital images, *Virginia Memory - Digital Collections* (http://www.lva.virginia.gov/ : accessed 13 Jun 2010).

75. 1810 U.S. census, Bedford, Virginia, p. 10, line 7B, Elisha Hall; digital images, *Ancestry.com* (www.ancestry.com/ : accessed 4 Apr 2010); citing National Archives and Records Administration microfilm M252, roll 67.

76. 1850 U.S. census, Bedford, Virginia, population schedule, Southern Division, p. 249A; Image: 496, dwelling 566, family 566, Hezikiah; digital images, *Ancestry.com* (www.ancestry.com/ : accessed 20 Mar 2010); citing National Archives and Records Administration microfilm M432, roll M432_ 935.

77. Carrol Carmen Hall, *The Grandfathers, The Hall and Overstreet Families* , 2 Volumes (Springfield, Illinois: Illinois Ancestors.org - Menard County (http://www.illinoisancestors.org/menard/), 1981-2007), Section VI, Chapter 21, Page 225.

78. Carrol Carmen Hall, *The Grandfathers, The Hall and Overstreet Families* , 2 Volumes (Springfield, Illinois: Illinois Ancestors.org - Menard County (http://www.illinoisancestors.org/menard/), 1981-2007), Section 6, Chapter 21: 225. .... 1820 U.S. census, Bedford, Virginia population schedule, Southern District, p. 74; Image: 25., line 14, Elisha Hall; digital images, *Ancestry.com* (www.ancestry.com/ : accessed 4 Apr 2010); citing National Archives and Records Administration microfilm M33, roll M33_133.

79. Carrol Carmen Hall, *The Grandfathers, The Hall and Overstreet Families* , 2 Volumes (Springfield, Illinois: Illinois Ancestors.org - Menard County (http://www.illinoisancestors.org/menard/), 1981-2007), Section 6, Chapter 21: 225.

80. Marcia Witt, "Witt Family of Bedford County, Virginia," genealogy modified register report, *Witt Family of Bedford County, Virginia* (http://wc.rootsweb.ancestry.com/cgi-bin/igm.cgi?op=REG&db=wittm&id=I127 : accessed 21 Feb 2010), Keziah Hall; Contact: Marcia Witt 7991 West Lake Drive West Palm Beach, Fla 33406 USA; e-mail: witt_k@firn.edu

81. The Church of Jesus Christ of Latter-day Saints, "Pedigree Resource File," database, *FamilySearch* (http://www.familysearch.org : accessed 30 Sep 2013), entry for John Hall Jr (PIN (Ancestral File Number: 35HF-N8V)); submitted by Culps W.

82. Bedford, Virginia, Chancery Court 042, Mathew Hall v. Magdelin Hall, etc., May 1806; digital images, Library of Virginia, *Virginia Memory* (http://www.lva.virginia.gov/ : accessed 29 Sep 2013).

83. 1830 U.S. census, Bledsoe, Tennessee, p. 278, line 22, John Hall, Sr; digital images, *Ancestry.com* (www.ancestry.com/ : accessed 30 Sep 2013); citing National Archives and Records Administration microfilm M19, roll 175; Family History Film: 0024533.

84. Carrol Carmen Hall, *The Grandfathers, The Hall and Overstreet Families* , 2 Volumes (Springfield, Illinois: Illinois Ancestors.org - Menard County (http://www.illinoisancestors.org/menard/), 1981-2007), Section 1, Chapter 4: Page 44. .... Earle S. Dennis and Jane Estelle Smith, *Marriage Bonds of Bedford County, Virginia, 1755-1800* (Baltimore, Maryland: Genealogical Publishing Company, 1981), Page 34. .... William Wade Hinshaw, *Encyclopedia of American Quaker Genealogy. Vol. VI: (Virginia)* (Baltimore, Maryland: Genealogical Publishing Co., Reprint 1993), John Hall & Molly Wills; p. 926; "Molly Wills, dt. Euclid. Euclid Wills, surety."

85. Eddlemon, Sherida K, *Genealogical Abstracts from Tennessee Newspapers 1803-1812* (Bowie, Maryland: Heritage Books, 1989), page 6. .... Bedford, Virginia, Deed Book 26 - 1836-1837 Pages 190-191, Hall/Brown Power of Attorney, Jun 7 1837; Library of Virginia, Richmond; FHL microfilm 0100; Reel 11; ILL Film 173.

86. Carrol Carmen Hall, *The Grandfathers, The Hall and Overstreet Families* , 2 Volumes (Springfield, Illinois: Illinois Ancestors.org - Menard County (http://www.illinoisancestors.org/menard/), 1981-2007), I, Section VI.: 225.

87. Tennessee. Davidson. County Clerk, *Davidson County, Tennessee - Register of Deeds Vol. G-I Dates 1805-1813,* Nashville, TN:.

88. Tennessee. Davidson. County Clerk, *Davidson County, Tennessee - Register of Deeds Vol. K-M Date 1813-1819,* Nashville, TN:, Deed Book "L" Davidson County Court - page 263. Microfilm Roll #4

89. Prof. W. W. Clayton, *History of Davidson County, Tennessee* (Philadelphia, Pennsylvania: J. W. Lewis & Co., 1880), page 373; On-line document: http://www.tngenweb.org/records/davidson/history/clayton/367-376-PT_3_Dist.pdf

90. 1820 U.S. census, Davidson, Tennessee population schedule, Nashville, p. 84, line 35, William Hall; digital images, *Ancestry.com* (www.ancestry.com/ : accessed 10 Nov 2012); citing National Archives and Records Administration microfilm M33, roll 122.

91. 1830 U.S. census, Yazoo, Mississippi, "within the division allotted to Joseph--", p. 292, line 1, William Hall; digital images, *Ancestry.com*

Source Citations

(www.ancestry.com/ : accessed 5 Dec 2012); citing National Archives and Records Administration microfilm M19, roll 71; Family History Film: 0014839.

92. Yazoo, Mississippi, Chancery Court - Probate Cases 1841-1873, Box 119, Estate of William Hall - 1844; FHL microfilm #2438941, item 1.

93. Nan Harvey, "Officials of Yazoo County, Mississippi - Registers of Commissions," database,*MSGenWeb Archives* (http://files.usgwarchives.net/ms/yazoo/history/officials.txt : accessed 26 Nov 2010), Officials of Yazoo County, Mississippi; citing: Registers of Commissions at The Mississippi Department of Archives and History, Jackson, Mississippi, Series 1097, RG 28.

94. Linda Mason, "Yazoo County, MS 1823 Tax List," database,*MSGenWeb - Special Projects - Library Project* (http://www.msgw.org/library/yazoo-1823tax.html : accessed 24 Jan 2010), John B. Hall, William Hall, Archebib C. Hall, Elisha S. Hall; citing: MDAH microfilm. .... Linda Armstrong, "Yazoo County Tax Lists 1823 and 1825," database,*Yazoo County Mississippi - Yazoo County Tax Lists 1823 and 1825* (http://www.rootsweb.ancestry.com/~msyazoo/taxlists.htm : accessed 29 Jan 2010), Yazoo County Tax Lists 1823 - 1825; citing: microfilm at the Mississippi Department of Archives and History.

95. United States. Department of the Interior,*United States Bureau of Land Management - Records,* Washington D.C, Document Nr.: 6334; Land Office: Mt Salus.

96. United States. Department of the Interior,*United States Bureau of Land Management - Records,* Washington D.C, Document Nr.: 10650; Land Office: Mt Salus.

97. James Logan Morgan,*Arkansas Newspaper Index 1819-1845 - Biographical Notes, Probate and Chancery Notices from Arkansas Newspapers, 1819-1845,* 4 volumes: v. 1. Obituaries and biographical notes from Arkansas newspapers, 1819-1835 -- v. 2. Obituaries and biographical notes from Arkansas newspapers, 1836-1840 -- v. 3. Obituaries and biographical notes from Arkansas newspapers, 1841-1845 -- v. 4. Probate and chancery notices from Arkansas newspapers, 1819-1845 (Conway, Arkansas: Arkansas Research, 1992, c1981).

98. Yazoo, Mississippi, Chancery Court - Probate Cases 1841-1873, Box 119, Estate of William Hall - 1844; FHL microfilm #2438941, item 1. .... Yazoo, Mississippi, Probate Minute Book Vol. B 1838-1842, B: 30, Estate of William Hall, deceased; Case #210; FHL microfilm 0,885,171. .... Yazoo, Mississippi, Probate Minute Book Vol. B 1838-1842, B: 57, Estate of William Hall, deceased; Case #210; FHL microfilm 0,885,171. .... Yazoo, Mississippi, Probate Minute Book Vol. B 1838-1842, B: 72, Estate of William Hall, deceased; Case #210; FHL microfilm 0,885,171. .... Yazoo, Mississippi, Probate Minute Book Vol. B 1838-1842, B: 98, Estate of William Hall, deceased; Case #210; FHL microfilm 0,885,171. .... Betty Couch Wiltshire, *Yazoo County, Mississippi Pioneers* (Bowie, Maryland: Heritage Books, 1992), 86, 87, 93, 102, 106. .... George, James Z., Reporter to the State, Mississippi Supreme Court,*Cases Argued and Decided in the Supreme Court of Mississippi*, Vol. 31- Vol. 2 (Philadelphia, Pennsylvania: E. W. Stephens Publishing Co./ T & J.W. Johnson & Co., 1858), 644 - 653; Digitized August 25, 2007 - Google Books Search

99. Lucy Harrision Miller Baber and Hazel Letts Williamson,*Marriages of Campbell County Virginia 1782-1810* (Lynchburg, Virginia: n.p., 1971), Chapter H, page 43.

100. Knox County, Tennessee, Wills Vol. 0-3 July 1792-1824 Vol. 0-3, April Session 1802, Microfilm Roll #155: Page 30-31, Archibald Campbell Will - 8 September 1801; Dallas Public Library - J. Eric Jonsson, Dallas.

101. *Yazoo County, Mississippi - Probate Records* (Yazoo City, Mississippi, Yazoo County, Mississippi, County Clerk), Minute Book A, page 167.

102. Yazoo, Mississippi, Chancery Court - Probate Cases 1841-1873, Box 122, Estate of Samuel S. Hall - 1847; FHL microfilm #2438941.

103. Harriet DeCell and JoAnne Prichard,*Yazoo : its legends and legacies* (Yazoo City, Mississippi: Yazoo Delta Press, 1976), 60.

104. Betty Couch Wiltshire,*Carroll County, Mississippi, pioneers* (Carrollton, Mississippi: Pioneer Publishing Co., c1990), 60.

105. Jane Henry Thomas and J. G. M. Ramsey contributor,*Old Days in Nashville* (1897; reprint, Nashville, Tennessee: Charles Elder, 196?), 105; Reprint of the 1897 ed., to which is added an historical sketch of Nashville as of 1854, by J. G. M. Ramsey.

106. Jane Henry Thomas and J. G. M. Ramsey contributor,*Old Days in Nashville* (1897; reprint, Nashville, Tennessee: Charles Elder, 196?), 107; Reprint of the 1897 ed., to which is added an historical sketch of Nashville as of 1854, by J. G. M. Ramsey.

107. Lindsey C. Hall, non-graduate card file, Princeton University, 1818-1819; supplied by Princeton University, Seeley G. Mudd Manuscript Library, Princeton, New Jersey, 10 February 2005.

108. Jonathan Pearson, *A general catalogue of the officers, graduates and students of Union College from 1795 to 1854* (New York: S. S. Riggs, 1854; Digitized 2009, Google Books), 29.

109. Smith, Mary Sue,*Davidson County, Tennessee Deed Book "P"* (Bowie, Maryland: Heritage Books, Inc., 1997), page 76.

110. Linda Armstrong, "Yazoo County Tax Lists 1823 and 1825," database,*Yazoo County Mississippi - Yazoo County Tax Lists 1823 and 1825* (http://www.rootsweb.ancestry.com/~msyazoo/taxlists.htm : accessed 29 Jan 2010), Yazoo County Tax Lists 1823 - 1825; citing: microfilm at the Mississippi Department of Archives and History.

111. Betty Couch Wiltshire,*Yazoo County, Mississippi Pioneers* (Bowie, Maryland: Heritage Books, 1992), 1. .... United States. Department of the Interior, *United States Bureau of Land Management - Records,* Washington D.C, Certificate No's. 1954, 1956, 1957, 1960, 1961, 3471, 3681, 4830.

112. Robert Lowry and Wuilliam H. McCardle,*A history of Mississippi: from the discovery of the great river by Hernando DeSoto, including the earliest settlement made by the French under Iberville, to the death of Jefferson Davis* (Jackson, Mississippi: R. H. Henry & Co., 1891), p. 614.

113. United States Senate - Second Session of the Twenty-third Congress,*Public Documents Printed by Order of the Senate of the United States*, 4

Source Citations

Volumes (Washington, District of Columbia: Duff Green, 1834), 2: 52, 54.

114. United States. Department of the Interior, *United States Bureau of Land Management - Records,* Washington D.C, Certificate No. 2343, 2278.

115. United States. Department of the Interior, *United States Bureau of Land Management - Records,* Washington D.C, Certificate No. 449.

116. Betty Couch Wiltshire, *Carroll County, Mississippi, pioneers* (Carrollton, Mississippi: Pioneer Publishing Co., c1990), 60, 81.

117. The Church of Jesus Christ of Latter-day Saints [LDS], "International Genealogical Index - Individual Record," database on-line *FamilySearch* (http://www.familysearch.org/eng/Search/frameset_search.asp : accessed 23 Oct 2011), North America Region, entry for Archibald C. Hall, birth 25 Oct 1792, Tennessee; Record submitted after 1991 by a member of the LDS Church. No additional information is available.

118. Reed, Verna [Verna@carlsbadnm.com], "Modified Register for Hall" (Carlsbad, New Mexico: Sept 2002), page 18. The report is part of a series of e-mail correspondence with Verna Reed all dated 2002-2007. Verna Reed's address is: 1512 E. Fiesta Drive, Carlsbad, NM 88220. She was also in contact with Stephen Hatch, another researcher primarily interested in the Bonney family. .... The Church of Jesus Christ of Latter-day Saints [LDS], "International Genealogical Index - Individual Record," database on-line *FamilySearch* (http://www.familysearch.org/eng/Search/frameset_search.asp : accessed 23 Oct 2011), North America Region, entry for Archibald C. Hall, death 30 Jun 1863; Record submitted after 1991 by a member of the LDS Church. No additional information is available.

119. Betty Couch Wiltshire, *Carroll County, Mississippi, pioneers* (Carrollton, Mississippi: Pioneer Publishing Co., c1990), 199, Russell Family.

120. Russell Family Tree - Ancestry.com, Annabel and Wade Russell, compiler (Wm. Ross Russell Family Bible, July 30 2008; privately held by Scott Russell Redmond, Washington); Scott Russell.

121. Jackson, Ron V., Accelerated Indexing Systems, compiler, *U.S. Federal Census Mortality Schedules Index [database on-line],* *Ancestry.com.* www.ancestry.com/ : 1999, ID# MRT197_262100.

122. "Revolutionary War Pension and Bounty-Land Warrant Application Files," database and images *FootNote.com* (FootNote.com/ : accessed 25 Jan 2010); Mathew Hall, affidavit regarding Abram Blankenship, deceased.

123. 1810 U.S. census, Bedford, Virginia, p. 10, line 8B, Mathew Hall; digital images, *Ancestry.com* (www.ancestry.com/ : accessed 4 Apr 2010); citing National Archives and Records Administration microfilm M252, roll 67.

124. 1820 U.S. census, Bedford, Virginia population schedule, Southern District, p. 76; Image: 26., line 10, Mathew Hall; digital images, *Ancestry.com* (www.ancestry.com/ : accessed 4 Apr 2010); citing National Archives and Records Administration microfilm M33, roll M33_133.

125. 1850 U.S. census, Bedford, Virginia, population schedule, Southern Division, p. 230B; Image: 459, dwelling 292, family 292, Mathew Hall; digital images, *Ancestry.com* (www.ancestry.com/ : accessed 10 Feb 2010); citing National Archives and Records Administration microfilm M432, roll M432_935.

126. Carrol Carmen Hall, *The Grandfathers, The Hall and Overstreet Families* , 2 Volumes (Springfield, Illinois: Illinois Ancestors.org - Menard County (http://www.illinoisancestors.org/menard/), 1981-2007), Section 1, Chapter 3: Page 19. .... Earle S. Dennis and Jane Estelle Smith *Marriage Bonds of Bedford County, Virginia, 1755-1800* (Baltimore, Maryland: Genealogical Publishing Company, 1981), Page 33. .... William Wade Hinshaw, *Encyclopedia of American Quaker Genealogy. Vol. VI: (Virginia)* (Baltimore, Maryland: Genealogical Publishing Co., Reprint 1993), Mathew Hall & Mary Banks; p. 926; "Mary Banks, dt. Samuel. Levi Best, surety. Married by John Ayers, January 1, 1795."; The marriage bond is dated 29 Dec 1794.

127. 1850 U.S. census, Bedford, Virginia, population schedule, Southern Division, p. 231B; Image: 460, dwelling 292, family 292, Mathew Hall; digital images, *Ancestry.com* (www.ancestry.com/ : accessed 10 Feb 2010); citing National Archives and Records Administration microfilm M432, roll M432_935.

128. 1860 U.S. census, Bedford, Virginia, population schedule, Southern Revenue District, p. 580; Image: 286, dwelling 924, family 924, Mathew Hall, Jr; digital images, *Ancestry.com* (www.ancestry.com/ : accessed 23 Mar 2010); citing National Archives and Records Administration microfilm M653, roll M653_1335.

129. Carrol Carmen Hall, *The Grandfathers, The Hall and Overstreet Families* , 2 Volumes (Springfield, Illinois: Illinois Ancestors.org - Menard County (http://www.illinoisancestors.org/menard/), 1981-2007), Section 1, Chapter 3: Page 19. .... William Wade Hinshaw *Encyclopedia of American Quaker Genealogy. Vol. VI: (Virginia)* (Baltimore, Maryland: Genealogical Publishing Co., Reprint 1993), Jessee Hall & Elizabeth Williams; p. 926; "John Thrasher, surety. Married by William Johnson, March 1, 1797."; The marriage bond is dated 27 February 1797.

130. 1810 U.S. census, Bedford, Virginia, p. 10, line 9B, Elizabeth Hall; digital images, *Ancestry.com* (www.ancestry.com/ : accessed 4 Apr 2010); citing National Archives and Records Administration microfilm M252, roll 67.

131. 1820 U.S. census, Bedford, Virginia population schedule, Southern District, p. 76; Image: 26., line 7, Elizabeth Hall; digital images, *Ancestry.com* (www.ancestry.com/ : accessed 4 Apr 2010); citing National Archives and Records Administration microfilm M33, roll M33_133.

132. Bedford, Virginia, Deed Book 27 Page 337, Hall to Hall Deed, 19 November 1838; Library of Virginia, Richmond; FHL microfilm.

133. 1840 U.S. census, Patrick, Virginia, p. 42, line 28, Jesse Hall; digital images, *Ancestry.com* (www.ancestry.com/ : accessed 15 Jan 2013); citing National Archives and Records Administration microfilm M704, roll 573; Family History Library Film: 0029691.

134. 1820 U.S. census, Bedford, Virginia population schedule, Southern District, p. 74; Image: 25., line 14, Elisha Hall; digital images, *Ancestry.com* (www.ancestry.com/ : accessed 4 Apr 2010); citing National Archives and Records Administration microfilm M33, roll M33_133.

135. Carrol Carmen Hall, *The Grandfathers, The Hall and Overstreet Families* , 2 Volumes (Springfield, Illinois: Illinois Ancestors.org - Menard

Source Citations

County (http://www.illinoisancestors.org/menard/), 1981-2007), Section 6, Chapter 21: 225. .... Earle S. Dennis and Jane Estelle Smith,*Marriage Bonds of Bedford County, Virginia, 1755-1800* (Baltimore, Maryland: Genealogical Publishing Company, 1981), Page 30. .... William Wade Hinshaw, *Encyclopedia of American Quaker Genealogy. Vol. VI: (Virginia)* (Baltimore, Maryland: Genealogical Publishing Co., Reprint 1993), Elisha Hall & Sarah Best; p. 926; "Sarah Best, dt. Drusala. Levi Best, surety."

136. Earle S. Dennis and Jane Estelle Smith,*Marriage Bonds of Bedford County, Virginia, 1755-1800* (Baltimore, Maryland: Genealogical Publishing Company, 1981), Page 30.

137. 1840 U.S. census, Bedford, Tennessee, p. Page: 26; Image: 60, line 22, S. S. Brown; digital images,*Ancestry.com* (www.ancestry.com/ : accessed 26 Jan 2010); citing National Archives and Records Administration microfilm M704, roll 519.

138. 1850 U.S. census, Bedford, Tennessee, population schedule, District 6, p. 139A; Image: 280, dwelling 106, family 106, Tabitha Brown; digital images, *Ancestry.com* (www.ancestry.com/ : accessed 9 Feb 2010); citing National Archives and Records Administration microfilm M432, roll M432_869.

139. 1860 U.S. census, Bedford, Tennessee, population schedule, Shelbyville - Western Division District 6, p. 189; Image: 384, dwelling 222, family 203, Tabitha Brown; digital images, *Ancestry.com* (www.ancestry.com/ : accessed 8 Sep 2010); citing National Archives and Records Administration microfilm M653, roll M653_1239.

140. Helen Crawford Marsh, *Bedford County Tennessee Wills and Vital Records from Newspapers* (Greenville, South Carolina: Southern Historical Press, Inc., 1996), Page 2.

141. Carrol Carmen Hall, *The Grandfathers, The Hall and Overstreet Families* , 2 Volumes (Springfield, Illinois: Illinois Ancestors.org - Menard County (http://www.illinoisancestors.org/menard/), 1981-2007), Section 1, Chapter 3: Page 19. .... Barbara Brown Eakley,*The Browns of Bedford County, Virginia 1748-1840* (Westminister, Maryland: Heritage Books, 1998), page 129. .... C. T. Spear, editor,*Bedford County, Tennessee - Family History Book* (Paducah, Kentucky: Turner Publishing Company, 2002), Page 225. .... Earle S. Dennis and Jane Estelle Smith,*Marriage Bonds of Bedford County, Virginia, 1755-1800* (Baltimore, Maryland: Genealogical Publishing Company, 1981), Page 10.

142. C. T. Spear, editor, *Bedford County, Tennessee - Family History Book* (Paducah, Kentucky: Turner Publishing Company, 2002), Page 225. .... Jill K. Garrett, "Circuit Court Records, Maury County, Tennessee,"*The River Counties* Vol. 12 (1983): Page 117; "Shaderick Brown, age 50, Bedford County made deposition Feb. 1828-"

143. C. T. Spear, editor, *Bedford County, Tennessee - Family History Book* (Paducah, Kentucky: Turner Publishing Company, 2002), Page 225.

144. Earle S. Dennis and Jane Estelle Smith,*Marriage Bonds of Bedford County, Virginia, 1755-1800* (Baltimore, Maryland: Genealogical Publishing Company, 1981), Page 10.

145. Lucy D. Zeier, "Tennessee, Bedford County - Index County Court Minute Book, Volume 1, 1848-1852," transcript,*Tennessee, Bedford County - Index County Court Minute Book, Volume 1, 1848-1852* (http://www.tngenweb.org/bedford/County_minutes/CNC_V1_index.htm : accessed 20 Feb 2010), Shadrack Brown transactions; citing: Bedford County, Tennessee, County Court Minute Book.

146. Helen Crawford Marsh, *Bedford County Tennessee Wills and Vital Records from Newspapers* (Greenville, South Carolina: Southern Historical Press, Inc., 1996), Pages 104, 149.

147. C. T. Spear, editor, *Bedford County, Tennessee - Family History Book* (Paducah, Kentucky: Turner Publishing Company, 2002), page 226.

148. Carrol Carmen Hall, *The Grandfathers, The Hall and Overstreet Families* , 2 Volumes (Springfield, Illinois: Illinois Ancestors.org - Menard County (http://www.illinoisancestors.org/menard/), 1981-2007), Section 2, Chapter 21: Page 225. .... C. T. Spear, editor,*Bedford County, Tennessee - Family History Book* (Paducah, Kentucky: Turner Publishing Company, 2002), page 226.

149. Marcia Witt, "Witt Family of Bedford County, Virginia," genealogy modified register report,*Witt Family of Bedford County, Virginia* (http://wc.rootsweb.ancestry.com/cgi-bin/igm.cgi?op=REG&db=wittm&id=I127 : accessed 21 Feb 2010), Keziah Hall.

150. 1820 U.S. census, Bedford, Virginia population schedule, Southern District, p. 85; Image: 30, line 13, Benjamin Musgrove; digital images, *Ancestry.com* (www.ancestry.com/ : accessed 5 Apr 2010); citing National Archives and Records Administration microfilm M33, roll M33_133.

151. 1830 U.S. census, Bedford, Virginia, p. 174, line 1, Benjamin Musgrove; digital images,*Ancestry.com* (www.ancestry.com/ : accessed 5 Apr 2010); citing National Archives and Records Administration microfilm M19, roll M19- 194; Family History Film: 0029673.

152. 1850 U.S. census, Bedford, Virginia, population schedule, Southern Division, p. 249A; Image: 496, dwelling 566, family 566, Keziah Musgrove; digital images,*Ancestry.com* (www.ancestry.com/ : accessed 20 Mar 2010); citing National Archives and Records Administration microfilm M432, roll M432_935.

153. 1860 U.S. census, Bedford, Virginia, population schedule, Southern Revenue District, p. 563; Image: 269; Family History Library Film: 805335., dwelling 805, family 805, Keziah Musgrove; digital images,*Ancestry.com* (www.ancestry.com/ : accessed 20 Mar 2010); citing National Archives and Records Administration microfilm M653, roll M653_1335.

154. Carrol Carmen Hall, *The Grandfathers, The Hall and Overstreet Families* , 2 Volumes (Springfield, Illinois: Illinois Ancestors.org - Menard County (http://www.illinoisancestors.org/menard/), 1981-2007), Section 1, Chapter 3: Page 19. .... Marcia Witt, "Witt Family of Bedford County, Virginia," genealogy modified register report,*Witt Family of Bedford County, Virginia* (http://wc.rootsweb.ancestry.com/cgi-bin/igm.cgi?op=REG&db=wittm&id=I127 : accessed 21 Feb 2010), Keziah Hall. .... Earle S. Dennis and Jane Estelle Smith,*Marriage Bonds of Bedford County, Virginia, 1755-1800* (Baltimore, Maryland: Genealogical Publishing Company, 1981), Page 44.

155. Carrol Carmen Hall, *The Grandfathers, The Hall and Overstreet Families* , 2 Volumes (Springfield, Illinois: Illinois Ancestors.org - Menard

Source Citations

County (http://www.illinoisancestors.org/menard/), 1981-2007), Section 2, Chapter 21: Page 225. .... Marcia Witt, "Witt Family of Bedford County, Virginia," genealogy modified register report, *Witt Family of Bedford County, Virginia* (http://wc.rootsweb.ancestry.com/cgi-bin/igm.cgi?op=REG&db=wittm&id=I127 : accessed 21 Feb 2010), Benjamin B. Musgrove.

156. Earle S. Dennis and Jane Estelle Smith, *Marriage Bonds of Bedford County, Virginia, 1755-1800* (Baltimore, Maryland: Genealogical Publishing Company, 1981), Page 44.

157. 1840 U.S. census, Bedford, Virginia, Southern District, p. 263; Image: 540, line 20, Benjamin Musgrove; digital images, *Ancestry.com* (www.ancestry.com/ : accessed 5 Apr 2010); citing National Archives and Records Administration microfilm M704, roll 550; Family History Library Film: 0029683.

158. Carrol Carmen Hall, *The Grandfathers, The Hall and Overstreet Families* , 2 Volumes (Springfield, Illinois: Illinois Ancestors.org - Menard County (http://www.illinoisancestors.org/menard/), 1981-2007), Section VI, Chapter 21, Page 225. .... Marcia Witt, "Witt Family of Bedford County, Virginia," genealogy modified register report, *Witt Family of Bedford County, Virginia* (http://wc.rootsweb.ancestry.com/cgi-bin/igm.cgi?op=REG&db=wittm&id=I127 : accessed 21 Feb 2010), Christopher Musgrove.

159. Marcia Witt, "Witt Family of Bedford County, Virginia," genealogy modified register report, *Witt Family of Bedford County, Virginia* (http://wc.rootsweb.ancestry.com/cgi-bin/igm.cgi?op=REG&db=wittm&id=I127 : accessed 21 Feb 2010), Christopher Musgrove.

160. Carrol Carmen Hall, *The Grandfathers, The Hall and Overstreet Families* , 2 Volumes (Springfield, Illinois: Illinois Ancestors.org - Menard County (http://www.illinoisancestors.org/menard/), 1981-2007), Section VI, Chapter 21, Page 225. .... Marcia Witt, "Witt Family of Bedford County, Virginia," genealogy modified register report, *Witt Family of Bedford County, Virginia* (http://wc.rootsweb.ancestry.com/cgi-bin/igm.cgi?op=REG&db=wittm&id=I127 : accessed 21 Feb 2010), Henry Musgrove.

161. Carrol Carmen Hall, *The Grandfathers, The Hall and Overstreet Families* , 2 Volumes (Springfield, Illinois: Illinois Ancestors.org - Menard County (http://www.illinoisancestors.org/menard/), 1981-2007), Section VI, Chapter 21, Page 225. .... Marcia Witt, "Witt Family of Bedford County, Virginia," genealogy modified register report, *Witt Family of Bedford County, Virginia* (http://wc.rootsweb.ancestry.com/cgi-bin/igm.cgi?op=REG&db=wittm&id=I127 : accessed 21 Feb 2010), Mary Magdalene Musgrove.

162. Marcia Witt, "Witt Family of Bedford County, Virginia," genealogy modified register report, *Witt Family of Bedford County, Virginia* (http://wc.rootsweb.ancestry.com/cgi-bin/igm.cgi?op=REG&db=wittm&id=I127 : accessed 21 Feb 2010), Mary Magdalene Musgrove.

163. Carrol Carmen Hall, *The Grandfathers, The Hall and Overstreet Families* , 2 Volumes (Springfield, Illinois: Illinois Ancestors.org - Menard County (http://www.illinoisancestors.org/menard/), 1981-2007), Section VI, Chapter 21, Page 225. .... Marcia Witt, "Witt Family of Bedford County, Virginia," genealogy modified register report, *Witt Family of Bedford County, Virginia* (http://wc.rootsweb.ancestry.com/cgi-bin/igm.cgi?op=REG&db=wittm&id=I127 : accessed 21 Feb 2010), Rebekah Hall Musgrove.

164. Marcia Witt, "Witt Family of Bedford County, Virginia," genealogy modified register report, *Witt Family of Bedford County, Virginia* (http://wc.rootsweb.ancestry.com/cgi-bin/igm.cgi?op=REG&db=wittm&id=I127 : accessed 21 Feb 2010), Rebekah Hall Musgrove.

165. Carrol Carmen Hall, *The Grandfathers, The Hall and Overstreet Families* , 2 Volumes (Springfield, Illinois: Illinois Ancestors.org - Menard County (http://www.illinoisancestors.org/menard/), 1981-2007), Section VI, Chapter 21, Page 225. .... Marcia Witt, "Witt Family of Bedford County, Virginia," genealogy modified register report, *Witt Family of Bedford County, Virginia* (http://wc.rootsweb.ancestry.com/cgi-bin/igm.cgi?op=REG&db=wittm&id=I127 : accessed 21 Feb 2010), John Hall Musgrove.

166. Marcia Witt, "Witt Family of Bedford County, Virginia," genealogy modified register report, *Witt Family of Bedford County, Virginia* (http://wc.rootsweb.ancestry.com/cgi-bin/igm.cgi?op=REG&db=wittm&id=I127 : accessed 21 Feb 2010), John Hall Musgrove.

167. Carrol Carmen Hall, *The Grandfathers, The Hall and Overstreet Families* , 2 Volumes (Springfield, Illinois: Illinois Ancestors.org - Menard County (http://www.illinoisancestors.org/menard/), 1981-2007), Section VI, Chapter 21, Page 225. .... Marcia Witt, "Witt Family of Bedford County, Virginia," genealogy modified register report, *Witt Family of Bedford County, Virginia* (http://wc.rootsweb.ancestry.com/cgi-bin/igm.cgi?op=REG&db=wittm&id=I127 : accessed 21 Feb 2010), Rachel Musgrove.

168. Marcia Witt, "Witt Family of Bedford County, Virginia," genealogy modified register report, *Witt Family of Bedford County, Virginia* (http://wc.rootsweb.ancestry.com/cgi-bin/igm.cgi?op=REG&db=wittm&id=I127 : accessed 21 Feb 2010), Rachel Musgrove.

169. Drema Swader, "Keziah Stovel Musgrove," genealogy report, *Keziah Stovel Musgrove* (http://genealogy.drema.com/genealogy/ksm.html : accessed 20 Feb 2010), Keziah Stovel Musgrove Wilkerson; Citing: Janie Moseley Garraghty Jordan, Descendants of Joseph Wilkerson (12 May 1729-15 March 1829) and Allied Families of Bedford County, Virginia, (Warwick House Publishing, Lynchburg, Virginia: 1995).

170. Carrol Carmen Hall, *The Grandfathers, The Hall and Overstreet Families* , 2 Volumes (Springfield, Illinois: Illinois Ancestors.org - Menard County (http://www.illinoisancestors.org/menard/), 1981-2007), Section VI, Chapter 21, Page 225. .... Marcia Witt, "Witt Family of Bedford County, Virginia," genealogy modified register report, *Witt Family of Bedford County, Virginia* (http://wc.rootsweb.ancestry.com/cgi-bin/igm.cgi?op=REG&db=wittm&id=I127 : accessed 21 Feb 2010), Tabitha Musgrove.

171. Marcia Witt, "Witt Family of Bedford County, Virginia," genealogy modified register report, *Witt Family of Bedford County, Virginia* (http://wc.rootsweb.ancestry.com/cgi-bin/igm.cgi?op=REG&db=wittm&id=I127 : accessed 21 Feb 2010), Tabitha Musgrove.

172. Carrol Carmen Hall, *The Grandfathers, The Hall and Overstreet Families* , 2 Volumes (Springfield, Illinois: Illinois Ancestors.org - Menard County (http://www.illinoisancestors.org/menard/), 1981-2007), Section VI, Chapter 21, Page 225. .... Marcia Witt, "Witt Family of Bedford County, Virginia," genealogy modified register report, *Witt Family of Bedford County, Virginia* (http://wc.rootsweb.ancestry.com/cgi-bin/igm.cgi?op=REG&db=wittm&id=I127 : accessed 21 Feb 2010), Minerva Musgrove.

173. Marcia Witt, "Witt Family of Bedford County, Virginia," genealogy modified register report, *Witt Family of Bedford County, Virginia*

(http://wc.rootsweb.ancestry.com/cgi-bin/igm.cgi?op=REG&db=wittm&id=I127 : accessed 21 Feb 2010), Minerva Musgrove.

174. Carrol Carmen Hall, *The Grandfathers, The Hall and Overstreet Families* , 2 Volumes (Springfield, Illinois: Illinois Ancestors.org - Menard County (http://www.illinoisancestors.org/menard/), 1981-2007), Section VI, Chapter 21, Page 225. .... Marcia Witt, "Witt Family of Bedford County, Virginia," genealogy modified register report,*Witt Family of Bedford County, Virginia* (http://wc.rootsweb.ancestry.com/cgi-bin/igm.cgi?op=REG&db=wittm&id=I127 : accessed 21 Feb 2010), Millicent Musgrove.

175. Marcia Witt, "Witt Family of Bedford County, Virginia," genealogy modified register report*Witt Family of Bedford County, Virginia* (http://wc.rootsweb.ancestry.com/cgi-bin/igm.cgi?op=REG&db=wittm&id=I127 : accessed 21 Feb 2010), Millicent Musgrove.

176. Carrol Carmen Hall, *The Grandfathers, The Hall and Overstreet Families* , 2 Volumes (Springfield, Illinois: Illinois Ancestors.org - Menard County (http://www.illinoisancestors.org/menard/), 1981-2007), Section VI, Chapter 21, Page 225. .... Marcia Witt, "Witt Family of Bedford County, Virginia," genealogy modified register report,*Witt Family of Bedford County, Virginia* (http://wc.rootsweb.ancestry.com/cgi-bin/igm.cgi?op=REG&db=wittm&id=I127 : accessed 21 Feb 2010), Benjamin Musgrove, Jr.

177. Marcia Witt, "Witt Family of Bedford County, Virginia," genealogy modified register report*Witt Family of Bedford County, Virginia* (http://wc.rootsweb.ancestry.com/cgi-bin/igm.cgi?op=REG&db=wittm&id=I127 : accessed 21 Feb 2010), Benjamin Musgrove, Jr.

178. Carrol Carmen Hall, *The Grandfathers, The Hall and Overstreet Families* , 2 Volumes (Springfield, Illinois: Illinois Ancestors.org - Menard County (http://www.illinoisancestors.org/menard/), 1981-2007), Section VI, Chapter 21, Page 225. .... Marcia Witt, "Witt Family of Bedford County, Virginia," genealogy modified register report,*Witt Family of Bedford County, Virginia* (http://wc.rootsweb.ancestry.com/cgi-bin/igm.cgi?op=REG&db=wittm&id=I127 : accessed 21 Feb 2010), Demetrius Polyclitus Musgrove.

179. Marcia Witt, "Witt Family of Bedford County, Virginia," genealogy modified register report*Witt Family of Bedford County, Virginia* (http://wc.rootsweb.ancestry.com/cgi-bin/igm.cgi?op=REG&db=wittm&id=I127 : accessed 21 Feb 2010), Demetrius Polyclitus Musgrove.

180. "Revolutionary War Pension Files," database and images,*Folld3.com* (http://www.fold3.com/ : accessed 28 Sep 2013); Moses B. Crawford; citing entire pension file, M804.

181. 1830 U.S. census, Bledsoe, Tennessee, p. 278, line 21, John Hall; digital images,*Ancestry.com* (www.ancestry.com/ : accessed 30 Sep 2013); citing National Archives and Records Administration microfilm M19, roll 175; Family History Film: 0024533.

182. 1840 U.S. census, Bledsoe, Tennessee, p. 148, line 21, John Hale [Hall]; digital images,*Ancestry.com* (www.ancestry.com/ : accessed 28 Sep 2013); citing National Archives and Records Administration microfilm M704, roll 517.

183. 1850 U.S. census, Meigs, Tennessee, population schedule, Subdivision 22, p. 361A, dwelling 63, family 63, John Hall; digital images, *Ancestry.com* (www.ancestry.com/ : accessed 21 Jun 2013); citing National Archives and Records Administration microfilm M432, roll 890.

184. 1860 U.S. census, Collin, Texas, population schedule, Precinct 4, p. 19; Sheet 65, dwelling 125, family 135, John Hall; digital images, *Ancestry.com* (www.ancestry.com/ : accessed 19 Jun 2013); citing National Archives and Records Administration microfilm M653, roll 1291; Family History Library Film: 805291.

185. Timothy E. Hall, Texas to Ronald C. Hall, e-mail, March 1, 2013, "RE: DNA Results from 67 marker test"; privately held by Hall, Fort Worth, Texas; Includes Excel file containing research of E. Ann Patterson, Timothy's sister. .... The Church of Jesus Christ of Latter-day Saints, "Pedigree Resource File," database, *FamilySearch* (http://www.familysearch.org : accessed 30 Sep 2013), entry for John Hall Jr (PIN (Ancestral File Number): 35HF-N8V)); submitted by Culps W.

186. Ancestry.com Operations, Inc, "U.S. Federal Census Mortality Schedules, 1850-1885," database and images,*Ancestry.com* (www.ancestry.com/ : accessed 21 Jun 2013); Delilah Hall, Oct 1869, Collin County, Texas; Archive Collection: T1134; Archive Roll Number: 55; Census Year: 1870; Census Location: Precinct 5, Collin, Texas; Page: 64; Line: 27.

187. The Church of Jesus Christ of Latter-day Saints, "Pedigree Resource File," database,*FamilySearch* (http://www.familysearch.org : accessed 30 Sep 2013), entry for Jesse F. Hall (PIN (Ancestral File Number: 43CC-DKK); submitted by Morris R.

188. The Church of Jesus Christ of Latter-day Saints, "Pedigree Resource File," database,*FamilySearch* (http://www.familysearch.org : accessed 30 Sep 2013), entry for Joseph Marion Hall.

189. Diane Miller, "CHISUM - BLUFORD ESTES FAMILY,"*Estes Trails Family Newsletter* XXII (March 2004): 6.

190. Brown, Texas, "U.S., Confederate Pensions, 1884-1958," Mrs Lucitia Hall, widow of William Houston Hall; Pension file no. 17386; digital images, Ancestry.com Operations, Inc., "Confederate Pension Applications, 1899-1975; Collection #: CPA17376; Roll #: 202; Roll Description: Pension File Nos 17376 to 17390, Application Years 1909 to 1910.," *Ancestry.com* (www.ancestry.com/ : accessed 21 Jun 2013).

191. Texas. Texas Bureau of Vital Statistics., "Texas Deaths 1890 - 1976," database,*Family Search* (www.familysearch.org/ : accessed 23 Jun 2013), Martha Delilah Brown, 4 Sep 1921, Montague County, Texas; Death Certificate #25994.

192. 1820 U.S. census, Davidson, Tennessee population schedule, Nashville, p. 84, line 4, John Hall; digital images,*Ancestry.com* (www.ancestry.com/ : accessed 10 Nov 2012); citing National Archives and Records Administration microfilm M33, roll 122.

193. 1830 U.S. census, Yazoo, Mississippi, "within the division allotted to Joseph--", p. 295, line 24, J. C. Hall; digital images,*Ancestry.com* (www.ancestry.com/ : accessed 29 Nov 2012); citing National Archives and Records Administration microfilm M19, roll 71; Family History Film: 0014839.

194. Yazoo, Mississippi, Probate Minute Book Vol. A 1834-1838, A: 279, Estate of John C. Hall, deceased; Case #61; FHL microfilm 0,885,171. ....

Source Citations

Yazoo, Mississippi, Probate Minute Book Vol. A 1834-1838, A: 402, Estate of John C. Hall, deceased; Case #61; FHL microfilm 0,885,171. .... Yazoo, Mississippi, Probate Minute Book Vol. A 1834-1838, A: 412, 437, Estate of John C. Hall, deceased; Case #61; FHL microfilm 0,885,171. .... Yazoo, Mississippi, Chancery Court - Probate Cases 1841-1873, Box 119, Estate of William Hall - 1844; FHL microfilm #2438941, item 1. .... Betty Couch Wiltshire, *Yazoo County, Mississippi Pioneers* (Bowie, Maryland: Heritage Books, 1992), 65, 80, 113, 115.

195. Dodd, Jordan, *Tennessee Marriages to 1825 [database on-line]*, Ancestry.com. www.ancestry.com/ : 1997.

196. *Yazoo County, Mississippi - Probate Records* (Yazoo City, Mississippi, Yazoo County, Mississippi, County Clerk), Minute Book A, page 167. December Term 1834 - Elizabeth Hall and Samuel Dilley were granted letters of administration of the estate of John C. Hall, deceased.

November Term 1837 - Citation to Campbell Hall, Jane and Nancy Ann Hall, heirs of John C. Hall, deceased, to appear and show cause why land of the estate should not be sold.

197. Yazoo, Mississippi, Chancery Court - Probate Cases 1841-1873, Box 119, Estate of William Hall - 1844; FHL microfilm #2438941, item 1. .... Yazoo, Mississippi, Probate Minute Book Vol. B 1838-1842, B: 72, Estate of William Hall, deceased; Case #210; FHL microfilm 0,885,171.

198. Betty Couch Wiltshire, *Yazoo County, Mississippi Pioneers* (Bowie, Maryland: Heritage Books, 1992), 113.

199. Reed, Verna [Verna@carlsbadnm.com], "Modified Register for Hall" (Carlsbad, New Mexico: Sept 2002), page 21. .... Jackson, Ron V., Accelerated Indexing Systems, compiler, *U.S. Federal Census Mortality Schedules Index [database on-line]*, Ancestry.com. www.ancestry.com/ : 1999, Mississippi; MRT197_200663.

200. Elvis E. Fleming, "Part I of II William W. Wildy: "Grandfather of Roswell", *Roswell Daily Record*, February 2, 2002, p. 46; digital images, *NewspaperArchives.com* (http://www.newspaperarchive.com/ : accessed 9 Oct 2011), Historical Newspapers.

201. Jerry Morrison, transcriber Arkansas USGenWeb Project Archives, "Arkansas -Territorial Papers 1819-1825," database, *Arkansas Archives - Territorial Papers* (http://www.usgwarchives.net/ar/territory.htm : accessed 27 Feb 2007), Executives with surnames D-H, Samuel S. Hall; Transcribed from: U.S. Government Publication "Territorial Papers - Arkansas 1819-1825" page 789-874, Part Seven. "Executive Register for the Arkansas Territory, 1819-1836". .... "Laws of Arkansas," *Arkansas Gazette*, Decemeber 18, 1827, p. 1, col. 4; digital images, *GenealogyBank.com* (http://www.genealogybank.com/ : accessed 10 Mar 2012), Historical Newspapers. .... "General Assembly," *Arkansas Gazette*, November 6, 1827, p. 1, col. 4; digital images, *GenealogyBank.com* (http://www.genealogybank.com/ : accessed 10 Mar 2012), Historical Newspapers.

202. Pris Weathers, "Arkansas Gazette (1819-1930)," database, *Arkansas Ties* (http://www.arkansasties.com/), Samuel S. Hall; citing: Arkansas Gazette transcription. .... "50 Dollars Reward," *Arkansas Weekly Gazette*, 25 January 1825, p. 4; digital images, *GenealogyBank.com* (http://www.genealogybank.com/ : accessed 4 Feb 2012), Historical Newspapers.

203. Butler Center for Arkansas Studies, "The Encyclopedia of Arkansas History and Culture," database, *The Encyclopedia of Arkansas History and Culture* (http://www.encyclopediaofarkansas.net/default.aspx : accessed 3 May 2011), Samuel S. Hall - "Churches of Christ in Arkansas"; citing works by Paul D. Haynie of Harding University.

204. George S. Yerger, *Reports of Cases Argued and Determined in the Supreme Court of Tennessee During the Year 1836*, Volume IX (Nashville, Tennessee: S. Nye & Co. State Printers, 1836), IX: 358-382.

205. "To the Citizens of White, Saline, and Pulaski Counties," *(Little Rock) Arkansas Gazette Weekly*, November 24, 1835; Authored by Samuel S. Hall. .... John Hallum, *Biographical and Pictorial History of Arkansas* (Albany, New York: Weed, Parsons and Company, 1887), 67-70. .... James Logan Morgan, *Arkansas Newspaper Index 1819-1845 - Biographical Notes, Probate and Chancery Notices from Arkansas Newspapers, 1819-1845*, 4 volumes: v. 1. Obituaries and biographical notes from Arkansas newspapers, 1819-1835 -- v. 2. Obituaries and biographical notes from Arkansas newspapers, 1836-1840 -- v. 3. Obituaries and biographical notes from Arkansas newspapers, 1841-1845 -- v. 4. Probate and chancery notices from Arkansas newspapers, 1819-1845 (Conway, Arkansas: Arkansas Research, 1992, c1981), Vol. 1: 77. .... Arkansas. Eastern District - The United States Attorney's Office, *The United States Attorney's Office - Eastern District of Arkansas* (http://www.justice.gov/usao/are/meetattorney.html : accessed 17 Feb 2013), United States Attorney Listing of District of Arkansas and Eastern District of Arkansas, District of Arkansas.

206. United States. Department of the Interior, *United States Bureau of Land Management - Records*, Washington D.C, Certificate No. 26.

207. 1830 U.S. census, Pulaski, Arkansas Territory, p. 237; image 5 of 24, line 15, Samuel S. Hall; digital images, *Ancestry.com* (www.ancestry.com/ : accessed 11 Oct 2012); citing National Archives and Records Administration microfilm M19, roll 5; Family History Film: 0002473.

208. Ron V. Jackson, compiler. Accelerated Indexing Systems, "Arkansas Census, 1819-70," database, *Ancestry.com* (www.ancestry.com/ : accessed 2 May 2011), Samuel S. Hall; p. 13.

209. 1840 U.S. census, Yazoo, Mississippi, p. 323, line 15, Samuel S. Hall; digital images, *Ancestry.com* (www.ancestry.com/ : accessed 10 Dec 2012); citing National Archives and Records Administration microfilm M704, roll 217; Family History Library Film: 0014841.

210. Yazoo, Mississippi, Chancery Court - Probate Cases 1841-1873, Box 122, Estate of Samuel S. Hall - 1847; FHL microfilm #2438941. .... Betty Couch Wiltshire, *Yazoo County, Mississippi Pioneers* (Bowie, Maryland: Heritage Books, 1992), 107, 119. .... Yazoo, Mississippi, Probate Minute Book Vol. C 1842-1846, C: 44; Case #343, Samuel S. Hall, Deceased; FHL microfilm 0,885,172. .... Yazoo, Mississippi, Probate Minute Book Vol. C 1842-1846, C: 431; Case #47, Samuel S. Hall, Deceased; Wm. Hall, minor; FHL microfilm 0,885,172.

211. Turner Publishing Company, *Daughters of Republic of Texas, Volume I* (Texas: Turner Publishing Company, 1995), 105.

212. "The following minutes of the Convention...," *Telegraph and Texas Register*, October 17, 1835 , p. 3, col. 2; digital images, *GenealogyBank.com* (www.genealogybank.com/ : accessed 8 Dec 2012), Newspaper archives.

213. Reed, Verna [Verna@carlsbadnm.com], "Modified Register for Hall" (Carlsbad, New Mexico: Sept 2002), page 25. Verna cites a transcript of

the family Bible of Ada Byron Wildy Holloman Edwards Davis for this information. There is a difference in the birth date calculation given later: "Laurena Wildy died on the 13th day of Nov 1871 age 52 years 2 months 13 days." 31st of August?. .... The Church of Jesus Christ of Latter-day Saints [LDS], "International Genealogical Index," database,*FamilySearch* (http://www.familysearch.org : accessed 17 May 2009), North America Region, entry for Laurena Matilda Hall, born 3 Aug 1819, Arkansas.

214. Reed, Verna [Verna@carlsbadnm.com], "Modified Register for Hall" (Carlsbad, New Mexico: Sept 2002), page 25. .... The Church of Jesus Christ of Latter-day Saints [LDS], "International Genealogical Index," database*FamilySearch* (http://www.familysearch.org : accessed 17 May 2009), North America Region, entry for Laurena Matilda Hall, died 13 Nov 1871, Yazoo, Mississippi.

215. Coody, Marianna, copier; Schneider, Betty Aron, Coordinator, "Wesley Chapel Methodist Church Cemetery" (Yazoo County, Mississippi GenWeb, updated July 5, 2008.) .... *Mississippi Cemetery and Bible Records Vol. V* (Jackson, Mississippi: Mississippi Genealogical Society, September 1958), 147-151.

216. Reed, Verna [Verna@carlsbadnm.com], "Modified Register for Hall" (Carlsbad, New Mexico: Sept 2002), page 18. .... The Church of Jesus Christ of Latter-day Saints [LDS], "International Genealogical Index - Individual Record," database on-line*FamilySearch* (http://www.familysearch.org/eng/Search/frameset_search.asp : accessed 23 Oct 2011), North America Region, entry for Archibald C. Hall, death 30 Jun 1863; Record submitted after 1991 by a member of the LDS Church. No additional information is available.

217. Byron and Samuel Sistler transcribers,*Tennesseans in the War of 1812* (Nashville, Tennessee: Byron Sistler and Associates, Inc., 1992), 230.

218. Westin A. Goodspeed,*Goodspeed's History of Tennessee - Carroll County* (Nashville, Tennessee: Goodspeed Publishing Co., 1887; Southern Historical Press, Reprinted 1978).

219. United States. Department of the Interior,*United States Bureau of Land Management - Records,* Washington D.C, Document Nr.: 3264, 3265; Land Office: Mt Salus; SW 13/ 9N 4W Choctaw Mississippi.

220. United States. Department of the Interior,*United States Bureau of Land Management - Records,* Washington D.C, Document Nr.: 17228; Land Office: Columbus; N??W??SE 13/ 17N 1E Choctaw, Mississippi.

221. 1830 U.S. census, Yazoo, Mississippi, "within the division allotted to Joseph--", p. 295, line 20, A. C. Hall; digital images*Ancestry.com* (www.ancestry.com/ : accessed 29 Nov 2012); citing National Archives and Records Administration microfilm M19, roll 71; Family History Film: 0014839.

222. 1840 U.S. census, Carroll, Mississippi, p. 44, line 5, Archibald Hall; digital images,*Ancestry.com* (www.ancestry.com/ : accessed 3 Nov 2012); citing National Archives and Records Administration microfilm M704, roll 215; FHL Film: 0014841.

223. 1850 U.S. census, Yazoo, Mississippi, population schedule, p. 486A, dwelling 97, family 99, Archibald C. Hall; digital images*Ancestry.com* (www.ancestry.com/ : accessed 15 Dec 2012); citing National Archives and Records Administration microfilm M432, roll 382.

224. 1860 U.S. census, Yazoo, Mississippi, population schedule, p. 49; 977, dwelling 477, family 397, A. C. Hall; digital images*Ancestry.com* (www.ancestry.com/ : accessed 16 Dec 2012); citing National Archives and Records Administration microfilm M653, roll 594; Family History Library Film: 803594.

225. Hunting For Bears, comp,*Mississippi Marriages, 1776-1935 [database on-line],* Ancestry.com. www.ancestry.com/: The Generations Network, Inc., 2004. .... The Church of Jesus Christ of Latter-day Saints [LDS], "International Genealogical Index - Individual Record," database on-line, *FamilySearch* (http://www.familysearch.org/eng/Search/frameset_search.asp : accessed 23 Oct 2011), North America Region, entry for Archibald C. Hall and Mary B. Hamilton, marriage 23 Mar 1826 , Wilkinson, Mississippi; citing FHL microfilm 0877598 (Marriages, 1804-1952; register of marriages, births and deaths, 1879-1887 (Wilkinson County, Mississippi)), batch no. M520424, reference no. 1820 - 1828; V. C-D; Microfilm of original record in the Wilkinson County Courthouse at Woodville, Mississippi.

226. Reed, Verna [Verna@carlsbadnm.com], "Modified Register for Hall" (Carlsbad, New Mexico: Sept 2002), page 19.

227. 1840 U.S. census, Carroll, Mississippi, p. 44, line 5, Archibald Hall; digital images*Ancestry.com* (www.ancestry.com/ : accessed 3 Nov 2012); citing National Archives and Records Administration microfilm M704, roll 215; Family History Library Film: 0014841.

228. 1870 U.S. census, Yazoo, Mississippi, population schedule, District 3, p. 121; 359A, dwelling 1105, family 1087, M. D. Hall; digital images, *Ancestry.com* (www.ancestry.com/ : accessed 19 Dec 2012); citing National Archives and Records Administration microfilm M593, roll 754; Family History Library Film: 552253.

229. Brown, "Our Family Tree - James Nathaniel Bradshaw"; Limited documentation; contact email: 'bloubrown45@yahoo.com'; database, Rootsweb.com, "Rootsweb's WorldConnect Project - Our Family Tree,"*Rootsweb's World Connect* (http://www.rootsweb.ancestry.com/ : accessed 15 Feb 2012).

230. Yazoo, Mississippi, Will Records Volume A-B 1833-1908, A: 293, Laurena M. Hall; FHL microfilm #879249.

231. Reed, Verna [Verna@carlsbadnm.com], "Modified Register for Hall" (Carlsbad, New Mexico: Sept 2002), page 20.

232. 1830 U.S. census, Yazoo, Mississippi, "within the division allotted to Joseph--", p. 292, line 18, Wm. Russell; digital images*Ancestry.com* (www.ancestry.com/ : accessed 5 Dec 2012); citing National Archives and Records Administration microfilm M19, roll 71; Family History Film: 0014839.

233. 1840 U.S. census, Carroll, Mississippi, p. 31, line 16, William Russell; digital images*Ancestry.com* (www.ancestry.com/ : accessed 10 Dec 2012); citing National Archives and Records Administration microfilm M704, roll 215.

234. 1850 U.S. census, Carroll, Mississippi, population schedule, Northern Division, p. 277B; 552, dwelling 333, family 338, Tobitha Ross; digital images, *Ancestry.com* (www.ancestry.com/ : accessed 4 Nov 2012); citing National Archives and Records Administration microfilm M432, roll 369.

235. Tennessee. Davidson. County Clerk, *Davidson County, Tennessee - Marriage Book 1,* Nashville, TN:, page 15.

236. Yazoo, Mississippi, Probate Minute Book Vol. A 1834-1838, A: 387, Estate of William Russell - Case #40; FHL microfilm 0,885,171. .... Yazoo, Mississippi, Probate Minute Book Vol. A 1834-1838, A: 432, Estate of William Russell - Case #40; FHL microfilm 0,885,171. .... Yazoo, Mississippi, Probate Minute Book Vol. B 1838-1842, B: 159, Estate of William Russell, deceased; Case #40; FHL microfilm 0,885,171. .... Yazoo, Mississippi, Probate Minute Book Vol. B 1838-1842, B: 43, Estate of William Russell, deceased; Case #40; FHL microfilm 0,885,171.

237. Betty Couch Wiltshire, *Carroll County, Mississippi, pioneers* (Carrollton, Mississippi: Pioneer Publishing Co., c1990), 80, 82.

238. Russell Family Tree - Ancestry.com, Annabel and Wade Russell, compiler (Wm. Ross Russell Family Bible, July 30 2008; privately held by Scott Russell Redmond, Washington); Scott Rusell. .... Betty Couch Wiltshire, *Carroll County, Mississippi, pioneers* (Carrollton, Mississippi: Pioneer Publishing Co., c1990), 199, Russell Family.

239. Russell Family Tree - Ancestry.com, Annabel and Wade Russell, compiler (Wm. Ross Russell Family Bible, July 30 2008; privately held by Scott Russell Redmond, Washington); Scott Russell. .... Betty Couch Wiltshire, *Carroll County, Mississippi, pioneers* (Carrollton, Mississippi: Pioneer Publishing Co., c1990), 199, Russell Family.

240. Reed, Verna [Verna@carlsbadnm.com], "Modified Register for Hall" (Carlsbad, New Mexico: Sept 2002), page 20. .... Betty Couch Wiltshire, *Carroll County, Mississippi, pioneers* (Carrollton, Mississippi: Pioneer Publishing Co., c1990), 199, Russell Family.

241. Reed, Verna [Verna@carlsbadnm.com], "Modified Register for Hall" (Carlsbad, New Mexico: Sept 2002), page 21. .... Betty Couch Wiltshire, *Carroll County, Mississippi, pioneers* (Carrollton, Mississippi: Pioneer Publishing Co., c1990), 199, Russell Family.

242. Yazoo, Mississippi, Chancery Court - Probate Cases 1841-1873, Box 119, Estate of William Hall - 1844; FHL microfilm #2438941, item 2 of 2.

243. Linda Mason, "Yazoo County, MS 1823 Tax List," database, *MSGenWeb - Special Projects - Library Project* (http://www.msgw.org/library/yazoo-1823tax.html : accessed 24 Jan 2010), Elisha S. Hall.

244. Jill K. Garrett, "Circuit Court Records, Maury County, Tennessee," *The River Counties* Vol. 12 (1983): 116-117. .... Steve Carson, "Hall and related deeds, part 2," *RootsWeb - TNBEDFOR-L Archives,* message board, 24 Jul 2005 (http://archiver.rootsweb.ancestry.com : accessed 8 Feb 2010); Bedford Roll #118 .... Bedford, Tennessee, Deed Records X-BB; Roll #118: 397-398, Abraham B. Morton to Hall heirs, 1 Dec 1831; Tennessee State Library and Archives, Nashville, Tennessee.

245. Claudia Brumbalow, "[BROWN] Browns in TN, MS, TX, NC," *BROWN-L Archives,* mailing list archives, 25 Jan 2008 (http://archiver.rootsweb.ancestry.com/th/read/BROWN/ : accessed 15 Feb 2010).

246. Claudia Brumbalow, "[BROWN] Browns in TN, MS, TX, NC," *BROWN-L Archives,* mailing list archives, 25 Jan 2008 (http://archiver.rootsweb.ancestry.com/th/read/BROWN/ : accessed 13 Feb 2010); Citing: "Desc. of William and Margaret Brown", by Helen Rugely

247. Helen Crawford Marsh, *Bedford County Tennessee Wills and Vital Records from Newspapers* (Greenville, South Carolina: Southern Historical Press, Inc., 1996), Page 285.

248. Jane Henry Thomas and J. G. M. Ramsey contributor, *Old Days in Nashville* (1897; reprint, Nashville, Tennessee: Charles Elder, 196?), 105-107; Reprint of the 1897 ed., to which is added an historical sketch of Nashville as of 1854, by J. G. M. Ramsey.

249. 1830 U.S. census, Yazoo, Mississippi, "within the division allotted to Joseph--", p. 295, line 19, Marcus Pierce; digital images *Ancestry.com* (www.ancestry.com/ : accessed 29 Nov 2012); citing National Archives and Records Administration microfilm M19, roll 71; Family History Film: 0014839.

250. 1840 U.S. census, Carroll, Mississippi, p. 40, line 29, Marcus Pierce; digital images, *Ancestry.com* (www.ancestry.com/ : accessed 3 Nov 2012); citing National Archives and Records Administration microfilm M704, roll 215; Family History Library Film: 0014841.

251. 1850 U.S. census, Carroll, Mississippi, population schedule, Southern Division, p. 240A, dwelling 614, family 674, Rhoda Pierce; digital images, *Ancestry.com* (www.ancestry.com/ : accessed 4 Nov 2012); citing National Archives and Records Administration microfilm M432, roll 369.

252. 1860 U.S. census, Choctaw, Mississippi, population schedule, Township 17; Poplar Creek P. O., p. 9; 199, dwelling 55, family 55, Rhoda Pierce; digital images, *Ancestry.com* (www.ancestry.com/ : accessed 4 Nov 2012); citing National Archives and Records Administration microfilm M653, roll 579; Family History Library Film: 803579.

253. 1870 U.S. census, Choctaw, Mississippi, population schedule, Township 11, Range 6, p. 255A, dwelling 18, family 18, Benjamin Pierce; digital images, *Ancestry.com* (www.ancestry.com/ : accessed 4 Nov 2012); citing National Archives and Records Administration microfilm M593, roll 725; Family History Library Film: 552224.

254. George, James Z., Reporter to the State, Mississippi Supreme Court, *Cases Argued and Decided in the Supreme Court of Mississippi*, Vol. 31-Vol. 2 (Philadelphia, Pennsylvania: E. W. Stephens Publishing Co./ T & J.W. Johnson & Co., 1858), Vol. 31 - Vol. 2: page 646. .... Betty Couch Wiltshire, *Carroll County, Mississippi, pioneers* (Carrollton, Mississippi: Pioneer Publishing Co., c1990), 101; From Carroll County Probate Records - Probate Book A 1834-41, December Term 1844, page 242. "Rhoda Pierce, widow of Marcus Pierce, deceased..."

255. George, James Z., Reporter to the State, Mississippi Supreme Court, *Cases Argued and Decided in the Supreme Court of Mississippi*, Vol. 31-Vol. 2 (Philadelphia, Pennsylvania: E. W. Stephens Publishing Co./ T & J.W. Johnson & Co., 1858), Vol. 31- Vol. 2: page 646. .... Betty Couch Wiltshire, *Carroll County, Mississippi, pioneers* (Carrollton, Mississippi: Pioneer Publishing Co., c1990), 97; From Carroll County Probate Records -

Source Citations

Probate Book A 1834-41, May Term 1844, page 205. "William Sanders was appointed Administrator of the Estate of Marcus Pierce, dec'd."

256. Yazoo, Mississippi, Chancery Court - Probate Cases 1841-1873, Box 119, Estate of Willliam Hall - 1844; FHL microfilm #2438941, item 1.

257. Betty Couch Wiltshire, *Yazoo County, Mississippi Pioneers* (Bowie, Maryland: Heritage Books, 1992), 118. .... Yazoo, Mississippi, Probate Minute Book Vol. C 1842-1846, C: 391; Case #36, Marcus Pierce, Deceased; Rhoda Pierce, Widow; FHL microfilm 0,885,172; Date entry in court records says "1843". This was a mistake. It has to be "1844" according to its position in the volume, page numbering, etc.. [rch]

258. Betty Couch Wiltshire, *Carroll County, Mississippi, pioneers* (Carrollton, Mississippi: Pioneer Publishing Co., c1990), 97, 101.

259. 1850 U.S. census, Carroll, Mississippi, population schedule, Southern Division, p. 478; 240B, dwelling 614, family 674, Rhoda Pierce; digital images, *Ancestry.com* (www.ancestry.com/ : accessed 4 Nov 2012); citing National Archives and Records Administration microfilm M432, roll 369.

260. 1860 U.S. census, Choctaw, Mississippi, population schedule, Township 17; Poplar Creek P. O., p. 9; 199, dwelling 55, family 55, Rhoda Pierce; digital images, *Ancestry.com* (www.ancestry.com/ : accessed 4 Nov 2012); citing National Archives and Records Administration microfilm M653, roll 579; Family History Library Film: 803579.

261. 1880 U.S. census, Montgomery, Mississippi, population schedule, enumeration district (ED) 144, p. 412A; 114, dwelling 121, family 123, Henry Pierce; digital images, *Ancestry.com* (www.ancestry.com/ : accessed 4 Nov 2012); citing National Archives and Records Administration microfilm T9, roll 658; Family History Film: 1254658.

262. Carrol Carmen Hall, *The Grandfathers, The Hall and Overstreet Families* , 2 Volumes (Springfield, Illinois: Illinois Ancestors.org - Menard County (http://www.illinoisancestors.org/menard/), 1981-2007), Section 2, Chapter 21: Page 225. .... Virginia, Virginia Marriages, 1785-1940 page 15, Carter-Hall, 1820; FHL microfilm 30591.

263. 1850 U.S. census, Bedford, Virginia, population schedule, Southern Division, p. 245B; Image: 489, dwelling 517, family 517, John Hall; digital images, *Ancestry.com* (www.ancestry.com/ : accessed 10 Feb 2010); citing National Archives and Records Administration microfilm M432, roll M432_935.

264. 1860 U.S. census, Bedford, Virginia, population schedule, Davis Mills - Southern Revenue District, p. 588; Image: 294, dwelling 984, family 984, M. A. Hall; digital images, *Ancestry.com* (www.ancestry.com/ : accessed 11 Nov 2011); citing National Archives and Records Administration microfilm M653, roll M653_1335.

265. Carrol Carmen Hall, *The Grandfathers, The Hall and Overstreet Families* , 2 Volumes (Springfield, Illinois: Illinois Ancestors.org - Menard County (http://www.illinoisancestors.org/menard/), 1981-2007), Section 2, Chapter 21: Page 225. .... William Wade Hinshaw *Encyclopedia of American Quaker Genealogy. Vol. VI: (Virginia)* (Baltimore, Maryland: Genealogical Publishing Co., Reprint 1993), John Hall & Melinda Hall; p. 926; "Melinda Hall, dt. Mathew. Mathew Hall, Jr., surety. Married by William Leftwich, 18 February 1830."; The marriage bond is dated 15 February 1830.

266. 1860 U.S. census, Bedford, Virginia, population schedule, Davis Mills - Southern Revenue District, p. 588; Image: 294, dwelling 984, family 984, Jno. Hall; digital images, *Ancestry.com* (www.ancestry.com/ : accessed 8 Sep 2010); citing National Archives and Records Administration microfilm M653, roll M653_1335.

267. 1860 U.S. census, Bedford, Virginia, population schedule, Davis Mills - Southern Revenue District, p. 588; Image: 294, dwelling 985, family 985, A. J. Hall; digital images, *Ancestry.com* (www.ancestry.com/ : accessed 11 Nov 2011); citing National Archives and Records Administration microfilm M653, roll M653_1335.

268. 1850 U.S. census, Bedford, Virginia, population schedule, Southern Division, p. 246A; Image: 490, dwelling 517, family 517, John Hall; digital images, *Ancestry.com* (www.ancestry.com/ : accessed 10 Feb 2010); citing National Archives and Records Administration microfilm M432, roll M432_935.

269. 1830 U.S. census, Bedford, Virginia, p. 174, line 14, Joel Hall; digital images, *Ancestry.com* (www.ancestry.com/ : accessed 5 Apr 2010); citing National Archives and Records Administration microfilm M19, roll M19- 194; Family History Film: 0029673.

270. 1850 U.S. census, Bedford, Virginia, population schedule, Southern Division, p. 240A; Image: 478, dwelling 427, family 427, Joel Hall; digital images, *Ancestry.com* (www.ancestry.com/ : accessed 10 Feb 2010); citing National Archives and Records Administration microfilm M432, roll M432_935.

271. William Wade Hinshaw, *Encyclopedia of American Quaker Genealogy. Vol. VI: (Virginia)* (Baltimore, Maryland: Genealogical Publishing Co., Reprint 1993), Joel Hall & Sally B. Jones; p. 926; "Sally B. Jones, dt. Elizabeth. Christopher Musgrove, surety."

272. Carl Hanson, "Re: Turner, Heptinstall, Snow, Craighead, Craghead," *Virginia. Bedford - Family History & Genealogy Message Board*, message board - rootsweb.com, 13 Aug 2004; edited 5 Mar 2006 (http://boards.rootsweb.com/localities.northam.usa.states.virginia.counties.bedford/ : accessed 21 Oct 2011).

273. 1850 U.S. census, Henry, Tennessee, population schedule, District 9, p. 313A; Image: 145, dwelling 9, family 9, Bird Greer; digital images, *Ancestry.com* (www.ancestry.com/ : accessed 4 Apr 2010); citing National Archives and Records Administration microfilm M432, roll M432_884.

274. 1860 U.S. census, Henry, Tennessee, population schedule, District 9, p. 402; Image: 451, dwelling 949, family 969, Bird Greer; digital images, *Ancestry.com* (www.ancestry.com/ : accessed 4 Apr 2010); citing National Archives and Records Administration microfilm M653, roll M653_1256.

275. 1830 U.S. census, Bedford, Virginia, p. 175, line 3, John Hall; digital images, *Ancestry.com* (www.ancestry.com/ : accessed 5 Apr 2010); citing National Archives and Records Administration microfilm M19, roll M19- 194.

276. Carrol Carmen Hall, *The Grandfathers, The Hall and Overstreet Families* , 2 Volumes (Springfield, Illinois: Illinois Ancestors.org - Menard

County (http://www.illinoisancestors.org/menard/), 1981-2007), Section 6, Chapter 21: 225. .... Genealogical Society of Utah, "Virginia, Marriages, 1785-1940," database, The Church of Jesus Christ of Latter-day Saints, *FamilySearch* (https://familysearch.org/ : accessed 1 Jan 2013), John Hall and Elizabeth Moon, 17 Feb 1824; citing reference page 80, FHL microfilm #33326. .... Bedford, Virginia, Chancery Court Index No. 1846-045, Case No. 6122, Moon v. Hall, abt 1841; digital images, *Virginia Memory - Digital Collections* (http://www.lva.virginia.gov/ : accessed 13 Jun 2010).

277. Bedford, Virginia, Chancery Court Index No. 1846-045, Case No. 6122, Moon v. Hall, abt 1841; digital images, *Virginia Memory - Digital Collections* (http://www.lva.virginia.gov/ : accessed 13 Jun 2010).

278. Carrol Carmen Hall, *The Grandfathers, The Hall and Overstreet Families* , 2 Volumes (Springfield, Illinois: Illinois Ancestors.org - Menard County (http://www.illinoisancestors.org/menard/), 1981-2007), Section 6, Chapter 21: 225. .... "Waddie *Bos'n Mate*" Salmon, "Burnett Marriage Records," *BURNETT-L Archives*, message board, 19 Aug 1999 (http://archiver.rootsweb.ancestry.com/th/read/BURNETT/ : accessed 23 Mar 2010); Dec. 25, 1826; William Burnett & Katherine Hall, dt Elisha; John Hall,
Jr., Surety; Married
by William Leftwich, Jan. 10, 1827.

279. 1850 U.S. census, Bedford, Virginia, population schedule, Southern Division, p. 248A; Image: 494, dwelling 547, family 547, James K. Shaon; digital images, *Ancestry.com* (www.ancestry.com/ : accessed 28 Feb 2010); citing National Archives and Records Administration microfilm M432, roll M432_935.

280. 1840 U.S. census, Audrain, Missouri, Wilson, p. 7, line 9, B. B. Hall; digital images, *Ancestry.com* (www.ancestry.com/ : accessed 31 Dec 2012); citing National Archives and Records Administration microfilm M704, roll 220; Family History Library Film: 0014855.

281. 1850 U.S. census, Audrain, Missouri, population schedule, District 4, p. 176A; Image: 359, dwelling 292, family 311, Banks B. Hall; digital images, *Ancestry.com* (www.ancestry.com/ : accessed 23 Mar 2010); citing National Archives and Records Administration microfilm M432, roll M432_391.

282. 1860 U.S. census, Audrain, Missouri, population schedule, Loutre, p. 745; Image: 249, dwelling 20, family 25, Bank Hall; digital images, *Ancestry.com* (www.ancestry.com/ : accessed 4 Apr 2010); citing National Archives and Records Administration microfilm M653, roll M653_606.

283. Genealogical Society of Utah. Missouri Marriages, "Missouri, Marriages, 1750-1920," database, *FamilySearch* (https://familysearch.org/ : accessed 31 Dec 2012), Banks B. Hall and Mary H. Reed, 1835; FHL Microfilm #901383.

284. 1870 U.S. census, St. Louis, Missouri, population schedule, St Louis Ward 5, p. 865A; Image: 343, dwelling 737, family 1512, Mary H. Hall; digital images, *Ancestry.com* (www.ancestry.com/ : accessed 4 Apr 2010); citing National Archives and Records Administration microfilm M593, roll M593_814.

285. 1880 U.S. census, St. Louis, Missouri, population schedule, Saint Louis, enumeration district (ED) 270, p. 204.1000; Image: 0418, dwelling 31, family 41, Mary H. Hall; digital images, *Ancestry.com* (www.ancestry.com/ : accessed 4 Apr 2010); citing National Archives and Records Administration microfilm T9, roll T9_732.

286. 1850 U.S. census, Bedford, Tennessee, population schedule, District 6, p. 139A; Image: 280, dwelling 105, family 105, Elizabeth Robertson; digital images, *Ancestry.com* (www.ancestry.com/ : accessed 9 Feb 2010); citing National Archives and Records Administration microfilm M432, roll M432_869.

287. 1850 U.S. census, Bedford, Tennessee, population schedule, District 6, p. 139A; Image: 280, dwelling 107, family 107, George W. Brown; digital images, *Ancestry.com* (www.ancestry.com/ : accessed 9 Feb 2010); citing National Archives and Records Administration microfilm M432, roll M432_869.

288. 1860 U.S. census, Bedford, Tennessee, population schedule, Shelbyville - Western Division District 6, p. 189; Image: 384, dwelling 223, family 204, G. W. Brown; digital images, *Ancestry.com* (www.ancestry.com/ : accessed 8 Sep 2010); citing National Archives and Records Administration microfilm M653, roll M653_1239.

289. Turner Publishing Company, *Rover & Bedford County, Tn, Volume 2* (Paducah, Kentucky: Turner Publishing Company, 2000), Page 270.

290. 1850 U.S. census, Bedford, Virginia, population schedule, Southern Division, p. 249B; Image: 497, dwelling 570, family 570, Christopher Musgrove; digital images, *Ancestry.com* (www.ancestry.com/ : accessed 20 Mar 2010); citing National Archives and Records Administration microfilm M432, roll M432_935.

291. University of Virginia Library, "Valley of the Shadow - Civil War- Era Newspapers," database, *Valley of the Shadow - Civil War- Era Newspapers* (http://valley.lib.virginia.edu/news/ss1858/va.au.ss.1858.07.27.xml : accessed 20 Feb 2010), Christopher Musgrove.

292. 1850 U.S. census, Clark, Illinois, population schedule, Marshall, p. 176B; Image: 111, dwelling 188, family 188, Henry Musgrove; digital images, *Ancestry.com* (www.ancestry.com/ : accessed 20 Mar 2010); citing National Archives and Records Administration microfilm M432, roll M432_100.

293. Marcia Witt, "Witt Family of Bedford County, Virginia," genealogy modified register report, *Witt Family of Bedford County, Virginia* (http://wc.rootsweb.ancestry.com/cgi-bin/igm.cgi?op=REG&db=wittm&id=I127 : accessed 21 Feb 2010), Henry Musgrove.

294. 1850 U.S. census, Bedford, Virginia, population schedule, Northern Division, p. 175B; Image: 350, dwelling 533, family 509, Wm. Wilkerson; digital images, *Ancestry.com* (www.ancestry.com/ : accessed 20 Mar 2010); citing National Archives and Records Administration microfilm M432, roll M432_935.

295. 1850 U.S. census, Bedford, Virginia, population schedule, Northern Division, p. 175A; Image: 349, dwelling 527, family 504, Hall Pearson; digital images, *Ancestry.com* (www.ancestry.com/ : accessed 20 Mar 2010); citing National Archives and Records Administration microfilm M432,

roll M432_935.

296. 1850 U.S. census, Franklin, Virginia, population schedule, p. 79B; Image: 162., dwelling 288, family 287, John H. Musgrove; digital images, *Ancestry.com* (http://www.ancestry.com/ : accessed 20 Mar 2010); citing National Archives and Records Administration microfilm M432, roll M432_944.

297. 1850 U.S. census, Bedford, Virginia, population schedule, Northern Division, p. 144A; Image: 287, dwelling 61, family 61, Owin Wilkerson; digital images, *Ancestry.com* (www.ancestry.com/ : accessed 20 Mar 2010); citing National Archives and Records Administration microfilm M432, roll M432_935.

298. Drema Swader, "Keziah Stovel Musgrove," genealogy report,*Keziah Stovel Musgrove* (http://genealogy.drema.com/genealogy/ksm.html : accessed 20 Feb 2010), Keziah Stovel Musgrove Wilkerson.

299. 1850 U.S. census, Bedford, Virginia, population schedule, Northern Division, p. 175B; Image: 350, dwelling 534, family 510, Wm. L. Wilkerson; digital images,*Ancestry.com* (www.ancestry.com/ : accessed 20 Mar 2010); citing National Archives and Records Administration microfilm M432, roll M432_935.

300. Marcia Witt, "Witt Family of Bedford County, Virginia," genealogy modified register report,*Witt Family of Bedford County, Virginia* (http://wc.rootsweb.ancestry.com/cgi-bin/igm.cgi?op=REG&db=wittm&id=I127 : accessed 21 Feb 2010), Keziah Stover Musgrove.

301. 1850 U.S. census, Franklin, Virginia, population schedule, p. 79B; Image: 162., dwelling 293, family 292, Parmesias English; digital images, *Ancestry.com* (http://www.ancestry.com/ : accessed 20 Mar 2010); citing National Archives and Records Administration microfilm M432, roll M432_944.

302. 1850 U.S. census, Independence, Arkansas, population schedule, White River, p. 332B; Image: 662, dwelling 287, family 287, Harrison Baker; digital images, *Ancestry.com* (www.ancestry.com/ : accessed 20 Mar 2010); citing National Archives and Records Administration microfilm M432, roll M432_26.

303. 1850 U.S. census, Bedford, Virginia, population schedule, Southern Division, p. 249B; Image: 497, dwelling 567, family 567, Benjamin B. Musgrove; digital images,*Ancestry.com* (www.ancestry.com/ : accessed 20 Mar 2010); citing National Archives and Records Administration microfilm M432, roll M432_935.

304. 1850 U.S. census, Bedford, Virginia, population schedule, Southern Division, p. 249A; Image: 496, dwelling 565, family 565, D. P. Musgrove; digital images, *Ancestry.com* (www.ancestry.com/ : accessed 20 Mar 2010); citing National Archives and Records Administration microfilm M432, roll M432_935.

305. 1870 U.S. census, Collin, Texas, population schedule, Precinct 5; P. O. Plano, p. 484B, dwelling 312, family 315, Jesse Hall; digital images, *Ancestry.com* (www.ancestry.com/ : accessed 21 Jun 2013); citing National Archives and Records Administration microfilm M593, roll 1579; Family History Library Film: 553078.

306. 1880 U.S. census, Collin, Texas, population schedule, Justice Precinct 5, enumeration district (ED) 26, p. 2B; Sheet 221B, dwelling 15, family 16, Jesse Hall; digital images,*Ancestry.com* (www.ancestry.com/ : accessed 21 Jun 2013); citing National Archives and Records Administration microfilm T9, roll 1296; Family History Film: 1255296.

307. The Church of Jesus Christ of Latter-day Saints, "Pedigree Resource File," database,*FamilySearch* (http://www.familysearch.org : accessed 30 Sep 2013), entry for Elizabeth Jane Houston (PIN (Ancestral File Number: 43CC-BNT)); submitted by Morris R.

308. The Church of Jesus Christ of Latter-day Saints, "Pedigree Resource File," database,*FamilySearch* (http://www.familysearch.org : accessed 30 Sep 2013), entry for Fidelia N. (Della) Hall (PIN (Ancestral File Number: 42W2-Z5C)); submitted by Morris R.

309. 1860 U.S. census, Collin, Texas, population schedule, Precinct 4, p. 19; Sheet 65, dwelling 124, family 134, J. M. Hall; digital images, *Ancestry.com* (www.ancestry.com/ : accessed 19 Jun 2013); citing National Archives and Records Administration microfilm M653, roll 1291; Family History Library Film: 805291.

310. 1870 U.S. census, Limestone, Texas, population schedule, District 48 West Texas, p. 189B, dwelling 575, family 608, Joseph M. Hall; digital images, *Ancestry.com* (www.ancestry.com/ : accessed 17 Jun 2013); citing National Archives and Records Administration microfilm M593, roll 1596; Family History Library Film: 553095.

311. 1880 U.S. census, Lampasas, Texas, population schedule, Precinct 6, enumeration district (ED) 090, p. 339B, dwelling 9, family 9, James Hall (Joseph Hall); digital images,*Ancestry.com* (www.ancestry.com/ : accessed 17 Jun 2013); citing National Archives and Records Administration microfilm T9, roll 1316; Family History Film: 1255316.

312. 1900 U.S. census, Collin, Texas, population schedule, Justice Precint 1, enumeration district (ED) 2, sheet 3B, dwelling 57, family 59, Joseph M. Hall; digital images,*Ancestry.com* (www.ancestry.com/ : accessed 20 Jun 2013); citing National Archives and Records Administration microfilm T623, roll 1620; FHL microfilm: 1241620.

313. Hunting For Bears, compilers, "Missouri Marriages, 1766-1983," database,*Ancestry.com* (www.ancestry.com/ : accessed 20 Jun 2013), Joseph M. Hall m. Mary Ann Estes, 1853.

314. Diane Miller, "CHISUM - BLUFORD ESTES FAMILY,"*Estes Trails Family Newsletter* XXII (March 2004): 5. .... Find A Grave, Inc. database, *Find A Grave.com/* (http://www.findagrave.com/ : accessed 20 Jun 2013), Polly Ann Estes Hall (1834 - 1912); Memorial #25326866; Created by: G. Mounger; Mar 16, 2008

315. Find A Grave, Inc. database,*Find A Grave.com/* (http://www.findagrave.com/ : accessed 20 Jun 2013), Polly Ann Estes Hall (1834 - 1912); Memorial #25326866; Created by: G. Mounger; Mar 16, 2008

Source Citations

316. Collin, Texas, "Confederate Pension Applications, 1899-1975," Mrs Polly Ann Hall, Pension File No. 00570; digital images, Ancestry.com Operations, Inc., "Collection #: CPA16526; Roll #: 337; Roll Description: Pension File Nos. 00133 to 04752,"*Ancestry.com* (www.ancestry.com/ : accessed 20 Jun 2013); Texas State Library and Archives Commission; Austin, Texas; Confederate Pension Applications, 1899-1975.

317. 1850 U.S. census, Lawrence, Arkansas, population schedule, Black River, p. 214B, dwelling 338, family 338, Blueford Estes; digital images, *Ancestry.com* (www.ancestry.com/ : accessed 21 Jun 2013); citing National Archives and Records Administration microfilm M432, roll 27.

318. 1860 U.S. census, Collin, Texas, population schedule, Precinct 4, p. 65, dwelling 124, family 134, J. M. Hall; digital images, *Ancestry.com* (www.ancestry.com/ : accessed 19 Jun 2013); citing National Archives and Records Administration microfilm M653, roll 1291; Family History Library Film: 805291.

319. 1910 U.S. census, Collin, Texas, population schedule, Justice Precinct 1, enumeration district (ED) 5, sheet 3B, dwelling 51, family 51, William S. Murphy; digital images, *Ancestry.com* (www.ancestry.com/ : accessed 20 Jun 2013); citing National Archives and Records Administration microfilm T624, roll 1539; FHL microfilm: 1375552.

320. Texas. Texas Bureau of Vital Statistics., "Texas Deaths 1890 - 1976," database, *Family Search* (www.familysearch.org/ : accessed 23 Jun 2013), John Andrew Houston Hall, 11 Feb 1943, Tom Green County, Texas; Death Certificate #9738.

321. Texas. Texas Department of Health, State Vital Statistics Unit, *Texas Death Index, 1903-2000 [database on-line].*, Ancestry.com. www.ancestry.com/ : 2006, John Andrew H. Hall, 11 Feb 1943, Tom Green County, Texas, Death Certificate #9738. .... Texas. Texas Bureau of Vital Statistics., "Texas Deaths 1890 - 1976," database, *Family Search* (www.familysearch.org/ : accessed 23 Jun 2013), John Andrew Houston Hall, 11 Feb 1943, Tom Green County, Texas; Death Certificate #9738; Informant: Mrs. C. M. Jones,

322. Texas. Texas Bureau of Vital Statistics., "Texas Deaths 1890 - 1976," database, *Family Search* (www.familysearch.org/ : accessed 23 Jun 2013), John Andrew Houston Hall, 11 Feb 1943, Tom Green County, Texas; Death Certificate #9738; Informant: Mrs. C. M. Jones,

323. Texas. Texas Bureau of Vital Statistics., "Texas Deaths 1890 - 1976," database, *Family Search* (www.familysearch.org/ : accessed 23 Jun 2013), William J. G. Hall, 11 Dec 1955, Haskell County, Texas; Death Certificate #65317.

324. Texas. Texas Bureau of Vital Statistics., "Texas Deaths 1890 - 1976," database, *Family Search* (www.familysearch.org/ : accessed 23 Jun 2013), Mrs. Hariette D. Murphy, 18 Jan 1959, Collin County, Texas; Death Certificate #1085.

325. 1860 U.S. census, Collin, Texas, population schedule, Precinct 4, p. 20, dwelling 125, family 135, Wm. H. Hall; digital images, *Ancestry.com* (www.ancestry.com/ : accessed 19 Jun 2013); citing National Archives and Records Administration microfilm M653, roll 1291; Family History Library Film: 805291.

326. Yates Publishing, "U.S. and International Marriage Records 1590-1900 [database on-line]," database, *Ancestry.com* (www.ancestry.com/ : accessed 28 Sep 2013), Martha Delilah Lovelady m. William Basil Brown, Texas.

327. 1840 U.S. census, Yazoo, Mississippi, p. 322, line 30, Robert Mebane; digital images, *Ancestry.com* (www.ancestry.com/ : accessed 10 Dec 2012); citing National Archives and Records Administration microfilm M704, roll 217; Family History Library Film: 0014841.

328. 1850 U.S. census, Yazoo, Mississippi, population schedule, p. 485B, dwelling 85, family 86, Robert M. Mabin; digital images, *Ancestry.com* (www.ancestry.com/ : accessed 15 Dec 2012); citing National Archives and Records Administration microfilm M432, roll 382.

329. 1860 U.S. census, Yazoo, Mississippi, population schedule, p. 56; 984, dwelling 476, family 396, R. M. Maben; digital images, *Ancestry.com* (www.ancestry.com/ : accessed 16 Dec 2012); citing National Archives and Records Administration microfilm M653, roll 594; Family History Library Film: 803594.

330. 1870 U.S. census, Vermillion, Louisiana, population schedule, Subdivision 109; Abbeyville P. O., p. 20, 171B, dwelling 146, family 139, Robert Maben; digital images, *Ancestry.com* (www.ancestry.com/ : accessed 1 Nov 2012); citing National Archives and Records Administration microfilm M593, roll 534; Family History Library Film: 552033.

331. Reed, Verna [Verna@carlsbadnm.com], "Modified Register for Hall" (Carlsbad, New Mexico: Sept 2002), page 21.

332. 1850 U.S. census, Yazoo, Mississippi, population schedule, p. 485B, dwelling 89, family 90, Thomas S. Mabin; digital images, *Ancestry.com* (www.ancestry.com/ : accessed 15 Dec 2012); citing National Archives and Records Administration microfilm M432, roll 382.

333. 1860 U.S. census, Yazoo, Mississippi, population schedule, p. 56; 984, dwelling 477, family 397, T. S. Maben; digital images, *Ancestry.com* (www.ancestry.com/ : accessed 16 Dec 2012); citing National Archives and Records Administration microfilm M653, roll 594; Family History Library Film: 803594.

334. 1870 U.S. census, Carroll, Louisiana, population schedule, Ward 6, p. 19; Sheet 291, dwelling 147, family 147, Thomas M. Mabin; digital images, *Ancestry.com* (www.ancestry.com/ : accessed 28 Jan 2012); citing National Archives and Records Administration microfilm M593, roll M593 _509.

335. Reed, Verna [Verna@carlsbadnm.com], "Modified Register for Hall" (Carlsbad, New Mexico: Sept 2002), page 22. .... Jackson, Ron V., Accelerated Indexing Systems, compiler, *U.S. Federal Census Mortality Schedules Index [database on-line]*, Ancestry.com. www.ancestry.com/ : 1999, Mississippi; MRT197_200664.

336. "William Garrett vs. William Nash et als. - advertisement,"*Texas Union*, Feb 5 1848, p. 3; digital images, *GenealogyBank.com* (GenealogyBank.com/ : accessed 19 Nov 2011), citing Historical newspapers; They must be related through Matilda Garrett's family. .... San Augustine, Texas, Loose Probate Court Record, Catalog #B-35; Box 4; Folder 16; Pages: 3, San Augustine County, Texas Courthouse Records and Loose Papers, 1831-1906, p.31, 28 July 1847; East Texas Research Center/Stephen F. Austin State University Library, Nacogdoches.

337. 1850 U.S. census, Yazoo, Mississippi, population schedule, p. 485A, dwelling 76, family 76, William W. Wildy; digital images,*Ancestry.com* (www.ancestry.com/ : accessed 15 Dec 2012); citing National Archives and Records Administration microfilm M432, roll 382.

338. 1860 U.S. census, Yazoo, Mississippi, population schedule, p. 49; 977, dwelling 426, family 345, W. W. Wildy; digital images,*Ancestry.com* (www.ancestry.com/ : accessed 16 Dec 2012); citing National Archives and Records Administration microfilm M653, roll 594; Family History Library Film: 803594.

339. 1870 U.S. census, Yazoo, Mississippi, population schedule, District 3, p. 127; 362A, dwelling 1152, family 1133, W. W. Wildy; digital images, *Ancestry.com* (www.ancestry.com/ : accessed 16 Dec 2012); citing National Archives and Records Administration microfilm M593, roll 754; Family History Library Film: 552253.

340. Lucas, Silas Emmett Rev., editor,*Marriages from Early Tennessee Newspapers 1794-1851* (Easley, South Carolina: Southern Historical Press, 1978), p. 198. .... Jordan R, et. al. Dodd, "Arkansas Marriages to 1850," database, Ancestry.com Operations Inc.,*Ancestry.com* (www.ancestry.com/ : accessed 27 Mar 2011), Laurena Hall to Robertson Childress. .... James Logan Morgan,*Arkansas Marriage Notices, 1819-1845* (Newport, Arkansas: Morgan Books, 1984), 9.

341. The Church of Jesus Christ of Latter-day Saints [LDS], "International Genealogical Index," database*FamilySearch* (http://www.familysearch.org : accessed 17 May 2009), North America Region, entry for Elisha Robertson Childress, born 5 April 1807, Davidson, Tennessee, USA.

342. Lucas, Silas Emmett Rev., editor,*Marriages from Early Tennessee Newspapers 1794-1851* (Easley, South Carolina: Southern Historical Press, 1978), page 198. .... James Logan Morgan, *Arkansas Marriage Notices, 1819-1845* (Newport, Arkansas: Morgan Books, 1984), 9.

343. Patrick Childress, "Childers/ress DNA Project," database - genealogy report,*Childress/Mathis Family Tree Photographs* (http://freepages.genealogy.rootsweb.ancestry.com/~jpcfamily/childress_observations.htm : accessed 2 Feb 2009), Samuel Hall Childress; citing DNA study.

344. Pris Weathers, "Arkansas Gazette (1819-1930)," database, *Arkansas Ties* (http://www.arkansasties.com/), Elisha Robertson; citing: Arkansas Gazette transcription.

345. Reed, Verna [Verna@carlsbadnm.com], "Modified Register for Hall" (Carlsbad, New Mexico: Sept 2002), page 22.

346. Grissette, Sharon, "Hart-Childress Cemetery, Yazoo County, Mississippi" (2003). USGenWeb Project - http://www.rootsweb.ancestry.com/~msyazoo/index.htm

347. Childress, J. Patrick <londonwildcat@earthlink.net>, "Childress/Mathis Family Tree" (04 December 2007 (Updated)). Patrick Childress, the author of this web-site, attributes most of the information to the sister of Samuel Hall Childress III, Annie Laura Childress Lichte.
--
Web site address: http://worldconnect.rootsweb.ancestry.com/cgi-bin/igm.cgi?db=patchildress

348. Reed, Verna [Verna@carlsbadnm.com], "Modified Register for Hall" (Carlsbad, New Mexico: Sept 2002), page 23.

349. Grissette, Sharon, "Hart-Childress Cemetery, Yazoo County, Mississippi" (2003).

350. Reed, Verna [Verna@carlsbadnm.com], "Modified Register for Hall" (Carlsbad, New Mexico: Sept 2002), pages 23-25.

351. Reed, Verna [Verna@carlsbadnm.com], "Modified Register for Hall" (Carlsbad, New Mexico: Sept 2002), page 25. .... Elvis Fleming, "Maj. William W. Wildy's Children - Part II of II,"*Roswell Daily Record*, March 2, 2001, p. 20; digital images,*NewspaperArchive.com* (http://www.newspaperarchive.com/ : accessed 9 Oct 2011), Historical newspapers.

352. Elvis Fleming, "Wildy Brought Leas' to Roswell,"*Roswell Daily Record*, July 30, 1989, p. 27; digital images, *NewspaperArchives.com* (http://www.newspaperarchive.com/ : accessed 9 Oct 2011), Historical Newspapers.

353. 1840 U.S. census, Yazoo, Mississippi, p. 323, line 16, W. W. Wildy; digital images,*Ancestry.com* (www.ancestry.com/ : accessed 10 Dec 2012); citing National Archives and Records Administration microfilm M704, roll 217; Family History Library Film: 0014841.

354. 1880 U.S. census, Yazoo, Mississippi, population schedule, Phoenix, enumeration district (ED) 118, p. 11; 281C, family 101, W. W. Wildy; digital images, *Ancestry.com* (www.ancestry.com/ : accessed 18 Dec 2012); citing National Archives and Records Administration microfilm T9, roll 669; Family History Film: 1254669.

355. Reed, Verna [Verna@carlsbadnm.com], "Modified Register for Hall" (Carlsbad, New Mexico: Sept 2002). ....*Mississippi Cemetery and Bible Records Vol. V* (Jackson, Mississippi: Mississippi Genealogical Society, September 1958), 147-151.

356. Bonney, Caleb Dawley,*Bonney Family Bible,* Vicksburg, MS.: Vicksburg Genealogical Society Publications, Mississippi River Routes, Winter 1994, page 20. .... *Mississippi Cemetery and Bible Records Vol. V* (Jackson, Mississippi: Mississippi Genealogical Society, September 1958), 147-151.

357. Reed, Verna [Verna@carlsbadnm.com], "Modified Register for Hall" (Carlsbad, New Mexico: Sept 2002), page 24. Cites Wildy Family Bible.

358. "Glimpses of the Past in San Diego's Life,"*The San Diego Union*, December 20, 1918, p. 4, col. 7; digital images,*GenealogyBank.com* (www.GenealogyBank.com/ : accessed 19 Nov 2011).

359. University of Mississippi,*Historical catalogue of the University of Mississippi: 1849-1909* (Marshall and Bruce Company, 1910), 152; digital images, *Google Books* (http://books.google.com/ : downloaded 20 Nov 2011).

360. "The Journal of San Diego History - SAN DIEGO HISTORICAL SOCIETY QUARTERLY" (Quarterly Journal, San Diego, California); digital

images, San Diego History Center - University of San Diego, "San Diego's Centennial Celebration,"*The Journal of San Diego History* (http://www.sandiegohistory.org/ : accessed 23 Sep 2011); Article written by Wayne M. Fabert and Ann Kantor.

361. "Latest from Campo - Two Gangs of Mexican Bandits - Reported Revolution in Sonora,"*San Francisco Bulletin*, 23 December 1875, p. 1; digital images, *GenealogyBank.com* (www.GenealogyBank.com/ : accessed 19 Nov 2011), citing Historical Newpapers.

362. Reed, Verna [Verna@carlsbadnm.com], "Modified Register for Hall" (Carlsbad, New Mexico: Sept 2002), page 24. Sally appears on the 1850 Census, age 2. I changed her date of birth to reflect that. [rch].

363. Elvis Fleming, "Maj. William W. Wildy's Children - Part II of II,"*Roswell Daily Record*, March 2, 2001, p. 20; digital images, *NewspaperArchive.com* (http://www.newspaperarchive.com/ : accessed 9 Oct 2011), Historical newspapers.

364. Reed, Verna [Verna@carlsbadnm.com], "Modified Register for Hall" (Carlsbad, New Mexico: Sept 2002), page 30. Ada appears on the 1850 Census. Age 1. I changed her date of birth to 1849 to reflect that. [rch].

365. Reed, Verna [Verna@carlsbadnm.com], "Modified Register for Hall" (Carlsbad, New Mexico: Sept 2002), page 30-31.

366. Reed, Verna [Verna@carlsbadnm.com], "Modified Register for Hall" (Carlsbad, New Mexico: Sept 2002), page 32.

367. Reed, Verna [Verna@carlsbadnm.com], "Modified Register for Hall" (Carlsbad, New Mexico: Sept 2002), page 25.

368. Coody, Marianna, copier; Schneider, Betty Aron, Coordinator, "Wesley Chapel Methodist Church Cemetery" (Yazoo County, Mississippi GenWeb, updated July 5, 2008.), Willy and Ella Wildy. Web site accessed 26 January 2009. ...*Mississippi Cemetery and Bible Records Vol. V* (Jackson, Mississippi: Mississippi Genealogical Society, September 1958), 147-151.

369. *Mississippi Cemetery and Bible Records Vol. V* (Jackson, Mississippi: Mississippi Genealogical Society, September 1958), 147-151.

370. Yazoo, Mississippi, Chancery Court - Probate Cases 1841-1873, Box 122, Estate of Samuel S. Hall - 1847; FHL microfilm #2438941. .... Yazoo, Mississippi, Chancery Court - Probate Cases 1841-1873, Box 119, Estate of William Hall - 1844; FHL microfilm #2438941, item 1. .... "William Garrett vs. William Nash et als. - advertisement,"*Texas Union*, Feb 5 1848, p. 3; digital images, *GenealogyBank.com* (GenealogyBank.com/ : accessed 19 Nov 2011), citing Historical newspapers; They must be related through Matilda Garrett's family.

371. Hunting For Bears, comp,*Mississippi Marriages, 1776-1935 [database on-line]*, Ancestry.com. www.ancestry.com/: The Generations Network, Inc., 2004, Wm. C. Hall m. Mary E. Pace.

372. 1850 U.S. census, Warren, Mississippi, population schedule, p. Page: 213; Image: 434, dwelling 736, family 760, Mary E. Pace; digital images, *Ancestry.com* (www.ancestry.com/); citing National Archives and Records Administration microfilm M432, roll M432_382.

373. 1870 U.S. census, Warren, Mississippi, population schedule, Warrenton, p. 390; Image: 782., dwelling 346, family 346, W. E. Hall; digital images, *Ancestry.com* (www.ancestry.com/); citing National Archives and Records Administration microfilm M593, roll M593_751.

374. 1900 U.S. census, Chaves, New Mexico, population schedule, Roswell, enumeration district (ED) 30, sheet 17A, p. 17, dwelling 249, family 249, Earnest L. Wildy; digital images,*Ancestry.com* (www.ancestry.com/ : accessed 14 Nov 2012); citing National Archives and Records Administration microfilm T623, roll 999.

375. "Death of Mrs. Hall," *Evening Tribune*, August 19, 1904, p. 3, col. 3; digital images,*GenealogyBank.com* (www.GenealogyBank.com/ : accessed 19 Nov 2011).

376. California Department of Health Services, Center for Health Statistics., "California, Death Index, 1940-1997," database,*Ancestry.com* (www.ancestry.com/ : accessed 8 Dec 2012), Willie Hall Wildy.

377. 1860 U.S. census, Yazoo, Mississippi, population schedule, p. 49; 977, dwelling 429, family 347, Elvira Bradshaw; digital images, *Ancestry.com* (www.ancestry.com/ : accessed 16 Dec 2012); citing National Archives and Records Administration microfilm M653, roll 594; Family History Library Film: 803594.

378. 1870 U.S. census, Yazoo, Mississippi, population schedule, District 3; Yazoo City, p. 124; 360B, dwelling 1124, family 1106, J. N. Bradshaw; digital images, *Ancestry.com* (www.ancestry.com/ : accessed 16 Dec 2012); citing National Archives and Records Administration microfilm M593, roll 754; Family History Library Film: 552253.

379. 1900 U.S. census, Yazoo, Mississippi, population schedule, Beat 1, enumeration district (ED) 0109, sheet 17A, p. 85, dwelling 329, family 331, Elvira Bradshaw; digital images,*Ancestry.com* (www.ancestry.com/ : accessed 20 Dec 2012); citing National Archives and Records Administration microfilm T623, roll 835; FHL microfilm: 1240835.

380. Reed, Verna [Verna@carlsbadnm.com], "Modified Register for Hall" (Carlsbad, New Mexico: Sept 2002), Verna Reed Cites Yazoo County Marriage Book A, page 83. J. T. Russell, Jr. Bondsman. .... Hunting For Bears, comp,*Mississippi Marriages, 1776-1935 [database on-line]*, Ancestry.com. www.ancestry.com/: The Generations Network, Inc., 2004.

381. 1860 U.S. census, Yazoo, Mississippi, population schedule, p. 49; 977, dwelling 429, family 347, Lauretta Wallace; digital images, *Ancestry.com* (www.ancestry.com/ : accessed 16 Dec 2012); citing National Archives and Records Administration microfilm M653, roll 594; Family History Library Film: 803594.

382. Hunting For Bears, comp., "Mississippi Marriages, 1776-1935 [database on-line]," database, Ancestry.com Operations Inc,*Ancestry.com* (www.ancestry.com/ : accessed 29 Jan 2012), Mrs. Elvira Wallis m. James N. Bradshaw.

Source Citations

383. 1860 U.S. census, Yazoo, Mississippi, population schedule, p. 49; 977, dwelling 429, family 347, Jas. N. Bradshaw; digital images, *Ancestry.com* (www.ancestry.com/ : accessed 16 Dec 2012); citing National Archives and Records Administration microfilm M653, roll 594; Family History Library Film: 803594.

384. Find A Grave, Inc. database, *Find A Grave.com/* (http://www.findagrave.com/ : accessed 15 Feb 2012), John Wesley Bradshaw (1865-1938); Memorial #75964378; Created by: Marilyn Smith; Sep 04, 2011

385. Reed, Verna [Verna@carlsbadnm.com], "Modified Register for Hall" (Carlsbad, New Mexico: Sept 2002), page 20. .... "Yazoo County Marriage Book B," database, Genealogy Trails, *Mississippi Genealogy Trails* (http://genealogytrails.com/miss/yazoo/marriage_book_b.htm : accessed 20 Feb 2012), Page 188. Octavia E. Hall m. W. S. Elkins; citing transcript submitted by Debora Reese.

386. Betty Couch Wiltshire, *Yazoo County, Mississippi Pioneers* (Bowie, Maryland: Heritage Books, 1992), 41. .... Yazoo, Mississippi, Will Records Volume A-B 1833-1908, A: 293, Laurena M. Hall; FHL microfilm #879249.

387. 1850 U.S. census, Carroll, Mississippi, population schedule, Northern Division, p. 277B; 552, dwelling 332, family 337, William R. Russell; digital images, *Ancestry.com* (www.ancestry.com/ : accessed 4 Nov 2012); citing National Archives and Records Administration microfilm M432, roll 369.

388. Hunting For Bears, comp, *Mississippi Marriages, 1776-1935 [database on-line],* Ancestry.com. www.ancestry.com/: The Generations Network, Inc., 2004, "Mrs." Elizabeth Morehead. .... Betty Couch Wiltshire, *Carroll County, Mississippi, pioneers* (Carrollton, Mississippi: Pioneer Publishing Co., c1990), 199, Russell Family.

389. 1840 U.S. census, Carroll, Mississippi, p. 31, line 15, William Morehead; digital images, *Ancestry.com* (www.ancestry.com/ : accessed 10 Dec 2012); citing National Archives and Records Administration microfilm M704, roll 215.

390. Russell Family Tree - Ancestry.com, Annabel and Wade Russell, compiler (Wm. Ross Russell Family Bible, July 30 2008; privately held by Scott Russell Redmond, Washington); Tabitha Ann Russell, Scott Russell.

391. 1860 U.S. census, Carroll, Mississippi, population schedule, Police District 2; Jefferson P. O., p. 4; 800, dwelling 27, family 29, Donna Russell; digital images, *Ancestry.com* (www.ancestry.com/ : accessed 4 Nov 2012); citing National Archives and Records Administration microfilm M653, roll 578; Family History Library Film: 803578.

392. 1910 U.S. census, Carroll, Mississippi, population schedule, Beat 1, enumeration district (ED) 28, p. 1A, dwelling 1; digital images, *Ancestry.com* (www.ancestry.com/); citing National Archives and Records Administration microfilm T624, roll T624_734.

393. 1920 U.S. census, Carroll, Mississippi, population schedule, Beat 1, enumeration district (ED) 27, sheet 7B, p. 86, dwelling 133; Fam 133; digital images, *Ancestry.com* (www.ancestry.com/); citing National Archives and Records Administration microfilm T625, roll T625_869.

394. 1850 U.S. census, Carroll, Mississippi, population schedule, Northern Division, p. 288B; 574, dwelling 492, family 501, William Morehead; digital images, *Ancestry.com* (www.ancestry.com/ : accessed 4 Nov 2012); citing National Archives and Records Administration microfilm M432, roll 369.

395. 1860 U.S. census, Carroll, Mississippi, population schedule, Police District 2; Jefferson P. O., p. 4; 800, dwelling 27, family 29, W. L. Russell; digital images, *Ancestry.com* (www.ancestry.com/ : accessed 4 Nov 2012); citing National Archives and Records Administration microfilm M653, roll 578; Family History Library Film: 803578.

396. Hunting For Bears, comp, *Mississippi Marriages, 1776-1935 [database on-line],* Ancestry.com. www.ancestry.com/: The Generations Network, Inc., 2004. .... Betty Couch Wiltshire, *Carroll County, Mississippi, pioneers* (Carrollton, Mississippi: Pioneer Publishing Co., c1990), 199, Russell Family; She is listed as Susan J. Carpenter in this source.

397. Russell Family Tree - Ancestry.com, Annabel and Wade Russell, compiler (Wm. Ross Russell Family Bible, July 30 2008; privately held by Scott Russell Redmond, Washington); reported by Scott Russell, Wm. Ross Russell Family Bible.

398. 1860 U.S. census, Carroll, Mississippi, population schedule, Police District 4, p. 784; 48, dwelling 358, family 358, Rufus K. Beene; digital images, *Ancestry.com* (www.ancestry.com/ : accessed 4 Nov 2012); citing National Archives and Records Administration microfilm M653, roll 578; Family History Library Film: 803578.

399. Russell Family Tree - Ancestry.com, Annabel and Wade Russell, compiler (Wm. Ross Russell Family Bible, July 30 2008; privately held by Scott Russell Redmond, Washington); vital statistics, reported by Scott Russell, Wm. Ross Russell Family Bible. .... Betty Couch Wiltshire, *Carroll County, Mississippi, pioneers* (Carrollton, Mississippi: Pioneer Publishing Co., c1990), 199, Russell family.

400. Russell Family Tree - Ancestry.com, Annabel and Wade Russell, compiler (Wm. Ross Russell Family Bible, July 30 2008; privately held by Scott Russell Redmond, Washington); reported by Scott Russell, Wm. Ross Russell Family Bible, Thomas Benton Maddox Family Bible.

401. Russell Family Tree - Ancestry.com, Annabel and Wade Russell, compiler (Wm. Ross Russell Family Bible, July 30 2008; privately held by Scott Russell Redmond, Washington); reported by Scott Russell, Wm. Ross Russell Family Bible and Thomas Benton Maddox Family Bible.

402. 1860 U.S. census, Fayette, Texas, population schedule, Plum Grove P. O., p. 139;328, dwelling 1044, family 1404, L. W. [H.] Russell; digital images, *Ancestry.com* (www.ancestry.com/ : accessed 12 Nov 2012); citing National Archives and Records Administration microfilm M653, roll 1294; Family History Library Film: 805294.

403. Hunting For Bears, comp, *Mississippi Marriages, 1776-1935 [database on-line],* Ancestry.com. www.ancestry.com/: The Generations Network, Inc., 2004.

171

Source Citations

404. 1870 U.S. census, Tallahatchie, Mississippi, population schedule, Township 24; Range 3; Tillataba P. O., p. 583A; 23, dwelling 177, family 180, Louisa A. Russell; digital images, *Ancestry.com* (www.ancestry.com/ : accessed 4 Nov 2012); citing National Archives and Records Administration microfilm M593, roll 749; Family History Library Film: 552248.

405. 1880 U.S. census, Montgomery, Mississippi, population schedule, enumeration district (ED) 144, p. 413D; dwelling 189, family 201, William Pierce; digital images, *Ancestry.com* (www.ancestry.com/ : accessed 4 Nov 2012); citing National Archives and Records Administration microfilm T9, roll 658; Family History Film: 1254658.

406. 1860 U.S. census, Carroll, Louisiana, population schedule, Ward 7; Delhi P. O., p. 9; Sheet 325, dwelling 63, family 60, Moses M. Munholland; digital images, *Ancestry.com* (www.ancestry.com/ : accessed 22 Oct 2012); citing National Archives and Records Administration microfilm M653, roll 409; Family History Library Film: 803409.

407. 1880 U.S. census, Montgomery, Mississippi, population schedule, enumeration district (ED) 144, p. 412A; 114, dwelling 119, family 121, Frank Pierce; digital images, *Ancestry.com* (www.ancestry.com/ : accessed 4 Nov 2012); citing National Archives and Records Administration microfilm T9, roll 658; Family History Film: 1254658.

408. David Murray Raper, "David Murray Raper Family Tree," database, *Ancestry.com* (www.ancestry.com/ : accessed 26 Jan 2009), Antionette T. Crook, wife of B. F. Pierce.

409. 1860 U.S. census, Choctaw, Mississippi, population schedule, Township 17; Poplar Creek P. O., p. 9; 199, dwelling 58, family 58, Antinett T. Crook; digital images, *Ancestry.com* (www.ancestry.com/ : accessed 4 Nov 2012); citing National Archives and Records Administration microfilm M653, roll 579; Family History Library Film: 803579.

410. David Murray Raper, "David Murray Raper Family Tree," database, *Ancestry.com* (www.ancestry.com/ : accessed 26 Jan 2009), Ada Beatrice Pierce, daughter of B. F. Pierce.

411. William Wade Hinshaw, *Encyclopedia of American Quaker Genealogy. Vol. VI: (Virginia)* (Baltimore, Maryland: Genealogical Publishing Co., Reprint 1993), David Hall & Minerva Overstreet; p. 926; "David [Hall], s of Joel & Minerva A. Overstreet. Milton J. Hall, surety. Married by Abner Anthony, 19 February 1852."

412. 1850 U.S. census, Bedford, Virginia, population schedule, Southern Division, p. 248A; Image: 494, dwelling 547, family 547, Manerva Overstreet; digital images, *Ancestry.com* (www.ancestry.com/ : accessed 9 Nov 2011); citing National Archives and Records Administration microfilm M432, roll M432_935.

413. The Church of Jesus Christ of Latter-day Saints, "Pedigree Resource File," database, *FamilySearch* (http://www.familysearch.org : accessed 30 Sep 2013), entry for Fountain Lee Myrick (PIN (Ancestral File Number: 42W2-VMQ)); submitted by Morris R.

414. 1900 U.S. census, Lampasas, Texas, population schedule, Justice Precinct 6, enumeration district (ED) 102, sheet 23A, p. 210, dwelling 319, family 323, Jno. A. Hall; digital images, *Ancestry.com* (www.ancestry.com/ : accessed 23 Jun 2013); citing National Archives and Records Administration microfilm T623, roll 1653; FHL microfilm: 1241653.

415. 1910 U.S. census, Burnet, Texas, population schedule, Burnet, enumeration district (ED) 111, sheet 7A, p. 209, dwelling 137, family 139, John A. Hall; digital images, *Ancestry.com* (www.ancestry.com/ : accessed 23 Jun 2013); citing National Archives and Records Administration microfilm T624, roll 1535; FHL microfilm: 1375548.

416. Texas. Texas Department of State Health Services, "Texas Marriages, 1837-1973," database, *Family Search - Record Search* (http://familysearch.org/ : accessed 4 Jul 2013), John A. Hall m. Ora Bean, June 9, 1881; Index includes the IGI, digital copies of original records, and compiled records. FHL digital and microfilm copies. Family History Library, Salt Lake City, Utah.

417. Find A Grave, Inc. database, *Find A Grave.com/* (http://www.findagrave.com/ : accessed 12 Oct 2013), Ora Hall (1867-1900); Memorial # 79134337; Created by Nichol Rogers Wiebe; Oct 23, 2011.

418. 1870 U.S. census, Burnet, Texas, population schedule, Precinct 2, p. 38, dwelling 292, family 292, Charles Bean; digital images, *Ancestry.com* (www.ancestry.com/ : accessed 12 Oct 2013); citing National Archives and Records Administration microfilm M593, roll 1577.

419. 1880 U.S. census, Lampasas, Texas, population schedule, Precinct 6, enumeration district (ED) 090, p. 1; Sheet 339A, dwelling 2, family 2, Charles Bean; digital images, *Ancestry.com* (www.ancestry.com/ : accessed 12 Oct 2013); citing National Archives and Records Administration microfilm T9, roll 1316; Family History Film: 1255316.

420. Find A Grave, Inc. database, *Find A Grave.com/* (http://www.findagrave.com/ : accessed 4 Jul 2013), Jessie L. Jones (1884-1986); Memorial # 41032086; Created by: Carolyn Mackey-Byrum; Aug 23, 2009

421. Find A Grave, Inc. database, *Find A Grave.com/* (http://www.findagrave.com/ : accessed 4 Jul 2013), Belle Hall Smiley (1890-1927); Memorial #10171695; Created by: E. J. Brown; Dec 24, 2004.

422. Find A Grave, Inc. database, *Find A Grave.com/* (http://www.findagrave.com/ : accessed 4 Jul 2013), Ora Hall MacAtee (1892-1977); Memorial # 78328602; Created by: Cheri Bogowitz; Oct 13, 2011

423. Find A Grave, Inc. database, *Find A Grave.com/* (http://www.findagrave.com/ : accessed 4 Jul 2013), William Leonard MacAtee, Sr. (1885-1950); Memorial #78328006; Created by: Cheri Bogowitz; Oct 13, 2011.

424. "Texas Births and Christenings 1840-1981," database, *Family Search - Record Search* (http://search.labs.familysearch.org/recordsearch/ : accessed 4 Jul 2013), John Reagan Hall, 08 Oct 1893; Citing GS Film #1433154 V. 4-6.

Source Citations

425. U. S. Social Security Administration,*Social Security Death Index [database on-line]*, Ancestry.com. www.ancestry.com/ : 2011, John Hall, SS #462-22-1830. .... Texas. Texas Department of Health, State Vital Statistics Unit,*Texas Death Index, 1903-2000 [database on-line].*, Ancestry.com. www.ancestry.com/ : 2006, John Hall; Death County: Tom Green; widowed.

426. 1910 U.S. census, Burnet, Texas, population schedule, Burnet, enumeration district (ED) 111, sheet 7A, p. 209, dwelling 137, family 139, John A. Hall; digital images,*Ancestry.com* (www.ancestry.com/ : accessed 4 Jul 2013); citing National Archives and Records Administration microfilm T624, roll 1535; FHL microfilm: 1375548.

427. Texas. Texas Bureau of Vital Statistics., "Texas Deaths 1890 - 1976," database,*Family Search* (www.familysearch.org/ : accessed 27 Jun 2013), George Dewey Hall; Death Certificate #55742; Hidalgo County, Texas; George Dewey Hall; Chronic Alcoholism; Information given by Archie Hall (his brother); Skinner Mortuary.

428. Texas. Texas Bureau of Vital Statistics., "Texas Deaths 1890 - 1976," database,*Family Search* (www.familysearch.org/ : accessed 7 Jul 2013), Archie Andrew Hall, 1960; Citing: Texas Death Certificate #46819; Archie Andrew Hall; Informant: Charles Hall.

429. Find A Grave, Inc. database,*Find A Grave.com/* (http://www.findagrave.com/ : accessed 21 Jun 2013), William Stephen Murphy (1876-1960); Memorial #25326872; Created by: G. Mounger; Mar 16, 2008

430. 1880 U.S. census, Yazoo, Mississippi, population schedule, Phoenix, enumeration district (ED) 118, p. 9; 280A, family 83, W. G. Childress; digital images,*Ancestry.com* (www.ancestry.com/ : accessed 19 Dec 2012); citing National Archives and Records Administration microfilm T9, roll 669; Family History Film: 1254669.

431. 1900 U.S. census, Yazoo, Mississippi, population schedule, Beat 1, enumeration district (ED) 0109, sheet 17A, p. 85, dwelling 327, family 329, W. G. Childress; digital images,*Ancestry.com* (www.ancestry.com/ : accessed 20 Dec 2012); citing National Archives and Records Administration microfilm T623, roll 835; FHL microfilm: 1240835.

432. 1910 U.S. census, Yazoo, Mississippi, population schedule, Mechanicsburg, Beat 1, enumeration district (ED) 0073, sheet 2B, dwelling 45, family 45, S. A. Childress; digital images,*Ancestry.com* (www.ancestry.com/ : accessed 20 Dec 2012); citing National Archives and Records Administration microfilm T624, roll 765, FHL microfilm: 1374778.

433. 1920 U.S. census, Yazoo, Mississippi, population schedule, Satartia, enumeration district (ED) 89, sheet 1A, p. 189, dwelling 1, family 1, Wm. Gordon Childress, Sr; digital images,*Ancestry.com* (www.ancestry.com/ : accessed 27 Dec 2012); citing National Archives and Records Administration microfilm T625, roll 900.

434. Grissette, Sharon, "Hart-Childress Cemetery, Yazoo County, Mississippi" (2003), "Wife of W. G. Childress". Web site accessed 26 January 2009.

435. 1850 U.S. census, Yazoo, Mississippi, population schedule, p. 486A, dwelling 96, family 98, Susan E. Hart; digital images,*Ancestry.com* (www.ancestry.com/ : accessed 15 Dec 2012); citing National Archives and Records Administration microfilm M432, roll 382.

436. U. S. Selective Service System,*World War I Draft Registration Cards, 1917-1918 [database on-line]*, Ancestry.com. www.ancestry.com/ : 2005, Yazoo County, Mississippi; Roll: 1684098; Draft Board: 2; Sep 12, 1918. citing National Archives and Records Administration microfilm M1509.

437. Grissette, Sharon, "Hart-Childress Cemetery, Yazoo County, Mississippi" (2003), Lillye Childress Long. Web site accessed 26 January 2009.

438. Childress, J. Patrick <londonwildcat@earthlink.net>, "Childress/Mathis Family Tree" (04 December 2007 (Updated)).

439. 1870 U.S. census, Yazoo, Mississippi, population schedule, District 3; Yazoo City, p. 35; 316A, dwelling 286, family 294, S. H. Childress; digital images, *Ancestry.com* (www.ancestry.com/ : accessed 16 Dec 2012); citing National Archives and Records Administration microfilm M593, roll 754; Family History Library Film: 552253.

440. 1880 U.S. census, Yazoo, Mississippi, population schedule, Phoenix, enumeration district (ED) 118, p. 11; 281C, family 108, S. H. Childress; digital images, *Ancestry.com* (www.ancestry.com/ : accessed 18 Dec 2012); citing National Archives and Records Administration microfilm T9, roll 669; Family History Film: 1254669.

441. 1910 U.S. census, Yazoo, Mississippi, population schedule, Mechanicsburg, Beat 1, enumeration district (ED) 0073, sheet 3A, p. 8, dwelling 45, family 45, W. G. Childress; digital images,*Ancestry.com* (www.ancestry.com/ : accessed 20 Dec 2012); citing National Archives and Records Administration microfilm T624, roll 765, FHL microfilm: 1374778.

442. Childress, J. Patrick <londonwildcat@earthlink.net>, "Childress/Mathis Family Tree" (04 December 2007 (Updated)), http://worldconnect.genealogy.rootsweb.com/cgi-bin/igm.cgi?op=GET&db=patchildress&id=I5146. .... nomoney6 , "[CHILDRESS RESEARCH] [Fwd: CHILDRESS-CHILDERS MISC MARRIAGES FYI ONLY.......K],"*CHILDRESS-RESEARCH-L Archives*, mailing list, 09 Jan 2003 (http://archiver.rootsweb.ancestry.com/ : accessed 29 Jan 2010).

443. 1850 U.S. census, Yazoo, Mississippi, population schedule, p. 486A, dwelling 96, family 98, Georgana Hart; digital images*Ancestry.com* (www.ancestry.com/ : accessed 15 Dec 2012); citing National Archives and Records Administration microfilm M432, roll 382.

444. Grissette, Sharon, "Hart-Childress Cemetery, Yazoo County, Mississippi" (2003), Ada Viola Childress. Web Site accessed 26 January 2009.

445. Childress, J. Patrick <londonwildcat@earthlink.net>, "Childress/Mathis Family Tree" (04 December 2007 (Updated)), http://worldconnect.genealogy.rootsweb.com/cgi-bin/igm.cgi?op=GET&db=patchildress&id=I5146.

446. Grissette, Sharon, "Hart-Childress Cemetery, Yazoo County, Mississippi" (2003), William G. Childress. Web site accessed 26 January 2009.

Source Citations

447. Grissette, Sharon, "Hart-Childress Cemetery, Yazoo County, Mississippi" (2003), Childress, infant son, Child of S.H & G. A. Childress.

448. Grissette, Sharon, "Hart-Childress Cemetery, Yazoo County, Mississippi" (2003), H. R. Childress. Web site accessed 26 January 2009.

449. Grissette, Sharon, "Hart-Childress Cemetery, Yazoo County, Mississippi" (2003), Childress, infant son, Child of S. H. and G. A. Childress.

450. 1870 U.S. census, Yazoo, Mississippi, population schedule, District 3; Yazoo City, p. 27; 312A, dwelling 210, family 218, F. M. Bonney; digital images, *Ancestry.com* (www.ancestry.com/ : accessed 16 Dec 2012); citing National Archives and Records Administration microfilm M593, roll 754; Family History Library Film: 552253.

451. 1880 U.S. census, Yazoo, Mississippi, population schedule, Sataria, enumeration district (ED) 119, p. 51; 314C, dwelling 38, family 38, J. M. Bonney; digital images, *Ancestry.com* (www.ancestry.com/ : accessed 19 Dec 2012); citing National Archives and Records Administration microfilm T9, roll 670; Family History Film: 1254670.

452. 1900 U.S. census, Yazoo, Mississippi, population schedule, Beat 1, enumeration district (ED) 0109, sheet 27B, dwelling 181, family 186, Jas. M. Bonny; digital images, *Ancestry.com* (www.ancestry.com/ : accessed 20 Dec 2012); citing National Archives and Records Administration microfilm T623, roll 835; FHL microfilm: 1240835.

453. 1910 U.S. census, Yazoo, Mississippi, population schedule, Mechanicsburg, Beat 1, enumeration district (ED) 0073, sheet 3B, dwelling 22, family 22, Mattie Bonney; digital images, *Ancestry.com* (www.ancestry.com/ : accessed 20 Dec 2012); citing National Archives and Records Administration microfilm T624, roll 765, FHL microfilm: 1374778.

454. Hunting For Bears, comp, *Mississippi Marriages, 1776-1935 [database on-line]*, Ancestry.com. www.ancestry.com/: The Generations Network, Inc., 2004. .... Bonney, Caleb Dawley, *Bonney Family Bible,* Vicksburg, MS.: Vicksburg Genealogical Society Publications, Mississippi River Routes, Winter 1994, page 17.

455. Bonney, Caleb Dawley, *Bonney Family Bible,* Vicksburg, MS.: Vicksburg Genealogical Society Publications, Mississippi River Routes, Winter 1994, page 18.

456. Bonney, Caleb Dawley, *Bonney Family Bible,* Vicksburg, MS.: Vicksburg Genealogical Society Publications, Mississippi River Routes, Winter 1994, page 20.

457. Lawrence W. Long, "Bonney Cemetery (AKA Churchill Plantation Cemetery)," database *Yazoo County Mississippi - MS GenWeb* (http://www.rootsweb.ancestry.com/~msyazoo/BonneyCem.htm : accessed 26 Jan 2009), James M. Bonney. ...*Mississippi Cemetery and Bible Records Vol. XI* (Jackson, Mississippi: Mississippi Genealogical Society, 1965), 156.

458. 1850 U.S. census, Shelby, Kentucky, population schedule, District 1, p. 271B, dwelling 11, family 11, C. D. Bonney; digital images, *Ancestry.com* (www.ancestry.com/ : accessed 15 Oct 2012); citing National Archives and Records Administration microfilm M432, roll 218.

459. 1860 U.S. census, Shelby, Kentucky, population schedule, District 1; Simpsonville, P. O., p. 71; Sheet 223, dwelling 573, family 529, C. D. Bonney; digital images, *Ancestry.com* (www.ancestry.com/ : accessed 16 Oct 2012); citing National Archives and Records Administration microfilm M653, roll 395; Family History Library Film: 803395.

460. M. B. Fields, "J. M. Bonney," *Confederate Veteran Magazine*, Vol. XVIII, No. 6; 1910, p. 289; This article was taken from a sketch by M. B. (Mary Bonney) Fields, James's sister. A photo is attached to the article. .... Ellmo Howell *Mississippi Back Roads: Notes on Literature and History* (Memphis, Tennessee: Roscoe Langford, 1998), 260. .... NARA, "Compiled Service Records of Confederate Soldiers Who Served in Organizations from the State of Texas," database, *Fold3.com* (http://www.fold3.com/ : accessed 15 Dec 2011), James M. Bonney.

461. "Legislative- Bonney vs. Bowman, Appeal from the Chancery Court of Yazoo County," *The Clarion*, April 21, 1886, p. 2; digital images, *GenealogyBank.com* (www.genealogybank.com/ : accessed 10 Dec 2011).

462. Reed, Verna [Verna@carlsbadnm.com], "Modified Register for Hall" (Carlsbad, New Mexico: Sept 2002), page 24. Cites Wildy Family Bible. .... *Mississippi Cemetery and Bible Records Vol. V* (Jackson, Mississippi: Mississippi Genealogical Society, September 1958), 147-151.

463. Coody, Marianna, copier; Schneider, Betty Aron, Coordinator, "Wesley Chapel Methodist Church Cemetery" (Yazoo County, Mississippi GenWeb, updated July 5, 2008.), Ella Bonney. Web site accessed 26 January 2009.

464. Coody, Marianna, copier; Schneider, Betty Aron, Coordinator, "Wesley Chapel Methodist Church Cemetery" (Yazoo County, Mississippi GenWeb, updated July 5, 2008.), Mary Bonney. Web site accessed 26 January 2009. ....*Mississippi Cemetery and Bible Records Vol. V* (Jackson, Mississippi: Mississippi Genealogical Society, September 1958), 147-151.

465. Bonney, Caleb Dawley, *Bonney Family Bible,* Vicksburg, MS.: Vicksburg Genealogical Society Publications, Mississippi River Routes, Winter 1994, page 19.

466. Hatch, Stephen W, "Descendants of Caleb Dawley Bonney," 20 February 2007. This report was included as part of a series of e-mail correspondence with Stephen Hatch all dated February 2007.

467. Lawrence W. Long, "Bonney Cemetery (AKA Churchill Plantation Cemetery)," database *Yazoo County Mississippi - MS GenWeb* (http://www.rootsweb.ancestry.com/~msyazoo/BonneyCem.htm : accessed 26 Jan 2009), Caleb Wildy, M.D. ...*Mississippi Cemetery and Bible Records Vol. XI* (Jackson, Mississippi: Mississippi Genealogical Society, 1965), 156.

468. 1900 U.S. census, Tensas, Louisiana, population schedule, Newellton Ward 2, enumeration district (ED) 106, sheet 13B, dwelling 342, family 371, C. Wildy Bonney; digital images, *Ancestry.com* (www.ancestry.com/ : accessed 27 Nov 2010); citing National Archives and Records Administration microfilm T623, roll T623_ 583.

469. 1920 U.S. census, Yazoo, Mississippi, population schedule, Mechanicsburg, enumeration district (ED) 90, sheet 9B, dwelling 157, family 161, Wildy C. Bonney; digital images,*Ancestry.com* (www.ancestry.com/ : accessed 27 Dec 2012); citing National Archives and Records Administration microfilm T625, roll 900.

470. 1930 U.S. census, Yazoo, Mississippi, population schedule, Beat 1; Satartia, enumeration district (ED) 2, sheet 18A, p. 209, dwelling 382, family 401, Caleb W. Bonney; digital images,*Ancestry.com* (www.ancestry.com/ : accessed 27 Dec 2012); citing National Archives and Records Administration microfilm T626, roll 1172; FHL microfilm: 2340907.

471. 1880 U.S. census, Lincoln, New Mexico, population schedule, 5th Precinct, enumeration district (ED) 19, p. 1; 405A, dwelling 2, family 2, Joseph C. Lea; digital images,*Ancestry.com* (www.ancestry.com/ : accessed 8 Nov 2012); citing National Archives and Records Administration microfilm T9, roll 802; Family History Film: 1254802.

472. Elvis Fleming, "Maj. William W. Wildy's Children - Part II of II,"*Roswell Daily Record*, March 2, 2001, p. 20; digital images, *NewspaperArchive.com* (http://www.newspaperarchive.com/ : accessed 9 Oct 2011), Historical newspapers; A photo is included in the article.

473. Reed, Verna [Verna@carlsbadnm.com], "Modified Register for Hall" (Carlsbad, New Mexico: Sept 2002), page 27.

474. Elvis Fleming, "Leas Make Roswell Their Home,"*Roswell Daily Record*, Aug 6 1989, p. 27; digital images, *NewspaperArchives.com* (http://www.newspaperarchive.com/ : accessed 9 Oct 2011), Historical Newspapers.

475. Chaves, New Mexico, SUPREME COURT OF NEW MEXICO, 1947-NMSC-019, 51 N.M. 100, 179 P.2d 524, Harry Wildy Lea, 1947; digital images, *New Mexico Compilation Commission* (http://www.nmcompcomm.us/nmcases/NMSC/1947/1947-NMSC-019.pdf : accessed 23 Aug 2013).

476. Find A Grave, Inc. database,*Find A Grave.com/* (http://www.findagrave.com/ : accessed 23 Aug 2013), Harry Wildy Lea (1877-1938); Find A Grave: Memorial #15453969; Created by Delma Ingram; August 21, 2006

477. Jennifer Lamson, "Lamson," database - family tree,*Ancestry.com* (www.ancestry.com/ : accessed 27 Jan 2009), Hall - Wildy - Lea Families.

478. Find A Grave, Inc. database,*Find A Grave.com/* (http://www.findagrave.com/ : accessed 23 Aug 2013), Eleanor Laurena "Ella" Lea Dow (1881-1962); Find A Grave Memorial #17424695; Maintained by Whisper Stockton; January 13, 2007.

479. 1910 U.S. census, Chaves, New Mexico, population schedule, Roswell; Ward 2, enumeration district (ED) 22, sheet 9B, p. 58, dwelling 243, family 254, George T. Davis; digital images,*Ancestry.com* (www.ancestry.com/ : accessed 14 Nov 2012); citing National Archives and Records Administration microfilm T624, roll 913; FHL microfilm: 1374926.

480. 1920 U.S. census, Chaves, New Mexico, population schedule, Roswell; Ward 2, enumeration district (ED) 4, sheet 9A, p. 43, dwelling 181, family 191, George T. Davis; digital images,*Ancestry.com* (www.ancestry.com/ : accessed 14 Nov 2012); citing National Archives and Records Administration microfilm T625, roll 1074.

481. Hunting For Bears, comp., "Mississippi Marriages, 1776-1935 [database on-line]," database, Ancestry.com Operations Inc,*Ancestry.com* (www.ancestry.com/ : accessed 29 Jan 2012), Ada B. Wildy m. W. E. Holloman.

482. Reed, Verna [Verna@carlsbadnm.com], "Modified Register for Hall" (Carlsbad, New Mexico: Sept 2002), page 25. Cites Wildy Family Bible.

483. Coody, Marianna, copier; Schneider, Betty Aron, Coordinator, "Wesley Chapel Methodist Church Cemetery" (Yazoo County, Mississippi GenWeb, updated July 5, 2008.), William E. Holloman. Web site accessed 26 January 2009. ...*Mississippi Cemetery and Bible Records Vol. V* (Jackson, Mississippi: Mississippi Genealogical Society, September 1958), 147-151.

484. Sharon Grissett, "Mt. Olivet Confederate Cemetery," database,*Yazoo County, Mississippi - Confederate Cemetery* (http://www.rootsweb.ancestry.com/~msyazoo/ConfederateCem.htm : accessed 26 Jan 2009), William E. Holloman.

485. Hunting For Bears, comp,*Mississippi Marriages, 1776-1935 [database on-line],* Ancestry.com. www.ancestry.com/: The Generations Network, Inc., 2004, W. D. Edwards m. Alla B. Holloman.

486. Reed, Verna [Verna@carlsbadnm.com], "Modified Register for Hall" (Carlsbad, New Mexico: Sept 2002), page 31.

487. Reed, Verna - submitter, Family Group Record: "George Tennel Davis," The Church of Jesus Christ of Latter Day Saints. www.familysearch.org/ Accessed March 6, 2008.

488. 1880 U.S. census, Tulare, California, population schedule, Village of Tulare, enumeration district (ED) 101, p. 101B, dwelling 158, family 158, J. H. Wildy; digital images,*Ancestry.com* (www.ancestry.com/ : accessed 11 Oct 2012); citing National Archives and Records Administration microfilm T9, roll 85; Family History Film: 1254085.

489. University of Mississippi,*Announcements and Catalogue*, Digitized 2009 - Google Books (Mississippi: University of Mississippi, 1883), Page 69.

490. Helen Coughlin transcriber, "Virginia Military Institute - Class of 1874," database,*Rockbridge County, Virginia Genealogy Trails* (http://genealogytrails.com/vir/rockbridge/vmi/cadet_class_registers/cadets_1874.html : accessed 23 Sep 2011), Wildy, John Hall; citing: Register of Former Cadets, Centennial Edition, Virginia Military Institute, Lexington, Virginia. Published 1939. .... Elvis Fleming, "Maj. William W. Wildy's Children - Part II of II," *Roswell Daily Record*, March 2, 2001, p. 20; digital images, *NewspaperArchive.com* (http://www.newspaperarchive.com/ : accessed 9 Oct 2011), Historical newspapers.

491. Elvis Fleming, "Maj. William W. Wildy's Children - Part II of II,"*Roswell Daily Record*, March 2, 2001, p. 20; digital images, *NewspaperArchive.com* (http://www.newspaperarchive.com/ : accessed 9 Oct 2011), Historical newspapers. .... "Personal,"*Mesilla Valley Democrat,*

Source Citations

March 22, 1889, p. 3; digital images, *GenealogyBank.com* (www.GenealogyBank.com/ : accessed 19 Nov 2011).

492. "Local News," *Las Cruces Democrat*, November 15, 1893, p. 3; digital images, *GenealogyBank.com* (www.GenealogyBank.com/ : accessed 19 Nov 2011), Citing Historical Newspapers.

493. 1910 U.S. census, Los Angeles, California, population schedule, Los Angeles; Assembly District 70, enumeration district (ED) 218, sheet 1B, dwelling 22, family 22, Ernest Wildy; digital images, *Ancestry.com* (www.ancestry.com/ : accessed 7 Oct 2012); citing National Archives and Records Administration microfilm T624, roll 80; FHL microfilm: 1374093.

494. Reed, Verna [Verna@carlsbadnm.com], "Modified Register for Hall" (Carlsbad, New Mexico: Sept 2002), page 33.

495. "Milverton Cleared for Europe," *The San Diego Union*, September 1, 1903, p. 7, col. 1; digital images, *GenealogyBank.com* (http://www.genealogybank.com/ : accessed 1 Sep 1903), historical newspaper.

496. 1930 U.S. census, Los Angeles, California, population schedule, Los Angeles; Assembly District 60, enumeration district (ED) 724, sheet 13B, dwelling 95, family 231, Willie H. Wildy; digital images, *Ancestry.com* (www.ancestry.com/ : accessed 7 Oct 2012); citing National Archives and Records Administration microfilm T626, roll 163; FHL microfilm: 2339898.

497. 1940 U.S. census, Los Angeles, California, population schedule, Monrovia Township, enumeration district (ED) 19-391A, sheet 7B, Willie Wildy; digital images, *Famly Search* (www.familysearch.org/ : accessed 20 Sep 2012); citing National Archives and Records Administration microfilm T627, roll 237.

498. Los Angeles, California, California Voter Registrations, 1900-1968 [database on-line], Willie H. Wildy; digital images, Ancestry.com Operations Inc, "California Voter Registrations, 1900-1968 [database on-line]," *Ancestry.com* (www.ancestry.com/ : accessed 27 Sep 2011); Los Angeles City Precinct No. 737

499. California Department of Health Services, Center for Health Statistics., "California, Death Index, 1940-1997," database *Ancestry.com* (www.ancestry.com/ : accessed 8 Dec 2012), Mary Wildy; This source correctly shows her mother's maiden name as Hall. The birth state is listed (incorrectly) as Michigan, instead of Mississippi.

500. 1930 U.S. census, San Bernadino, California, population schedule, Highland - Patton State Hospital, enumeration district (ED) 36-29, sheet 16B; Image: 192.0, p. 96; digital images, *Ancestry.com* (www.ancestry.com/); citing National Archives and Records Administration microfilm T626, roll 188.

501. 1940 U.S. census, Ventura, California, population schedule, Camarillo, enumeration district (ED) 56-5, sheet 24B, Mary Wildy; digital images, *Ancestry.com* (www.ancestry.com/ : accessed 8 Dec 2012); citing National Archives and Records Administration microfilm T627, roll 363.

502. U. S. Selective Service System, *World War I Draft Registration Cards, 1917-1918 [database on-line]*, Ancestry.com. www.ancestry.com/ : 2005, Harry Hill Wildy; single; Los Angeles, California; Roll: 1531188; Draft Board: 17.

503. U. S. Social Security Administration, *Social Security Death Index [database on-line]*, Ancestry.com. www.ancestry.com/ : 2011, Number: 563-66-0137;Issue State: California;Issue Date: 1962. .... California Department of Health Services, Center for Health Statistics., "California, Death Index, 1940-1997," database, *Ancestry.com* (www.ancestry.com/ : accessed 8 Dec 2012), Harry Hill Wildy.

504. Coody, Marianna, copier; Schneider, Betty Aron, Coordinator, "Wesley Chapel Methodist Church Cemetery" (Yazoo County, Mississippi GenWeb, updated July 5, 2008.), William Hall Wildy. Web site accessed 26 January 2009. ....*Mississippi Cemetery and Bible Records Vol. V* (Jackson, Mississippi: Mississippi Genealogical Society, September 1958), 147-151.

505. U. S. Selective Service System, *World War I Draft Registration Cards, 1917-1918 [database on-line]*, Ancestry.com. www.ancestry.com/ : 2005, Leon Rudolph Wildey. Los Angeles; Roll: 1531188; Draft Board: 17; Sept 12, 1918.

506. U. S. Social Security Administration, *Social Security Death Index [database on-line]*, Ancestry.com. www.ancestry.com/ : 2011, Number: 547-80-7449; Issue State: California;Issue Date: 1965. .... California Department of Health Services, Center for Health Statistics., "California, Death Index, 1940-1997," database, *Ancestry.com* (www.ancestry.com/ : accessed 8 Dec 2012), Leon Wildy.

507. 1930 U.S. census, San Bernadino, California, population schedule, Highland - Patton State Hospital, enumeration district (ED) 29, sheet 2B, p. 82; digital images, *Ancestry.com* (www.ancestry.com/); citing National Archives and Records Administration microfilm T626, roll 188.

508. 1940 U.S. census, Ventura, California, population schedule, Camarillo, enumeration district (ED) 56-5, sheet 29A, p. 66, Leon Wildy; digital images, *Ancestry.com* (www.ancestry.com/ : accessed 8 Dec 2012); citing National Archives and Records Administration microfilm T627, roll 363.

509. 1870 U.S. census, Carroll, Mississippi, population schedule, Township 19; Range 5 East, p. 9; sheet 630, dwelling 55, family 55, Thomas Russell; digital images, *Ancestry.com* (www.ancestry.com/ : accessed 26 Jan 2009); citing National Archives and Records Administration microfilm M593, roll M593_723.

510. 1880 U.S. census, Tarrant, Texas, population schedule, Justice Precinct No. 4, enumeration district (ED) 96, p. 171C; Sheet 11, dwelling 83, family 84; digital images, *Ancestry.com* (www.ancestry.com/); citing National Archives and Records Administration microfilm T9, roll T9_1328; Family History Film: 1255328.

511. 1900 U.S. census, Tarrant, Texas, population schedule, Ft. Worth; Precinct No. 1, enumeration district (ED) 82, sheet 22, p. 22A, dwelling 423; Fam 433; digital images, *Family Search Labs* (www.familysearchlabs.org/); citing National Archives and Records Administration microfilm T623, roll GSU 1241671.

512. 1910 U.S. census, Tarrant, Texas, population schedule, Fort Worth, enumeration district (ED) 0144, sheet 1A, p. 237, dwelling 5, family 5, Thomas S. Russell; digital images, *Ancestry.com* (www.ancestry.com/ : accessed 2 Oct 2012); citing National Archives and Records Administration

microfilm T624, roll 1591.

513. Russell Family Tree - Ancestry.com, Annabel and Wade Russell, compiler (Wm. Ross Russell Family Bible, July 30 2008; privately held by Scott Russell Redmond, Washington); reported by Scott Russell, Wm. Ross Russel Family Bible.

514. Russell Family Tree - Ancestry.com, Annabel and Wade Russell, compiler (Wm. Ross Russell Family Bible, July 30 2008; privately held by Scott Russell Redmond, Washington); reported by Scott Russell, Thomas Benton Maddox Family Bible.

515. Russell Family Tree - Ancestry.com, Annabel and Wade Russell, compiler (Wm. Ross Russell Family Bible, July 30 2008; privately held by Scott Russell Redmond, Washington); reported by Scott Russell, Wm. Ross Russell Family Bible and Thomas Benton Maddox Family Bible. .... Tarrant, Texas, Death Certificate no. 41302 (1928), Sallie Russell; digital image, LDS Family Search, "Texas Deaths 1890-1976,"*FamilySearch.org* (http://familysearch.org/ : accessed 26 Jan 2009); Informant: C. C. Russell; Ft. Worth Undertakers Co.

516. U. S. Selective Service System,*World War I Draft Registration Cards, 1917-1918 [database on-line], Ancestry.com.* www.ancestry.com/ : 2005, Claude Caperton Russell; FHL Roll #1953362. .... Texas. Texas Bureau of Vital Statistics., "Texas Deaths 1890 - 1976," database*Family Search* (www.familysearch.org/ : accessed 17 Nov 2011), Claude Capperton Russell; citing: Texas Death Certificate #33172; FHL Film #2117826; Digital Film #4028302; image #384; Claude Capperton Russell; widower;

517. U. S. Social Security Administration,*Social Security Death Index [database on-line],* Ancestry.com. www.ancestry.com/ : 2011, Number: 458-54-3214; Issue State: Texas; Issue Date: 1952. .... Texas. Texas Bureau of Vital Statistics., "Texas Deaths 1890 - 1976," database*Family Search* (www.familysearch.org/ : accessed 17 Nov 2011), Claude Capperton Russell; citing: Texas Death Certificate #33172; FHL Film #2117826; Digital Film #4028302; image #384; Claude Capperton Russell; widower;

518. Russell Family Tree - Ancestry.com, Annabel and Wade Russell, compiler (Wm. Ross Russell Family Bible, July 30 2008; privately held by Scott Russell Redmond, Washington); reported by Scott Russell, Wm. Ross Russell Family Bible, Hendley Mathews Russell Family Bible and Thomas Benton Maddox Family Bible.

519. Tarrant, Texas, Death Certificate no. 21370 (1951), Hendley M. Russell; digital image, LDS Family Search, "Texas Deaths 1890-1976," *FamilySearch.org* (http://familysearch.org/ : accessed 26 Jan 2009); Informant: ? Russell; Hugh M. Moore Funeral Home.

520. David Murray Raper, "David Murray Raper Family Tree," database,*Ancestry.com* (www.ancestry.com/ : accessed 26 Jan 2009), Ada B. Pierce, marriage.

521. David Murray Raper, "David Murray Raper Family Tree," database,*Ancestry.com* (www.ancestry.com/ : accessed 26 Jan 2009).

522. 1910 U.S. census, Tom Green, Texas, population schedule, Justice Precinct 2, enumeration district (ED) 284, sheet 8B, dwelling 138, family 140, Charley M. Jones; digital images,*Ancestry.com* (www.ancestry.com/ : accessed 4 Jul 2013); citing National Archives and Records Administration microfilm T624, roll 1592; FHL microfilm: 1375605.

523. 1920 U.S. census, Tom Green, Texas, population schedule, Justice Precinct 2, enumeration district (ED) 202, sheet 7A, p. 253, dwelling 124, family 134, Charles M. Jones; digital images,*Ancestry.com* (www.ancestry.com/ : accessed 4 Jul 2013); citing National Archives and Records Administration microfilm T625, roll 1844.

524. 1930 U.S. census, Tom Green, Texas, population schedule, Precinct 2, enumeration district (ED) 14, sheet 7B, dwelling 144, family 145, Charley M. Jones; digital images,*Ancestry.com* (www.ancestry.com/ : accessed 4 Jul 2013); citing National Archives and Records Administration microfilm T626, roll 2401; FHL microfilm: 2342135.

525. 1940 U.S. census, Tom Green, Texas, population schedule, enumeration district (ED) 226-19, sheet 19A, p. 457, household 374, Charlie M. Jones; digital images, *Ancestry.com* (www.ancestry.com : accessed 4 Jul 2013); citing National Archives and Records Administration microfilm T627, roll 4147.

526. Texas. Texas Department of State Health Services, "Texas Marriages, 1837-1973," database,*Family Search - Record Search* (http://familysearch.org/ : accessed 6 Jul 2013), C. M. Jones and Jessie Hall, 20 Jul 1902.

527. Find A Grave, Inc. database,*Find A Grave.com/* (http://www.findagrave.com/ : accessed 4 Jul 2013), Charlie M. Jones (1877-1940); Memorial # 41032028; Created by: Carolyn Mackey-Byrum; Aug 23, 2009

528. Find A Grave, Inc. database,*Find A Grave.com/* (http://www.findagrave.com/ : accessed 4 Jul 2013), Charlie M. Jones (1877-1940); Memorial # 41032028; Created by: Carolyn Mackey-Byrum; Aug 23, 2009 .... Texas. Texas Bureau of Vital Statistics., "Texas Deaths 1890 - 1976," database, *Family Search* (www.familysearch.org/ : accessed 6 Jul 2013), Charles Marion Jones, 1940, Tom Green County, Texas; Citing Death Certificate #25737; Charles Marion Jones; Stock Farmer; Informant: Mrs. Aubrey L. Lewis.

529. "Tornado Tears Hole in Garland and Nevada With Heavy Loss of Life,"*The Richardson Echo*, May 13, 1927, p. 1, col. 1; digital images, *GenealogyBank.com* (http://www.genealogybank.com/ : accessed 4 Jul 2013), Newspaper Archives.

530. Find A Grave, Inc. database,*Find A Grave.com/* (http://www.findagrave.com/ : accessed 4 Jul 2013), Chas Oscar Smiley (1890 - 1927); Memorial #10171689; Created by: E. J. Brown; December 24, 2004.

531. "Bury Tornado Dead; Relief Work Hurried,"*The Dallas Morning News*, May 11, 1927, p. 1, col. 14; digital images,*GenealogyBank.com* (http://www.genealogybank.com/ : accessed 4 Jul 2013), Historical Obituaries.

532. 1930 U.S. census, Hidalgo, Texas, population schedule, Mercedes, enumeration district (ED) 1, sheet 6A, p. 6, dwelling 132, family 137, Dewey Hall; digital images,*Ancestry.com* (www.ancestry.com/ : accessed 27 Jun 2013); citing National Archives and Records Administration microfilm T626, roll 2355; FHL microfilm: 2342089.

Source Citations

533. 1940 U.S. census, Hidalgo, Texas, population schedule, Edinburg, Justice Precinct 6, enumeration district (ED) 108-39, sheet 62B, household 355, Dewey Hall; digital images, *FamiltSearch* (https://familysearch.org/ : accessed 28 Jun 2013); citing National Archives and Records Administration microfilm T627, roll 4063.

534. Texas, birth certificate no. 23891 (1931), Allen Dee Arlyn Hall; digital image, The Church of Jesus Christ of Latter-day Saints, "Texas, Birth Certificates, 1903-1935," *Family Search* (https://familysearch.org/ : accessed 23 Jun 2013).

535. Texas. Texas Department of Health, State Vital Statistics Unit, *Texas Death Index, 1903-2000 [database on-line].*, Ancestry.com. www.ancestry.com/ : 2006, Certificate #28426.

536. 1900 U.S. census, Limestone, Texas, population schedule, Groesbeck, enumeration district (ED) 52, sheet 11A, p. 41, dwelling 179, family 181, Harvey R. Adair; digital images, *Ancestry.com* (www.ancestry.com/ : accessed 23 Jun 2013); citing National Archives and Records Administration microfilm T623, roll 1654; FHL microfilm: 1241654.

537. 1910 U.S. census, Limestone, Texas, population schedule, Justice Precinct 1, enumeration district (ED) 32, sheet 5A, p. 148, dwelling 67, family 70, Reuben H. Adair; digital images, *Ancestry.com* (www.ancestry.com/ : accessed 23 Jun 2013); citing National Archives and Records Administration microfilm T624, roll 1573.

538. 1920 U.S. census, Limestone, Texas, population schedule, Justice Precinct 8, enumeration district (ED) 38, sheet 3A, p. 86, dwelling 41, family 41, Reuben H. Adair; digital images, *Ancestry.com* (www.ancestry.com/ : accessed 23 Jun 2013); citing National Archives and Records Administration microfilm T625, roll 1784.

539. Texas. Texas Department of State Health Services, *Texas Birth Index 1903 - 1997 [database on-line]*, Ancestry.com. www.ancestry.com/ : 2005, Timothy Elijah Hall; Roll #1948_0006; p. 1345.

540. "George Dewey Hall, Jr.," *The Bay City Tribune*, Aug 7, 2012, online archives (http://search.ancestry.com/oldsearch/obit/view.aspx?db=web-obituary&kw=Hall+George+Dewey&pid=148559589&url=http://search.ancestry.com/cgi-bin/sse.dll%3Frank%3d1%26new%3d1%26MSAV%3d1%26msT%3d1%26gss%3dangs-i%26gsfn%3dGeorge%2bDewey%26gsln%3dHall%26msbpn__ftp%3dUSA%26msbpn%3d2%26msbpn_PInfo%3d3-%257c0%257c1652393%257c0%257c2%257c0%257c0%257c0%257c0%257c0%257c0%257c%26msrpn__ftp%3dTexas%252c%2bUSA%26msrpn%3d46%26msrpn_PInfo%3d5-%257c0%257c1652393%257c0%257c2%257c3249%257c46%257c0%257c0%257c0%257c0%257c%26msfns0%3dHall%26uidh%3dyz5%26_83004003-n_xcl%3df%26db%3dweb-obituary : accessed 16 Jun 2013); United States Obituary Collection .... Texas. Texas Department of State Health Services, *Texas Birth Index 1903 - 1997 [database on-line]*, Ancestry.com. www.ancestry.com/ : 2005, George Dewey Hall, Jr; Roll: 1921_0007; Certificate #77710.

541. "George Dewey Hall, Jr.," *The Bay City Tribune*, Aug 7, 2012, online archives (http://search.ancestry.com/oldsearch/obit/view.aspx?db=web-obituary&kw=Hall+George+Dewey&pid=148559589&url=http://search.ancestry.com/cgi-bin/sse.dll%3Frank%3d1%26new%3d1%26MSAV%3d1%26msT%3d1%26gss%3dangs-i%26gsfn%3dGeorge%2bDewey%26gsln%3dHall%26msbpn__ftp%3dUSA%26msbpn%3d2%26msbpn_PInfo%3d3-%257c0%257c1652393%257c0%257c2%257c0%257c0%257c0%257c0%257c0%257c0%257c%26msrpn__ftp%3dTexas%252c%2bUSA%26msrpn%3d46%26msrpn_PInfo%3d5-%257c0%257c1652393%257c0%257c2%257c3249%257c46%257c0%257c0%257c0%257c0%257c%26msfns0%3dHall%26uidh%3dyz5%26_83004003-n_xcl%3df%26db%3dweb-obituary : accessed 16 Jun 2013); United States Obituary Collection

542. "George Dewey Hall, Jr.," *The Bay City Tribune*, Aug 7, 2012, online archives (http://search.ancestry.com/oldsearch/obit/view.aspx?db=web-obituary&kw=Hall+George+Dewey&pid=148559589&url=http://search.ancestry.com/cgi-bin/sse.dll%3Frank%3d1%26new%3d1%26MSAV%3d1%26msT%3d1%26gss%3dangs-i%26gsfn%3dGeorge%2bDewey%26gsln%3dHall%26msbpn__ftp%3dUSA%26msbpn%3d2%26msbpn_PInfo%3d3-%257c0%257c1652393%257c0%257c2%257c0%257c0%257c0%257c0%257c0%257c0%257c%26msrpn__ftp%3dTexas%252c%2bUSA%26msrpn%3d46%26msrpn_PInfo%3d5-%257c0%257c1652393%257c0%257c2%257c3249%257c46%257c0%257c0%257c0%257c0%257c%26msfns0%3dHall%26uidh%3dyz5%26_83004003-n_xcl%3df%26db%3dweb-obituary : accessed 16 Jun 2013); United States Obituary Collection .... Find A Grave, Inc. database, *Find A Grave.com/* (http://www.findagrave.com/ : accessed 16 Jun 2013), George Dewey Hall, Jr. (1921-2012); Memorial# 95151512; Created by: Marsha Newton Kirchmeier; Aug 10, 2012

543. "United States Obituary Collection," database, *Ancestry.com* (www.ancestry.com/ : accessed 29 Jun 2013), Allen D. Hall, obituary; Brownsville Herald, 6 Dec 2003, Brownsville, TX.

544. 1920 U.S. census, Tom Green, Texas, population schedule, Justice Precinct 2, enumeration district (ED) 202, sheet 7B, dwelling 124, family 134, Archie A. Hall; digital images, *Ancestry.com* (www.ancestry.com/ : accessed 4 Jul 2013); citing National Archives and Records Administration microfilm T625, roll 1844.

545. The Church of Jesus Christ of Latter-Day Saints, "Texas County Marriage Records, 1837-1977," database, *FamilySearch* (https://familysearch.org/ : accessed 7 Jul 2013), Archie Hall and Beulah Mae Bean, 1923; Citing: Tom Green County, Texas Marriage Certificate # 4120.

546. 1900 U.S. census, Yazoo, Mississippi, population schedule, Beat 1, enumeration district (ED) 0109, sheet 17A, p. 85, dwelling 327, family 329, E. G. Childress; digital images, *Ancestry.com* (www.ancestry.com/ : accessed 20 Dec 2012); citing National Archives and Records Administration microfilm T623, roll 835; FHL microfilm: 1240835.

547. 1910 U.S. census, Yazoo, Mississippi, population schedule, Mechanicsburg, Beat 1; Satartia, enumeration district (ED) 0073, sheet 1A, p. 1, dwelling 3, family 3, E. G. Childress; digital images, *Ancestry.com* (www.ancestry.com/ : accessed 20 Dec 2012); citing National Archives and Records Administration microfilm T624, roll 765, FHL microfilm: 1374778.

548. 1920 U.S. census, Yazoo, Mississippi, population schedule, Satartia, enumeration district (ED) 89, sheet 1A, p. 189, dwelling 13, family 13, Edward G. Childress; digital images, *Ancestry.com* (www.ancestry.com/ : accessed 27 Dec 2012); citing National Archives and Records Administration microfilm T625, roll 900.

549. 1920 U.S. census, Yazoo, Mississippi, population schedule, Satartia, enumeration district (ED) 89, sheet 1B, dwelling 13, family 13, Edward G.

Childress; digital images,*Ancestry.com* (www.ancestry.com/ : accessed 27 Dec 2012); citing National Archives and Records Administration microfilm T625, roll 900.

550. U. S. Selective Service System,*World War I Draft Registration Cards, 1917-1918 [database on-line], Ancestry.com*. www.ancestry.com/ : 2005, Yazoo County, Mississippi; Roll: 1684098; Draft Board: 2; Sep 12, 1918.

551. 1920 U.S. census, Yazoo, Mississippi, population schedule, Satartia, enumeration district (ED) 89, sheet 1A, p. 189, dwelling 1, family 1, Samuel A. Childress; digital images,*Ancestry.com* (www.ancestry.com/ : accessed 27 Dec 2012); citing National Archives and Records Administration microfilm T625, roll 900.

552. 1930 U.S. census, Yazoo, Mississippi, population schedule, Satartia, enumeration district (ED) 1, sheet 1A, p. 190, dwelling 5, family 5, Samuel A. Childress; digital images,*Ancestry.com* (www.ancestry.com/ : accessed 27 Dec 2012); citing National Archives and Records Administration microfilm T626, roll 1172; FHL microfilm: 2340907.

553. Social Security Administration, "U. S. Social Security Death Index," database,*Family Search* (www.familysearch.org/ : accessed 20 Dec 2012), entry for Flora Childress, 1967, SS no. 425-07-9436.

554. 1900 U.S. census, Yazoo, Mississippi, population schedule, Beat 1, enumeration district (ED) 0109, sheet 27B, dwelling 190, family 196, Henry C. Bonney; digital images,*Ancestry.com* (www.ancestry.com/ : accessed 20 Dec 2012); citing National Archives and Records Administration microfilm T623, roll 835; FHL microfilm: 1240835.

555. 1900 U.S. census, Caddo, Louisiana, population schedule, Township 18- Parish Ward 4; Shreveport - City Ward 2, enumeration district (ED) 40, sheet 11B, dwelling 211, family 252, Lawrence W. Long; digital images,*Ancestry.com* (www.ancestry.com/ : accessed 20 Oct 2012); citing National Archives and Records Administration microfilm T623, roll 560; FHL microfilm: 1240560.

556. 1910 U.S. census, Pulaski, Arkansas, population schedule, Little Rock Ward 6, enumeration district (ED) 128, sheet 149, p. 13A, dwelling 236, family 279, Lawrence W. Long; digital images,*Ancestry.com* (www.ancestry.com/ : accessed 27 Nov 2010); citing National Archives and Records Administration microfilm T624, roll T624_62.

557. Louisiana. Secretary of State, Division of Archives, Records Management, and History. Vital Records Indices,*Louisiana Statewide Death Index, 1900-1949 [database on-line]*, Baton Rouge, Louisiana: Ancestry.com. www.ancestry.com/ : 2002, Lawrence Long; Volume 9; Certificate #4109.

558. Find A Grave, Inc. database,*Find A Grave.com/* (http://www.findagrave.com/ : accessed 15 Feb 2012), Dr Lawrence Wilbun Long, Jr (1902-1986); Memorial #64363709; Created by: John Van Zandt; Jan 18, 2011

559. 1900 U.S. census, Yazoo, Mississippi, population schedule, Beat 1, enumeration district (ED) 0109, sheet 30B, dwelling 245, family 252, Will G. Childress; digital images,*Ancestry.com* (www.ancestry.com/ : accessed 20 Dec 2012); citing National Archives and Records Administration microfilm T623, roll 835; FHL microfilm: 1240835.

560. Grissette, Sharon, "Hart-Childress Cemetery, Yazoo County, Mississippi" (2003), Elizabeth H. Childress. Web site accessed 26 January 2009.

561. Grissette, Sharon, "Hart-Childress Cemetery, Yazoo County, Mississippi" (2003), Georgia Russell Childress. Web site accessed 26 January 2009.

562. Childress, J. Patrick <londonwildcat@earthlink.net>, "Childress/Mathis Family Tree" (04 December 2007 (Updated)), Samuel Hall Childress, son of William Gordon Childress.

563. Grissette, Sharon, "Hart-Childress Cemetery, Yazoo County, Mississippi" (2003), Robert Lee Childress. Web site accessed 26 January 2009.

564. 1910 U.S. census, Chaves, New Mexico, population schedule, Roswell; Ward 1, enumeration district (ED) 21, sheet 3A, p. 34, dwelling 41, family 46, Edgar L. Bedell; digital images,*Ancestry.com* (www.ancestry.com/ : accessed 14 Nov 2012); citing National Archives and Records Administration microfilm T624, roll 913; FHL microfilm: 1374926.

565. Find A Grave, Inc. database,*Find A Grave.com/* (http://www.findagrave.com/ : accessed 23 Aug 2013), Hiram Millet Dow (1885-1969); Find A Grave Memorial# 17424680; Maintained by: Whisper Stockton; Jan 13, 2007

566. 1920 U.S. census, Chaves, New Mexico, population schedule, Roswell; Ward 2, enumeration district (ED) 4, sheet 9A, p. 43, dwelling 182, family 192, Thomas H. Watts; digital images,*Ancestry.com* (www.ancestry.com/ : accessed 14 Nov 2012); citing National Archives and Records Administration microfilm T625, roll 1074.

567. Los Angeles, California, California Voter Registrations, 1900-1968 [database on-line], vol. - Precinct 971: Sheet 2, Harry H. Wildy; digital images, Ancestry.com Operations Inc,*Ancestry.com* (www.ancestry.com/ : accessed 4 Jan 2012).

568. 1930 U.S. census, Los Angeles, California, population schedule, Los Angeles; Assembly District 57, enumeration district (ED) 130, sheet 8A, p. 254, dwelling 165, family 165, H. H. Wildy; digital images,*Ancestry.com* (www.ancestry.com/ : accessed 7 Oct 2012); citing National Archives and Records Administration microfilm T626, roll 137.

569. 1940 U.S. census, Los Angeles, California, population schedule, San Gabriel/Alhambra, enumeration district (ED) 19-661, sheet 4A, p. 12322, household 84, Harry H. Wildy; digital images,*Famly Search* (www.familysearch.org/ : accessed 8 Dec 2012); citing National Archives and Records Administration microfilm T627, roll 251.

570. U. S. Social Security Administration,*Social Security Death Index [database on-line]*. Ancestry.com. www.ancestry.com/ : 2011, Number: 555-80-1718;Issue State: California;Issue Date: 1965. .... California Department of Health Services, Center for Health Statistics., "California, Death Index, 1940-1997," database, *Ancestry.com* (www.ancestry.com/ : accessed 4 Jan 2012), Vivian Rose Wildy.

571. 1900 U.S. census, Los Angeles, California, population schedule, Los Angeles Ward 6,, enumeration district (ED) 52, sheet 8B, dwelling 178, family 187, Rose Dee; digital images,*Ancestry.com* (www.ancestry.com/ : accessed 4 Jan 2012); citing National Archives and Records Administration microfilm T623, roll T623_ 90.

572. Los Angeles, California, California Voter Registrations, 1900-1968 [database on-line], vol. - Precinct 971: Sheet 2, Mrs. Vivian R. Wildy; digital images, Ancestry.com Operations Inc,*Ancestry.com* (www.ancestry.com/ : accessed 4 Jan 2012).

573. 1930 U.S. census, Tarrant, Texas, population schedule, Fort Worth, enumeration district (ED) 0040, sheet 12A, family 211, Claude Russell; online database, *Family Search* (www.familysearch.org/ : accessed 17 Nov 2011); citing National Archives and Records Administration microfilm T626, roll 2394.

574. 1930 U.S. census, Tarrant, Texas, population schedule, Fort Worth, enumeration district (ED) 0040, sheet 12A, family 211, Josephine Russell; online database, *Family Search* (www.familysearch.org/ : accessed 17 Nov 2011); citing National Archives and Records Administration microfilm T626, roll 2394.

575. Russell Family Tree - Ancestry.com, Annabel and Wade Russell, compiler (Wm. Ross Russell Family Bible, July 30 2008; privately held by Scott Russell Redmond, Washington); reported by Scott Russell, Hendley Mathews Russell Family Bible and Wm. Ross Russell Family Bible.

576. Russell Family Tree - Ancestry.com, Annabel and Wade Russell, compiler (Wm. Ross Russell Family Bible, July 30 2008; privately held by Scott Russell Redmond, Washington); reported by Scott Russell, John Dent Spain Family Bible.

577. Russell Family Tree - Ancestry.com, Annabel and Wade Russell, compiler (Wm. Ross Russell Family Bible, July 30 2008; privately held by Scott Russell Redmond, Washington); reported by Scott Russell, Hendley Mathews Russell Family Bible, Wm. Ross Russell Family Bible and John Dent Spain Family Bible.

578. Texas. Texas Department of State Health Services,*Texas Birth Index 1903 - 1997 [database on-line],* Ancestry.com. www.ancestry.com/ : 2005, Francis Brandell Moseley, 1929; Roll #1929_0005.

579. 1930 U.S. census, Yazoo, Mississippi, population schedule, Satartia, enumeration district (ED) 1, sheet 1A, p. 190, dwelling 2, family 2, Sam H. Childress; digital images,*Ancestry.com* (www.ancestry.com/ : accessed 27 Dec 2012); citing National Archives and Records Administration microfilm T626, roll 1172; FHL microfilm: 2340907.

580. Carrol Carmen Hall,*The Grandfathers, The Hall and Overstreet Families* , 2 Volumes (Springfield, Illinois: Illinois Ancestors.org - Menard County (http://www.illinoisancestors.org/menard/), 1981-2007), Section 1, Chapter 4: Page 31. .... Volume 309; Elisha Hall, Nancy Overstreet, SAR Membership Number 61766, U. S., Sons of the American Revolution, Ancestry.com: The Generations Network, Inc., Provo. .... Zeb Motley McCormick, 40399, U. S., Sons of the American Revolution, Ancestry.com: The Generations Network, Inc., Provo; A descendant of John Overstreet and Elisha Hall

581. Carrol Carmen Hall,*The Grandfathers, The Hall and Overstreet Families* , 2 Volumes (Springfield, Illinois: Illinois Ancestors.org - Menard County (http://www.illinoisancestors.org/menard/), 1981-2007), Section 1, Chapter 4: Page 31. .... Abner Hall; Vol. 243; 48500, U. S., Sons of the American Revolution, Ancestry.com: The Generations Network, Inc., Provo; Citing original data*Sons of the American Revolution Membership Applications, 1889-1970.* Louisville, Kentucky: National Society of the Sons of the American Revolution. Microfilm, 508 rolls.

582. Carrol Carmen Hall,*The Grandfathers, The Hall and Overstreet Families* , 2 Volumes (Springfield, Illinois: Illinois Ancestors.org - Menard County (http://www.illinoisancestors.org/menard/), 1981-2007), Section 1, Chapter 4: Page 31. .... William Wade Hinshaw*Encyclopedia of American Quaker Genealogy. Vol. VI: (Virginia)* (Baltimore, Maryland: Genealogical Publishing Co., Reprint 1993), William Hall & Nancy Dixon; p. 926; "James Dixon, surety."

583. 1850 U.S. census, Lawrence, Ohio, population schedule, Rome, p. 410B, dwelling 42, family 42, Nancy Hall; digital images,*Ancestry.com* (www.ancestry.com/ : accessed 5 Jan 2012); citing National Archives and Records Administration microfilm M432, roll M432_701.

584. Carrol Carmen Hall,*The Grandfathers, The Hall and Overstreet Families* , 2 Volumes (Springfield, Illinois: Illinois Ancestors.org - Menard County (http://www.illinoisancestors.org/menard/), 1981-2007), Section 1, Chapter 4: Page 31. .... William Wade Hinshaw*Encyclopedia of American Quaker Genealogy. Vol. VI: (Virginia)* (Baltimore, Maryland: Genealogical Publishing Co., Reprint 1993), Thomas Hall & Elizabeth Radford; p. 926; "Elizabeth Radford, dt. Polly. Tubal Dixon, surety."

585. Find A Grave, Inc. database,*Find A Grave.com/* (http://www.findagrave.com/ : accessed 15 Feb 2012), Wesley Hall (1811-1893); Memorial # 35184794; Mar 26, 2009

586. 1820 U.S. census, Lawrence, Ohio population schedule, Union, p. 105, line 19, Elisha Hall; digital images,*Ancestry.com* (www.ancestry.com : accessed 27 Dec 2012); citing National Archives and Records Administration microfilm M33, roll 88.

587. 1830 U.S. census, Sangamon, Illinois, p. 193, line 5, Elisha Hall; digital images,*Ancestry.com* (www.ancestry.com/ : accessed 30 Nov 2011); citing National Archives and Records Administration microfilm M19, roll M19- 24.

588. Find A Grave, Inc. database,*Find A Grave.com/* (http://www.findagrave.com/ : accessed 15 Feb 2012), Elisha Hall (1783-1838); Memorial # 41841732; Created by: SUSAN HILL DAVIS; Sep 11, 2009

589. Virginia, Virginia Marriages, 1785-1940, Hall-Overstreet, 1811; FHL microfilm 30,591, item : pg 12. .... William Wade Hinshaw, *Encyclopedia of American Quaker Genealogy. Vol. VI: (Virginia)* (Baltimore, Maryland: Genealogical Publishing Co., Reprint 1993), Elisha Hall & Nancy Overstreet; p. 926; "Nancy Overstreet, dt. John, Sr; James Hall, surety. Married by James Scott 17 July 1811."

590. Volume 309; Nancy Overstreet, Elisha Hall, SAR Membership Number 61766, U. S., Sons of the American Revolution, Ancestry.com: The Generations Network, Inc., Provo.

591. 1850 U.S. census, Menard, Illinois, population schedule, p. 290A; Image: 420, dwelling 342, family 356, Nancy Hall; digital images, *Ancestry.com* (www.ancestry.com/ : accessed 21 Mar 2010); citing National Archives and Records Administration microfilm M432, roll M432_120.

592. 1860 U.S. census, Menard, Illinois, population schedule, Township 18, Range 6, p. 205; Sheet 953, dwelling 1443, family 1581, Nancy Hall; digital images, *Ancestry.com* (www.ancestry.com/ : accessed 8 Nov 2011); citing National Archives and Records Administration microfilm M653, roll M653_205; FHL Film 803205.

593. Find A Grave, Inc. database, *Find A Grave.com/* (http://www.findagrave.com/ : accessed 15 Feb 2012), Elisha Hall (1783-1838); Memorial # 41841732; Created by: SUSAN HILL DAVIS; Sep 11, 2009 .... Zeb Motley McCormick, 40399, U. S., Sons of the American Revolution, Ancestry.com: The Generations Network, Inc., Provo; A descendant of John Overstreet and Elisha Hall

594. Zeb Motley McCormick, 40399, U. S., Sons of the American Revolution, Ancestry.com: The Generations Network, Inc., Provo; A descendant of John Overstreet and Elisha Hall

595. Find A Grave, Inc. database, *Find A Grave.com/* (http://www.findagrave.com/ : accessed 15 Feb 2012), James Pembroke Hall (1818-1892); Memorial #30299361; Created by: Susan Hill Davis; Oct 04, 2008

596. Find A Grave, Inc. database, *Find A Grave.com/* (http://www.findagrave.com/ : accessed 5 Jan 2012), William M. Hall (-1864); Memorial # 16611561; Nov 11, 2006

597. 1850 U.S. census, Menard, Illinois, population schedule, p. 290B; Image: 421, dwelling 342, family 356, Wm. Hall; digital images, *Ancestry.com* (www.ancestry.com/ : accessed 8 Nov 2011); citing National Archives and Records Administration microfilm M432, roll M432_120.

598. 1820 U.S. census, Lawrence, Ohio population schedule, Union, p. 106A, line 12, Augustine Smith; digital images, *Ancestry.com* (www.ancestry.com : accessed 27 Dec 2012); citing National Archives and Records Administration microfilm M33, roll 88.

599. Carrol Carmen Hall, *The Grandfathers, The Hall and Overstreet Families* , 2 Volumes (Springfield, Illinois: Illinois Ancestors.org - Menard County (http://www.illinoisancestors.org/menard/), 1981-2007), Section 1, Chapter 4: 31; Chapter 5: 50. .... Earle S. Dennis and Jane Estelle Smith, *Marriage Bonds of Bedford County, Virginia, 1755-1800* (Baltimore, Maryland: Genealogical Publishing Company, 1981), Page 62.

600. 1820 U.S. census, Lawrence, Ohio population schedule, Union, p. 105, line 20, John Overstreet, Jr; digital images, *Ancestry.com* (www.ancestry.com : accessed 27 Dec 2012); citing National Archives and Records Administration microfilm M33, roll 88.

601. 1820 U.S. census, Lawrence, Ohio population schedule, Union, p. 106, line 5, Sam'l Hall; digital images, *Ancestry.com* (www.ancestry.com : accessed 27 Dec 2012); citing National Archives and Records Administration microfilm M33, roll 88.

602. 1850 U.S. census, Van Buren, Iowa, population schedule, Village, p. 347A; Image: 210., dwelling 17, family 17, Samuel Hall; digital images, *Ancestry.com* (www.ancestry.com/ : accessed 21 Mar 2010); citing National Archives and Records Administration microfilm M432, roll M432_189.

603. Iowa State Census -1856, Van Buren, Iowa, population schedule, Village, p. 172, dwelling 171, line 22, Samuel Hall; digital images, Ancestry.com Operations Inc., *Ancestry.com* (www.ancestry.com/ : accessed 21 Mar 2010); Roll: IA_66

604. 1850 U.S. census, Van Buren, Iowa, population schedule, Village, p. 26; Image: 269, dwelling 150, family 150, Saml. Hall; digital images, *Ancestry.com* (www.ancestry.com/ : accessed 21 Mar 2010); citing National Archives and Records Administration microfilm M432, roll M653_342; Family History Library Film: 803342.

605. 1830 U.S. census, Sangamon, Illinois, p. 193, line 6, James Hall; digital images, *Ancestry.com* (www.ancestry.com/ : accessed 30 Nov 2011); citing National Archives and Records Administration microfilm M19, roll M19- 24.

606. 1850 U.S. census, Menard, Illinois, population schedule, p. 281A, dwelling 207, family 214, Eleanor Hall; digital images, *Ancestry.com* (www.ancestry.com/ : accessed 8 Nov 2011); citing National Archives and Records Administration microfilm M432, roll M432_120.

607. 1850 U.S. census, Menard, Illinois, population schedule, p. 281A, dwelling 207, family 214, Minerva Hall; digital images, *Ancestry.com* (www.ancestry.com/ : accessed 8 Nov 2011); citing National Archives and Records Administration microfilm M432, roll M432_120.

608. 1850 U.S. census, Menard, Illinois, population schedule, p. 281A, dwelling 207, family 214, John Hall; digital images, *Ancestry.com* (www.ancestry.com/ : accessed 8 Nov 2011); citing National Archives and Records Administration microfilm M432, roll M432_120.

609. 1850 U.S. census, Menard, Illinois, population schedule, p. 281A, dwelling 207, family 214, S. M. Hall; digital images, *Ancestry.com* (www.ancestry.com/ : accessed 8 Nov 2011); citing National Archives and Records Administration microfilm M432, roll M432_120.

610. 1850 U.S. census, Menard, Illinois, population schedule, p. 281A, dwelling 207, family 214, James Hall; digital images, *Ancestry.com* (www.ancestry.com/ : accessed 8 Nov 2011); citing National Archives and Records Administration microfilm M432, roll M432_120.

611. 1820 U.S. census, Lawrence, Ohio population schedule, Union, p. 106, line 3, Abahan Hall; digital images, *Ancestry.com* (www.ancestry.com : accessed 27 Dec 2012); citing National Archives and Records Administration microfilm M33, roll 88.

612. 1830 U.S. census, Sangamon, Illinois, p. 193, line 7, Abner Hall; digital images, *Ancestry.com* (www.ancestry.com/ : accessed 30 Nov 2011); citing National Archives and Records Administration microfilm M19, roll M19- 24.

613. Certificate no. 8926; Abner Hall and Joseph B. Ayres; "U. S. General Land Office Records, 1796-1907 [database on-line]," database and images, *Ancestry.com* (www.ancestry.com/ : accessed 8 Nov 2011); Citing United States. Bureau of Land Management, General Land Office Records. *Automated Records Project; Federal Land Patents, State Volumes. http://www.glorecords.blm.gov/.* Springfield, Virginia: Bureau of Land Management, Eastern States, 2007.

Source Citations

614. 1850 U.S. census, Menard, Illinois, population schedule, p. 281B, dwelling 21, family 222, Jenny Hall; digital images*Ancestry.com* (www.ancestry.com/ : accessed 8 Nov 2011); citing National Archives and Records Administration microfilm M432, roll M432_120.

615. Find A Grave, Inc. database,*Find A Grave.com/* (http://www.findagrave.com/ : accessed 5 Jan 2012), James Wesley Hall (1815-1870); Memorial # 76568358; Created by: Susan Hill Davis; Sep 15, 2011

616. James Wesley Hall; Vol. 243; 48499, U. S., Sons of the American Revolution, Ancestry.com: The Generations Network, Inc., Provo; Citing original data: *Sons of the American Revolution Membership Applications, 1889-1970*. Louisville, Kentucky: National Society of the Sons of the American Revolution. Microfilm, 508 rolls.

617. Find A Grave, Inc. database,*Find A Grave.com/* (http://www.findagrave.com/ : accessed 5 Jan 2012), Catherine Hall Ayers (1817-1900); Memorial #79976142; Nov 06, 2011

618. Kristin Vaughn, Illinois Genealogy Trails, "Menard County, Illinois - History & Genealogy - Obituaries," database*Menard County, Illinois - History & Genealogy* (http://genealogytrails.com/ill/menard/index.html : accessed 18 Sep 2011), Abner Banks Hall; citing a newspaper obituary of Abner Banks Hall.

619. Find A Grave, Inc. database,*Find A Grave.com/* (http://www.findagrave.com/ : accessed 5 Jan 2012), Abner Banks "A.B." Hall (1820-1896); Memorial #16611610; Nov 11, 2006; Tombstone photos attached.

620. 1820 U.S. census, Lawrence, Ohio population schedule, Union, p. 106, line 1, John Neal; digital images*Ancestry.com* (www.ancestry.com . accessed 27 Dec 2012); citing National Archives and Records Administration microfilm M33, roll 88.

621. 1850 U.S. census, Menard, Illiinois, population schedule, p. 28?, dwelling 315, family 323, Wesley Hall; digital images*FamilySearch* (https://familysearch.org/ : accessed 28 Dec 2012); citing National Archives and Records Administration microfilm M432, roll 119; FHL Film #442908.

622. Illinois, "Illinois, State Census, 1855," database,*FamilySearch* (https://familysearch.org/ : accessed 28 Dec 2012), Westley Hall, Menard, Illinois; FHL Film #976671.

623. 1880 U.S. census, Menard, Illinois, population schedule, Sugar Grove, enumeration district (ED) 135, p. 17; 171A, dwelling 127, family 131, Wesley Hall; digital images,*Ancestry.com* (www.ancestry.com/ : accessed 28 Dec 2012); citing National Archives and Records Administration microfilm T9, roll 236; Family History Film: 1254236.

624. Find A Grave, Inc. database,*Find A Grave.com/* (http://www.findagrave.com/ : accessed 15 Feb 2012), Nancy Ferguson Hall (1821-1904); Memorial #35184722; Mar 26, 2009

625. 1900 U.S. census, Menard, Illinois, population schedule, Fancy Prairie, enumeration district (ED) 71, sheet 1A, p. 166, dwelling 12, family 13, Thomas H. Hall; digital images,*Ancestry.com* (www.ancestry.com : accessed 28 Dec 2012); citing National Archives and Records Administration microfilm T623, roll 329; FHL microfilm: 1240329.

626. 1850 U.S. census, Menard, Illinois, population schedule, p. 282B, dwelling 231, family 239, Nelson Hall; digital images*Ancestry.com* (www.ancestry.com/ : accessed 15 Feb 2012); citing National Archives and Records Administration microfilm M432, roll M432_120.

627. 1900 U.S. census, Menard, Illinois, population schedule, Athens, enumeration district (ED) 70, sheet 26A, p. 164, dwelling 521, family 530, John N. Hall; digital images,*Ancestry.com* (www.ancestry.com : accessed 15 Feb 2012); citing National Archives and Records Administration microfilm T623, roll T623 329.

628. John Nelson Hall/Sarah Parker, National #61766; State #602, U. S., Sons of the American Revolution, Ancestry.com: The Generations Network, Inc., Provo.

629. Find A Grave, Inc. database,*Find A Grave.com/* (http://www.findagrave.com/ : accessed 15 Feb 2012), Mary Jane Pierce Hall (1830-1905); Memorial #30299636; Created by: SUSAN HILL DAVIS, Oct 04, 2008

630. 1870 U.S. census, Mason, Illinois, population schedule, Mason City, p. 133B, dwelling 160, family 159, Dabney Hall; digital images, *Ancestry.com* (www.ancestry.com/ : accessed 8 Nov 2011); citing National Archives and Records Administration microfilm M593, roll M593_255; FHL Film: 545754.

631. Dabney Hall Photograph of Tombstone; digital images, Ancestry.com, "Dabney Hall (1828-1874) - Tombstone,"*Ancestry.com* (www.ancestry.com/ : accessed 30 Nov 2011).

632. 1870 U.S. census, Mason, Illinois, population schedule, Mason City, p. 133B, dwelling 160, family 159, Tobetha Hall; digital images, *Ancestry.com* (www.ancestry.com/ : accessed 8 Nov 2011); citing National Archives and Records Administration microfilm M593, roll M593_255; FHL Film: 545754.

633. 1850 U.S. census, Menard, Illinois, population schedule, p. 290B; Image: 421, dwelling 342, family 356, Virginia Pierce; digital images, *Ancestry.com* (www.ancestry.com/ : accessed 8 Nov 2011); citing National Archives and Records Administration microfilm M432, roll M432_120.

634. 1880 U.S. census, Brown, Kansas, population schedule, Washington, enumeration district (ED) 20, p. 2B, dwelling 14, family 14, Virginia Pierce; digital images,*Ancestry.com* (www.ancestry.com/ : accessed 30 Nov 2011); citing National Archives and Records Administration microfilm T9, roll 374.

635. 1850 U.S. census, Menard, Illinois, population schedule, p. 290B; Image: 421, dwelling 342, family 356, George Pierce; digital images, *Ancestry.com* (www.ancestry.com/ : accessed 8 Nov 2011); citing National Archives and Records Administration microfilm M432, roll M432_120.

Source Citations

636. 1880 U.S. census, Brown, Kansas, population schedule, Washington, enumeration district (ED) 20, p. 2B, dwelling 14, family 14, George Pierce; digital images, *Ancestry.com* (www.ancestry.com/ : accessed 30 Nov 2011); citing National Archives and Records Administration microfilm T9, roll 374.

637. 1850 U.S. census, Menard, Illinois, population schedule, p. 290A; Image: 420, dwelling 342, family 356, N. J. Hall; digital images, *Ancestry.com* (www.ancestry.com/ : accessed 21 Mar 2010); citing National Archives and Records Administration microfilm M432, roll M432_120.

638. Jordan Dodd compilers, Liahona Research, "Illinois Marriages, 1851-1900 [database on-line]," database, Ancestry.com Operations Inc, *Ancestry.com* (www.ancestry.com/ : accessed 4 Jan 2012), Oliver P. Pierce m. Nancy J. Hall; citing: County Court Records, FHL Film # 1311614 - 1311615.

639. 1860 U.S. census, Menard, Illinois, population schedule, Township 18, Range 6, p. 205; Sheet 953, dwelling 1443, family 1581, Oliver Pierce; digital images, *Ancestry.com* (www.ancestry.com/ : accessed 8 Nov 2011); citing National Archives and Records Administration microfilm M653, roll M653_205; FHL Film 803205.

640. 1840 U.S. census, Sangamon, Illinois, p. 45, line 30, James W. Hall; digital images, *Ancestry.com* (www.ancestry.com/ : accessed 8 Nov 2011); citing National Archives and Records Administration microfilm M704, roll 69; FHL Film: 0007644.

641. 1850 U.S. census, Menard, Illinois, population schedule, p. 283A, dwelling 234, family 242, James Hall; digital images, *Ancestry.com* (www.ancestry.com/ : accessed 8 Nov 2011); citing National Archives and Records Administration microfilm M432, roll M432_120.

642. 1860 U.S. census, Menard, Illinois, population schedule, Athens, p. 991, James W. Hall; digital images, *Ancestry.com* (www.ancestry.com/ : accessed 8 Nov 2011); citing National Archives and Records Administration microfilm M653, roll M653_205; FHL Film: 803205.

643. Henry E. Hall/ John Overstreet, National No. 48500; State No. 3178, Sons of the American Revolution, Illinois Society of the Sons of the American Revolution, Springfield.

644. 1850 U.S. census, Menard, Illinois, population schedule, p. 283A, dwelling 234, family 242, Catharine Hall; digital images, *Ancestry.com* (www.ancestry.com/ : accessed 8 Nov 2011); citing National Archives and Records Administration microfilm M432, roll M432_120.

645. 1860 U.S. census, Menard, Illinois, population schedule, Athens, p. 991, Catharine Hall; digital images, *Ancestry.com* (www.ancestry.com/ : accessed 8 Nov 2011); citing National Archives and Records Administration microfilm M653, roll M653_205; FHL Film: 803205.

646. 1850 U.S. census, Menard, Illinois, population schedule, p. 282B, dwelling 233, family 241, Joseph Ayres; digital images, *Ancestry.com* (www.ancestry.com/ : accessed 8 Nov 2011); citing National Archives and Records Administration microfilm M432, roll M432_120.

647. 1860 U.S. census, Menard, Illinois, population schedule, Township 18 Range 6, p. 953, dwelling 1444, family 1382, Jas. B. Ayres; digital images, *Ancestry.com* (www.ancestry.com/ : accessed 8 Nov 2011); citing National Archives and Records Administration microfilm M653, roll M653_205; FHL Film: 803205.

648. 1870 U.S. census, Menard, Illinois, population schedule, Athens; Township 18 Range 6, p. 44B, dwelling 54, family 52, Joseph Ayers; digital images, *Ancestry.com* (www.ancestry.com/); citing National Archives and Records Administration microfilm M593, roll M593_260.

649. Find A Grave, Inc. database, *Find A Grave.com/* (http://www.findagrave.com/ : accessed 5 Jan 2012), Catherine Hall Ayers (1817-1900); Memorial #76569103; Created by: Susan Hill Davis; Sep 15, 2011; Tombstone photos attached.

650. Ancestry.com Operations, Inc., "U.S. Federal Census Mortality Schedules, 1850-1885 [database on-line].," database and images, *Ancestry.com* (www.ancestry.com/ : accessed 8 Nov 2011); Joseph B. Ayres; T1133; Archive Roll Number: 63; Census Year: 1880; Census Location: Athens, Menard, Illinois; Page: 1; Line: 5.

651. Find A Grave, Inc. database, *Find A Grave.com/* (http://www.findagrave.com/ : accessed 5 Jan 2012), Joseph B Ayers (1807-1880); Memorial# 79976257; Nov 06, 2011

652. Certificate no. 8926; Abner Hall and Joseph B. Ayres; "U. S. General Land Office Records, 1796-1907 [database on-line]," database and images, *Ancestry.com* (www.ancestry.com/ : accessed 8 Nov 2011).

653. 1850 U.S. census, Menard, Illinois, population schedule, p. 281A, dwelling 215, family 223, A. B. Hall; digital images, *Ancestry.com* (www.ancestry.com/ : accessed 8 Nov 2011); citing National Archives and Records Administration microfilm M432, roll M432_120.

654. Find A Grave, Inc. database, *Find A Grave.com/* (http://www.findagrave.com/ : accessed 5 Jan 2012), Jeanette Francis Hall (unknown); Memorial # 38106534; Jun 08, 2009; Tombstone photo attached.

655. 1850 U.S. census, Menard, Illinois, population schedule, p. 281A, dwelling 215, family 223, F. J. Hall; digital images, *Ancestry.com* (www.ancestry.com/ : accessed 8 Nov 2011); citing National Archives and Records Administration microfilm M432, roll M432_120.

656. 1850 U.S. census, Menard, Illinois, population schedule, p. 281B, dwelling 214, family 221, Matilda Clarke; digital images, *Ancestry.com* (www.ancestry.com/ : accessed 8 Nov 2011); citing National Archives and Records Administration microfilm M432, roll M432_120.

657. Edward Nevill McAllister and Annabelle Cox McAllister, *Estes Family of old Clay County, Missouri, their ancestors and their descendants* (N.p.: n.p., 1972), Page 253. .... Peggy Loveless Contreras, "Re: Alse DePriest," *Depreist - Family History & Genealogy Message Board*, message board, 16 May 2004 (http://boards.ancestry.co.uk/surnames.depreist/ : accessed 21 Mar 2010).

658. Carrol Carmen Hall, *The Grandfathers, The Hall and Overstreet Families* , 2 Volumes (Springfield, Illinois: Illinois Ancestors.org - Menard County (http://www.illinoisancestors.org/menard/), 1981-2007), Section VI, Chapter 20, page 222. .... Peggy Loveless Contreras, "Re: Alse DePriest,"

Source Citations

Depreist - Family History & Genealogy Message Board, message board, 16 May 2004 (http://boards.ancestry.co.uk/surnames.depreist/ : accessed 21 Mar 2010).

659. Find A Grave, Inc. database,*Find A Grave.com/* (http://www.findagrave.com/ : accessed 18 Sep 2011), Jerimiah S. Hall (1783-1859); Record added: Nov 26, 2007; Find A Grave Memorial# 23111722.

660. Edward Nevill McAllister and Annabelle Cox McAllister,*Estes Family of old Clay County, Missouri, their ancestors and their descendants* (N.p.: n.p., 1972), Page 253.

661. 1840 U.S. census, Clay, Missouri, p. 35, line 29, Elisha Hall; digital images,*Ancestry.com* (www.ancestry.com/ : accessed 29 Dec 2012); citing National Archives and Records Administration microfilm M704, roll 222; Family History Library Film: 0014855.

662. 1850 U.S. census, Clinton, Missouri, population schedule, District 16, p. 428A; Image: 384, dwelling 520, family 520, Elisha Hall; digital images, *Ancestry.com* (www.ancestry.com/ : accessed 20 Mar 2010); citing National Archives and Records Administration microfilm M432, roll M432_396.

663. Carrol Carmen Hall,*The Grandfathers, The Hall and Overstreet Families* , 2 Volumes (Springfield, Illinois: Illinois Ancestors.org - Menard County (http://www.illinoisancestors.org/menard/), 1981-2007), Section VI; Chapter 20; Page 222. .... Peggy Loveless Contreras, "Re: Alse DePriest," *Depreist - Family History & Genealogy Message Board*, message board, 16 May 2004 (http://boards.ancestry.co.uk/surnames.depreist/ : accessed 21 Mar 2010).

664. Peggy Loveless Contreras, "Re: Alse DePriest,"*Depreist - Family History & Genealogy Message Board*, message board, 16 May 2004 (http://boards.ancestry.co.uk/surnames.depreist/ : accessed 21 Mar 2010).

665. Edward Nevill McAllister and Annabelle Cox McAllister,*Estes Family of old Clay County, Missouri, their ancestors and their descendants* (N.p.: n.p., 1972), Page 253, 255.

666. Find A Grave, Inc. database,*Find A Grave.com/* (http://www.findagrave.com/ : accessed 18 Sep 2011), Jerimiah S. Hall (1783-1859); Memorial # 23111722; Record added: Nov 26, 2007.

667. 1830 U.S. census, Clay, Missouri, p. 279, line 12, Jeremiah Hall, Sr; digital images,*Ancestry.com* (www.ancestry.com/ : accessed 29 Dec 2012); citing National Archives and Records Administration microfilm M19, roll 73; Family History Film: 0014854.

668. 1850 U.S. census, Clay, Missouri, population schedule, Gallatin, p. 327A; Image: 180., dwelling 355, family 355, Jerimiah Hall; digital images, *Ancestry.com* (www.ancestry.com/ : accessed 21 Mar 2010); citing National Archives and Records Administration microfilm M432, roll M432_396.

669. Find A Grave, Inc. database,*Find A Grave.com/* (http://www.findagrave.com/ : accessed 18 Sep 2011), Sarah Cochran Hall (1786-1867); Record added: Nov 26, 2007; Find A Grave Memorial# 23111712;
Jeremiah S. Hall and his wife, Sarah (Cochran) Hall, were among the earliest settlers of Clay County in western Missouri. He was born in Virginia and she in North Carolina. We know almost nothing of their family origins. They probably came as children or young adults to Kentucky, where they married, apparently in Madison County on September 12, 1807. At that date, he would have been about 24 years old; she about 21.

The family moved to Bedford County, Tennessee by 1811 (according to a county tax list) and on to Missouri, first to Boone County about 1818, and then to Clay County, where Jeremiah Hall purchased land from the government beginning in June 1823. These migrations were shared by the family of Elisha (sometimes recorded as Elijah) Hall (born about 1773). Due to the similarity in their histories and in the first names among their children, it seems very likely that Jeremiah and Elisha were brothers. This agrees with a single, unverified source which indicates that Jeremiah's father may have been an Elisha Hall who had two sons named Elisha and Jeremiah, both of whom migrated to Missouri.
Jeremiah and Sarah lived and farmed east of Liberty, near the old Stockdale crossroads, for many years. They were apparently successful in farming, as the size and value of their holdings increased over the years. Sometime after 1850 they moved to Clinton County where several of their children were living.

Jeremiah died in Clinton County in 1859. In 1860, Sarah was living with her son Andrew in Clinton County. Andrew died in 1863 and she probably lived with other of her children in Clinton County until her own death in 1867. Jeremiah and Sarah share a tombstone in the Pleasant Hill Cemetery in southwestern Clinton County that is unusual in that it is a single block about two feet square and four feet high. It stands solid and erect over many newer stones that have toppled.

670. 1830 U.S. census, Clay, Missouri, p. 279, line 14, William Hall; digital images,*Ancestry.com* (www.ancestry.com/ : accessed 30 Dec 2012); citing National Archives and Records Administration microfilm M19, roll 73; Family History Film: 0014854.

671. 1840 U.S. census, Clay, Missouri, p. 30, line 4, Wm. Hall; digital images,*Ancestry.com* (www.ancestry.com/ : accessed 27 Sep 2013); citing National Archives and Records Administration microfilm M704, roll 222; Family History Library Film: 0014855.

672. Edward Nevill McAllister and Annabelle Cox McAllister,*Estes Family of old Clay County, Missouri, their ancestors and their descendants* (N.p.: n.p., 1972), Page 254.

673. 1850 U.S. census, Clinton, Missouri, population schedule, District 16, p. 428A; Image: 384, dwelling 518, family 518, Mrs. Hall; digital images, *Ancestry.com* (www.ancestry.com/ : accessed 20 Mar 2010); citing National Archives and Records Administration microfilm M432, roll M432_396.

674. 1850 U.S. census, Tarrant, Texas, population schedule, Navarro, p. 86B; Image: 266, dwelling 4, family 4, Wm. W. Hall; digital images, *Ancestry.com* (www.ancestry.com/ : accessed 21 Mar 2010); citing National Archives and Records Administration microfilm M432, roll M432_910.

675. 1830 U.S. census, Clay, Missouri, p. 279, line 13, James E. Hall; digital images,*Ancestry.com* (www.ancestry.com/ : accessed 30 Dec 2012); citing National Archives and Records Administration microfilm M19, roll 73; Family History Film: 0014854.

Source Citations

676. 1840 U.S. census, Clay, Missouri, p. 30, line 1, Jame[s] E. Hall; digital images,*Ancestry.com* (www.ancestry.com/ : accessed 27 Sep 2013); citing National Archives and Records Administration microfilm M704, roll 222; Family History Library Film: 0014855.

677. 1850 U.S. census, Marion, Oregon, population schedule, p. 78A; Image: 147, dwelling 73, family 73, James E. Hall; digital images,*Ancestry.com* (www.ancestry.com/ : accessed 4 Apr 2010); citing National Archives and Records Administration microfilm M432, roll M432_742.

678. 1830 U.S. census, Clay, Missouri, p. 279, line 7, John D. Hall; digital images,*Ancestry.com* (www.ancestry.com/ : accessed 30 Dec 2012); citing National Archives and Records Administration microfilm M19, roll 73; Family History Film: 0014854.

679. 1850 U.S. census, Clay, Missouri, population schedule, Gallatin, p. 329B; Image: 185., dwelling 396, family 396, John D. Hall; digital images, *Ancestry.com* (www.ancestry.com/ : accessed 8 Mar 2010); citing National Archives and Records Administration microfilm M432, roll M432_396.

680. 1860 U.S. census, Clay, Missouri, population schedule, Liberty, p. 900; Image: 356, dwelling 438, family 437, John D. Hall; digital images, *Ancestry.com* (www.ancestry.com/ : accessed 8 Mar 2010); citing National Archives and Records Administration microfilm M653, roll M653_614; Original data: 1860 U.S. census, population schedule. NARA microfilm publication M653, 1,438 rolls. Washington, D.C.: National Archives and Records Administration, n.d.

681. Edward Nevill McAllister and Annabelle Cox McAllister,*Estes Family of old Clay County, Missouri, their ancestors and their descendants* (N.p.: n.p., 1972), Page 255.

682. Carrol Carmen Hall,*The Grandfathers, The Hall and Overstreet Families* , 2 Volumes (Springfield, Illinois: Illinois Ancestors.org - Menard County (http://www.illinoisancestors.org/menard/), 1981-2007), Section VI: Chapter 20; Page 222.

683. 1860 U.S. census, Clay, Missouri, population schedule, Liberty, p. 900; Image: 356, dwelling 438, family 437, John D. Hall; digital images, *Ancestry.com* (www.ancestry.com/ : accessed 8 Mar 2010); citing National Archives and Records Administration microfilm M653, roll M653_614.

684. Edward Nevill McAllister and Annabelle Cox McAllister,*Estes Family of old Clay County, Missouri, their ancestors and their descendants* (N.p.: n.p., 1972), Page 256.

685. 1830 U.S. census, Clay, Missouri, p. 279, line 9, Samuel Hall; digital images,*Ancestry.com* (www.ancestry.com/ : accessed 30 Dec 2012); citing National Archives and Records Administration microfilm M19, roll 73; Family History Film: 0014854.

686. Edward Nevill McAllister and Annabelle Cox McAllister,*Estes Family of old Clay County, Missouri, their ancestors and their descendants* (N.p.: n.p., 1972), Page 103.

687. 1850 U.S. census, Clay, Missouri, population schedule, Liberty, p. 311B, dwelling 149, family 149, Thomas Fry; digital images,*Ancestry.com* (www.ancestry.com/ : accessed 26 Sep 2013); citing National Archives and Records Administration microfilm M432, roll 396.

688. 1860 U.S. census, Clay, Missouri, population schedule, Platte, p. 229; 1065, dwelling 1578, family 1578, Thos. Fry; digital images, *Ancestry.com* (www.ancestry.com/ : accessed 27 Sep 2013); citing National Archives and Records Administration microfilm M653, roll 614; Family History Library Film: 803614.

689. Edward Nevill McAllister and Annabelle Cox McAllister,*Estes Family of old Clay County, Missouri, their ancestors and their descendants* (N.p.: n.p., 1972), Page 253. .... Jordan Dodd, "Missouri Marriages to 1850," database,*Ancestry.com* (www.ancestry.com : accessed 26 Sep 2013), Thomas Fry m. Elizabeth A. Hall, 1823; citing transcripts of county marriage records.

690. 1840 U.S. census, Clay, Missouri, p. 30, line 3, Thomas Fry; digital images,*Ancestry.com* (www.ancestry.com/ : accessed 27 Sep 2013); citing National Archives and Records Administration microfilm M704, roll 222; Family History Library Film: 0014855.

691. 1850 U.S. census, Daviess, Missouri, population schedule, District 27, p. 372B; Image: 228, dwelling 267, family 271, David M. Hall; digital images, *Ancestry.com* (www.ancestry.com/ : accessed 21 Mar 2010); citing National Archives and Records Administration microfilm M432, roll M432_398.

692. 1850 U.S. census, Clinton, Missouri, population schedule, District 16, p. 428A; Image: 384, dwelling 520, family 520, Jefferson Fry; digital images, *Ancestry.com* (www.ancestry.com/ : accessed 20 Mar 2010); citing National Archives and Records Administration microfilm M432, roll M432_396.

693. 1850 U.S. census, Tarrant, Texas, population schedule, Navarro, p. 86B; Image: 266, dwelling 4, family 4, Little B. Hall; digital images, *Ancestry.com* (www.ancestry.com/ : accessed 21 Mar 2010); citing National Archives and Records Administration microfilm M432, roll M432_910.

694. 1880 U.S. census, Josephine, Oregon, population schedule, Williamsburg, enumeration district (ED) 57, p. 16D, dwelling 142, family 150, Litte B. G. Hall; digital images,*Ancestry.com* (www.ancestry.com/ : accessed 1 Dec 2011); citing National Archives and Records Administration microfilm T9, roll 1081.

695. 1880 U.S. census, Josephine, Oregon, population schedule, Williamsburg, enumeration district (ED) 57, p. 16D, dwelling 142, family 150, Lucy A. Hall; digital images,*Ancestry.com* (www.ancestry.com/ : accessed 1 Dec 2011); citing National Archives and Records Administration microfilm T9, roll 1081.

696. Carrol Carmen Hall,*The Grandfathers, The Hall and Overstreet Families* , 2 Volumes (Springfield, Illinois: Illinois Ancestors.org - Menard County (http://www.illinoisancestors.org/menard/), 1981-2007), Section VI: Chapter 20; Page 222. .... Edward Nevill McAllister and Annabelle Cox McAllister, *Estes Family of old Clay County, Missouri, their ancestors and their descendants* (N.p.: n.p., 1972), Page 255.

697. 1850 U.S. census, Clay, Missouri, population schedule, Gallatin, p. 329B; Image: 185., dwelling 394, family 394, Alijah Ecton; digital images, *Ancestry.com* (www.ancestry.com/ : accessed 8 Mar 2010); citing National Archives and Records Administration microfilm M432, roll M432_396.

Source Citations

698. Edward Nevill McAllister and Annabelle Cox McAllister,*Estes Family of old Clay County, Missouri, their ancestors and their descendants* (N.p.: n.p., 1972), Page 255-256.

699. Harris, Texas, death certificate no. 23888 (1940), Ida Mosby Campbell; digital image, LDS Family Search, "Texas Deaths 1890 - 1976," *FamilySearch.org* (http://familysearch.org/ : accessed 6 Apr 2010); Ida Mosby Campbell. Widow. Informant: Mrs. E. R. Hail. Fogle-West Funeral Home

700. Edward Nevill McAllister and Annabelle Cox McAllister,*Estes Family of old Clay County, Missouri, their ancestors and their descendants* (N.p.: n.p., 1972), Page 255. .... Harris, Texas, death certificate no. 23888 (1940), Ida Mosby Campbell; digital image, LDS Family Search, "Texas Deaths 1890 - 1976," *FamilySearch.org* (http://familysearch.org/ : accessed 6 Apr 2010); Ida Mosby Campbell. Widow. Informant: Mrs. E. R. Hail. Fogle-West Funeral Home

Bibliography

Acklen, Jeanette Tillotson, compiler. *Tennessee Records*. 2 volumes. Nashville, Tennessee: Cullom & Ghertner Co., 1933.

Aiken, Leona Taylor. *Donelson, Tennessee It's History and Landmarks*. Kingsport, Tennessee: Kingsport Press, Inc., 1968.

Ancestry.com Operations, Inc. "U.S. Federal Census Mortality Schedules, 1850-1885 ." Database and images. *Ancestry.com*. www.ancestry.com/ : 2010.

Ancestry.com Operations, Inc. "U.S. Federal Census Mortality Schedules, 1850-1885 [database on-line]." Database and images. *Ancestry.com*. www.ancestry.com/ : 2010.

Ancestry.com. *Historical Sketch of Bedford County, Virginia, 1753-1907*. Provo, Utah: The Generations Network, Inc., 2005.

"Ansearchin' News." Quarterly Journal. Memphis, Tennessee, 1954-2008. Digital images. Tennessee Genealogical Society. *Welcome to the Ansearchin' News Archives*. http://www.tngs.org/ : 2010.

Arkansas Territory. Pulaski. 1830 U.S. census. Digital images. *Ancestry.com*. www.ancestry.com/ : 2010.

Arkansas. Eastern District - The United States Attorney's Office. *The United States Attorney's Office - Eastern District of Arkansas*. http://www.justice.gov/usao/are/meetattorney.html : 2012.

Arkansas. Independence. 1850 U.S. census, population schedule. Digital images. *Ancestry.com*. www.ancestry.com/ : 2009.

Arkansas. Lawrence. 1850 U.S. census, population schedule. Digital images. *Ancestry.com*. www.ancestry.com/ : 2009.

Arkansas. Little Rock. *Arkansas Gazette Weekly*.

Arkansas. Little Rock. *Arkansas Gazette*.

Arkansas. Little Rock. *Arkansas Weekly Gazette*.

Arkansas. Pulaski. 1910 U.S. census, population schedule. Digital images. *Ancestry.com*. www.ancestry.com/ : 2006.

Armstrong, Linda. "Yazoo County Tax Lists 1823 and 1825." Database. MSGenWeb. *Yazoo County Mississippi - Yazoo County Tax Lists 1823 and 1825*. http://www.rootsweb.ancestry.com/~msyazoo/taxlists.htm : 2002-2003.

Baber, Lucy Harrision Miller and Hazel Letts Williamson. *Marriages of Campbell County Virginia 1782-1810*. Lynchburg, Virginia: n.p., 1971.

Barnes, Robert and Thomas L. Hollowak. *Maryland Genealogies : a consolidation of articles from the Maryland historical magazine*. 2 volumes. Baltimore, Maryland: Genealogical Publishing Co., 1980.

Barnes, Robert William. *Baltimore County Families, 1659-1759*. Baltimore, Maryland: Genealogical Publisher Company, 1989.

Bell, Landon C. *Sunlight on the South Side - Lists of Tithes Lunenburg County, Virginia 1748-1783*. Philadelphia, Pennsylvania: George S. Ferguson Co., 1931, Baltimore, MD.: Genealogical Publishing Co., Inc., Reprinted for Clearfield Company, Inc. 1974, 1991.

Bonney, Caleb Dawley, Bonney Family Bible, Vicksburg, MS.: Vicksburg Genealogical Society Publications, Mississippi River Routes, Winter 1994.

Boogher, William Fletcher. *Gleanings of Virginia History: An historical and genealogical collection, largely from original sources*. Washington, D. C.: W. F. Boogher, 1903; Digitized February 10, 2009.

Brown. "Our Family Tree - James Nathaniel Bradshaw." Database. Rootsweb.com. *Rootsweb's World Connect*. http://www.rootsweb.ancestry.com/ : September 22, 2005.

BROWN-L Archives, mailing list archives. http://archiver.rootsweb.ancestry.com/th/read/BROWN/.

Bibliography

Bureau of Land Management. "U. S. General Land Office Records, 1796-1907 [database on-line]." Database and images. *Ancestry.com.* www.ancestry.com/ : 2008.

BURNETT-L Archives, message board. http://archiver.rootsweb.ancestry.com/th/read/BURNETT/.

Butler Center for Arkansas Studies. "The Encyclopedia of Arkansas History and Culture." Database. The Central Arkansas Library System. *The Encyclopedia of Arkansas History and Culture*. http://www.encyclopediaofarkansas.net/default.aspx : 2011.

California Department of Health Services, Center for Health Statistics. "California, Death Index, 1940-1997." Database. Ancestry.com Operations Inc. *Ancestry.com.* www.ancestry.com/ : 2000.

California. Los Angeles. 1900 U.S. census, population schedule. Digital images. *Ancestry.com.* www.ancestry.com/ : 2004.

California. Los Angeles. 1910 U.S. census, population schedule. Digital images. *Ancestry.com.* www.ancestry.com/ : 2006.

California. Los Angeles. 1930 U.S. census, population schedule. Digital images. *Ancestry.com.* www.ancestry.com/ : 2002.

California. Los Angeles. 1940 U.S. census, population schedule. Digital images. *Famly Search.* www.familysearch.org/ : 2012.

California. Los Angeles. California Voter Registrations, 1900-1968 [database on-line]. Digital images. Ancestry.com Operations Inc. *Ancestry.com.* www.ancestry.com/ : 2008.

California. San Bernadino. 1930 U.S. census, population schedule. Digital images. *Ancestry.com.* www.ancestry.com/ : 2002.

California. San Diego. *Evening Tribune.*

California. San Diego. *The San Diego Union.*

California. San Francisco. *San Francisco Bulletin.*

California. Tulare. 1880 U.S. census, population schedule. Digital images. *Ancestry.com.* www.ancestry.com/ : 2010.

California. Ventura. 1940 U.S. census, population schedule. Digital images. *Ancestry.com.* www.ancestry.com/ : 2012.

Callaway, William. (Bedford, Virginia) to George Washington. Letter. May 15 1758.Digital images. The Library of Congress. *American Memory.* http://memory.loc.gov/cgi-bin/ampage?collId=mgw4&fileName=gwpage031.db&recNum=487 : March 31, 2010.

Cartmell, Thomas K. *Shenandoah Valley pioneers and their descendants; a history of Frederick County, Virginia, from its formation in 1738 to 1908.* Winchester, Virgtinia, Eddy Press Corp., 1909. Reprint, Westminister, Maryland: Heritage Books, Inc, 1989; 2007.

Chalkley, Lyman. *Chronicles of the Scot-Irish Settlement of Virginia, extracted from the original court records of Augusta County, 1745-1800 – Augusta County (Va.).* 3 Volumes. Roselyn, Virginia: National Society of the Daughters of the American Revolution, 1912.

Chesnut, Don. "Chronology of Robert Benge, aka Chief Bench ." Report . 1997. Don Chesnut's Homepage.

Childress, J. Patrick <londonwildcat@earthlink.net>, Childress/Mathis Family Tree (04 December 2007 (Updated)).

Childress, Patrick. "Childers/ress DNA Project." Database - Genealogy Report. RootsWeb.com. *Childress/Mathis Family Tree Photographs.* http://freepages.genealogy.rootsweb.ancestry.com/~jpcfamily/childress_observations.htm : November 23 2008.

CHILDRESS-RESEARCH-L Archives, mailing list. http://archiver.rootsweb.ancestry.com/.

Chilton, Ann, Bedford County, Virginia Will Book 1 & Will Book 2, Signal Mountain, TN: Mountain Press, 1988.

Chilton, Ann. *Bedford Co., Virginia Deed Book A-1 1754-1762.* Signal Mountain, Tennessee: Mountain Press, 1987.

Bibliography

Choate-L Archives, mailing list. http://archiver.rootsweb.ancestry.com/th/index/CHOATE.

The Church of Jesus Christ of Latter-day Saints [LDS]. "International Genealogical Index - Individual Record." Database on-line. *FamilySearch*. http://www.familysearch.org/eng/Search/frameset_search.asp : 2011.

The Church of Jesus Christ of Latter-day Saints [LDS]. "International Genealogical Index." Database. *FamilySearch*. http://www.familysearch.org : 2009.

The Church of Jesus Christ of Latter-day Saints [LDS]. "International Genealogical Index." Database. *FamilySearch*. http://www.familysearch.org : May 17, 2009.

The Church of Jesus Christ of Latter-day Saints. "Ancestral File," database. *FamilySearch*. http://www.familysearch.org : 2008.

The Church of Jesus Christ of Latter-day Saints. "FamilySearch - Maryland Births and Christenings, 1650-1995." Database. *FamilySearch*. http://new.familysearch.org : 2011.

The Church of Jesus Christ of Latter-day Saints. "Pedigree Resource File," database. *FamilySearch*. http://www.familysearch.org : 2008.

The Church of Jesus Christ of Latter-Day Saints. "Texas County Marriage Records, 1837-1977." Database. The Church of Jesus Christ of Latter-Day Saints. *FamilySearch*. https://familysearch.org/ : 2013.

Clayton, Prof. W. W. *History of Davidson County, Tennessee*. Philadelphia, Pennsylvania: J. W. Lewis & Co., 1880.

Clement, Maud Carter. *The History of Pittsylvania County, Virginia*. Lynchburg, Virginia: J. P. Bell Company, 1929.

Clements, Paul. *A Past Remembered Volume I*. Nashville, Tennessee: Clearview Press, 1987.

Confederate Veteran Magazine.

Coody, Marianna, copier; Schneider, Betty Aron, Coordinator, Wesley Chapel Methodist Church Cemetery (Yazoo County, Mississippi GenWeb, updated July 5, 2008.)

Coughlin, Helen, transcriber. "Virginia Military Institute - Class of 1874." Database. Virginia Genealogy Trails . *Rockbridge County, Virginia Genealogy Trails* . http://genealogytrails.com/vir/rockbridge/vmi/cadet_class_registers/cadets_1874.html : 2011.

Cox, Debie. E-mail correspondence with Ronald Hall. Privately held by Hall, Fort Worth, Texas.

CROSS-L Archives, mailing list. http://archiver.rootsweb.ancestry.com/th/read/CROSS/.

Dalton, Timothy. (Bedford, Virginia) to George Washington. Letter/ Sworn Testimony/Affidavit on Indian Raid. May 9, 1758.Digital images. The Library of Congress. *American Memory*. http://memory.loc.gov/cgi-bin/ampage?collId=mgw4&fileName=gwpage031.db&recNum=444 : 31 March 2010.

Davidson County, Tennessee - County Court Minutes 1824-1826 (Nashville, TN: Davidson County, Tennessee, County Clerk).

Davis, John David. *Baltimore County, Maryland Deed Records: 1727-1757* . Volume 2 of Baltimore County, Maryland Deed Records. Heritage Books, 1997. Digital images - Preview. *Google Books*. http://books.google.com/ : 2009.

DeCell, Harriet and JoAnne Prichard. *Yazoo : its legends and legacies* . Yazoo City, Mississippi: Yazoo Delta Press, 1976.

Dennis, Earle S. and Jane Estelle Smith. *Marriage Bonds of Bedford County, Virginia, 1755-1800*. Baltimore, Maryland: Genealogical Publishing Company, 1981.

Depreist - Family History & Genealogy Message Board, message board. http://boards.ancestry.co.uk/surnames.depreist/.

Dodd, Jordan R, et. al. "Arkansas Marriages to 1850." Database. Ancestry.com Operations Inc. *Ancestry.com*. www.ancestry.com/ : 1997.

Bibliography

Dodd, Jordan, compilers, Liahona Research. "Illinois Marriages, 1851-1900 [database on-line]." Database. Ancestry.com Operations Inc. *Ancestry.com*. www.ancestry.com/ : 2005.

Dodd, Jordan, Tennessee Marriages to 1825 [database on-line], Ancestry.com. www.ancestry.com/ : 1997.

Dodd, Jordan. "Missouri Marriages to 1850." Database. The Generations Network, Inc. *Ancestry.com*. www.ancestry.com : 1997.

Eakley, Barbara Brown. *The Browns of Bedford County, Virginia 1748-1840*. Westminister, Maryland: Heritage Books, 1998.

Eddlemon, Sherida K, Genealogical Abstracts from Tennessee Newspapers 1803-1812 (Bowie, Maryland: Heritage Books, 1989).

Estes Trails Family Newsletter, newsletter.

Fassnacht, Grace Spencer. *Campbell Kith and Kin: Campbell Kith and Kin: Descendants of Archibald Campbell and Elizabeth Baker, Who Came from Campbell County, Virginia, to Knox County, Tennessee, 1796*. Chattanooga, Tennessee: n.p., 1983.

Find A Grave, Inc. Database. *Find A Grave.com/*. http://www.findagrave.com/ : 2012.

Genealogical Society of Utah. "Virginia, Marriages, 1785-1940." Database. The Church of Jesus Christ of Latter-day Saints. *FamilySearch*. https://familysearch.org/ : 2013.

Genealogical Society of Utah. Missouri Marriages. "Missouri, Marriages, 1750-1920 ." Database. The Church of Jesus Christ of Latter-day Saints. *FamilySearch*. https://familysearch.org/ : 2012.

George, James Z., Reporter to the State, Mississippi Supreme Court. *Cases Argued and Decided in the Supreme Court of Mississippi*. Vol. 31- Vol. 2. Philadelphia, Pennsylvania: E. W. Stephens Publishing Co./ T & J.W. Johnson & Co., 1858.

Glass, George W. *Glass Family Notes - Volume I*. Houston, Texas: n.p., n.d.

Goodspeed, Westin A. *Goodspeed's History of Tennessee - Carroll County*. Nashville, Tennessee: Goodspeed Publishing Co., 1887; Southern Historical Press, Reprinted 1978.

Grissett, Sharon. "Mt. Olivet Confederate Cemetery." Database. *Yazoo County, Mississippi - Confederate Cemetery*. http://www.rootsweb.ancestry.com/~msyazoo/ConfederateCem.htm : 2005.

Grissette, Sharon, Hart-Childress Cemetery, Yazoo County, Mississippi (2003).

Gwathmey, John H. *Historical Register of Virginians in the Revolution 1775-1783*. Baltimore, Maryland: Genealogical Publishing Co., Inc., 1987.

Hall, Carrol Carmen. *The Grandfathers, The Hall and Overstreet Families*. 2 Volumes. Springfield, Illinois: Illinois Ancestors.org - Menard County (http://www.illinoisancestors.org/menard/), 1981-2007.

Hall, Dabney. Photograph of Tombstone. Digital images. Ancestry.com. *Ancestry.com*. www.ancestry.com/ : 2011-.

Hall, Lindsey C. non-graduate card file. Princeton University, 1818-1819. Supplied by Princeton University, Seeley G. Mudd Manuscript Library, Princeton, New Jersey. 10 February 2005.

Hall, Timothy E. E-mail correspondence with Ronald C. Hall. Privately held by Hall, Fort Worth, Texas.

Hallum, John. *Biographical and Pictorial History of Arkansas*. Albany, New York: Weed, Parsons and Company, 1887.

Harvey, Nan. "Officials of Yazoo County, Mississippi - Registers of Commissions." Database. www.usgwarchives.net. *MSGenWeb Archives*. http://files.usgwarchives.net/ms/yazoo/history/officials.txt : 2010.

Hatch, Stephen W, Descendants of Caleb Dawley Bonney, 20 February 2007.

HELM-L Archives, mailing list. http://archiver.rootsweb.ancestry.com/th/read/HELM/1996-06/0835342679.

Bibliography

Hening, William Waller. *The Statutes at Large, a collection of all the laws of Virginia*. 7 Volumes. Richmond, Virginia: Franklin Press, 1820.

Hinshaw, William Wade. *Encyclopedia of American Quaker Genealogy. Vol. VI: (Virginia)*. Baltimore, Maryland: Genealogical Publishing Co., Reprint 1993.

The Historical Committee of the Bicentennial Commission of Campbell County, Virginia. *Lest it be Forgotten - A Scrapbook of Campbell County, Virginia*. Virginia: Alta Vista Printing Co., 1976.

Hoobler, James A. *A Guide to Historic Nashville, Tennessee* . Charleston, South Carolina: The History Press, 2008.

Houston, Florence and Laura Blaine. *Maxwell history and genealogy*. Indianapolis, Indiana: Press of C.E. Pauley, Indianapolis Engraving Co., 1916.

Howell, Ellmo. *Mississippi Back Roads: Notes on Literature and History*. Memphis, Tennessee: Roscoe Langford, 1998.

Hunting For Bears, comp, Mississippi Marriages, 1776-1935 [database on-line], Ancestry.com. www.ancestry.com/: The Generations Network, Inc., 2004.

Hunting For Bears, comp. "Mississippi Marriages, 1776-1935 [database on-line]." Database. Ancestry.com Operations Inc. *Ancestry.com*. www.ancestry.com/ : 2004.

Hunting For Bears, compilers. "Missouri Marriages, 1766-1983 ." Database. Ancestry.com Operations Inc. *Ancestry.com*. www.ancestry.com/ : 2004.

Illiinois. Menard. 1850 U.S. census, population schedule. Digital images. *FamilySearch*. https://familysearch.org/ : 2012.

Illinois. "Illinois, State Census, 1855." Database. The Church of Jesus Christ of Latter-day Saints. *FamilySearch*. https://familysearch.org/ : 2012.

Illinois. Clark. 1850 U.S. census, population schedule. Digital images. *Ancestry.com*. www.ancestry.com/ : 2009.

Illinois. Mason. 1870 U.S. census, population schedule. Digital images. *Ancestry.com*. www.ancestry.com/ : 2009.

Illinois. Menard. 1850 U.S. census, population schedule. Digital images. *Ancestry.com*. www.ancestry.com/ : 2009.

Illinois. Menard. 1860 U.S. census, population schedule. Digital images. *Ancestry.com*. www.ancestry.com/ : 2009.

Illinois. Menard. 1870 U.S. census, population schedule. Digital images. *Ancestry.com*. www.ancestry.com/ : 2009.

Illinois. Menard. 1880 U.S. census, population schedule. Digital images. *Ancestry.com*. www.ancestry.com/ : 1999.

Illinois. Menard. 1900 U.S. census, population schedule. Digital images. *Ancestry.com*. www.ancestry.com : 2004.

Illinois. Sangamon. 1830 U.S. census. Digital images. *Ancestry.com*. www.ancestry.com/ : 2010.

Illinois. Sangamon. 1840 U.S. census. Digital images. *Ancestry.com*. www.ancestry.com/ : 2010.

Iowa. Van Buren. 1850 U.S. census, population schedule. Digital images. *Ancestry.com*. www.ancestry.com/ : 2009.

Iowa. Van Buren. 1850 U.S. census, population schedule. Digital images. *Ancestry.com*. www.ancestry.com/ : 2009.

Iowa. Van Buren. Iowa State Census -1856, population schedule. Digital images. Ancestry.com Operations Inc. *Ancestry.com*. www.ancestry.com/ : 2007.

Jackson, Ron V., Accelerated Indexing Systems, compiler, U.S. Federal Census Mortality Schedules Index [database on-line], *Ancestry.com*. www.ancestry.com/ : 1999.

Bibliography

Jackson, Ron V., compiler. Accelerated Indexing Systems. "Arkansas Census, 1819-70." Database. The Generations Network, Inc. *Ancestry.com*. www.ancestry.com/ : 1999.

"The Journal of San Diego History - SAN DIEGO HISTORICAL SOCIETY QUARTERLY." Quarterly Journal. San Diego, California. Digital images. San Diego History Center - University of San Diego. *The Journal of San Diego History*. http://www.sandiegohistory.org/ : 2011.

Kansas. Brown. 1880 U.S. census, population schedule. Digital images. *Ancestry.com*. www.ancestry.com/ : 2010.

Kentucky. Shelby. 1850 U.S. census, population schedule. Digital images. *Ancestry.com*. www.ancestry.com/ : 2009.

Kentucky. Shelby. 1860 U.S. census, population schedule. Digital images. *Ancestry.com*. www.ancestry.com/ : 2009.

Lamson, Jennifer. "Lamson." Database - Family Tree. The Generations Network. *Ancestry.com*. www.ancestry.com/ : 2009.

Long, Lawrence W. "Bonney Cemetery (AKA Churchill Plantation Cemetery) ." Database. *Yazoo County Mississippi - MS GenWeb*. http://www.rootsweb.ancestry.com/~msyazoo/BonneyCem.htm : 2003.

Louisiana. Caddo. 1900 U.S. census, population schedule. Digital images. *Ancestry.com*. www.ancestry.com/ : 2004.

Louisiana. Carroll. 1860 U.S. census, population schedule. Digital images. *Ancestry.com*. www.ancestry.com/ : 2009.

Louisiana. Carroll. 1870 U.S. census, population schedule. Digital images. *Ancestry.com*. www.ancestry.com/ : 2009.

Louisiana. Secretary of State, Division of Archives, Records Management, and History. Vital Records Indices, Louisiana Statewide Death Index, 1900-1949 [database on-line], Baton Rouge, Louisiana: Ancestry.com. www.ancestry.com/ : 2002.

Louisiana. Tensas. 1900 U.S. census, population schedule. Digital images. *Ancestry.com*. www.ancestry.com/ : 2004.

Louisiana. Vermillion. 1870 U.S. census, population schedule. Digital images. *Ancestry.com*. www.ancestry.com/ : 2009.

Lowry, Robert and Wuilliam H. McCardle. *A history of Mississippi: from the discovery of the great river by Hernando DeSoto, including the earliest settlement made by the French under Iberville, to the death of Jefferson Davis* . Jackson, Mississippi: R. H. Henry & Co., 1891.

Lucas, Jr., Rev. Silas Emmett, ed, Obituaries from Early Tennessee Newspapers 1794 - 1851 (Easley, South Carolina: Southern Historical Press, 1978).

Lucas, Silas Emmett Rev., editor, Marriages from Early Tennessee Newspapers 1794-1851 (Easley, South Carolina: Southern Historical Press, 1978).

Maas, Russell. *Bullock Genealogy*. http://bullockgenealogy.net/index.html : 2004.

Marsh, Helen C. and Marsh, Timothy R, Davidson County, Tennessee Wills & Inventories Volume One 1783-1816 (Greenville, South Carolina: Southern Historical Press, Inc., 1990).

Marsh, Helen C. and Timothy R Marsh. *Land and Deed Genealogy of Davidson County, Tennessee*. Greenville, South Carolina: Southern Historical Press, 1992.

Marsh, Helen Crawford. *Bedford County Tennessee Wills and Vital Records from Newspapers*. Greenville, South Carolina: Southern Historical Press, Inc., 1996.

Maryland Historical Magazine, Volume 15.

Maryland Historical Magazine.

Mason, Linda. "Yazoo County, MS 1823 Tax List ." Database. MSGenWeb - Special Projects. *MSGenWeb - Special Projects - Library Project*. http://www.msgw.org/library/yazoo-1823tax.html : Feb 5 2000.

Bibliography

Mc Donald, Cecil D., Jr. "Augusta County, VA Marriages 1700-1799." Database. transcribed on-line by Wes Blair and Pam Miller . *USGenWeb Archives* . http://files.usgwarchives.org/va/augusta/vitals/marriages/1700-99.txt : 2011.

McAllister, Edward Nevill and Annabelle Cox McAllister. *Estes Family of old Clay County, Missouri, their ancestors and their descendants*. N.p.: n.p., 1972.

McDowell, William L., Jr., editor. *Documents Related to Indian Affairs, 1754-1765*. Columbia, South Carolina: University of South Carolina Press, 1970.

Mississippi Cemetery and Bible Records Vol. V. Jackson, Mississippi: Mississippi Genealogical Society, September 1958.

Mississippi Cemetery and Bible Records Vol. XI. Jackson, Mississippi: Mississippi Genealogical Society, 1965.

Mississippi. Carroll. 1840 U.S. census. Digital images. *Ancestry.com*. www.ancestry.com/ : 2010.

Mississippi. Carroll. 1850 U.S. census, population schedule. Digital images. *Ancestry.com*. www.ancestry.com/ : 2009.

Mississippi. Carroll. 1860 U.S. census, population schedule. Digital images. *Ancestry.com*. www.ancestry.com/ : 2009.

Mississippi. Carroll. 1870 U.S. census, population schedule. Digital images. *Ancestry.com*. www.ancestry.com/ : 2003.

Mississippi. Carroll. 1910 U.S. census, population schedule. Digital images. *Ancestry.com*. www.ancestry.com/ : 2006.

Mississippi. Carroll. 1920 U.S. census, population schedule. Digital images. *Ancestry.com*. www.ancestry.com/ : 2005.

Mississippi. Choctaw. 1860 U.S. census, population schedule. Digital images. *Ancestry.com*. www.ancestry.com/ : 2009.

Mississippi. Choctaw. 1870 U.S. census, population schedule. Digital images. *Ancestry.com*. www.ancestry.com/ : 2009.

Mississippi. Jackson. *The Clarion*.

Mississippi. Montgomery. 1880 U.S. census, population schedule. Digital images. *Ancestry.com*. www.ancestry.com/ : 2010.

Mississippi. Tallahatchie. 1870 U.S. census, population schedule. Digital images. *Ancestry.com*. www.ancestry.com/ : 2009.

Mississippi. Warren. 1850 U.S. census, population schedule. Digital images. *Ancestry.com*. www.ancestry.com/ : 2005.

Mississippi. Warren. 1870 U.S. census, population schedule. Digital images. *Ancestry.com*. www.ancestry.com/ : 2003.

Mississippi. Yazoo. 1830 U.S. census. Digital images. *Ancestry.com*. www.ancestry.com/ : 2010.

Mississippi. Yazoo. 1840 U.S. census. Digital images. *Ancestry.com*. www.ancestry.com/ : 2010.

Mississippi. Yazoo. 1850 U.S. census, population schedule. Digital images. *Ancestry.com*. www.ancestry.com/ : 2009.

Mississippi. Yazoo. 1860 U.S. census, population schedule. Digital images. *Ancestry.com*. www.ancestry.com/ : 2009.

Mississippi. Yazoo. 1870 U.S. census, population schedule. Digital images. *Ancestry.com*. www.ancestry.com/ : 2009.

Mississippi. Yazoo. 1880 U.S. census, population schedule. Digital images. *Ancestry.com*. www.ancestry.com/ : 2010.

Mississippi. Yazoo. 1900 U.S. census, population schedule. Digital images. *Ancestry.com*. www.ancestry.com/ : 2004.

Mississippi. Yazoo. 1910 U.S. census, population schedule. Digital images. *Ancestry.com*. www.ancestry.com/ : 2006.

Mississippi. Yazoo. 1920 U.S. census, population schedule. Digital images. *Ancestry.com*. www.ancestry.com/ : 2010.

Mississippi. Yazoo. 1930 U.S. census, population schedule. Digital images. *Ancestry.com*. www.ancestry.com/ : 2002.

Bibliography

Mississippi. Yazoo. Chancery Court - Probate Cases 1841-1873. Yazoo County Court, Yazoo City. FHL microfilm #2438941. Family History Library, Salt Lake City, Utah.

Mississippi. Yazoo. Chancery Court - Probate Cases 1841-1873. Yazoo County Court, Yazoo City. FHL microfilm #2438942. Family History Library, Salt Lake City, Utah.

Mississippi. Yazoo. Probate Minute Book Vol. A 1834-1838. Yazoo County Court, Yazoo City. FHL microfilm. Family History Library, Salt Lake City, Utah.

Mississippi. Yazoo. Probate Minute Book Vol. B 1838-1842. Yazoo County Court, Yazoo City. FHL microfilm. Family History Library, Salt Lake City, Utah.

Mississippi. Yazoo. Probate Minute Book Vol. C 1842-1846. Yazoo County Court, Yazoo City. FHL microfilm. Family History Library, Salt Lake City, Utah.

Mississippi. Yazoo. Will Records Volume A-B 1833-1908. Yazoo County Court, Yazoo City. FHL microfilm #879249. Family History Library, Salt Lake City, Utah.

Missouri. Audrain. 1840 U.S. census. Digital images. *Ancestry.com.* www.ancestry.com/ : 2010.

Missouri. Audrain. 1850 U.S. census, population schedule. Digital images. *Ancestry.com.* www.ancestry.com/ : 2009.

Missouri. Audrain. 1860 U.S. census, population schedule. Digital images. *Ancestry.com.* www.ancestry.com/ : 2009.

Missouri. Clay. 1830 U.S. census. Digital images. *Ancestry.com.* www.ancestry.com/ : 2010.

Missouri. Clay. 1840 U.S. census. Digital images. *Ancestry.com.* www.ancestry.com/ : 2010.

Missouri. Clay. 1850 U.S. census, population schedule. Digital images. *Ancestry.com.* www.ancestry.com/ : 2009.

Missouri. Clay. 1860 U.S. census, population schedule. Digital images. *Ancestry.com.* www.ancestry.com/ : 2009.

Missouri. Clinton. 1850 U.S. census, population schedule. Digital images. *Ancestry.com.* www.ancestry.com/ : 2009.

Missouri. Daviess. 1850 U.S. census, population schedule. Digital images. *Ancestry.com.* www.ancestry.com/ : 2009.

Missouri. St. Louis. 1870 U.S. census, population schedule. Digital images. *Ancestry.com.* www.ancestry.com/ : 2009.

Missouri. St. Louis. 1880 U.S. census, population schedule. Digital images. *Ancestry.com.* www.ancestry.com/ : 2005.

Morgan, James Logan. *Arkansas Marriage Notices, 1819-1845*. Newport, Arkansas: Morgan Books, 1984.

Morgan, James Logan. *Arkansas Newspaper Index 1819-1845 - Biographical Notes, Probate and Chancery Notices from Arkansas Newspapers, 1819-1845*. 4 volumes: v. 1. Obituaries and biographical notes from Arkansas newspapers, 1819-1835 -- v. 2. Obituaries and biographical notes from Arkansas newspapers, 1836-1840 -- v. 3. Obituaries and biographical notes from Arkansas newspapers, 1841-1845 -- v. 4. Probate and chancery notices from Arkansas newspapers, 1819-1845. Conway, Arkansas: Arkansas Research, 1992, c1981.

Morrison,, Jerry, transcriberArkansas USGenWeb Project Archives. "Arkansas -Territorial Papers 1819-1825." Database. *Arkansas Archives - Territorial Papers*. http://www.usgwarchives.net/ar/territory.htm : March 1999.

Moser, Harold D. and Shannon Macpherson, editors. *The Papers of Andrew Jackson Vol. II 1804-1813*. Knoxville, Tennessee: University of Tennessee Press, 1984.

NARA - Publication Number M246. Record Group 93. Digital images. Footnote.com. *Footnote.com.* www.Footnote.com/ : 2007.

NARA. "Compiled Service Records of Confederate Soldiers Who Served in Organizations from the State of Texas." Database. Fold3. *Fold3.com.* http://www.fold3.com/ : 2008.

Bibliography

The Nashville Room - The Public Library of Nashville - Davidson County. *Nashville Families & Homes*. Nashville, Tennessee: Williams Printing Co., 1983.

New Mexico. Chaves. 1900 U.S. census, population schedule. Digital images. *Ancestry.com*. www.ancestry.com/ : 2004.

New Mexico. Chaves. 1910 U.S. census, population schedule. Digital images. *Ancestry.com*. www.ancestry.com/ : 2006.

New Mexico. Chaves. 1920 U.S. census, population schedule. Digital images. *Ancestry.com*. www.ancestry.com/ : 2010.

New Mexico. Chaves. SUPREME COURT OF NEW MEXICO, 1947-NMSC-019, 51 N.M. 100, 179 P.2d 524. Digital images. *New Mexico Compilation Commission* . http://www.nmcompcomm.us/nmcases/NMSC/1947/1947-NMSC-019.pdf.

New Mexico. Las Cruces. *Las Cruces Democrat*.

New Mexico. Las Cruces. *Mesilla Valley Democrat*.

New Mexico. Lincoln. 1880 U.S. census, population schedule. Digital images. *Ancestry.com*. www.ancestry.com/ : 2010.

New Mexico. Roswell. *Roswell Daily Record*.

Obert, Isabelle Board. *The Board Family Chronicle: from Maryland to Bedford County, Virginia* . Baltimore, Maryland: I. B. Obert, 1997; Digitized 2007 Google Books.

O'Dell, Jeffrey M. "Frederick County, Virginia Poor Farm." Report to Hugh C. Miller. July 6 1993. National Register of Historic Places, United States Department of Interior - National Park Service, Washington.

Oglesby, Victor. E-mail correspondence with Ronald C. Hall. Privately held by Hall, Ft. Worth, Texas.

Ohio. Lawrence. 1820 U.S. census, population schedule. Digital images. *Ancestry.com*. www.ancestry.com : 2010.

Ohio. Lawrence. 1850 U.S. census, population schedule. Digital images. *Ancestry.com*. www.ancestry.com/ : 2009.

Oregon. Josephine. 1880 U.S. census, population schedule. Digital images. *Ancestry.com*. www.ancestry.com/ : 2010.

Oregon. Marion. 1850 U.S. census, population schedule. Digital images. *Ancestry.com*. www.ancestry.com/ : 2009.

PA-OLD-CHESTER-L Archives, mailing list. http://archiver.rootsweb.ancestry.com/th/index/PA-OLD-CHESTER/.

Pearson, Jonathan. *A general catalogue of the officers, graduates and students of Union College from 1795 to 1854* . New York: S. S. Riggs, 1854; Digitized 2009, Google Books.

Raper, David Murray. "David Murray Raper Family Tree." Database. The Generations Network. *Ancestry.com*. www.ancestry.com/ : 2009.

Reed, Verna - submitter, Family Group Record: "George Tennel Davis," The Church of Jesus Christ of Latter Day Saints. www.familysearch.org/ Accessed March 6, 2008.

Reed, Verna [Verna@carlsbadnm.com], Modified Register for Hall (Carlsbad, New Mexico: Sept 2002).

"Revolutionary War Pension and Bounty-Land Warrant Application Files." Database and images. *FootNote.com*. FootNote.com/ : 2008.

"Revolutionary War Pension Files." Database and images. *Folld3.com*. http://www.fold3.com/ : 2013.

Rhodes, Carl/Rhodes Family.org. Database. *William Rhodes and his Descendants "1745 to 1825"*. http://wm.rhodesfamily.org/Wm2ndVA.htm : 2009.

RootsWeb - TNBEDFOR-L Archives, message board. http://archiver.rootsweb.ancestry.com.

Bibliography

Russell Family Tree - Ancestry.com. Annabel and Wade Russell, compiler. Wm. Ross Russell Family Bible, July 30 2008. Privately held by Scott Russell Redmond, Washington.

Sanders, Justin. E-mail correspondence with Ronald C. Hall. Privately held by Hall, Fort Worth, Texas.

Sistler, Byron and Samuel, transcribers. *Tennesseans in the War of 1812*. Nashville, Tennessee: Byron Sistler and Associates, Inc., 1992.

Smith, Mary Sue, Davidson County, Tennessee Deed Book "P" (Bowie, Maryland: Heritage Books, Inc., 1997).

Social Security Administration. "U. S. Social Security Death Index." Database. *Family Search*. www.familysearch.org/ : 2010.

Sons of the American Revolution. Application Files. Illinois Society of the Sons of the American Revolution, Springfield.

Spear, C. T., editor. *Bedford County, Tennessee - Family History Book*. Paducah, Kentucky: Turner Publishing Company, 2002.

Spradlin, Freddie . "Military-French & Indian War: Providers of Provisions for Militia." Database. USGenWeb Archives . *USGenWeb Archives* . http://files.usgwarchives.net/va/bedford/military/frenchindian/fiwbedf.txt : 2009.

Swader, Drema. "Keziah Stovel Musgrove." Genealogy Report. *Keziah Stovel Musgrove*. http://genealogy.drema.com/genealogy/ksm.html : 2009.

Tennessee. Bedford. 1840 U.S. census. Digital images. *Ancestry.com*. www.ancestry.com/ : 2009.

Tennessee. Bedford. 1850 U.S. census, population schedule. Digital images. *Ancestry.com*. www.ancestry.com/ : 2009.

Tennessee. Bedford. 1860 U.S. census, population schedule. Digital images. *Ancestry.com*. www.ancestry.com/ : 2009.

Tennessee. Bedford. Deed Records. Tennessee State Library and Archives, Nashville, Tennessee.

Tennessee. Bledsoe. 1830 U.S. census. Digital images. *Ancestry.com*. www.ancestry.com/ : 2010.

Tennessee. Bledsoe. 1840 U.S. census. Digital images. *Ancestry.com*. www.ancestry.com/ : 2010.

Tennessee. Davidson. 1820 U.S. census, population schedule. Digital images. *Ancestry.com*. www.ancestry.com/ : 2010.

Tennessee. Davidson. County Clerk, Davidson County, Tennessee - Marriage Book 1, Nashville, TN:.

Tennessee. Davidson. County Clerk, Davidson County, Tennessee - Minutes of the Circuit Court - Vol. G 1828-1831, Nashville, TN:.

Tennessee. Davidson. County Clerk, Davidson County, Tennessee - Register of Deeds Vol. G-I Dates 1805-1813, Nashville, TN:.

Tennessee. Davidson. County Clerk, Davidson County, Tennessee - Register of Deeds Vol. K-M Date 1813-1819, Nashville, TN:.

Tennessee. Davidson. County Clerk, Davidson County, Tennessee - Will Book Vol. 9, Nashville, TN:.

Tennessee. Henry. 1850 U.S. census, population schedule. Digital images. *Ancestry.com*. www.ancestry.com/ : 2009.

Tennessee. Henry. 1860 U.S. census, population schedule. Digital images. *Ancestry.com*. www.ancestry.com/ : 2009.

Tennessee. Knox County. Wills Vol. 0-3 July 1792-1824. Dallas Public Library - J. Eric Jonsson, Dallas.

Tennessee. Meigs. 1850 U.S. census, population schedule. Digital images. *Ancestry.com*. www.ancestry.com/ : 2009.

Tennessee. Nashville. *Impartial Review and Cumberland Repository*.

Tennessee. Nashville. *National Banner and Nashville Whig*.

Bibliography

"Texas Births and Christenings 1840-1981." Database. The Church of Jesus Christ of Latter-day Saints . *Family Search - Record Search*. http://search.labs.familysearch.org/recordsearch/ : 2010.

Texas. Austin. *Telegraph and Texas Register*.

Texas. Bay City. *The Bay City Tribune*. Online archives. www.ancestry.com/ : August 7, 2012.

Texas. Brown. "U.S., Confederate Pensions, 1884-1958." Digital images. Ancestry.com Operations, Inc. *Ancestry.com*. www.ancestry.com/ : 2010.

Texas. Burnet. 1870 U.S. census, population schedule. Digital images. *Ancestry.com*. www.ancestry.com/ : 2009.

Texas. Burnet. 1910 U.S. census, population schedule. Digital images. *Ancestry.com*. www.ancestry.com/ : 1910.

Texas. Collin. "Confederate Pension Applications, 1899-1975." Digital images. Ancestry.com Operations, Inc. *Ancestry.com*. www.ancestry.com/ : 2010.

Texas. Collin. 1860 U.S. census, population schedule. Digital images. *Ancestry.com*. www.ancestry.com/ : 2009.

Texas. Collin. 1870 U.S. census, population schedule. Digital images. *Ancestry.com*. www.ancestry.com/ : 2009.

Texas. Collin. 1880 U.S. census, population schedule. Digital images. *Ancestry.com*. www.ancestry.com/ : 2010.

Texas. Collin. 1900 U.S. census, population schedule. Digital images. *Ancestry.com*. www.ancestry.com/ : 2004.

Texas. Collin. 1910 U.S. census, population schedule. Digital images. *Ancestry.com*. www.ancestry.com/ : 1910.

Texas. Dallas. *The Dallas Morning News*.

Texas. Digital Images of Birth Certificates. The Church of Jesus Christ of Latter-day Saints. *Family Search*. https://familysearch.org/ : 2011-2012.

Texas. Fayette. 1860 U.S. census, population schedule. Digital images. *Ancestry.com*. www.ancestry.com/ : 2009.

Texas. Harris. Digital Images of Death Certificates. LDS Family Search. *FamilySearch.org*. http://familysearch.org/ : 2008 - 2012.

Texas. Hidalgo. 1930 U.S. census, population schedule. Digital images. *Ancestry.com*. www.ancestry.com/ : 2002.

Texas. Hidalgo. 1940 U.S. census, population schedule. Digital images. *FamiltSearch*. https://familysearch.org/ : 2013.

Texas. Lampasas. 1880 U.S. census, population schedule. Digital images. *Ancestry.com*. www.ancestry.com/ : 2010.

Texas. Lampasas. 1900 U.S. census, population schedule. Digital images. *Ancestry.com*. www.ancestry.com/ : 2004.

Texas. Limestone. 1870 U.S. census, population schedule. Digital images. *Ancestry.com*. www.ancestry.com/ : 2009.

Texas. Limestone. 1900 U.S. census, population schedule. Digital images. *Ancestry.com*. www.ancestry.com/ : 2004.

Texas. Limestone. 1910 U.S. census, population schedule. Digital images. *Ancestry.com*. www.ancestry.com/ : 2006.

Texas. Limestone. 1920 U.S. census, population schedule. Digital images. *Ancestry.com*. www.ancestry.com/ : 2010.

Texas. Richardson. *The Richardson Echo*.

Texas. San Augustine. Loose Probate Court Record. East Texas Research Center/Stephen F. Austin State University Library, Nacogdoches.

Texas. San Augustine. *Texas Union*.

Bibliography

Texas. Tarrant. 1850 U.S. census, population schedule. Digital images. *Ancestry.com*. www.ancestry.com/ : 2009.

Texas. Tarrant. 1880 U.S. census, population schedule. Digital images. *Ancestry.com*. www.ancestry.com/ : 2005.

Texas. Tarrant. 1900 U.S. census, population schedule. Digital images. *Family Search Labs*. www.familysearchlabs.org/ : 2008.

Texas. Tarrant. 1910 U.S. census, population schedule. Digital images. *Ancestry.com*. www.ancestry.com/ : 2006.

Texas. Tarrant. 1930 U.S. census, population schedule. Online database. *Family Search*. www.familysearch.org/ : 2011.

Texas. Tarrant. Digital Images of Death Certificates. LDS Family Search. *FamilySearch.org*. http://familysearch.org/ : 2008 - 2012.

Texas. Texas Bureau of Vital Statistics. "Texas Deaths 1890 - 1976." Database. The Church of Jesus Christ of Latter Day Saints. *Family Search*. www.familysearch.org/ : 2011.

Texas. Texas Department of Health, State Vital Statistics Unit, Texas Death Index, 1903-2000 [database on-line], Ancestry.com. www.ancestry.com/ : 2006.

Texas. Texas Department of State Health Services, Texas Birth Index 1903 - 1997 [database on-line], Ancestry.com. www.ancestry.com/ : 2005.

Texas. Texas Department of State Health Services. "Texas Marriages, 1837-1973." Database. The Church of Jesus Christ of Latter- Day Saints. *Family Search - Record Search*. http://familysearch.org/ : 15 May 2010.

Texas. Tom Green. 1910 U.S. census, population schedule. Digital images. *Ancestry.com*. www.ancestry.com/ : 2006.

Texas. Tom Green. 1920 U.S. census, population schedule. Digital images. *Ancestry.com*. www.ancestry.com/ : 2010.

Texas. Tom Green. 1930 U.S. census, population schedule. Digital images. *Ancestry.com*. www.ancestry.com/ : 2002.

Texas. Tom Green. 1940 U.S. census, population schedule. Digital images. *Ancestry.com*. www.ancestry.com : 2012.

The River Counties.

Thomas, Jane Henry and J. G. M. Ramsey contributor. *Old Days in Nashville*. 1897. Reprint, Nashville, Tennessee: Charles Elder, 196?.

TLC Genealogy. *Campbell County, Virginia Deeds, 1784-1790*. Miami, Florida: TLC Genealogy, 1991.

Turner Publishing Company, . *Rover & Bedford County, Tn, Volume 2*. Paducah, Kentucky: Turner Publishing Company, 2000.

Turner Publishing Company. *Daughters of Republic of Texas, Volume I*. Texas: Turner Publishing Company, 1995.

U. S. Department of the Interior - National Park Service. "National Register of Historic Places; Notification of Pending Nominations and Related Actions ." Database. GPO Access [wais.access.gpo.gov]. http://edocket.access.gpo.gov/2010/2010-4451.htm : March 4, 2010.

U. S. Selective Service System, World War I Draft Registration Cards, 1917-1918 [database on-line], *Ancestry.com*. www.ancestry.com/ : 2005.

U. S. Social Security Administration, Social Security Death Index [database on-line], Ancestry.com. www.ancestry.com/ : 2011.

U. S., Sons of the American Revolution. Membership Applications, 1889-1970 [database on-line]. Ancestry.com: The Generations Network, Inc., Provo.

"United States Obituary Collection ." Database. Ancestry.com Operations Inc. *Ancestry.com*. www.ancestry.com/ : 2006.

Bibliography

United States Senate - Second Session of the Twenty-third Congress. *Public Documents Printed by Order of the Senate of the United States*. 4 Volumes. Washington, District of Columbia: Duff Green, 1834.

United States. Department of the Interior, United States Bureau of Land Management - Records, Washington D.C.

University of Mississippi. *Announcements and Catalogue*. Digitized 2009 - Google Books. Mississippi: University of Mississippi, 1883.

University of Mississippi. *Historical catalogue of the University of Mississippi: 1849-1909*. Marshall and Bruce Company, 1910. Digital images. *Google Books*. http://books.google.com/ : 5 Oct 2007.

University of Virginia Library. "Valley of the Shadow - Civil War- Era Newspapers." Database. Virginia Center for Digital History. *Valley of the Shadow - Civil War- Era Newspapers*. http://valley.lib.virginia.edu/news/ss1858/va.au.ss.1858.07.27.xml.

USHistory.org/. Database. USHistory.org/. *Historic Valley Forge - Who Served Here? Physicians, Surgeons and Mates with Washington at Valley Forge*. http://www.ushistory.org/valleyforge/served/surgeons.html : 2009.

Valley Forge National Historical Park. "Muster Roll Data Sheet." Database. Valley Forge National Historical Park. *Valley Forge Legacy*. http://valleyforgemusterroll.org/ : 2008.

Vaughn, Kristin Illinois Genealogy Trails. "Menard County, Illinois - History & Genealogy - Obituaries." Database. *Menard County, Illinois - History & Genealogy*. http://genealogytrails.com/ill/menard/index.html : 2008.

Virginia Cavalcade.

Virginia Genealogical Society Quarterly.

Virginia State Library. *Report of the Virginia State Library, Volumes 13-14* . 1917. Reprint, Richmond, Virginia: State of Virginia, Google Books, Digitized 2009.

Virginia. Bedford - Family History & Genealogy Message Board, message board - rootsweb.com. http://boards.rootsweb.com/localities.northam.usa.states.virginia.counties.bedford/.

Virginia. Bedford. 1810 U.S. census. Digital images. *Ancestry.com*. www.ancestry.com/ : 2010.

Virginia. Bedford. 1820 U.S. census, population schedule. Digital images. *Ancestry.com*. www.ancestry.com/ : 2009.

Virginia. Bedford. 1830 U.S. census. Digital images. *Ancestry.com*. www.ancestry.com/ : 2009.

Virginia. Bedford. 1840 U.S. census. Digital images. *Ancestry.com*. www.ancestry.com/ : 2009.

Virginia. Bedford. 1850 U.S. census, population schedule. Digital images. *Ancestry.com*. www.ancestry.com/ : 2009.

Virginia. Bedford. 1860 U.S. census, population schedule. Digital images. *Ancestry.com*. www.ancestry.com/ : 2009.

Virginia. Bedford. Chancery Court. Library of Virginia, Richmond. Digital images. Library of Virginia. *Virginia Memory*. http://www.lva.virginia.gov/ : 2013.

Virginia. Bedford. Chancery Court. Library of Virginia, Richmond. Digital images. *Virginia Memory - Digital Collections*. http://www.lva.virginia.gov/ : 2009.

Virginia. Bedford. County Clerk, Bedford County, Virginia Order Book 1, 1754-1761, Miami Beach, Florida: T. L. C. Genealogy, c2000.

Virginia. Bedford. Deed Book 26 - 1836-1837. Library of Virginia, Richmond. FHL microfilm. Family History Library, Salt Lake City, Utah.

Virginia. Bedford. Deed Book 27. Library of Virginia, Richmond. FHL microfilm. Family History Library, Salt Lake City, Utah.

Bibliography

Virginia. Bedford. Revolutionary War - Public Service Claims. Virginia State Library. JR 3280. Dallas Public Library - J. Eric Jonsson, Dallas.

Virginia. Campbell. "1785 Campbell County, Virginia Personal Property Tax List." New River Notes, Saltville.

Virginia. Campbell. Campbell County, Virginia - Land Tax Books 1797-1819. FHL microfilm. Family History Library, Salt Lake City, Utah.

Virginia. Campbell. Chancery Court Records Index. Library of Virginia, Richmond. Digital images. Library of Virginia. *Virginia Memory - Library of Virginia*. http://www.lva.virginia.gov/ : 2009.

Virginia. Campbell. Circuit Court Order Books and General Index. FHL microfilm. Family History Library, Salt Lake City, Utah.

Virginia. Campbell. Deed Books 1782-1896. FHL microfilm. Family History Library, Salt Lake City, Utah.

Virginia. Franklin. 1850 U.S. census, population schedule. Digital images. *Ancestry.com*. http://www.ancestry.com/ : 2009.

Virginia. Patrick. 1840 U.S. census. Digital images. *Ancestry.com*. www.ancestry.com/ : 2010.

Virginia. Virginia Marriages, 1785-1940. The Church of Jesus Christ of Latter Day Saints, Salt Lake City. FHL microfilm. Family History Library, Salt Lake City, Utah.

Virginia. Virginia, Auditor of Public Accounts. "Virginia, Auditor of Public Accounts 1776-1928 - Court Booklets, indexes and lists, 1781-1783." Database. Library of Virginia. *Library of Virginia Catalog*. http://lva1.hosted.exlibrisgroup.com/ : 2009.

Weathers, Pris. "Arkansas Gazette (1819-1930)." Database. *Arkansas Ties*. http://www.arkansasties.com/ : 2007.

Wells, Carol, Davidson County, Tennessee County Court Minutes 1792-1799 (Bowie, MD.: Heritage Books, Inc., 1991).

Whitley, Edythe Johns Rucker. *Pioneers of Davidson County, Tennessee*. Baltimore, Maryland: Genealogical Publishing Co., Inc., 1979.

Whitley, Edythe Rucker, compiler. *Marriages of Davidson County, Tennessee 1789-1847*. Baltimore, Maryland: Genealogical Publishing Co, 1981.

Whitley, Edythe Rucker. *Membership Roster and Soldiers of the Tennessee Society of the Daughters of the American Revolution 1960-1970*. Tennessee: The Tennessee Society of the Daughters of the American Revolution, 1970.

Whitten, Joida, Abstracts of Bedford County, Virginia Wills, Inventories and Accounts 1754-1787, Dallas, Texas: Taylor Publishing Co., 1968.

Wiltshire, Betty Couch. *Carroll County, Mississippi, pioneers* . Carrollton, Mississippi: Pioneer Publishing Co., c1990.

Wiltshire, Betty Couch. *Yazoo County, Mississippi Pioneers*. Bowie, Maryland: Heritage Books, 1992.

Witt, Marcia. "Witt Family of Bedford County, Virginia." Genealogy Modified Register Report. RootsWeb.com. *Witt Family of Bedford County, Virginia*. http://wc.rootsweb.ancestry.com/cgi-bin/igm.cgi?op=REG&db=wittm&id=I127 : 2010.

Yates Publishing. "U.S. and International Marriage Records 1590-1900 [database on-line]." Database. The Generations Network, Inc., Provo, UT, USA. *Ancestry.com*. www.ancestry.com/ : 2004.

"Yazoo County Marriage Book B." Database. Genealogy Trails. *Mississippi Genealogy Trails*. http://genealogytrails.com/miss/yazoo/marriage_book_b.htm : 2012.

Yazoo County, Mississippi - Probate Records (Yazoo City, Mississippi, Yazoo County, Mississippi, County Clerk).

Yerger, George S. *Reports of Cases Argued and Determined in the Supreme Court of Tennessee During the Year 1836*. Volume IX. Nashville, Tennessee: S. Nye & Co. State Printers, 1836.

Bibliography

Zeier, Lucy D. "Tennessee, Bedford County - Index County Court Minute Book, Volume 1, 1848-1852." Transcript. TnGenWeb.org. *Tennessee, Bedford County - Index County Court Minute Book, Volume 1, 1848-1852*. http://www.tngenweb.org/bedford/County_minutes/CNC_V1_index.htm : 2005.

Name Index

Name Index

Name Index

Name Index

Name Index

Name Index

Leftwich
Lucy, 36

Lewellen
Charles, 58

Locke
Mary, 59
Robert Weakley, 60
William, 60

Lockett
Rhoda, 62

Logue
(No Given Name.), 133

Long
Jane, 9, 118, 121, 122
L. H., 106
Lawrence W., 106
Lawrence Wilburn (Dr.), Jr., 106
Thomas (Maj.), 122

Lovelady
William Amos, 68

Maben
(No Given Name.), 70
Andrew S., 70
Audrey J., 70
Benjamin F., 69
Frank, 71
Julia, 71
Mary E., 70
Nancy J., 71
Robert M., 69
Thomas S., 70
William, 69, 70

MacAtee
George Washington, 102
William Leonard, Sr, 102

Maddox
Sarah "Sallie" Thomas, 99
Thomas Benton, 99

Marshall
Daniel, 41
Elizabeth, 41
John R., 54

Mchaffey
Mary F., 117

Merryman
Charles (Capt.), Sr., 121
Charles, Jr., 9, 118, 121, 122
John, 121
Mary, 9, 25, 118, 123, 137

Miller
Joe, 111
Josephine Theadore, 111

Mitchell
Thomas Albert, 63

Moon
Christopher, 57
Elizabeth, 57

More
(No Given Name.), 79

Morgan
Nathaniel, 58
Reece, 58

Morhead
Elizabeth, 79
William, 79

Mosby
Etta, 147, 149
Gertrude, 147, 149
Ida, 147, 149
John Henry, 147
Wade, 147

Moseley
Elijah M., 113
Frances Brondell, 113, 117

Munholland
Gesisim, 83
Julia L., 83
Moses M., 83
Moses M., Jr., 83

Murphy
Stephen S., 87
William Stephen, 87

Musgrove
(No Given Name.), 37

Name Index

Name Index

Robertson

James M., 60

John, 60

Michael, 60

Ross

Jesse S., 49

Russell

Bettie, 100

Claud Caperton, 100, 111

Donna Julia, 80

Felix G., 48

Hendley Mathews, 100, 111

James, 48

James R., 48

Lambert Hudson, 81

Lindsey H., 49, 81

Lindsey H., Jr., 82

Mary W., 82

Roxannah Green, 81

Roxie, 100

Sarah M., 82

Tabitha Ann, 80, 98

Thomas Shelton, 81, 99

Virginia, 82

Wesley, 48

William, 48

William L., 80

William Ross, 48, 79

Rutherford

Rosannah, 48

Sanders

(No Given Name.), 59

Eliza H., 59

George W., 59

Mary L., 59

Shaon

James K., 57

Martha K., 85

Shofner

Loton S., 60

Short

(No Given Name.), 132

Short

Tobetha, 132

Shouse

Rebecca, 147

Simmons

Louisa A., 81

Smiley

Charles Oscar, 102

Henry, 102

Smith

(No Given Name.), 10, 25, 118

Augustine, 126

Charity, 69, 70

Frances, 111

Jane, 127

John, 126

Keziah, 12, 124

Mary Magdalene, 10, 25, 118

Spain

Annie Lee "Tula", 111

John Dent, 111

Steele

Andrew, 22

Nancy Buchanan, 22

Stewart

(No Given Name.), 148

Stoker

Elizabeth Jane, 60

Stout

Daniel, 146

Suddarth

Samuel, 59

Swearingen

Eleanor, 128

Taylor

Charity, 45

Thomas

Laura Almada McCreary, 87

Sarah, 50

Tilford

David, 59

Name Index

Location Index

Location Index

Location Index